W9-CQR-921

The Old-House Lover's
GUIDE TO
INNS

and Bed & Breakfast Guest Houses

by the editors of
OLD-HOUSE JOURNAL

introduction by
PATRICIA POORE

THE STEPHEN GREENE PRESS
PELHAM BOOKS

THE STEPHEN GREENE PRESS/PELHAM BOOKS
Published by the Penguin Group
Viking Penguin Inc., 40 West 23rd Street, New York, New York 10010, U.S.A.
Penguin Books Ltd, 27 Wrights Lane, London W8 5TZ, England
Penguin Books Australia Ltd, Ringwood, Victoria, Australia
Penguin Books Canada Ltd, 2801 John Street, Markham, Ontario, Canada L3R 1B4
Penguin Books (N.Z.) Ltd, 182-190 Wairau Road, Auckland 10, New Zealand

Penguin Books Ltd, Registered Offices: Harmondsworth, Middlesex, England

First published in 1989 by The Stephen Greene Press
Published simultaneously in Canada
Distributed by Viking Penguin Inc.

10 9 8 7 6 5 4 3 2 1

Copyright © Old-House Journal Corporation, 1989
All rights reserved

The sketches of the establishments represented in this book are reproduced by arrangement of their proprietors.

Library of Congress Cataloging-in-Publication Data
The Old-house lover's guide to inns and bed & breakfast
  guest houses.
    Includes index.
    1. Bed and breakfast accommodations — United States — Guide-books.   2. Hotels,
taverns, etc. — United States — Guide-books.   I. Old-house journal.   II. Title: Guide
to inns and bed & breakfast guest houses.
TX907.2.043 1989   647'.947303   88-21453
ISBN 0-8289-0709-9

Printed in the United States of America

Except in the United States of America, this book is sold subject to the condition that it shall not, by way of trade or otherwise, be lent, re-sold, hired out, or otherwise circulated without the publisher's prior consent in any form of binding or cover other than that in which it is published and without a similar condition including this condition being imposed on the subsequent purchaser.

CONTENTS

PREFACE

This is a unique Inns Guide. It's for old-house buffs, people who care more about the woodwork than the muffins. What these inns have in common is not location, not the sumptuousness of their breakfasts, not breathtaking collections of antique furnishings. What they have in common is owners with an enthusiastic interest in old buildings.

For each inn, you'll find the indispensable information you need as a traveler: number of guest rooms and baths, price range, restrictions, breakfast. But more than that, you'll be introduced to the houses themselves. We'll tell you the style of each one and the date it was built; stories about the original owners or colorful past inhabitants; restoration work recently completed or underway. Nearly all of the listings are illustrated.

The Old-House Lover's Guide to Inns started out as a "family" project for readers of the magazine I publish. *Old-House Journal* is a 15-year-old nuts-and-bolts magazine about restoration. We knew that a substantial subgroup of our readers were people who owned inns or bed & breakfasts. We also knew that our readers can't resist visiting other old houses. They love house tours and check out house museums. And they like to stay at historic inns.

So the magazine's editors sent out a detailed questionnaire to subscribers who had previously identified themselves as innkeepers. The 400 + listings in this book were selected from respondents. We then interviewed the innkeepers by phone. What we got is an insider's list: members of the restoration club who are in the business of sharing their houses!

Of course, the project had mushroomed (doesn't *every* old-house project?). It was no longer an in-house referral list, but rather a full-length book. And, with the burgeoning interest in historic buildings, it had an appeal that went beyond the readers of *Old-House Journal*. Enter our publisher, the Stephen Greene Press. We hope you enjoy our book.

Patricia Poore

Patricia Poore
Old-House Journal
Brooklyn, New York

Finally, a brief note: Any guidebook of this nature contains information that may be dated shortly after publication. Room prices may rise, inns may be renovated, accommodations may change. It's a good idea to call ahead for the latest information.

CALIFORNIA

Northern California

Eureka

Ferndale ◆ Redding

◆ Chico

Wine Country

Santa Rosa ◆
Napa ◆ ◆ Sacramento

Oakland
San Francisco ◆ Bay Area
◆ San Jose
Santa Cruz
◆ Monterey ◆ Fresno

Central California

◆ Bakersfield
Southern California

◆ Santa Barbara

◆ Los Angeles ◆ Palm Springs

◆ San Diego

ALAMEDA

GARRATT MANSION
Royce and Betty Gladden
900 Union
Alameda, CA 94501
(415) 521-4779
Year-round

1893 Neo-Colonial

LOCATION: Alameda is a quiet island near Oakland and the San Francisco Bay Bridge, with a high concentration of Victorian homes. The inn's neighborhood, known as "the Gold Coast," is close to a tennis court and the beach and features "trees, beautiful flowers, and friendly squirrels."

"I really enjoy watching guests walking around 'discovering' the house —the wood carvings, mantels, leaded- and stained-glass windows..."

The Gladdens endured a classic restorer's nightmare: After they'd stripped layers of wallpaper from the walls, the lath and plaster came crumbling down. So some walls have been replastered, others Sheetrocked. Fortunately restoring the lovely woodwork in the house —bird's eye maple, walnut, oak, mahogany—proved much less traumatic; it needed only to be stripped of many years' accumulation of smoke, grime, and paint.

When the J. A. Leonard Company neared completion of the structure in 1893, the *Alameda Daily Argus* called it "the notable house of the year for this firm" and "a very fine residence." W. T. Garratt, the

7

first owner, lived there only a few years. Records show that when he sold in 1902 the house was altered and improved for one Dr. W. R. Cluness. When the grand house grew obsolete it was used as a rooming house; it had been one for 40 years when the Gladdens bought it in 1977.

In the entry you'll note a coffered ceiling and inset oak panels with egg-and-dart beading. Lincrusta-Walton wallpaper, stained to match the woodwork, covers the walls of the inner hallway, where there's also a tiled floor. In the "living hall"—generously sized, as are all the rooms—there's a classical fireplace, an orchestra loft, and a staircase with a Jacobean balustrade. The room's stained-glass window has an unusual pattern: a moon with a spider web. Elsewhere in the house the stained glass has the characteristic pattern of the turn of the century: stylized ribbons and bows with faceted red "rubies."

Restrictions: Babies and children only under special circumstances. No smoking. Check-in after 3 p.m., check-out at 11 a.m.
Beds: Two rooms have queens and private baths; three share baths.
Breakfast: Freshly squeezed orange juice, homemade muffins, cheese omelettes, and fruit in season, "for example," are served in guest's room or dining room. On Sunday a buffet is offered in the dining room.
Extras: Fresh lemonade on hot afternoons, hot tea on chilly days, plus cookies and milk "depending on guest's schedule" are served. noons, hot tea on chilly days, plus cookies and milk "depending on guest's schedule" are served.
Rates: $60 to $75 per room. Personal checks welcome.

CALIFORNIA: BAY AREA

HALF MOON BAY

SAN BENITO HOUSE
Carol Mickelsen
356 Main Street
Half Moon Bay, CA 94019
(415) 726-3425
Year-round

1908 California Stucco

LOCATION: Half Moon Bay is a small seaside town surrounded by acres of fields and flowers; it's known as "the Pumpkin Capital of California," and there's a pumpkin festival each October. The inn is adjacent to the water and has an English garden.

The first hotel in Half Moon Bay was built in 1908 by one Emanuele Daneri. For years it was called the Mosconi Hotel; in the 1930s the name was changed to Dominic's. The building was allowed to deteriorate, though the establishment kept its reputation for serving family-style, inexpensive Italian meals.

By the time Carol Mickelsen and her partners purchased the place in 1976, it was rundown and suffering from neglect. She used Half Moon Bay's original name, San Benito, to rename her inn, and set about extensive restoration and remodelling. The kitchen and dining rooms came first; there were thick layers of old paint on the beams and cornices.

Mickelsen haunted antique shops from San Francisco to Europe to furnish the building. She found a 15-foot pier mirror for the entry, brass chandeliers for the kitchen, along with clawfoot tubs for the baths. The tubs now stand underneath stained-glass portholes. And one unusual headboard in a guest room is comprised of carved double doors that stand from floor to ceiling.

The second floor now contains a sauna, and rear decks have been added that overlook the garden and ocean.

Restrictions: No children, babies, or pets. Check-in after 3 p.m., check-out at 11 a.m.

Beds: Ten rooms have doubles, one has a king and one a set of twins. Three share a bath.

Breakfast: Homemade whole-wheat bread, sweet butter, jam, juice, a special blend of coffee, and soft-cooked eggs.

Extras: There's a sauna, a lawn for playing croquet, a gourmet restaurant in the inn, and a saloon.

Rates: $40 (room over kitchen with shared bath) to $95 (suite with living room). Personal checks and credit cards welcome.

10% discount to OHJ members.

INVERNESS

TEN INVERNESS WAY
Sarah Thorpe, Mary Davies, and
Stephen Kimball
Ten Inverness Way
Inverness, CA 94937
(415) 669-1648
Year-round

1904 Shingle Style

LOCATION: Inverness is a village on Tomales Bay, minutes from Point Reyes National Seashore and Tomales Bay State Park. The house is situated in the midst of a country garden.

The owners say the vintage of the massive stone fireplace in the living room is "open to historical debate." But they're sure the Douglas fir panelling and floors are original. Some of the things they've added: heirloom rugs, books, and a player piano; there are also oval portraits of one innkeeper's grandparents, taken the day before their wedding.

Two of the rooms have sloping ceilings, the other three rows of dormer windows. All have handmade quilts and old-fashioned water pitchers.

An exuberant country garden surrounds the house. Around the benches, wisteria-covered arbor, and flagstone paths blooms a wide variety of flowers along with plum, lemon and apple trees.

Restrictions: Children welcome "at innkeeper's discretion." No pets ("our cat will keep you company"). Smoking in the living room only. Check-in between 5 and 7 p.m. except by special arrangement.
Beds: Four rooms, all with private baths and double or queen beds.
Breakfast: "Hearty, home style": blackberry or banana buttermilk pancakes, curried eggs with homemade chutney, homemade breads, jams, coffeecakes; coffee, fresh fruit.
Extras: Special events like Christmas story readings and a Valentine's Day harp concert are held periodically. Sherry is served in the evening.
Rates: $85 to $90, $5 extra on holidays and weekends. Personal checks

and credit cards accepted.

10% discount to OHJ members. mid-week and off-season.

Mailing Address: PO Box 63, Inverness, CA 94937

INVERNESS PARK

1939 Mission

HOLLY TREE INN
Diane and Tom Balogh
3 Silver Hills Road
Inverness Park, CA 94956
(415) 663-1554
Year-round

LOCATION: The inn sits on a small valley that abounds with coastal wildlife — deer, bobcats, 361 species of birds. Adjacent is the Point Reyes National Seashore, with miles of pine forests and rugged beaches. An English garden with holly, lilac, and boxwood surrounds the house.

Graffiti is one of the more unusual features of the Holly Tree Inn. Fifty-year-old graffiti, that is. On the patio steps you can see where the builders carved the construction date, "1939," into the concrete. And above the outdoor sink is the figure of a duck, also incised in concrete. The builders were prolific masons. They produced two outdoor fireplaces for the house, along with the outdoor sink and a stone "wishing well." The Baloghs found old plans left behind in the living room's built-in sideboard. From those documents they learned that the estate was once called Winchester, in honor of the original owners, Wilhelmina and Chester Noren.

This is the only house the Baloghs looked at when they were searching for a place to open an inn. Diane recalls that when she walked in, she saw the huge brick fireplace in the living room and the pheasant-patterned wallpaper: "The room reminded me of a hunting lodge, it seemed just perfect." The innkeepers have added little except a second-floor bath.

Restrictions: Children, but no pets, welcome. Smoking in the living room only. Check-in between 5 and 7 p.m. weekdays, 2 and 5 p.m. weekends.

Beds: Two kings, a queen, and a double all have private baths.

Breakfast: Fresh orange juice and fruit, cantaloupe with kiwi and strawberries, scrambled eggs with herbs or asparagus soufflés; croissant or homemade poppy seed bread with apricot-lemon butter; freshly roasted coffee, English teas, or herbal tea.

Extras: Tea and instant coffee are available anytime, and sherry is served at 5 p.m.

Rates: $60 (double with private entrance and garden) to $80 (large corner room with king bed, conversation area). Personal and traveler's checks and credit cards welcome.

10% discount to OHJ members.

Mailing Address: Box 642, Point Reyes Station, CA 94956

CALIFORNIA: BAY AREA

OLEMA

BEAR VALLEY INN
Ron and Jo Anne Nowell
88 Bear Valley Road
Olema, CA 94950
(415) 663-1777
Year-round

1899 Foursquare

LOCATION: Olema has many turn-of-the-century buildings, and a half-mile from the inn is the main trail of Point Reyes National Park. From there extend some 200 miles of hiking, biking, and riding trails along wide open beaches and woods. Horses and bicycles can be rented nearby.

The Nowells began with a structure that needed work. Fortunately much original detail remained, even the redwood rain gutters. But the redwood mudsill foundation had to be reconstructed with concrete, the floors had to be refinished, a new oak floor was laid from the living room to the dining room, and even the weighted cords in the windows had to be replaced. Then the Nowells applied the finishing touches of paint and wallpaper. "And that's just a partial list of what we did!" says Ron.

On the fir floors upstairs, below nine-foot-high ceilings, the couple arranged their accumulated antiques and decorated with quilts, lace, curtains, and a clawfoot tub. There's also a c. 1929 Wedgwood stove in the kitchen.

Restrictions: No children, pets, or smoking.
Beds: Two rooms have doubles, one has a king, and all three share a bath.
Breakfast: On Sundays they serve quiche, freshly squeezed orange juice, freshly baked muffins, and coffee or tea. "Something different" is offered every day of the week.
Rates: $60 all rooms; personal checks welcome.
10% discount to OHJ members for three or more consecutive days.
Mailing Address: PO Box 33, Olema, CA 94950

SAN FRANCISCO

1857 BED & BREAKFAST INN
Helvi O. and George Wamsley
1902 Filbert Street near Laguna
San Francisco, CA 94123
(415) 567-1526
Year-round

1857 Vernacular Italianate

LOCATION: The inn, between Fort Mason's views of the Bay and Union Street's stores, is convenient to most of the city's attractions.

The road to the Presidio, San Francisco's first settlement, was once a trail called the Filbert Path. It meandered next to a lagoon, and thieves plied their trade along its length, so it was given the nickname "Robber's Row." In the pastures of nearby Cow Hollow, cows as well as housewives took advantage of a freshwater river that flowed into the lagoon; the point where lagoon and river met was called "Washerwoman's Cove." The first permanent structure on the path was this inn. The rest of the city at that time consisted mostly of tents.

The lagoon was later filled in when it became putrid with industrial pollution and sewage (some freshwater springs still flow into this section of the city, however). The street built near where the lagoon stood is called, not surprisingly, Laguna. The inn was used as a rooming house in World War I, but had been converted into furnished apartments by the time the Wamsleys bought it in 1954. Twenty-seven years later they began restoration and started a B&B.

The structure was added to several times, and now contains five guest bedrooms, kitchens in every suite, a gallery/studio, small museum, and the owners' three-bedroom apartment. One of the suites has a piano, another a Swedish fireplace. "The Captain's Quarters" has an original brick fireplace, and some rooms open onto the small garden in the rear.

Restrictions: No smoking, please ("the odor lingers in the drapes and coverlets"); no pets also.
Beds: There are four suites with private baths and full kitchens, with a total of five bedrooms.
Breakfast: Self-service of "anything the guest wishes": eggs, jam, butter, bread, milk, coffee, tea, and cocoa. Cereals, fruit juice, and continental breakfast are served on the back deck.
Extras: Saturday art classes (full-day, $50) and 3-day seminars ($150) are available. Lunch on Saturday is a "potluck" gathering.
Rates: $65 (twin beds, piano, front porch entrance) $90 (three-room apartment) to $125 (two-bedroom apartment). 10% discount for two-week stay. Extra persons, 25% additional. Personal checks and credit cards welcome.

10% discount to OHJ members.

CALIFORNIA: BAY AREA

SAN FRANCISCO

ALAMO SQUARE INN
Wayne M. Corn and Klaus E.
May
719 Scott Street
San Francisco, CA 94117
(415) 922-2055
Year-round

1895 Queen Anne/neo-Colonial

LOCATION: The inn is on Alamo Square, a hilltop park that overlooks the city, part of the Alamo Square Historic District. The two adjacent buildings, together with the inn, form a three-building complex with decks and a garden.

Mr. Baum, it seems, never lived to see his lovely home completed. The details are sketchy, but apparently he was born in Germany, lived for some time in St. Petersburg, and became director of the Russian American Fur Trading Co. When he was traveling to the U.S. his ship was wrecked off the coast of Mexico near Vera Cruz. Once ashore he met Eliza, daughter of the first Mexican consul to San Francisco. Baum married her and they moved to San Francisco; he died soon after, and she lived in the house until the early '20s.

Architect Arthur Brown was probably inspired by the Midwinter Fair of 1894, where avant-garde architects were displaying progressive combinations of Queen Anne and classical. The house's facade, you'll note, has both Ionic columns and Queen Anne asymmetry.

Inside the prevailing material is oak, including the newel post and the panelling. The entire entry and much of the flooring have the grainy, dotted pattern characteristic of quarter-sawn oak. Above the dramatic multi-level staircase, which has French doors overlooking one landing, hangs a stained-glass skylight. In the drawing room there's a stained-glass oculus that the owners recently restored.

This is the fifth building they've worked on. After overhauling the woodwork, floors, and plaster details, they added a deck, enlarged the kitchen, and installed more baths. The resulting building now demonstrates, they say, how "the application of the new can be blended with the old."

Restrictions: No pets or smoking. Children "with prior approval." Check-in before 6 p.m., later by special arrangement.
Beds: Twelve rooms, ten with private baths.
Breakfast: A "hearty" meal is cooked by Klaus, the German chef-in-residence. Homemade breads, omelettes, other egg dishes "to order," fresh fruit and juice.
Extras: Afternoon tea and/or wine are served; sherry late at night is also provided. They also offer "special dinners by discussion/agreement."
Rates: $65 (double bed, smaller room) to $225 (two-bedroom suite, king bed); cots and cribs cost extra. Personal checks and credit cards welcome.
10% discount to OHJ members for stays of more than two days.

SAN FRANCISCO

HERMITAGE HOUSE
Marian Binkley
2224 Sacramento Street
San Francisco, CA 94115
(415) 921-5515
Year-round

1900 Georgian Revival

LOCATION: Streets of shops and restaurants (Union and Fillmore Streets) are within a five-minute walk. The house, in the residential Pacific Heights neighborhood, is also on a major bus line, one block from Lafayette Park, three blocks from Japan Town and five minutes from the Bay.

"The house has stood the test of time beautifully." Marian Binkley

When the smoke cleared after the San Francisco quake and fire, Judge Charles Slack discovered he had been very lucky. Only one chimney of his house had been destroyed (the other still stands, though it looks a bit lonely). Plus he possessed the only set of law books in the city that had not been damaged. When he decided to lend it to Hastings Law School (where he was dean) students arrived to carry the books to the school. They formed a human chain, all the way up to the Judge's study at the top of the house, and passed the books down one by one.

The building survived several changes of hand during the 1940s. Later it endured five years as a drug rehabilitation center that housed 52 people. The current owners give this partial listing of their activities after buying the house: sanding, scrubbing, rubbing, oiling, waxing, wallpapering, sewing, painting, gardening, and more. They also updated the wiring and heating systems, made bathrooms out of closets, repaired the leaded-glass doors of the china cabinets, and installed copper pipes.

The family is especially proud of the redwood panelling and ornament, such as pilasters, columns, inlaid floors, and scrollwork on the stair, along with original sliding doors. Little has been added in the kitchen except a new counter, a stainless sink, and track lighting. The original Wedgwood stove still works, aided by a new thermostat

16

and a self-starter. And many of the rooms are lit by the original lighting fixtures.

Restrictions: No babies, small children, or pets; smoking "discouraged (but allowed)." Check-in until 9 p.m.; later by special arrangement only.
Beds: The five rooms/suites have mostly king and queen beds. There are some two-bedroom, two-bath suites. All rooms have private baths.
Breakfast: "Finest blends" of coffee, tea, and chocolate; fresh orange juice; selection of pastries, bagels, toast, muffins, with butter, jam, or cream cheese; fruit bowl, and cereal.
Extras: Off-street parking is available, along with "copious maps" and event guides.
Rates: $70 (single), $80 (double) to $115 (fireplace, king bed). Personal checks and credit cards accepted.

SAN FRANCISCO

VICTORIAN INN ON THE PARK
Lisa and William Benau, Shirley and Paul Weber
301 Lyon Street
San Francisco, CA 94117
(415) 931-1830
Year-round

1897 Queen Anne

LOCATION: The area is "famed for its noble Victorians." Golden Gate Park is next door, Civic Center and downtown are a few minutes away.

Marble steps lead to a Honduras mahogany front door. Inside the entry ceiling has carved mahogany panels. In the parlor there's a maple fireplace with an oval mirror above. Four types of wood are inlaid in the floors; the dining room is panelled in oak and even has its original dish rack. In the guest rooms you'll find Victorian lighting

17

fixtures, William Morris wallpaper, and bathrooms furnished with marble sinks, pull-chain toilets, and clawfoot tubs. And if you climb to the top of the house, you'll stand on one of San Francisco's last remaining open belvedere towers.

The first owner, Thomas Clurie, was a lawyer who served as both congressman and senator. The house was later sold to the Cooke family, who were in the leather-tanning business. When Haight-Ashbury attracted the counterculture in the 1960s, underground cartoonist R. Crumb (of "Keep on Trucking" fame) lived in the house.

Restrictions: Babies and toddlers not allowed. Smoking discouraged. Check-in after 2 p.m., check-out at noon.
Beds: Ten queens, one double, and one room with twins all have private baths.
Breakfast: "Deluxe continental": fresh fruit, freshly squeezed orange juice, homemade breads, hot croissants, coffee and tea.
Extras: A decanter of sherry is provided in each room, and there's a nightly "wine hour" in the parlor with other guests and the innkeepers.
Rates: $75 (double bed) to $125 (tub for two, belvedere overlooking park, fireplace), payable in personal checks or credit cards.
10% discount to OHJ members.

CALIFORNIA: BAY AREA

SAUSALITO

CASA MADRONA HOTEL
John W. Mays
801 Bridgeway
Sausalito, CA 94965
(415) 332-0502
Year-round

1885 Italianate/Stick style

LOCATION: The inn covers a whole section of seaside cliff in Sausalito; its main entrance on Bridgeway leads to nearby seafood restaurants, quaint stores, and the bay, where seals bark.

The Casa Madrona Hotel's story is a classic tale of "riches to rags to riches"; the building survived trials by fire, storm, neglect, and hostile city councils to be transformed into a local landmark and an elegant 35-room hotel. In 1885 a wealthy Vermont-born lumber baron, William G. Barrett, moved his family into their fine new home perched on a hillside. *The Sausalito News* that year year reported that "the Barrett place is one of the finest improved sites in Susalito."

Even before construction was completed, the mansion was threatened by the fire that engulfed much of Sausalito in 1883. But the gardens and grounds sustained the only damage. Soon after the Barretts left, the building was converted into a guest house. Successively known as the Casa Madrona Hotel (named for a type of pine tree that grows in nearby) and the Gallagher Inn, it once served, rumor has it, as a bordello. During the 1950s "beatniks" used the house as a beer hall and "crash pad." In 1959 a hero of the French Resistance, Henri Deschamps, took over the lease and established a well-known French restaurant on the lower floor.

The heavy rains of 1973-4 left the structure's fate uncertain; it began to slip off it high perch, and there were threats of condemnation. But the citizens of Sausalito banded together — the Casa is the oldest structure in town—and had it declared a historic monument.

Enter John Mays, a San Francisco attorney, who purchased, renovated, and reopened the hotel. Soon afterward he announced plans for a 16-unit compatible addition to be built on the hillside below. While the hillside was being stabilized with steel and concrete, in 1982 the worst storm in nearly a century struck Sausalito. Only the new underpinnings saved the old building from crashing downhill onto the construction site.

Purists should be aware that the new addition looks new; but, to be fair, it must be said that a great effort was made to give it period detail like multiple gables, bay windows, and decorative panels.

Restrictions: No pets. Check-in after 3 p.m., check-out at noon.
Beds: The 35 rooms have either king or queen beds; at most two share a bath.
Breakfast: Juice, freshly sliced fruit salad, fresh croissants, homemade muffins or scones, coffee or tea are served in the restaurant (or, for $2.50 per person, in bed).
Extras: Valet parking, one-day dry cleaning, and use of the spa are available. Guests dining at the restaurant between 6 and 7 p.m. receive a free bottle of wine, and wine and cheese are provided daily between 5:30 and 6:30 p.m.
Rates: $60 (room in Old Casa with view and shared bath) to $275 (two-bedroom, two-bath suite/conference room with decks, fireplace, bay views, and wet bar). Personal checks and credit cards accepted.

19

APTOS

APPLE LANE INN
John and Carol Coakley
6265 Soquel Drive
Aptos, CA 95003
(408) 475-6868
Year-round

1876 Vernacular with Queen Anne elements

LOCATION: Aptos is on the north (Santa Cruz) side of Monterey Bay, with fine beaches and redwood parks. Activities include whale watching, sailing, or wandering along the Santa Cruz boardwalk. The Monterey Aquarium is 40 minutes away.

Benjamin Porter operated a local tannery. In the 1870s he planted an orchard of apple trees and built his house in their midst. He used a minimum of gingerbread on the outside, and what the current owners describe as "redwood, redwood, redwood" on the inside.

Two acres of gardens and fields still surround the building, and attached is a patio sheltered by grape and wisteria arbors. Antiques like pine and walnut furniture, brass beds, and clawfoot tubs furnish the interior. On the walls there's stencilling, and one room has a tin ceiling installed four years ago. The living room has a fireplace made of travertine, a light-colored limestone.

Restrictions: No pets or children under 12. Smoking in the parlor only. Check-in between 3 and 6 p.m., check-out at 11 a.m.
Beds: Three queens, one double, and one room with two double beds —two share a bath.
Breakfast: Eggs, ham, fresh fruit, homemade apple-cinnamon rolls, muffins, breads, freshly squeezed orange juice, and coffee.
Extras: Complimentary sherry is served in the evenings.
Rates: $65 (two doubles, "cozy attic room," shared bath) to $85 (queen canopied bed, skylight, clawfoot tub). Summer weekend rates $10 more. Personal checks and credit cards welcome.

APTOS

MANGELS HOUSE
Jacqueline and Ron Fisher
570 Aptos Creek Road
Aptos, CA 95001
(408) 688-7982
Year-round except December 23
to 27

1886 Italianate

LOCATION: The inn's four acres of gardens are bounded by the Forest of Nisene Marks (10,000 acres of redwoods, creeks, and trails). Monterey Bay is under a mile away. Museums, theater and wineries are nearby, and whale watching is popular from November to April.

The first owner, Claus Mangels, must have been a giant, or perhaps just a newly rich businessman who wanted to impress visitors. The ceilings are 14 feet high downstairs, 11 feet upstairs. In one guest room the Fishers have used long chains to hang the lighting fixture at a more reasonable height, lighting a sitting area of Victorian wicker pieces. In the living room as well, a fixture on chains hangs over the concert grand piano (made by Jacob Zech, the state's first piano builder).

Mangels and his brother-in-law, Claus Spreckels, earned their fortunes by pioneering the sugar-beet industry in California. Spreckels' identical house once stood half a mile away, but burned down 25 years ago.

The Fishers bought the house from Mangels' descendants. The couple soon discovered heart of redwood floors under layers of paint and linoleum; the boards have been refinished to a rich glow.

Restrictions: Children over 12, and outdoor pets, are welcome. Smoking permitted in the sitting room. Check-in after 3 p.m., check-out at noon.
Beds: One king and a double with private bath; one double and two queens share full bath; one queen has half-bath.
Breakfast: Fresh herb omelette, homemade bran muffins, croissants, rolls, fresh fruit or yogurt; fresh juice; tea or coffee.
Extras: An aperitif is served in the evening.

Rates: $70 to $88; cots, $10. 20% discount for stays of three days or more, Sunday through Thursday. Personal checks and credit cards accepted.

10% discount to OHJ members except Saturdays.

Mailing Address: PO Box 302, Aptos, CA 95001

CENTRAL CALIFORNIA

AUBURN

**LINCOLN HOUSE BED &
BREAKFAST**
Howard and Ginny Leal
191 Lincoln Way
Auburn, CA 95603
(916) 885-8880
Year-round

1933 English Country Revival

LOCATION: Many gold-rush towns are accessible via country roads from this inn, including Sutter's gold-discovery site. Nearby activities include river rafting and hiking, as well as shopping for antiques in the c. 1850 town of Auburn.

Furnishings from the 1920s through the 1940s fill this 1933 house. An exterior archway, tucked under the roofline, marks the path to the house. The sunroom has a stone fireplace, and the living room a brick hearth. Some of the ceilings are beamed; the one in the kitchen is made of tin. The dining room offers an expansive view of the Sierra Nevada Mountains, and koi inhabit the outdoor pond.

President Grover Cleveland granted the original 40-acre estate in 1889 to Clarence A. Johnson, a descendant of Mayflower Pilgrims. When Johnson's house burnt down in the early 1930s, Charles W. Hatch built the present house on the same site; most of the original 40 acres have been sold off.

Restrictions: Check-in between 2 and 11 p.m. Children over ten welcome, no pets, smoking on the grounds only.

Beds: All three rooms—one double, one double with single, and two twins—have private baths.

Breakfast: "Country and/or continental": homemade quiches, French toast, pancakes, assorted egg dishes, fresh fruits, freshly squeezed juices, freshly ground coffee, jams, and jellies.
Extras: Beverages, use of swimming pool, and pickup at local airport are complimentary.
Rates: $35 to $45 single, $45 to $55 double. Personal checks welcome.

CENTRAL CALIFORNIA

CARMEL

HAPPY LANDING INN
Bob Alberson and Dick Stewart
Monte Verde
Carmel, CA 93921
(408) 624-7917
Year-round

1925 English Country Revival

LOCATION: The inn's garden site is located four blocks from the beach and is convenient to central Carmel.

Hugh Comstock was a popular architect in Carmel in the 1920s. You'll find several of his "Hansel and Gretel" style homes in the area. This one was originally used by two families as a vacation retreat, though it's been an inn for about 40 years.

The owners have added stained glass and more fireplaces to the cathedral-ceilinged rooms. They've also decorated with antiques bought at auction (one of their favorite hobbies). Most rooms open onto a garden where flagstone paths lead to a fish pond and gazebo; some rooms also have an ocean view.

Restrictions: No children or pets; smoking is discouraged. Check-in after 1:30 p.m.
Beds: All seven units—one double, four queens, and two king suites —have their own baths.
Breakfast: Homemade breads, fresh fruit, orange juice, hot coffee, tea, and cocoa. "We bring it to your room as soon as you open the curtains in the morning."
Extras: Afternoon tea is served.

Rates: $75 to $120 (suite with fireplace and living room). Personal checks and credit cards accepted.
Mailing Address: PO Box 2619, Carmel, CA 93921

COLUMBIA

CITY HOTEL
Tom Bender and Ron Erickson
Main Street
Columbia, CA 95310
(209) 532-1479
Year-round

1856 Streetfront Hotel

LOCATION: Columbia is a state-owned, restored "living museum." Antique shops, the restored Fallon Theater, a stage depot with a running stagecoach, saloons, and a working blacksmith shop are within walking distance of the inn. Redwood parks, caverns, and the Stanislaus River for fishing are within driving distance.

The hotel has served as a backdrop for many a movie, the most famous being "High Noon." Mark Twain stayed here during his frequent trips to Columbia, and the first owner, George Morgan (after whom the dining room is named), was renowned as an "illustrious innkeeper," according to the current proprietors.

Guests have a choice of balcony, parlor, or hall rooms. There are four hall rooms; balcony rooms overlook tree-lined Main Street, while the three parlor rooms open onto an in-period parlor, complete with overstuffed couches, rocking chairs, and an oval hall mirror. The guest beds range from massive Victorian bedsteads to small-scale brass and iron twins. The "What Cheer" saloon boasts its original cherry Eastlake bar, which has paired round mirrors capped by decorative railings. Many of the pieces come from the state's collection (the building is currently owned by the state).

The whole town is gradually being restored. The most recent effort is the nearby Fallon House Hotel-Theatre, scheduled for completion this year.

Restrictions: No pets. Check-in after 2 p.m., check-out at noon.
Beds: There are six doubles, two rooms with two doubles, and one room with twins. All have half-baths, and showers are down the hall.
Breakfast: Breads, coffee, juices, cheese, and soft-boiled eggs.
Extras: Evening sherry is provided, babysitting can be arranged, and guests are given a wicker basket of "necessaries" for the bath. Wine tastings and dinners are also a highlight.
Rates: $55 (hall and parlor rooms) to $65 (balcony rooms). Cots, $10; cribs at no charge. $5 discount single occupancies. Personal checks and credit cards welcome.
Mailing Address: Box 1870, Main St., Columbia, CA 95310

CENTRAL CALIFORNIA

IONE

THE HEIRLOOM BED & BREAKFAST INN
Melisande Hubbs and Patricia Cross
214 Shakeley Lane
Ione, CA 95640
(209) 274-4468
Year-round

C. 1863 Greek Revival

LOCATION: The structure is set on one-and-a-half acres of English gardens, in the Sierra foothills of gold country. Nearby are lakes, rivers, wineries, antiques, and historic sites.

The inn's name is certainly appropriate, for many heirloom pieces furnish the interior, including a rosewood grand piano that Lola Montez once owned, and collections of fans, glass, and china.

The building's architecture is very unusual for gold-rush country; the place looks much like a Southern plantation. Two-storey porches wrap around the brick structure, and the deep-set windows are nearly six feet high. There's a transom over the front door and many brick arches over the windows. Inside, panelled walls surround a colonial-style staircase, and three fireplaces that sport new flues provide warmth.

Restrictions: No pets. Children over ten only. Check-in between 2 and 6 p.m., check-out at 11 a.m.
Beds: Three of the six rooms share a bath: two kings, two queens, and two doubles.
Breakfast: Fresh fruit and orange juice, homemade breads, "gourmet coffees," plus a quiche, crepe, soufflé, or eggs Benedict entree.
Extras: Afternoon refreshments are provided.
Rates: $50 (shared bath) to $75 (private bath, balcony, fireplace). Personal checks welcome.
Mailing Address: PO Box 322, Ione, CA 95640

JACKSON

COURT STREET INN
Mildred Burns
215 Court Street
Jackson, CA 95642
(209) 223-0416
Year-round

1872 Vernacular with Queen Anne

LOCATION: Downtown Jackson is two blocks away. Churches, a museum, courthouse, original Synagogue, and cemetery are adjacent to the inn. In the surrounding area are antique stores, rivers, lakes, ghost towns, as well as facilities for hiking and skiing.

Mildred Burns was in the middle of restoring the house when she opened it as a B&B in 1981, and she's still working on it today. The whole place, from basement to roof, needed work: like replumbing, rewiring, uncovering fireplaces, doors, windows, and panelling —"a great challenge," she calls it.

The parlor's been furnished in the high style of 1875, with a rococo sofa, chairs, and mirror, a marble fireplace, and a period lighting fixture (one of many in the house) complete with dangling prisms.

The guest rooms are named after successive owners of the house, beginning with Edward Muldoon, a mine owner; the Muldoon room has an oak mantel and a spoon-carved headboard. In 1874 came Isaac Peiser, a pioneer merchant; late 19th-century style prevails in his room, with its Queen Anne bed. The Blairs bought the place in 1900; the family owned a Wells Fargo office and the Jackson Water Works, and they also added another wing to the house. Their room features two iron beds and an oak washstand.

Their daughter, Grace Blair DePue, made another significant addition to the house. In 1930 she had a brick house in the back constructed to house her Indian artifacts collection. (The impressive collection has since been donated to the University of California at Berkeley.) The "Indian House" has two bedrooms, a bath with claw-foot tub, a fireplace, and an 1860 grand piano.

Restrictions: No pets or children under ten. Check-in after 2 p.m., check-out at 11 a.m.
Beds: Four queens, two doubles, and one room with a double and twin include two that share a bath—these have private half-baths, though.
Breakfast: Eggs Benedict, omelettes, waffles, and strada are served to guests' rooms at 9 a.m.
Extras: Local wine, tea, and snacks are served 5 to 7 p.m., and sherry is available in the parlor.
Rates: $55 (view of town, double with half-bath) to $115 (brick house behind main inn), $10 to $15 less mid-week. Personal checks welcome.
10% discount to OHJ members.

CENTRAL CALIFORNIA

JACKSON

1900 Queen Anne/neo-Colonial

GATE HOUSE INN
Frank and Ursel Walker
1330 Jackson Gate Road
Jackson, CA 95642
(209) 223-3500
Year-round

LOCATION: The inn is situated on a quiet country road within walking distance of restaurants and the town of Jackson (less than two miles). The Kennedy Tailing Wheels and old cemeteries are among the reminders of the area's gold-rush history.

One of the earliest settlers in Jackson was not a gold-seeker at all, but rather one A. Chichizola, merchant and rancher. While the miners worked 15-foot sections of the creek across from the present inn, Chichizola sold them food, clothing, and supplies in exchange for gold. His son Tom built this house at the turn of the century, and their descendants still live nearby, on a 380-acre estate.

Pieces of both house and summerhouse came from all over: the staircase from Italy, the front door and a brass chandelier from Leland Stanford's cottage; a stained-glass window was taken from the Comstock Mansion, and the brick wall with granite in the summerhouse (once the gardener's cottage) came from Los Angeles's Chinatown.

Original lighting fixtures and even wallpaper remained in the house, along with oak parquet floors, wainscotting, and marble and tile fireplaces. The Walkers have packed the house with their collections, which range from teddy bears to English bone china and some 100 antique clocks.

Restrictions: No children, pets, or smoking inside. Check-in after 2 p.m., check-out at 11 a.m.

Beds: Four queens and one double all have private baths.

Breakfast: Fresh fruit, coddled egg, fresh pastries, muffins, juice, tea or coffee.

Extras: There are large picnic grounds, screened-in barbecue areas, and a swimming pool for use in summer. Sherry is provided in the rooms.

Rates: $48 to $75 (summerhouse) weekdays, $60 to $85 weekends. Personal checks welcome.

CENTRAL CALIFORNIA

MARIPOSA

GRANNY'S GARDEN BED & BREAKFAST
Dave and Dixie Trabucco
7333 Highway 49 North
Mariposa, CA 95338
(209) 377-8342
Second Sunday in May to
October 31, weather permitting

1896 Queen Anne

LOCATION: Bear Valley is a tiny town near the county seat, where tours of the history center and 1854 Court House are offered. Surrounded by rolling pastures dotted with oak and pine, Bear Valley has a jailhouse, cemetery, and museum that date back to the gold rush. A 130-year-old restaurant is near the inn, and Yosemite is one hour (and one stoplight) away.

"One can sense their pride in owning and managing a house that Dave remembers as a child... We would recommend Granny's Garden to anyone." Scott and Carolyn Conti, Flourtown, Pa.

The first "granny" of the house was Dave Trabucco's grandmother Nancy. She and her husband were the original owners; Dave remembers visiting them as a child. When Nancy died, the house lay vacant for some thirty years. Dave and his wife Dixie bought it from other family members in 1977; miraculously it still had its original redwood interior and exterior, slate foundation, and even some brass fixtures. Dixie is now the granny of the house, "continuing a family heritage," as she puts it.

Six years have been spent restoring the place, with the help of a local carpenter. The Trabuccos are currently "95% done," they report. They've furnished the place with antiques, some inherited from his family and some from hers.

They've also purchased the building next door, saving it from a remuddler. Once a general store, it's the oldest building in Bear Valley. They plan to turn it into a community center or reception hall.

Restrictions: No pets or children under 16. They prefer guests smoke in bedrooms or outside. Check-in between 2 and 5 p.m. (other times by prior arrangement).
Beds: Five rooms, one with two twins and one double share split bath; double with private bath; queen suite with private bath.
Breakfast: Continental is served between 8:30 and 9 a.m.: fresh fruit, homemade muffins, breads, cereals, coffee, tea, or milk, plus champagne for special occasions.
Extras: Complimentary wine (choice of red or white) is provided, along with champagne on special occasions. In each room there's fresh flowers, instant coffee, tea, and a coffeepot. Yosemite-Mariposa airport pickup is available at no charge.
Rates: $40 (single, twin room); $50 (double, shared bath); $60 (queen suite). $5 discount for singles. Personal checks welcome.

10% discount to OHJ members.

MONTEREY

THE JABBERWOCK
Jim and Barbara Allen
598 Laine Street
Monterey, CA 93940
(408) 372-4777
Year-round

1911 Shingle Style with Queen Anne elements

LOCATION: The inn's residential area, overlooking Monterey Bay, is four blocks from Cannery Row and the Monterey Bay Aquarium. Carmel and 17-Mile Drive are nearby, and Big Sur is one hour away.

Once a convent, then a church, the Jabberwock now boasts rooms and even omelettes named for Alice in Wonderland characters (favorites from Jim Allen's childhood). Many rooms look out on Monterey Bay, as does the porch; "you can hear the seals and sea lions bark," says Barbara Allen. Her father built two waterfalls in the garden, and the resulting "fernfall," lined with rocks, evergreens, and ferns, can be seen from the sun porch.

The original woodwork remains, and some of the rooms have odd shapes. The Victorian walnut bed and mahogany clawfoot tub are antique, but the toothbrushes, bathrobes, and razors the management provides, Ms. Allen hastens to add, are new.

Restrictions: No young children; no pets ("our English bull terrier Turkey is affectionate to people, but their pets are a different story"); no smoking.
Beds: Two kings and five queens; two share a bath.
Breakfast: "Absolutely mouthwatering," with dishes named Razzelberry Flabjous, Snarkleberry Flumptious, and the like, plus fresh croissants and fresh fruit.
Extras: "We serve sherry and hors d'oeuvres at 5 p.m. (on the verandah overlooking the Bay) and tuck everyone in bed with cookies and milk." Soft drinks and juices are complimentary all day. Passes to the Aquarium are available for $7. Airport pick-up arrangements can also be made.
Rates: $80 (garden view, shared bath) to $155 (bay and garden view, fireplace, private bath). Personal checks welcome.

MURPHYS

DUNBAR HOUSE 1880 BED & BREAKFAST INN
Bob and Barbara Costa
271 Jones Street
Murphys, CA 95247
(209) 728-2897
Year-round

1880 Italianate

LOCATION: Within walking distance are Murphys Creek ("still a favorite with gold panners"), a museum, art gallery, old school and cemetery, the former jail, and other old homes and landmarks. Mercer and Moaning Caverns are one mile away, a winery is three miles away, and Calaveras Big Trees State Park is within 15 miles.

Though "Seven Brides for Seven Brothers" (the television version) was filmed here, Willis and Ellen Dunbar had only five sons. Willis built the house for his bride in 1880; as babies each of the five boys were fed in the high chair that, covered in many layers of worn paint, still stands in the dining room.

Willis came from New Hampshire, as did his father Freeman. The two operated a lumber mill on the property at one time, and Willis ran the nearby Old Utica Flume, which washed gold from ore. The house was named in honor of this first family. Ironically the owner who restored the structure in 1978 was named Dr. Malcolm Dunbar —no relation to the original Dunbars.

Among the new improvements are an updated kitchen, a pantry converted to a bath, and a closet made from a shower. The house also has new wiring, plumbing, air conditioning, electric heat, and a solar for water. Inside are original mouldings, wide-pine floors, graining on doors, and a freestanding woodburning stove.

Restrictions: Children over ten welcome. Smoking on verandahs only. Check-in between 3 and 6 p.m., other times by special arrangement.
Beds: One double and one queen share a bath; two doubles and one queen have private baths.

Breakfast: Gourmet breakfast served in dining room or in your own room.

Extras: Cheese and crackers served in the afternoon; piano, games, and books available.

Rates: $60 to $75. Credit cards, personal and traveler's checks accepted.

10% discount to OHJ members Sunday to Thursday.

Mailing Address: PO Box 1375, Murphys, CA 95247

PACIFIC GROVE

HOUSE OF SEVEN GABLES INN
John, Nora, Susan, Fred, Ed, and Heather Flatley
555 Ocean View Boulevard
Pacific Grove, CA 93950
(408) 372-4341
Year-round

1886 Queen Anne

LOCATION: Pacific Grove, "crammed with Victorians, from cottages to mansions," is a well-preserved seaside town on the edge of Monterey Bay. From the inn an oceanfront path leads to Cannery Row and the Monterey Aquarium.

The Chase family was delighted to sell the house in 1972 to the current innkeepers, the Flatleys; "they knew we weren't going to tear it down for its land value." Lucey Chase, the first owner, was a well-known philanthropist. One of her pet projects was the local natural history museum. She was a bit of a character, and was known to drive about town in a tiny electric car. Apparently the woman gave the house its name because of her roots in Salem, Massachusetts.

The only changes the Flatleys have made are enlarging some windows to take advantage of the ocean views, and doing some "artful planning" to install more private baths. All 14 guest rooms are part of the original floor plan.

Disliking dark Victorian colors, the Flatleys painted the exterior yellow with white gingerbread. They also gave the decorative iron fence a coat of white. Inside, beside the stained-glass windows, crystal chandeliers, and pier mirrors, Oriental rugs accompany the inlaid French furnishings.

Restrictions: No smoking or pets in the inn; children over 12 welcome. Check-in between 2 and 10 p.m.
Beds: All 14 rooms—13 queens, one double—have private baths.
Breakfast: "No one leaves hungry!" after a full, sit-down breakfast is served in the old dining room: several freshly baked items, fresh orange juice, fresh fruit, some homemade jams—"always *very* generous amounts."
Extras: High tea is served in the old parlor at 4 p.m., fruit is provided in the rooms, local and national newspapers and magazines ("including OHJ") are available, as is a turn-down with sweets. For an additional charge champagne and fresh flowers can be ordered.
Rates: $85 (ocean view, private bath, queen bed) to $125 (ocean view, stained-glass window, queen bed). Cots, $10. Personal and traveler's checks welcome.

PACIFIC GROVE

THE MARTINE INN
Marion and Don Martine
255 Oceanview Boulevard
Pacific Grove, CA 93950
(408) 373-3388
Year-round

1899 Mediterranean

LOCATION: Overlooking the rocky coastline of Monterey Bay, with its whales, sea otters, and fishing fleet, the inn is within walking distance of Cannery Row, Monterey Bay Aquarium, and repertory theatre; a short drive away are the Carmel Mission, 17-Mile Drive, and Fisherman's Wharf.

This mansion, which descends in various stages to the ocean, was built by James and Laura Parke, of Parke-Davis Pharmaceuticals fame. The numerous levels, protected by six-to-ten-foot walls along the street, now hold 19 guest rooms, along with a parlor, library, game room, conference center and spa. Exotic woods were used throughout the interior, from the Siamese teak gates and Honduras mahogany trim to the Spanish cedar main stair. Less esoteric materials like mahogany and oak provide the floor inlay and trim. Tucked in the baths are marble corner sinks and clawfoot tubs. On the doors are original brass hardware and hinges, and in the windows leaded glass.

The Martines completely restored the building, installing new electric, heating, and plumbing systems. Their extensive Victorian furniture collection is primarily American; many of the pieces are still in their original sets. The couple also collects antique pewter, tapestries, crystal, and silver. You'll eat breakfast with Old Sheffield and Victorian utensils.

Restrictions: No children or pets; smoking in fireplace rooms only. Check-in between 2 and 6 p.m.
Beds: 19 rooms—four kings, two doubles, 13 queens—have private baths.
Breakfast: Full.
Extras: Fresh flowers and fruit brought to the rooms daily; wine and hors d'oeuvres are served each evening from 6 to 8.
Rates: $85 to $175 (canopy bed, full ocean view). Personal checks and credit cards accepted.

CENTRAL CALIFORNIA

PACIFIC GROVE

ROSEROX COUNTRY INN BY-THE-SEA
D. Browncroft Family
557 Ocean View Boulevard
Pacific Grove, CA 93950
(408) 373-7673
Year-round

1904 Vernacular neo-Colonial

LOCATION: Within walking distance of this seaside inn are Fisherman's Wharf, Cannery Row, Monterey Bay Aquarium, and Lover's

34

Point Beach. Nearby are Point Lobos, the Carmel Mission, Pebble Beach, and 17-Mile Drive.

Dr. Julia Platt, a noted zoologist, was the house's first owner; she was also the first and only woman mayor of Pacific Grove. She left behind an odd collection of secret compartments and closed-off staircases that the Browncrofts discovered while renovating the building.

The main open stairway winds through four storeys of hardwood floors and redwood-beamed ceilings. The bathrooms have both claw-foot tubs and pull-chain commodes. Every room overlooks the ocean.

Restrictions: No children under 13, no pets, no smoking indoors. Check-in between 3 and 9 p.m.
Beds: One room has two twins, one has a king-sized trundle, four have doubles, and two have queens. Four share a bath.
Breakfast: "You will be spoiled by a sumptuous breakfast," served in bed, on the lower patio, or in the morning room.
Extras: "Happy hour" entails soft drinks, french spring water, beer, and hors d'oeuvres. Evening maid service, morning newspapers, and a special gift are provided in each room.
Rates: $85 to $185 ("truly breathtaking ocean views"). Personal checks welcome.
10% discount to OHJ members.

CENTRAL CALIFORNIA

PLACERVILLE

THE JAMES BLAIR HOUSE
Patsy and Richard Thompson
2985 Clay Street
Placerville, CA 95667
(916) 626-6136
Year-round

1901 Queen Anne

LOCATION: Old Hangtown, the Gold Bug Mine, several restaurants, and a museum are within walking distance. Local wineries and Apple Hill are within a short drive.

Somewhere among the stained-glass windows, in and out the panelled rooms, up the three-storey turret, and along the wraparound porch, wanders a ghost. One of the inn's guests reported sighting it on the main stair; and even before the Thompsons bought the house, a ghost was rumored to be "in residence."

The spirit must have plenty of toys to play with, because owners Patsy and Richard collect everything from antique dolls and stitchery to lamps and tools.

They spent two years restoring the house, using only authentic (not reproduced) materials. The rooms range from the canopy-bedded turret room with a private bath to an enclosed sleeping porch, equipped with quilts and a private entrance.

Restrictions: No babies, pets, or smoking in the house. Check-in between 4 and 8 p.m., other times by prior arrangement.
Beds: Three rooms have queen beds; one has a double bed, and two beds can accommodate roll-aways. Three share a bath.
Breakfast: "Expanded continental": hot muffins, fruit bread, fresh fruit, juice, and coffee, as well as homemade jams and jellies.
Extras: Sherry and nuts are served in the parlor; wine, coffee, and tea are offered upon arrival.
Rates: $35 (sleeping porch) to $70 (turret rooom); cots, $10. 20% discount mid-week in winter. Personal checks welcome.

10% discount to OHJ members mid-week.

CENTRAL CALIFORNIA

SACRAMENTO

THE BRIGGS HOUSE
S. Garmston/B. Stoltz/K. Yeates/
P. Rawles/S. Lewis
2209 Capitol Avenue
Sacramento, CA 95816
(916) 441-3214
Year-round

1901 Neo-Colonial/Foursquare

LOCATION: The house, surrounded by other early 20th- and late 19th-century homes, is seven blocks from the State Capitol and close

to Sutter's Fort, historic Sacramento, and the Governor's Mansion.

After studying medicine in Vienna, London, Paris, and Michigan, Dr. William Ellery Briggs came to Sacramento. Well-known as an ear, nose, and throat specialist, he was also an active conservationist who founded the Save the Redwoods League. He and his wife, Grace, raised a daughter Phoebe in the house; Pheobe's son (the Briggs' grandson), C. K. McClatchy, is currently the editor of the *Sacramento Bee*.

After Briggs' death in 1931, the house was used as a boarding house. It deteriorated until the 1970s, when a lawyer and an interior decorator undertook its restoration. With its condition stabilized by 1981, a group of teachers were able to buy it and turn it into a B&B.

About the only things that needed work were the exterior and roof; also a few extra baths had to be installed to make the place a serviceable inn. And the carriage house was completely overhauled and turned into two two-bedroom suites.

Much of the original detail remains, such as an Ionic-columned porch, Ionic pilasters and leaded-glass windows on the outside; pocket doors, inlaid floors, china cupboards, and coved ceilings inside. Plus the original lighting fixtures have survived.

The teachers—there are five of them—have brought many antiques and family heirlooms to the house. There are carved beds, china dolls, lace, china, and armoires, spiced with memorabilia like a framed photo of Dr. Briggs.

Restrictions: Small children allowed only in the carriage house. Smoking limited. No pets. Check-in after 4 p.m., check-out at 11 a.m.
Beds: Two suites have a double, queen, roll-away, and bath; two doubles have a private bath and two share; and one has twins and a semi-private bath.
Breakfast: Full: fresh orange juice, fresh fruit, baked egg dish (fritata or quiche), homemade muffins, freshly ground coffee or tea.
Extras: Bicycles, a spa, and a sauna are available for guest use. In the afternoons wine, lemonade, mineral water, iced or hot tea are served with nuts and fruits.
Rates: $50 (double with shared bath) to $90 (two-room suite); cots, $10; playpens available at no charge. Personal checks and credit cards accepted.

SANTA CRUZ

BABBLING BROOK INN
Tom and Helen King
1025 Laurel Street
Santa Cruz, CA 95060
(408) 427-2437
Year-round

1909 Vernacular

LOCATION: An acre of terraced gardens with redwoods, laurels, stone walls, patios, and a gazebo surrounds the inn. Laurel Creek meanders past the property's decks and under a covered footbridge. Beaches and redwood forests are within ten minutes; restaurants, wineries, and sailing charters are also close by.

The Babbling Brook Inn made the National Register solely on the basis of the people who've owned the site. The building itself was built in 1909 and has been substantially enlarged over the years.

The first in a series of fascinating uses of the property came long ago, when the Ohlone Indians bathed and fished in this bend of Laurel Creek. When the Spanish controlled the region, in 1796 the Mission fathers built a grist mill here; its foundation was incorporated into the present house. Next an entrepreneur named R. C. Kirby set up Santa Cruz's first tannery on the property. He'd come to California for the gold rush; he'd already made and lost three fortunes. Mr. and Mrs. Charles Place, actors who ran a touring stock company, built a five-room log cabin in 1909. Silent films were made at the house.

Peter Rovnianek bought the cabin in 1916. The last of the Czar's U.S. representatives, he spoke 13 languages and was a leader of the American Slovak community. He brought with him a friend, Ulysses S. Grant's son. Rovnianek added a lean-to to the cabin (which is now called the Countess Room), and there Grant wrote a biography of his father.

Rovnianek was famed as both gourmet and gourmand. One main course at his house was described as "suckling pig stuffed with a quail inside a pheasant." These excesses were soon upstaged by those of the next owners, Mr. and Mrs. Charles Chandler of San Francisco. She claimed to be the Countess Florenzo de Chandler (Rovnianek said he'd known her in Europe and that she was a fraud). She was given to wearing large quantities of pearls and diamonds, both real and fake. She entertained lavishly, though her guests made fun of her pretensions behind her back. She added the second storey, balcony, front bedroom, and bath to the house, and built the stone retaining walls that line the river bed.

In addition to the Countess's stone walls, there's a complex of decks overlooking the waterfall, as well as gazebos and a covered fastbridge.

Restrictions: No children under 12, no pets.
Beds: All 12 rooms have private baths. Ten have fireplaces. One has a king and rollaway, one has two queens, and the rest have queens.
Breakfast: "Large continental": warm, homemade breads and muffins, fresh fruits and juices, freshly ground coffee and herb teas.
Extras: "Delectable desserts" as well as cappuccino and espresso, beer, soft drinks, champagne, and local wine are available. The innkeepers can provide dry-cleaning services, wake-up calls, and picnic baskets.
Rates: $60 to $95 (honeymoon suite with waterfall view). 15% discount from September 16 to May 15 weekdays. $10 per person over double occupancy. Personal and traveler's checks and credit cards accepted.

CENTRAL CALIFORNIA

SANTA CRUZ

CHATEAU VICTORIAN, A
BED & BREAKFAST INN
Alice-June Benjamin
118 First Street
Santa Cruz, CA 95060
(408) 458-9458
Year-round

LOCATION: The inn is close to sailing and surfing (the beach is one block away) and near Santa Cruz's boardwalk and wharf.

The original owner is said to have been a New England sea captain, who eloped and sailed with his new bride to the West Coast. After his death the house was, at various times, a bordello, rooming house, and most recently, several apartments.

Franz Benjamin accomplished many major restoration tasks in a single year. The ceilings were restored to their original 11-foot height, the front bay window rebuilt, fireplaces were reconstructed, and the like. His family heirlooms—paintings, etchings, a 200-year-old clock —now fill the individually decorated rooms, many of which have ocean views.

Restrictions: No children, pets or smoking. Check-in 3:30 to 6:30 p.m., check-out at noon.
Beds: All seven rooms have queen-size beds and private baths; five have fireplaces as well.
Breakfast: "Expanded continental": croissants, fruit, fresh coffee, a variety of teas, hot chocolate, marmalades and preserves, cream cheese and butter.
Extras: Wine, sherry, cheese, and crackers are served in the afternoon at no charge, and after-dinner drinks are provided.
Rates: $70 (bay window and window seat) to $100 (large room with ocean view, fireplace). Personal checks and credit cards accepted.

CENTRAL CALIFORNIA

SANTA CRUZ

CLIFF CREST BED & BREAKFAST INN
Cheryl McEnery
407 Cliff Street
Santa Cruz, CA 95060
(408) 427-2609
Year-round except Christmas Eve and Day

1887 Queen Anne

LOCATION: The inn, located on Santa Cruz's historic Beach Hill, is less than two blocks from the ocean, on a landscaped half-acre. The wharf, boardwalk, and lighthouse are also within walking distance, and Pacific Garden Mall is close by.

Carved in Victorian lettering on a stone wall near the entrance are the words "Cliff-Crest." The landscaper of Golden Gate Park, John McLaren, planned the lush half-acre of grounds that surrounds the house. He was a good friend of one of the first owners, William Jeter, who served as Lieutenant Governor of California and Mayor of Santa Cruz. An early conservationist, Jeter is best remembered for helping establish the Henry Cowell Redwoods State Park.

After five years of searching, the McEnerys discovered this ideal B&B in 1984—it had already been restored in 1970 and operated as an inn. Their improvements consisted mainly of renovating the gardens, stripping paint and wallpaper in the interior, and highlighting the exterior details with five shades of paint.

Sunshine streams through geometric "Mondrian"-style stained glass in the solarium, overlooking the garden. There's more stained glass in the rooms, and the furnishings include a four-poster with pineapple-carved posts, a Victorian clawfoot tub, and an Eastlake queen-sized bed.

Restrictions: No smoking, pets, or children. Check-in between 2:30 and 6 p.m., check-out at 11:30 a.m.
Beds: There are three queens and two doubles, all with private baths.
Breakfast: Fresh fruit, yogurt, homemade muffins, fresh orange juice, jams; coffee, tea, or cocoa.
Extras: Evening wine and cheese are provided at no charge, as are coffee, tea, and iced tea.
Rates: $60 to $90. Personal checks and credit cards welcome.

10% discount to OHJ members.

CENTRAL CALIFORNIA

SONORA

BARRETTA GARDENS INN, BED & BREAKFAST
Bob and Julie Thiele, Beverly J. MacLauchlin
700 South Barretta Street
Sonora, CA 95370
(209) 532-6039
Year-round

1904 Vernacular

LOCATION: The inn is located on a hillside street overlooking Sonora, part of gold country. The downtown area is within walking distance, and many intriguing towns within driving distance, including the preserved state park at Columbia. Yosemite is 65 miles away.

Along with the lovely leaded-glass bookcases, arched doorways, and the collections of golden-oak furniture, silver, and china inside, you'll want to examine, of all places, the garage. There an unusual rotating platform turns the car around while it's still *inside the garage*, so that it faces out in the morning—the driver just pulls in and pushes the platform around manually.

The owners don't know the building's history—"we're still researching," says Julie Thiele—but they've put much effort into the house, including removing some five layers of wallpaper, scraping, sanding, painting, and papering.

Restrictions: Check-in after 4 p.m. Smoking on the porch only, children under 15 by prior arrangement, no pets.
Beds: All four rooms have queen beds, and one has an extra trundle. Three share a bath.
Breakfast: Orange juice, freshly ground coffee, homemade breads, cakes, fruit in season, plus a hot entree.
Extras: Complimentary sherry and wine are served, as well as, upon request, tea, coffee, and lemonade. And, "on occasion," snacks are available.
Rates: $50 on weekdays, $55 weekends and holidays; group and family rates are available, and rates are lower in winter. Personal check, and credit cards welcome.
10% discount to OHJ members.

CENTRAL CALIFORNIA

SONORA

**THE RYAN HOUSE BED &
BREAKFAST INN**
Nancy and Guy Hoffman
153 South Shepherd Street
Sonora, CA 95370
(209) 533-3445
Year-round

1855 Vernacular Greek Revival

LOCATION: This quiet neighborhood of Sonora, in gold country is five miles from the preserved town of Columbia, "a living history park." Yosemite is within an hour's drive, Stanislaus National Forest is a few minutes away, and there are many gold-rush attractions and antique shops to explore.

"Ours is not a pretentious home. It has a simple, lived-in feeling. It's not a museum, but rather a place to experience what old houses have to offer."

Since the original owners, the Ryan family, were involved in the banking and mining industries, their descendants expected that a safe found buried on the property would be full of gold, or at least banknotes. Just before the family sold the house, the safe was hoisted out of the ground and opened. Alas, like most such treasure chests, it turned out to be empty.

When Maureen Kelley purchased the place from the Ryans early in 1983, she embarked on an extensive restoration project. The house was rewired, replumbed, drywalled, carpeted, painted, and "generally spruced up." Only one room of the original floor plan (itself a product of the Ryans' successive additions) was changed, and several baths were added. Next, Ms. Kelley worked on the grounds, where rose bushes up to 80 years old still stand. And at the end of her efforts the county historical society gave her a "Gold Nugget Award" for historic restoration.

Original details like the doors, mouldings, siding, and foundation remain. The house is one of the oldest wooden-frame buildings left in Sonora, a town ravaged by several fires.

Restrictions: Children welcome by prior approval. No smoking inside the inn. "We have two cats so we ask guests to leave pets at home." Check-in between 3 and 8 p.m.
Beds: Three doubles and one queen: one has a private half-bath, and a full bath, and the other two share a bath.
Breakfast: A hearty breakfast is served each morning, including fresh nut breads, muffins, fruit, and juice. Coffee is freshly ground daily.
Extras: Sherry and a bowl of nuts or candy are set out each evening. Iced tea is available all day in the summer, and guests are welcome to use the refrigerator to chill wine.
Rates: $35 (shared bath) to $55 (private bath) weekdays, $50 to $60 weekends. Personal checks and credit cards welcome.
Mailing Address: PO Box 416, Sonora, CA 95370

SUTTER CREEK

BOTTO COUNTRY INN
Stan and Mary Ann Stanton
11 Sutter Hill Road
Sutter Creek, CA 95685
(209) 267-5519
Year-round

1913 Vernacular

LOCATION: The inn has a country setting across the street from the Central Eureka Mine, and features lawn and pasture complete with calves and ducks. Sutter Creek is a quarter-mile away, the county airport is nearby, and there are many historic sites on the inn's road (the old Highway 49).

"It's so nice having people visit who own or are restoring old houses —we have so many ideas to exchange and share."

Constantino Botto left his home in Italy in 1858, and travelled to America to seek his fortune. He found it in the mines of Sutter Creek, and by 1860 he was wealthy enough to purchase 40 acres across the street from the Central Eureka Mine. Botto built his residence, then voyaged back to Italy to bring his mother to the new home. He also planted the chestnut, olive, and walnut trees around the house, with seeds he'd brought back from Italy.

His was a high energy level, and among the businesses he became involved in were a boarding house in Sutter Creek, a partnership that constructed a ditch to bring water to the mines, and a liquor trading enterprise. He turned the building next door, intended as a grainery, into a saloon. Everything he touched, it seemed, thrived—even the trees, from which he was eventually able to cultivate fruit.

Of the Bottos' ten children five lived to a ripe old age, leaving behind quantities of grandchildren, great- and great-great-grandchildren.

Vines have overgrown the saloon, and the original house burnt down in 1913 (it was rebuilt that same year). Different "themes" characterize each guest room, and there's also period wallpaper and clawfoot tubs complete with showers.

44

Restrictions: Smoking restricted. Children over ten permitted any-time, babies and children under ten Monday to Thursday only.
Beds: Four doubles and a room with twins share two baths.
Breakfast: "Full country": fresh fruit compote, local smoked ham with orange-raisin sauce, sauteed apples, herb scrambled eggs with sauteed vegetables, basil tomatoes, potatoes, gourmet coffees.
Rates: All rooms are $58.50 ($48.50 single); cribs, $10. $10 discount mid-week December through February. Personal checks welcome.

  10% discount to OHJ members.

SUTTER CREEK

SUTTER CREEK INN
Jane Way
75 Main Street
Sutter Creek, CA 95685
(209) 267-5606
Year-round

1859 Greek Revival

LOCATION: Sutter Creek remains much as it was in the 19th cen-tury, a village of 1600 residents. Lakes, streams, and 16 mines are nearby, and Sacramento is one hour away. Plus the town boasts the only water-driven foundry in the nation, as well as many shops.

  "The inn has many French and English antiques, but we're most famous for our very comfortable beds."

A young man from Michigan, Edward Voorheis, came to Sutter Creek seeking his fortune in 1877. The gold rush was already well advanced, but the supply far from depleted: Voorheis was able to discover several new mines, and had such success that he eventually ran half of all mines in Sutter Creek. Later he served as president of the California Miners Association and as a state senator from 1890 to 1898, working on mining legislation.

  A local storeowner named John Keyes built the Sutter Creek Inn as his private home in 1859. He lived there with his wife Clara until he died in 1875; she was left a childless widow. Five years later, at the age of 39, she married Voorheis, who was a mere 30. He moved into the house, and she bore him a daughter in 1881—who, at age 85, sold the place to innkeeper Jane Way.

The passing generations added many rooms to the house; what looks like a small Greek Revival from the front actually holds nine guest rooms and shields ten bungalows behind it. Some of the bungalows have grape arbors and what Jane calls "secret gardens."

Her favorite anecdote about the place is that Elliott Roosevelt, FDR's son, was once visiting (before it became an inn). He was called to the phone early one morning, and came down dressed only in a towel wrapped around his waist. "The help was aghast; the old-timers still talk about it."

She collects antique cups, cow-shaped creamers and teapots, and has them on display.

Restrictions: Children over 15 welcome. No pets; no smoking in some rooms. Check-in after 2:30 p.m.

Beds: There are nine rooms in the main house and ten in the cottages, including ten queens, five twins, and four doubles. None share a bath.

Breakfast: All guests sit at a long table in front of the fireplace and are served, family-style, a hot breakfast, with a different menu each morning.

Extras: The spacious grounds are perfect for summer picnics, and the local pool, tennis courts, and museum are available at no charge.

Rates: $45 to $78 (fireplace, larger room), maximum of $58 on weekdays. Personal checks welcome.

Mailing Address: PO Box 385, Sutter Creek, CA 95685

CENTRAL CALIFORNIA

TUOLUMNE

OAK HILL RANCH BED & BREAKFAST
Sanford and Jane Grover
18550 Connally Lane
Tuolumne, CA 95379
(209) 928-4717
Year-round

1980 Victorian Revival

LOCATION: The inn is on 56 acres in the Sierra Nevada Mountains at an elevation of 3,000 feet. Native oaks, ponderosa pines, forested hillsides, and views of mountains grace the property, along with two large ponds and hilly pastures with farm animals. Yosemite is nearby, as are Columbia and other gold-rush attractions.

"**B**oy, you are sure doing a great job restoring that old house," a passer-by once told the Grovers, and they smiled. Because this isn't an old house at all; we're including it in this book because of the pains the Grovers took to make it look like one.

They began collecting Victorian building materials 25 years ago. And then, based on their philosophy that "we buy to use, not just collect," they hauled their collection by truck and trailer to a ranch site in Tuolumne. For his senior project in college, their architect son Donald produced plans for a "country Victorian" house. The Grovers set to work stripping, repairing, and refinishing the wood, a two-year undertaking. They found a "kind and very patient contractor" who helped them assemble the pieces, and that took another year and a half.

The new-old house has antique turned posts and rails on the porch, 34 redwood doors in the interior, as well as mahogany and walnut mantels, one of which has shelves with spindle rails and posts. There's also leaded glass throughout. Nearby is a new-old gazebo and a former milking barn converted to a honeymoon cottage.

In keeping with their policy of using, not just collecting, the Grovers don antique costumes when serving breakfast. They also actually drive the 1908 Maxwell two-cylinder they own. The heirloom furnishings range from barrel-top desks and marble-topped tables to china from the Orient. The Grovers collected the rest, with a predilection for Eastlake, including mirrors, beds, and a dining room set.

Restrictions: Check-in between 3 and 7 p.m. (later by arrangement). No smoking inside, children under 12, or pets.
Beds: Two doubles and one queen in the main house share two baths. The cottage has two queens, two twin roll-aways, and a bath.
Breakfast: Full, gourmet breakfasts are served daily: freshly squeezed orange or cranberry juice, fresh fruit, and beverages. Entrees include garden omelettes, eggs fantasia, crepes Normandy, pineapple pancakes, or square eggs-en-casserole with breakfast meats, fried potatoes, and broiled tomatoes.
Extras: Upon arrival guests are offered cold soft drinks, tea or coffee, and, of course, "a tour of the premises."
Rates: $50 (double) to $68 (cottage); cots, $15. Personal checks welcome.
   10% discount to OHJ members.
Mailing Address: PO Box 307, Tuolumne, CA 95379

VOLCANO

ST. GEORGE HOTEL
Marlene and Chuck Inman
Two Main Street
Volcano, CA 95689
(209) 296-4458
Closed all Mondays, Tuesdays,
and January to February 15

1862 Vernacular Italianate

LOCATION: There are many old buildings in town, as well as two gold-rush era cemeteries. Nearby are the Sierra foothills, dotted with oak and pine trees.

"There are no TVs or telephones in the rooms, so be prepared to listen to the sounds of frogs, crickets, and our great old jukebox."

With ivy crawling up the porch columns and dangling from the porch railings, the St. George Hotel looks a bit like a Southern plantation. It's actually one of the best preserved hotels left in gold-rush country.

When it was built it was called, "the tallest and most elegant hotel in the Mother Lode." The bar is literally crammed with old photos and memorabilia about the building, along with moose heads, cowboy hats, signs, and the like. In the lounge there's a stone fireplace, and there's also a vintage jukebox at the hotel.

The rooms, which come equipped with antique beds, are mostly named after mining towns. The rooms in the annex (a newer, c. 1961 structure, and like the main building recently repainted) are named after streets in Volcano.

Restrictions: No pets in the old building; children under 12 welcome in the annex.
Beds: In the old building, 14 rooms share two full and two half-baths. All annex rooms have private baths.
Extras: Babysitting can be arranged with 48-hour notice.
Rates: $40 and up. Weekends, $37.50 MAP. Personal checks welcome.

CLIO

**WHITE SULPHUR
SPRINGS RANCH BED &
BREAKFAST**
The Millers, the Vanellas, and
the Gordons
Highway 89 South
Clio, CA 96106
(916) 836-2387
May through November, other
times by special arrangement

1852 Greek Revival

LOCATION: The inn offers an expansive view of the Mohawk Valley. The Feather River, Johnsville State Park, lakes, and streams are nearby for recreation, as are four golf courses, riding stables, and skiing facilities.

Guests as far back as 1852 have been taking the plunge in the property's mineral-spring heated pool. The house originally served as a stagecoach stop on the Truckee-to-Quincy route.

In 1867, when George McLear purchased it, he and his family became determined to hang on to it at all costs. When Bing Crosby tried to buy the ranch from them, for an unspecified amount of money, George Jr. offered Bing the same amount to leave them alone!

George's family hung on to their furniture too, so the house is full of their accumulated oak, chestnut, walnut, and marble-topped pieces, along with a working pump organ, a piano shipped around Cape Horn, a fainting couch, and pieces crafted by George himself. The family also kept their papers; guests can view the ledger George used during his days as a shopkeeper (before he bought the ranch), and the letters George's brothers wrote during the Civil War.

The current owners have made a few changes in the floor plan, primarily by combining four separate areas into a large family room/kitchen. There the most singular feature is a three-door meat keeper, taken from the original meat house.

Restrictions: No smoking in the house, pets, or children under 12.

Check-in between 3 and 6 p.m.

Beds: Four doubles and one king; two or three share the baths.

Breakfast: Homemade muffins and jams, selections of coffees, teas, juices, and fruit are served in the formal dining room.

Extras: The Olympic-size swimming pool on the property is kept at a constant 70° by the 85° mineral springs that feed it; it reportedly has medicinal benefits. Complimentary wine and nuts are served from 5 to 7 p.m.

Rates: $65 to $140 (marble-topped furniture collection). Personal checks and credit cards accepted.

10% discount to OHJ members.

NORTHERN CALIFORNIA

EUREKA

THE CARTER HOUSE BED & BREAKFAST INN
Mark and Christi Carter
1033 Third Street
Eureka, CA 95501
(707) 445-1390
Year-round

1982 Victorian Revival

LOCATION: The inn has a view of the bay, the Carson Mansion, and Eureka, surrounded by foothills and redwood forests. It stands at the edge of historic Old Town. Local activities include hiking, bike trips, crabbing, hunting, and, of course, the ocean.

For years Mark Carter had admired the works of 19th-century architects Samuel and Joseph C. Newsom, the team who designed the famous Carson Mansion in Eureka. As a developer he'd even renovated a few of these buildings. When he found an old book containing the Newsoms' plans for a San Francisco house, built but burned to the ground in the 1906 fire, Carter was inspired. He decided to rebuild the house from scratch.

He chose a hillside spot that overlooks the bay and, appropriately, the Carson Mansion. He hired a crew of three and set about re-creating the four-storey redwood house, with its intricate details inside and out.

50

He changed only one feature, a bay window in the entry, in order to give the hallway more light. The interior is more open and airy than most of its Victorian counterparts; it has three open parlors, three large bays, and a light color scheme. The floors are of polished oak, and the accessories primarily contemporary paintings and ceramics.

Mark's 1958 Bentley is a "permanent guest," and is available for airport pickups.

Restrictions: Check-in between 3:30 and 6 p.m., check-out at 11 a.m. No pets; children ten and over welcome. Smoking in the main floor parlors only.

Beds: Two of the seven rooms have two doubles, one has a queen and a dressing room, and the rest doubles. Three share a bath.

Breakfast: Freshly squeezed orange juice, fresh fruit with cream; choice of eggs Benedict, eggs Florentine, apple crepes with sausage; smoked salmon platter, pecan tart, coffee, tea.

Extras: Wine and hors d'oeuvres are served each evening, and cookies, tea, and cordials are offered at bedtime.

Rates: $70 (shared bath) to $150 (suite with fireplace, dressing room, jacuzzi). Personal checks and credit cards welcome.

FERNDALE

1899 Queen Anne

GINGERBREAD MANSION BED & BREAKFAST INN
Wendy Hatfield and Ken Torbert
400 Berding Street
Ferndale, CA 95536
(707) 786-4000
Year-round

LOCATION: The whole village is a state historical landmark in honor of its brightly painted, well-preserved Victorians. Five miles from the ocean, it has shops, galleries, a museum, theatre, an old cemetery, and a blacksmith's shop.

In almost any other town the Gingerbread Mansion would stick out like a wonderful but sore thumb. But in Ferndale, where a colorful hodgepodge of bay windows, turrets, gazebos, cupolas and spires lines Main Street, the mansion fits right in.

Constructed by Dr. Hogan Ring, a Norwegian immigrant, the house was converted in 1920 to a hospital, with an annex that doubled the mansion's original size. Ferndale General, as the facility was named, failed after only three years. The addition was later used as an American Legion hall, rest home, and finally apartments.

When the annex was abandoned and began to deteriorate, the townspeople thought it best to demolish the entire mansion. Fortunately two sympathetic individuals purchased the house in the mid-1960s and spent 17 years carefully restoring it.

Inside the Gingerbread Mansion, the "most talked-about room," according to Wendy Hatfield, is the second-floor bath. It's 200 square feet, and contains an elevated clawfoot tub surrounded by a railing, a mirrored ceiling and walls, as well as a stained-glass window. For those in a hurry, a shower stands unobtrusively in one corner.

Clawfoot tubs, sometimes two to a room, are located in the bedrooms and come complete with reading lamps. Redwood moulding and trim line the walls, and a five-piece Eastlake parlor set is found in the parlor. Ken collects green Depression glass that he and Wendy serve breakfast on.

Recently the couple remodeled the annex into four more suites. They removed the cement operating-room floor "among other interesting things," and now, they say, visitors can't distinguish "where the old ends and the new begins."

Restrictions: Children ten and older welcome. Smoking permitted only on outside verandahs.
Beds: There are five queens, one queen with twin, one twin with double, and one room with two twins.
Breakfast: "Generous continental": homemade muffins, cakes, breads, cheeses, fruits, coffee, tea, and juice; early in the morning, coffee and tea are brought to the guest rooms as a starter.
Extras: Afternoon tea/coffee with cake is served in the parlor. The evening turn-down service leaves behind fresh hand-dipped chocolates. Bicycles, painted yellow and peach to match the inn, are provided as are bathrobes.
Rates: $75 (garden view, two twins plus private sink) to $125 (two-room suite with two clawfoot tubs). $10 less, mid-week in January and February. Personal checks and credit cards welcome.

10% discount to OHJ members.

GRASS VALLEY

ANNIE HORAN'S B&B
Ivan and Bette Nance
415 West Main Street
Grass Valley, CA 95945
(916) 272-2418
Year-round

1874 Queen Anne

LOCATION: Main and Mill Street shopping areas are within an easy stroll, and many pubs and restaurants are several blocks from the inn. And the Empire Mine is also close by, along with cross-country and downhill skiing areas.

With the money he'd earned by investing in rich local gold mines, James L. Horan built a new home for his wife, Mary, in 1874. But one fortune evidently wasn't enough for him, because when silver was discovered in nearby Nevada, he couldn't resist. He died there soon afterward of Rocky Mountain spotted fever.

He was a builder by trade, and among his handiworks, other than this house, was the first Catholic church in Grass Valley.

His widow deeded the house to her sons in 1893; they in turn passed it to their sister Annie. She, after having her brothers remodel it for her according to turn-of-the-century taste, opened it as a boarding house and Catholic retreat. She was very active in community affairs, and she let most of the newly-arrived priests in town stay with her. She ran the establishment until her death in the 1950s.

The interior remains as Annie maintained it, with the original configuration of entry hall, parlor, dining room, and guest quarters. Only an outdoor deck for dining was added by the Nances in 1984. To furnish the house Bette and Ivan collected antiques from Europe, Asia, and the American South.

Restrictions: Smoking only on the deck. No children or pets. Check-in between 4 and 6 p.m., check-out at 11 a.m.
Beds: The three queens and one double all have private baths.
Breakfast: Fresh fruit salad, two types of German pastry, tea, coffee, and juice.

Rates: $54 to $81; personal checks and credit cards welcome. 10% discount to OHJ members.

GRASS VALLEY

MURPHY'S INN
Marc and Rose Murphy
318 Neal Street
Grass Valley, CA 95945
(916) 273-6873
Year-round

1866 Vernacular Gothic Revival

LOCATION: The area offers restored miners' cottages, Victorian homes, the historic Holbrooke Hotel with California's oldest bar, as well as proximity to skiing, hiking, and fishing areas.

Long ago, two people who never knew one another set the stage for Murphy's Inn. One was Edward Coleman, a famous gold baron who owned the North Star and Idaho mines. He built this house as part of his personal estate. The other was innkeeper Marc Murphy's great-grandmother, who in 1902, near the Russian River, instituted the family tradition of innkeeping.

Original fireplaces and gas chandeliers, along with brass beds and other period furniture, characterize the interior. The vegetation on the property is particularly noteworthy; there's a giant sequoia in back of the house, and the ivy climbing up the porch columns has been trained to dangle from the porch roof in shapes that look just like hanging baskets.

Restrictions: Check-in between 2 and 6 p.m.
Beds: Two kings and four queens have private baths; one queen and one double share a bath.
Breakfast: Belgian waffles or coddled eggs, fresh juice's and coffee.
Extras: The innkeepers provide limousine and airport pickup service, complimentary wine, sherry, and "sun tea."
Rates: $51.20 (double, private entrance, shared bath) to $83.60 (king, private bath, fireplace). Extra occupant, $15; cots, $5. $10 discount

weekdays January through April. Personal checks and credit cards accepted.

10% discount to OHJ members.

GRASS VALLEY

SWAN-LEVINE HOUSE
Howard Levine and Margaret
Warner Swan
328 South Church Street
Grass Valley, CA 95945
(916) 272-1873
Year-round

1880 Queen Anne/neo-Colonial (modified 1895)

LOCATION: Grass Valley has parks, museums, and restored homes testifying to its past gold-mining days. The town is situated in the Sierra foothills at a 2500-foot elevation; many outdoor recreation areas are nearby.

"We have been working on this house for ten years and continue to improve and redecorate it—things are always changing!"

William Campbell, who built the house in 1880, was a merchant of a rather odd assortment of supplies, from mining equipment to baked goods. In 1895 he remodelled the place to keep up with popular taste, so there's both Queen Anne asymmetrical towers and a neo-Colonial hipped roof.

Two brothers, both doctors, turned the house into a community medical center around the turn of the century. It remained so for about 60 years, until 1968. The surgery room's white tiled floor and a bathroom with scrub-up sinks have survived.

The building stands nearly four stories in front, flanked by 80-foot magnolia trees. Four original fireplaces remain, two of which are encircled by ornamental tiles. The interior is furnished simply in what the Levines call "country Victorian." They've accumulated a number of Victorian oak pieces, including two bedsteads, to accompany some pieces they inherited.

Restrictions: Children are permitted. No smoking. Check-in "by arrangement." "Babies O.K. too!"

Beds: Two doubles and a king share two full and one half-bath; there's one queen suite with a private bath and sitting room.

Breakfast: "The menu depends on the season and what guests want to eat," but may include homemade breads, sausages, eggs, pancakes, fruit, juices, and coffeecake.

Extras: In general, odds and ends in the kitchen are accessible. And the cookie jar is always full. Many guests come to learn to make an etching so classes, materials, a studio, plus matting and framing are available.

Rates: $40 (double, sink) to $60 (suite). Personal checks and credit cards accepted.

NORTHERN CALIFORNIA

QUINCY

THE FEATHER BED
Chuck and Dianna Goubert
542 Jackson Street
Quincy, CA 95971
(916) 283-0102
Year-round

1893 Queen Anne; remodelled 1905 with neo-classical porch

LOCATION: The inn is along Quincy's "Heritage Walk." The town offers many gold-rush era buildings including a museum, courthouse, and the downtown area.

"Their impeccable taste has created an ambiance of elegance, charm, and tranquility. And we really enjoyed their warm hospitality." Mr. and Mrs. R.T., Palo Alto, Calif.

Edward Edwin Huskinson's mother whisked him off to America when he was only 14. They lived at first in a hotel in Quincy. Edward waited until he was 41 to marry a local girl named Jeannie Yeates, and soon afterward the couple had this house built.

An enterprising businessman, Huskinson was involved locally in both real estate and mining; he also helped organize the Plumas County Bank.

In 1905 the Huskinsons modernized their home. They added electricity and bathrooms to the inside, and a classical porch to the outside. At the same time columned woodwork (which has survived) to match the porch was installed in the parlor.

During restoration the Gouberts discovered many things, some of them depressing—that the original staircase had been removed, sold to a local hotel, and lost forever in a fire—others more cheerful, like many curious artifacts, a collection the couple has proudly on display.

The inn, named for the nearby Feather River, has rooms named after its previous inhabitants. Edward's room, appropriately, is the front bedroom that overlooks downtown Quincy, and it has stained-glass windows. Jeannie's room was once her sewing room. Son Barnett has a room named after him, as does daughter Gladys; her room has a view of the mountains.

The original fixtures remain in some of the baths, the wallpapers are all of period designs, and the furnishings are primarily pieces of antique American oak.

Restrictions: "We are unable to provide for children, pets, and have a non-smoking policy." Check-in usually 2 to 6 p.m., "but we're happy to accept other times with prior arrangement."
Beds: Both doubles and all four queens have private baths.
Breakfast: Freshly squeezed juice, blackberry smoothies, fresh fruit, baked apples and pears, poppyseed cake, bran muffins, coffee, and teas.
Extras: The inn offers a cross-country ski package, fishing guide, complimentary bicycles, and afternoon tea on the patio or porch.
Rates: $50 (double) to $65 (gardener's cottage), $10 discount in winter. Personal checks and credit cards accepted.
Mailing Address: PO Box 3200, Quincy, CA 95971

NORTHERN CALIFORNIA

TAHOE CITY

1929-30

MAYFIELD HOUSE
Janie Kaye
236 Grove Street
Tahoe City, CA 95730
(916) 583-1001
Year-round

LOCATION: The major ski resorts of the High Sierras are within an easy drive. Steps from the inn are the lake, shops, and restaurants of Tahoe City. Gambling casinos at Reno are also within driving distance.

Tahoe City would probably have about 150 fewer homes and no breakwater if it weren't for Norman Mayfield. And it might not have gotten a water utility as quickly as it did, nor have a boat company, if Mayfield hadn't been involved.

Mayfield, the inn's builder and first owner, started out as a caretaker on a Tahoe lakefront estate. Aided by his employer, he began a career as a contractor. Thirteen asphalt tennis courts were his first project. He soon tackled bridges, warehouses, houses, and then piers. Using a barge, tugboat, and pile driver he sank the first piers into Lake Tahoe. A tent by the lake shore served as his field office. At the peak of his 27-year career as a contractor, begun in 1925, he employed a group of 40 people, which frequently included a ten-man construction crew.

He built many houses for the leisure class of the Bay Area, though he himself took little part in their activities. At 95 he recalled, "There wasn't any of that pleasure stuff in the old days. We had to make a living." He frequently stayed in Tahoe each year until snows halted construction, though his wife preferred warmer climates and remained at their ranch in the San Joaquin Valley.

When he built his own home in 1930 he opted for a simple, cottage-like building. Like the larger houses he built, though, it's made of natural materials like wood shingles and stone. (In all his buildings he preferred to use local materials, including granite and native lumber.) He also hired the same mason that had worked on many of Tahoe's estates, so the property's stonework is well-crafted and extensive.

At age 90, in 1978, he finally agreed to sell the house, after years of hesitating. It opened as a B&B in 1979, on his 91st birthday. He not only attended the opening celebration but heartily approved of the changes that had been made.

Restrictions: No pets. Children over ten welcome. "We prefer no smoking but accept it."
Beds: The three king, two queen, and one twin rooms share three large, convenient central baths.
Breakfast: Different homemade pastries are served every day, along with fresh juice and coffee.
Extras: Afternoon tea and white wine are complimentary.
Rates: $60 to $82 (master bedroom). "We prefer personal checks, but accept Mastercard and Visa."
10% discount to OHJ members. with proof of membership.
Mailing Address: PO Box 5999, Tahoe City, CA 95730

ANAHEIM

ANAHEIM COUNTRY INN
Lois Ramont and
Marilyn Watson
856 South Walnut Street
Anaheim, CA 92806
(714) 778-0150
Year-round

1910 Post-Victorian with Bungalow-style details

LOCATION: The house's spacious lot is one mile from Disneyland, one-and-a-half miles to the Convention Center, 12 miles from the beaches, and within an hour of most of the Los Angeles area's attractions.

John Cook, the original owner, must have asked for a classic 1910 house. It has every typical detail of the period, in every possible style — Queen Anne and Shingle, Bungalow and neo-Colonial. For instance the porch is part neo-Colonial — the columns are classical — and part Queen Anne — the left side looks like the base of a turret. The foundation is concrete block, a material considered progressive at the time. The dormer is pure Bungalow, as is the plainly framed stained-glass window. And the eaves and center balcony speak of Shingle style.

Courses of bevelled, leaded diamond panes surmount the main parlor windows, while off to the side are diamond panes divided by simple wooden muntins. There are parquet floors and dark wood window frames; the parlor's arched entry is also typical of the period.

The owners' most recent restoration challenges included matching intricate mouldings and strengthening one of the exterior balconies. Many of the larger diamond panes needed replacing, but the smaller leaded ones survived.

John Cook was the mayor of Anaheim during Prohibition. He and his fellow "wets" held meetings at the house; the "drys" would have no part of it, the innkeepers report.

Restrictions: Smoking only on porches; children by arrangement.
Beds: Four rooms have private baths; the rest share.
Breakfast: Fresh fruit and juice; bacon, sausage, or ham; quiche,

blintzes, omelettes; rolls, croissants, or coffeecake; milk, tea, and coffee.

Extras: Lemonade, wine, and a light snack (cheese, crackers, fruit) are served during the afternoon "social hour." A hot tub, washer and dryer, and bicycles are available.

Rates: $50 to $75 (private bath and entrance); cots, $12. Personal checks and credit cards welcome.

10% discount to OHJ members.

JULIAN

JULIAN GOLD RUSH HOTEL
Steve and Gig Ballinger
2023 Main Street
Julian, CA 92036
(619) 765-0201
Year-round

1897 Queen Anne

LOCATION: The original false fronts from Julian's gold-rush days remain around town. The surrounding area offers mine tours, state parks, hiking trails, along with apple orchards, wildflowers and wild blackberry bushes.

Julian was a booming mine town when Albert Robinson married Margaret Tull there in the 1880s.

The Robinsons, both freed slaves, had come to Julian from separate directions. Albert was working as a cook, and Margaret too was working as a cook, so after the wedding the two decided to open a restaurant and bakery.

As the restaurant's reputation grew, the Robinsons decided to build a hotel on the site, which was conveniently located along the Butterfield stage route. During the construction, Albert planted the cypress, cedar, and locust trees which surround the hotel today.

The couple soon became famous for their hospitality and good Southern cooking. Word spread that "the Queen of the Back Country," as it was known, offered "the most modern mountain accommodations." The hotel's register confirms that it was a frequent stopping place for the famous: namely, Lady Bronston, the Scripps, the Whitneys, Admiral Nimitz, and Prime Minister Lloyd George, not to mention many a senator and congressman.

At that time Julian was the focus of southern California's Gold Rush. The town boasted two stage lines to San Diego, a dozen or more saloons, four general stores, and six hotels. Of these six the Julian Hotel is not only the sole survivor but also the oldest continuously operating hotel in southern California.

Originally named the Hotel Robinson, it was operated by its namesakes until Albert's death in 1915. A final touching entry in the register, penned in the widow's shaking hand, reads "Albert Robinson dide (sic) June 10, 1915."

Restrictions: No pets. Children only on weeknights (Sunday through Thursday). Check-in before 10 p.m.
Beds: Twelve rooms (ten doubles, one twin, one single) have shared baths (three per bath). Two doubles and a twin have private baths. The separate "Honeymoon Cottage" has a bath and double bed.
Breakfast: Eggs Florentine, granola cereal, date-nut raisin bread, fresh fruit in season, orange juice, coffee, and tea are served in the original dining room or on the sun porch/redwood deck.
Extras: The inn offers a guide to one-day tours of Julian and the area, and they'll book horse-drawn carriage rides as well.
Rates: $38 (weekdays) to $85 (weekends) for hotel; $105 to $135 for cottage. Personal and traveler's checks accepted.

10% discount to OHJ members. Sunday to Thursday only.
Mailing Address: PO Box 856, , Julian, CA 92036

LA JOLLA

1913 Cubist

THE BED & BREAKFAST INN AT LA JOLLA
Betty Albee
7753 Draper Avenue
La Jolla, CA 92037
(619) 456-2066
Year-round

LOCATION: La Jolla, a seaside resort, offers excellent snorkeling. Across the street from the inn is the Museum of Contemporary Art. The San Diego Zoo, Sea World, and many restaurants are close by.

The inn has many claims to fame: Cubist architect Irving Gill designed it; Kate Sessions, the noted horticulturist, planned its gardens; and the John Philip Sousa family lived there for seven years in the 1920s.

After spending a year restoring the house, Ms. Albee opened both the main building and an annex to guests. Above the smooth stucco arches are the leaded-glass multi-paned windows typical of the period; interior bookcases have leaded glass doors to match. The Craftsman-style ceilings are nine feet high.

Restrictions: Not equipped for small children or pets.
Beds: Ten rooms in the main house, six in the annex; 13 have queen beds and private baths, and of the three twin-bedded rooms one has a shared bath.
Breakfast: Freshly squeezed orange juice, hot bread, freshly ground coffee are "elegantly served on china with linen," on the sundeck or patio, in the dining room or guest's room.
Extras: Complimentary art museum passes are available; champagne and hors d'oeuvres can be obtained at cost. Picnic baskets are also available, and there's swimming at a nearby beach. Fresh fruit, sherry, and flowers are provided in the rooms.
Rates: $75 to $175 (ocean views, some fireplaces). Personal and traveler's checks welcome.

10% discount to OHJ members.

SOUTHERN CALIFORNIA

LOS ANGELES

EASTLAKE INN
Murray Burns and Planaria
Price
1442 Kellam Avenue
Los Angeles, CA 90026
(213) 250-1620
Year-round

1887 Eastlake

LOCATION: Angelino Heights, Los Angeles' first "suburb," over-looks downtown and has a high concentration of Victorian and Crafts-man homes. Within walking distance are Chinatown, the Pueblo (L.A.'s oldest street), downtown, Dodger Stadium, and Echo Lake Park.

Named after the architectural style in which it was built, this spa-cious duplex originally housed two young widows and their chil-dren. Innkeeper Planaria Price tells an interesting story: "The house was built for two widows named Annie Watson and Sarah Banholtz. Annie was married to John Watson, keeper of the port of Eureka. He came down with flu, and, feeling ill one night, went to the pantry for some cough medicine. By mistake, he drank carbolic acid. The young widow became quite wealthy and quickly moved to Los Angeles with her mother and daughter. Not that we're suspicious or anything, but carbolic acid in the pantry???" With the exception of the front stairrail, the house is exactly as it was in 1887, right down to the paint scheme. The etched, flashed glass is in perfect condition, as are the floors made of Douglas fir. Every room has a plaster ceiling medallion and the entire house is furnished with antiques.

Restrictions: Children under 11 and pets "discouraged." Smoking only on front porch. Check-in between 4 and 6 p.m., "flexible."
Beds: Four doubles, one twin, one queen, one queen with two twins, and a suite with a double in one room and a twin in the other. Six rooms have a choice of four baths.
Breakfast: "Fresh, wholesome, and nearly perfect": fresh juices from the garden, fresh croissants and muffins, fresh butters and jams, hard-boiled eggs, cheeses, freshly ground coffees and assorted teas, plus fresh kiwis (a house specialty).
Extras: Gourmet hors d'oeuvres (pâté, champagne, caviar) upon arrival. Fresh fruit is provided in rooms; the turn-down service leaves a bed-time "surprise." The owners give tours of their two National Register homes (an Eastlake and a Queen Anne one block away), and offer weekend activity packages: ballooning, "mystery" weekends, horseback riding.
Rates: $45 (single, "cozy") to $125 (four-room suite). Cots, $15 (for cost of breakfast and extras). Personal and traveler's checks, credit cards accepted.

10% discount to OHJ members "with pleasure."

LOS ANGELES

SALISBURY HOUSE
Kathleen and Bill Salisbury
2273 West 20th Street
Los Angeles, CA 90018
(213) 737-7817
Year-round

1909 Craftsman

LOCATION: This is but one of many homes in Arlington Heights that is being restored to its former charm and elegance. The residential neighborhood is convenient to downtown, Hollywood, Beverly Hills, the airport, and the beach.

F. M. Tyler designed this 1909 Craftsman house, which still has its original stained- and leaded-glass windows and beamed ceilings. Innkeepers Kathleen and Bill Salisbury have filled it with antiques to the point where it "abounds with dolls, stuffed animals, toys, and other collectibles," says Kathleen.

Restrictions: No pets or children under ten.
Beds: Of the five rooms, two share a bath.
Breakfast: "Full gourmet"
Extras: A wine rack is stocked with complimentary port, Sherry, and burgundy for guest's use.
Rates: $50 to $65; personal checks and credit cards welcome.
   10% discount to OHJ members.

LOS ANGELES

TERRACE MANOR
Sandy and Shirley Spillman
1353 Alvarado Terrace
Los Angeles, CA 90006
(213) 381-1478
Year-round

1902 Tudor Revival

LOCATION: The house is across from a small park and surrounded by six other large historic houses. The Convention Center, Chinatown, Little Tokyo, museums, Music Center, and University of Southern California are close by.

"Guests from all over the world stay with us ... and most love homes like ours. Nearly everyone is restoring a house, or contemplating it."

This large Tudor Revival sits, amazingly enough, in the center of Los Angeles. In fact, its whole neighborhood dates from the turn of the century, and is listed in the National Register. The house was built in 1902 by Sumner P. Hunt and Wesley A. Eager for glass manufacturer Robert H. Raphael. Some of the outstanding features include half timbering, two prominent gables, sequentially numbered terra cotta roof tiles, bevelled glass sidelights, and stained glass windows in Art Nouveau and medieval patterns. The entry and parlor are panelled in rare tiger oak. The dining room, panelled with mahogany, has an Ionic columned mantel with a built-in clock that still works! The butler's pantry and kitchen walls are tiled with original glass tiles.

Restrictions: "Sorry—no children, pets, or smoking." Check-in between 4 and 6 p.m. (later by special arrangement). Check-out at 11 a.m.
Beds: All five rooms, which contain two twins, two queens, two doubles, and one king, have private baths.
Breakfast: Fresh fruit and juice always served; main dish varies— Scotch eggs, blintzes, apricot French toast, eggs Florentine, for example.
Extras: Afternoon tea, hors d'oeuvres, and wine are complimentary,

as are guest cards to the Hollywood Magic Castle, a private club.
Rates: $45 to $75, personal checks and credit cards accepted.
10% discount to OHJ members.

NEWPORT BEACH

DORYMAN'S INN
Rick and Jeannie Lawrence
2102 West Ocean Front
Newport Beach, CA 92663
(714) 675-7300
Year-round

LOCATION: The pier and ocean are in front of the inn, an outdoor market is adjacent, and 16 restaurants are within walking distance.

"We have ten individually decorated, Victorian rooms—we suggest you not miss the fun of seeing them all before choosing one."

The original hotel housed both rail travelers to Newport Beach and tired fishermen. The new version has ten elegant rooms furnished with Victoriana, etched-glass light fixtures, plants, canopy beds, and draperies to match the bed hangings. There are sunken tubs and antique fireplaces in every room. Oak panelling lines the walls, ferns fill the hallway skylights, and the original facade—brick and stucco with bas-relief designs—remains.

Restrictions: No pets. Check-in after 3 p.m., check-out at noon.
Beds: The seven kings and three queens all have private baths.
Breakfast: Hard-boiled brown eggs, fresh pastries, croissants, seasonal fruits, yogurt, coffee, tea, juice, and assorted cheeses.
Rates: $135 (ocean view, fireplace, marble bath) to $275 (marble jacuzzi, ocean view, king bed with canopy). Personal checks and credit cards accepted.
10% discount to OHJ members.

NORTH HOLLYWOOD

LA MAIDA HOUSE
Megan and Helen Timothy
11159 La Maida Street
North Hollywood, CA 91601
(818) 769-3857
Year-round

1926 Mediterranean

LOCATION: This quiet, residential street (the inn has no exterior signage) is two minutes' walk from a lovely park with a running track and tennis courts. Universal City is two minutes away also, the Hollywood Bowl is five minutes away, and downtown Los Angeles within 15 minutes.

Antonio La Maida spared little expense when he built his house. He and an architect named Savage decided to fill it with mahogany, oak, brass, and wrought iron, and they had many fountains installed in the garden. They closely followed the style of La Maida's Mediterranean homeland: the walls are stucco, the roof tiled, the windows arched, and the interiors airy with open archways.

And innkeeper Megan Timothy has spared little effort to maintain La Maida's house as an elegant inn. She arrived in Los Angeles in 1965 with $5 in her pocket. By 1975 she had saved enough capital to buy the rundown building and restore it, especially the brass and woodwork. The house now holds the antiques she's collected from around the world: There are four-poster beds, wicker chaise lounges, Oriental rugs, and ceiling fans. Photographs, paintings, and stained-glass works she's created decorate the walls and doors; one room has a stained-glass ceiling. The bungalows across the street date from the 1930s; she bought and renovated them as the inn expanded.

Restrictions: No pets; no smoking on the premises.
Beds: Six rooms or suites are in the 1930s bungalows across the street, four are in the main house. In all there's three kings, four queens, two doubles, and one set of twins. Baths are all private.
Breakfast: "Nothing mixed or frozen used"—breads and pastries are made daily from scratch, fruit juices are squeezed less than an hour

before breakfast, jams and jellies are made from fruits taken from the inn's gardens. Plus, "much care is taken to accommodate special diets."

Extras: The nightly turn-down service leaves a freshly-dipped chocolate-covered fruit or homemade cookies; other complimentary extras include robes, toiletries, spring water, and fresh flowers. Telephones and TV are available at no extra charge. Afternoon tea, lunches, or dinner can be arranged (catered to guest's taste) for an extra fee.

Rates: $85 (in the bungalows, double bed) to $185 (suite with dining room, kitchen, and patio in the bungalows). Personal checks welcome.

10% discount to OHJ members.

SOUTHERN CALIFORNIA

SAN DIEGO

THE COTTAGE
Robert and Carol Emerick
3829 Albatross Street
San Diego, CA 92103
(619) 299-1564
Year-round

1916 Vernacular

LOCATION: Irving Gill, the Cubist architect, designed several buildings guests can view in the area. The waterfront area, established in the 1860s, is two miles away. The neighborhood offers many small restaurants and quaint shops.

Behind the main house, a leaf-shaded bungalow, lies a deceptively tiny cottage. Though it looks small from the outside it sleeps three comfortably (two in the bedroom, and one in the sitting room); there's also a kitchen, dining area, and bath.

The most interesting interior feature is a Victorian pump organ, whose pipes were recently restored. The wood-burning stove can heat the whole cottage. The other furnishings, which date from 1860 to 1920, include spool-legged stools, sleigh beds and an attractive Victorian bookcase. Lacy pillows and plenty of plants add to the cheerful clutter.

Restrictions: No pets, smoking outside only. Check-in after 4 p.m., check-out at noon.
Beds: The cottage—one king bed, one single—sleeps three and has a private bath, and an equipped kitchen.
Breakfast: "I bake bread or muffins every morning"—these, along with fruit and a beverage, are brought to the cottage.
Extras: A fresh-fruit and nut bowl is provided in the room.
Rates: $50, payable by personal check. Cots, $5.
Mailing Address: PO Box 3292, San Diego, CA 92103

SAN DIEGO

EDGEMONT INN
Rosemary Johnson
1955 Edgemont Street
San Diego, CA 92102
(619) 238-1677
Year-round

1900 Neo-Colonial

LOCATION: This residential neighborhood is some four blocks away from Balboa Park, the San Diego Zoo, theaters, and museums.

Mr. Renqua, a noted San Diego architect, typically built castles. But somehow he restrained himself when he bought this 1900 house and remodelled it in 1932. He added only French doors and balconies to the already existing Spanish arches.

The Davidsons purchased the building in 1981, and intended all along to turn it into a B&B. They used some 200 rolls of wallpaper to paper the guest rooms, each of which has its own "theme" and color scheme. Current owner Rosemary Johnson invites readers to come and enjoy the inn and its surroundings.

Restrictions: No children or pets.
Beds: One king has a private bath, the other shares; the two doubles share baths as well.
Breakfast: "Elegant full breakfast served on china, crystal, and silver."
Extras: There's no charge for afternoon refreshments, including

69

homemade "goodies," soda, beer, wine, and "holiday drinks." Plus the "snooze fairy" leaves a bedtime surprise after turning down the beds.

Rates: $50 to $90, lower for week-long stays. Personal checks and credit cards accepted.

10% discount to OHJ members.

SOUTHERN CALIFORNIA

SAN DIEGO

HERITAGE PARK BED &
BREAKFAST INN
Lori Chandler
2470 Heritage Park Row
San Diego, CA 92110
(619) 295-7088
Year-round

1889 Queen Anne

LOCATION: Heritage Park comprises seven once-endangered Victorians in a secluded park with cobblestone walkways and gardens. Old Town is within walking distance, as are the San Diego Zoo and Mission Valley's restaurants and nightclubs.

When *The Golden Era* magazine featured this house in 1890, they called it "an outstandingly beautiful home of Southern California." It still is, only now it's one of a row of equally beautiful Victorians. All were once endangered but have been moved to Heritage Park for safekeeping.

Harfield Timberlake Christian was not striving for simplicity when he built his home. There are numerous chimneys and surface textures on the outside; several levels, nooks, and two storeys of tower rooms on the inside. The redwood staircase is lit by stained-glass windows.

At one point, the first floor was turned into one large room and used as a restaurant; all the original walls were ripped out. The current owners had to replace them using floor plans found at the local historical society. Previous occupants also removed the seven-foot, six-inch four-panelled doors throughout the house; reproductions have been substituted.

In the rooms you'll find Eastlake, Victorian Renaissance, and

70

Bombe beds, along with fainting couches and other collectibles. If you want to take any of these home with you, you're in luck: they're all for sale.

Restrictions: No children under 14 or pets. Ashtrays provided for smoking on the outside porch only. Check-in between 4 and 9 p.m., check-out at 11 a.m.
Beds: Of the nine rooms—five queens, three doubles, one twin—six share three baths and the rest are private.
Breakfast: Full homemade, with giant stuffed croissants, soufflés, pots of oatmeal with "all the fixings," plus fresh breads, rolls, muffins, fruit, juices, and coffee/tea.
Extras: The "social hour," from 5 to 7 p.m., provides refreshments, and after 7 p.m. a vintage movie is shown. In-room candlelit dinners or gourmet picnic lunches can be obtained by request, 24 hours in advance.
Rates: $65 to $105; cots, $10. Personal checks and credit cards welcome.
10% discount to OHJ members.

SOUTHERN CALIFORNIA

SANTA BARBARA

THE BATH STREET INN
Nancy Stover and Susan Brown
1720 Bath Street
Santa Barbara, CA 93101
(805) 682-9680
Year-round

1873 Vernacular Queen Anne

LOCATION: Santa Barbara's historic downtown is a few blocks away. The beach, marina, and port are 17 blocks away. Old adobes, a botanical garden, children's zoo, and natural history museum are among the nearby attractions.

The Bath Street Inn has had no colorful owners—"I wish!" says the current one—a simple tailor from Massachusetts built the house for his wife. Nor have any colorful events occurred under its roof. But it does have an "eyelid" balcony, a semicircle that surrounds the single round dormer. The whole roof has an equally unusual outline, with a protrusion sloping over the part of the porch. Odd shapes prevail in the interior too, where eaves jut into antique-furnished rooms and alcoves lead off larger spaces.

French doors, clawfoot tubs, and hardwood floors also grace the interior, while 100-year-old trees shield the exterior. The owners recently built several new private baths and an addition. The rooms look out on the neighboring trees, the Santa Ynez Mountains, and the ocean (there's a window seat in one room that offers just a glimpse).

Restrictions: No children under 13, no pets.
Beds: All seven rooms—two kings, one with twins, and four queens —have private baths.
Breakfast: Fresh fruit, juice, homemade breads, ham-and-cheese croissants, coffee, tea.
Extras: Coffee and tea are served all day, wine and soft drinks are available in the late afternoon, and guests can use the inn's bicycles at no charge.
Rates: $75 ("wedgwood" color scheme, bath with shower only) to $85 (king bed, clawfoot tub); $10 to $15 less during winter mid-week. Personal checks and credit cards welcome.

10% discount to OHJ members (mid-week only) except June, July, August.

SOUTHERN CALIFORNIA

SANTA BARBARA

THE BAYBERRY INN
Keith Pomeroy and Carlton Wagner
111 West Valerio Street
Santa Barbara, CA 93101
(805) 682-3199
Year-round

1886 Shingle with Classical details

LOCATION: The beach is five minutes away; other nearby sights include the Spanish mission, Indian ruins, an art museum, and the wharf with its shops and tame pelicans.

With a Federal doorway topped by a gilded eagle, a Shingle-style roof, and Swiss-chalet-type balconies, the Bayberry Inn is an eclectic mixture of styles. Innkeeper Carlton Wagner decided to model the interior after the fashion of 1918 to 1920, so he's filled it with silk drapes, fringed lampshades, thick carpets, bevelled mirrors, and a crystal chandelier. There's also a grand piano in the living room. Some rooms have fireplaces and canopy beds; views are of the mountains or of the garden, where a wicker-furnished gazebo can be seen.

Restrictions: No pets; children over 12 accepted. Smoking outside only. Check-in between 3 and 7 p.m., check-out at 11 a.m.
Beds: Eight rooms, all with private baths.
Breakfast: Full: beverage, fresh juice or fruit, eggs, baked goods. And a champagne brunch is available on Sundays.
Extras: Bicycles and afternoon tea (served October through March) are complimentary, as is a glass of wine.
Rates: $75 (queen, mountain and garden views, shared bath) to $125 (sundeck, fireplace, private bath). Discounts mid-week October through March. Credit cards welcome.
   10% discount to OHJ members Monday through Thursday only.

SOUTHERN CALIFORNIA

SANTA BARBARA

GLENBOROUGH INN
Pat Hardy and Jo Ann Bell
1327 Bath Street
Santa Barbara, CA 93101
(805) 966-0589
Year-round

1906 California Craftsman/1880s Eastlake Stick Style

LOCATION: This tree-lined residential neighborhood includes many restored old homes. Santa Barbara's Old Town is three blocks away and there, too, preservation has prevailed.

Displayed on a table in the parlor is every old-house lover's delight: an album of "before" and "after" pictures. The house that Louis Brooks, a local fuel company executive, built was basically intact when Pat Hardy and Jo Ann Bell bought it in 1980. Not only did the original sliding doors, complete with hardware, remain but they had never been painted. Pat and Jo Ann still had to strip a lot of paint, refinish the floors, and add a bath before taking guests.

Next they tackled the circa 1880 cottage across the street. It has a hipped roof with a small center gable, an Eastlake sawtooth skirt under the eaves, and bay windows that extend onto its porches. The building was also basically intact (it was, the owners think, used as a summer home). So they stripped some more paint, added two baths, and repainted the outside in typical Victorian colors: beige with forest-green shutters and rust trim.

Pat also went antique hunting. You can easily see her and Jo Ann's preference for old fabrics: There are antique drapes transformed into bedspreads, coverlets made into curtains, old quilts, velvet, crochet, knitting, and lace; there are also framed tapestries on the walls.

Decorating themes run the gamut from feminine — the "French Rose" room has a bedspread and wallpaper to match the name — to nautical—the "Captain's Quarters" contains family heirlooms like an 1865 officer's armoire and a mica lampshade. Some rooms feature Mission pieces, others Eastlake; in the front hall there's an art nouveau secretary, and in the parlor an old Victrola stands near the green tiled fireplace.

Breakfast in bed comes on a tray with a lace mat, linen napkins, a silver coffeepot, silver flatware, and Haviland china. Pat has been known to bring it dressed in a Victorian nightdress and cap.

Restrictions: Smoking only in the cottage.
Beds: The four rooms in the main house share two baths; all cottage rooms have private baths. In total there's two doubles and six queens.
Breakfast: "Hearty gourmet": homemade breads, cheesy egg casseroles, fresh fruit and juices, blintzes, "decadent French toast," egg nachos, yogurt-fruit-granola parfait, and a choice of cinnamon-spiked coffee, tea, herbal tea, milk, or cocoa are served in the parlor, garden, or guest's room.
Extras: Evening "get-together" entails wine, juice, and homemade appetizers. The spa can be used privately.
Rates: $65 (shared bath, "cozy and popular") to $145 (private bath and entrance, canopied queen bed, fireplace). October 15 to June 15, mid-week rates, $55 to $119. "We prefer checks and cash, but accept Mastercard and Visa."

SANTA BARBARA

THE OLD YACHT CLUB INN
Nancy Donaldson, Lee Caruso, Sandy Hunt, Gay Swenson
431 Corona Del Mar Drive
Santa Barbara, CA 93103
(805) 962-1277
Year-round

1912 Tudor Revival/Craftsman; 1925 California Stucco

LOCATION: The inn is located in East Beach, a half-block from a white, sandy beach, and close to bicycle paths, the zoo, yacht harbor, as well as golf and tennis facilities and downtown Santa Barbara.

When a storm swept their headquarters out to sea in the 1920s, the Yacht Club used this building temporarily; hence its name. The inn's annex, a stucco building known as the Hitchcock House, was moved to its nearby site in 1928—"quite a large moving job!" the owners report.

The Old Yacht Club's parlor has a large brick fireplace. Guests can relax before it or on the porch, which is tucked under the house's extended roofline. Throughout the building there's original wood panelling and built-ins like dressers and window seats.

Restrictions: No pets or children under 12. Smoking in the rooms is discouraged. Check-in after 2 p.m., check-out at 11 a.m.
Beds: There are nine in total—one double, five queens, three kings. Four of the five in the main building share two baths. All four in the Hitchcock House have private baths.
Breakfast: Fresh juice, fresh fruit, home-baked breads and coffee-cakes, omelettes.
Extras: The complimentary evening social hour offers wine, tea, or soft drinks. Beach chairs and bicycles can be borrowed at no charge. Gourmet dinners (five courses) are available for a prix fixe of $17.50 by advance reservation.
Rates: $50 (double bed, shared bath) to $105 (king bed, private entrance, and bath). 10% to 15% less mid-week October through June. Cots, $15. Personal checks and credit cards accepted.

TEMPLETON

COUNTRY HOUSE INN
Dianne Garth
91 Main
Templeton, CA 93465
(805) 434-1598
Year-round

1886 Eastlake/Stick Style

LOCATION: This historic town, halfway between San Francisco and Los Angeles, is near Hearst Castle, 26 wineries, and Morro Bay and is surrounded by oak trees and rolling hills.

Templeton's founding father, C. H. Phillips, built his fashionable residence in 1886. That same year the Southern Pacific Railroad extended its line to terminate in Templeton, bringing with it a population boom. At one point the town had three hotels, 18 saloons, and a population of 5,000.

Above the delicate entry porch, and at the peak of the roof, stand the house's original iron railings. A well-manicured lawn surrounds large palm trees, and the Eastlake trim has been carefully highlighted in red.

Inside is the original redwood panelling, grained to resemble walnut.

Restrictions: No smoking or pets. Check-in after 3 p.m.
Beds: Five rooms share three baths.
Breakfast: Full breakfast.
Rates: $55 (twin bed) to $75 (queen bed, half-bath). Cots available for an extra charge. Personal checks welcome.
 10% discount to OHJ members.
Mailing Address: PO Box 179, Templeton, CA 93465

CALISTOGA

CULVER'S, A COUNTRY INN
George M. Hunt
1805 Foothill Boulevard
Calistoga, CA 94515
(707) 942-4535
Year-round

1875 Vernacular with Gothic Revival elements

LOCATION: Calistoga is located at the northern end of Napa Valley, enclosed by mountain ranges on both sides. The town's western-style Main Street still stands, and the area is known for its spas with mud baths, mineral waters and massages, and gourmet restaurants. Nearby activities include gliding, ballooning, bicycling, horseback riding, and canoeing.

California's first millionaire, Sam Brannan, began an ambitious development in 1859 on the site of several hot springs. He named his planned resort "Calistoga" (a combination of California and Saratoga, the famed New York resort). He hoped to attract San Franciscans in search of rejuvenation and relaxation.

He did attract one John Oscar Culver, a Wisconsin editor and publisher, to the area. Culver brought his wife, an artist named Minnie Bliss Culver, and their five children; they built a home the San Francisco papers called " the Culver mansion." The jerkinhead gable is unusual for Napa County, though the shiplap siding is pretty typical. The gable probably once had decorative bargeboards, since it still has a pointed finial. And the extended first floor doors and windows are most likely the result of remodeling.

George Hunt has put a player piano and oak dining tables in the public areas, where there's also an original mantel and ceiling rosette. The three downstairs bedrooms are decorated in, respectively, Edwardian, Art Nouveau, and Art Deco. The four upstairs rooms have Victorian or early 20th-century pieces. And each of the rooms has a quilt designed especially for its bed.

Restrictions: Check-in between 2:30 and 6 p.m., later by special arrangement. Check-out at 11 a.m. Children over 12 welcome. No pets or smoking in bedrooms.

Beds: There are three queens, two fulls, one king, and one room with twins; two share a bath.

Breakfast: "Sit-down breakfast" consists of freshly baked scones and other baked goods, choice of teas, and coffee.

Extras: Evening sherry, turn-down service, a pool, sauna, and spa/ jacuzzi are available.

Rates: $65 (mid-week winter rate) to $85 (weekends in summer). Personal checks and credit cards accepted.

CALIFORNIA: WINE COUNTRY

ELK

HARBOR HOUSE
Patricia Corcoran
5600 South Highway 1
Elk, CA 95432
(707) 877-3203
Year-round

1916 Bungalow/Prairie style

LOCATION: Harbor House is just outside the rural coastal town of Elk; a nearby cove accommodates fishing boats in their active season. The Navarro River is 15 minutes north, Van Damme State Park with its "fern walk" is ten minutes farther, and Mendocino, with its shops, galleries, and restaurants, is five minutes from there.

The staircase descends into the living room, a veritable cave of redwood. The ceiling is beamed, panelled, and coated from end to end in virgin redwood, as is the massive medieval-scale tiled fireplace. The floor is also covered in redwood. This and the rest of the interior woodwork was polished with hot beeswax in 1916, and it hasn't been refinished in any way since. The proprietor calls its deep golden sheen "truly remarkable."

The first owners had good reason for such a sumptuous use of redwood. They were the Goodyear Redwood Lumber Company, and this was where they lodged and entertained guests and executives.

The structure is an enlarged version of an exhibit shown at the 1915 International Exposition in San Francisco and called, not surprisingly, "The Home of Redwood." Architect Louis Christian Mullgardt designed this house, and it was constructed with wood taken from the nearby Albion forests.

The exterior has original siding and shingles. The oversize original fireplaces, excluding the one in the living room, are of brick. Some of the furniture was left by the first owners, and later inhabitants added several 19th-century Chinese pieces. Most recently the current owners purchased a 50-year-old, 10,000-gallon wine vat from Christian Brothers Winery in St. Helena, California. It is made of (what else?) redwood, and used to store water.

Restrictions: "Unsuitable for children or pets." Check-in after 1 p.m., check-out at noon.
Beds: All nine rooms—two with two queens, three with one queen, three with kings, and one with a queen and twin—have private baths.
Breakfast: Full: beginning with juice, coffee, and tea, followed by entree (omelette, quiche, eggs Benedict, souffled pancakes), homemade breads, and fresh fruit.
Extras: A selection of local wines, champagne, beer, and other beverages is available throughout the day. Dinner also included in room rate (for two): "exceptional country dining," with home-grown vegetables and local meats and fish, homemade soups, breads, and desserts—single seating begins at 7 p.m.
Rates: $110 (meadow view, cottage outside house with bath) to $165 (ocean view, two queens, in main house). Rates lower in winter midweek. Personal checks accepted.
Mailing Address: Box 369, Elk, CA 95432

CALIFORNIA: WINE COUNTRY

FORT BRAGG

THE GREY WHALE INN
John and Colette Bailey
615 North Main Street
Fort Bragg, CA 95437
(707) 964-0640
Year-round

1915 Georgian Revival

LOCATION: Fort Bragg, on the Mendocino coast, is in "Redwood Country." The inn, six blocks from the ocean, is near Noyo Harbor (with a fishing fleet and restaurants). A depot for a sightseeing railroad that travels through the forest is two blocks away.

"I would never have guessed that the old building had been anything but a hotel, the conversion was handled so skillfully." Jim Crain Historic Country Inns of California

Past lives as mansions, brothels, or garages are pretty common tales for B&Bs; but former hospitals are few and far between. The squeamish will be glad to know that one of the few traces of the past at the Grey Whale Inn is an old surgery lamp in one of the guest rooms (it hangs over the sitting area, by the way, not the bed). The old nursery and diet kitchen now form a breakfast area, with tongue-and-groove wainscotting that was taken from several closets in the building. The bath facility is now a parlor, equipped with a wet bar in an antique mahogany buffet.

Dr. Franklin Campbell convinced the Union Lumber Company to construct the imposing building in 1915. In June, 1920, Dr. Paul J. Bowman visited Campbell, whom he'd met while serving an internship in San Francisco. Apparently the blooming rhododendrons of the area attracted him, because he moved to Fort Bragg the next month.

Bowman bought the hospital, and succeeded Campbell to become its chief surgeon in 1923. He remained at the post until 1965.

Old photos of the hospital document that much is missing. It once had a decorative neo-classical cornice at the top and a balcony over the main entry. Mouldings surrounded the windows, and the solarium on the roof contained trellises supporting a partially open roof. The whole building was painted neo-classical white. The unusual rectangle-over-square windows are an original feature, however.

Restrictions: Pets not permitted, but smoking is. Check-in and check-out at noon.
Beds: There are two kings, six queens, two doubles, as well as three suites that accommodate up to four people. Two share a bath, some have kitchens.
Breakfast: Served buffet-style (can be carried back by guest to room) in the breakfast room, 7:30 a.m. to 11 a.m.: juices, fruit, homemade coffeecake or sweet bread, bagels, English muffins, cheddar eggs ("our famous recipe"), egg custard, yogurt, hot beverages.
Extras: The television, pool table, and kitchen are available for guests to use. Honeymooners are given complimentary champagne.
Rates: $50 (double, private bath, interior patio) to $75 (queen bed, kitchen, ocean view). Winter mid-week up to 25% less. Personal checks and credit cards welcome.

GEYSERVILLE

THE HOPE-BOSWORTH HOUSE
Bob and Rosalie Hope
21238 Geyserville Avenue
Geyserville, CA 95441
(707) 857-3356
Year-round

1904 Queen Anne

LOCATION: This rural agricultural community is within Sonoma County's premium wine-producing region. The Russian River flows a half-mile from town and has an enormous canoeing facility, and Warm Springs Dam and Lake Sonoma are six miles to the west. Trails for backpacking and biking are plentiful.

In 1904 George M. Bosworth picked a plan for a house out of a pattern book and had it built out of heart redwood. Bosworths continued to live in it until the mid-1960s. The family is still active in the community; grandson Harry continues the family feed and hardware stores. Family members called the house "The Palms," in honor of the 70-foot-high trees that once lined the street. Only two remain.

Oak-grained woodwork, from the sliding doors downstairs to the upstairs tower room, accompanies the polished fir floors. The upper windows have an unusual circle-and-diamond pattern. Antique fixtures light the rooms, which are often tucked under angled ceilings. The Hopes have used period designs for the wallpapers, curtains, and upholstery. Their biggest undertaking was removing the asbestos siding from the shiplap and remilling the missing trim. They also replastered and wallpapered some walls damaged 80 years before in the 1906 earthquake.

This is one of two neighboring houses the Hopes have restored and converted to B&Bs; the other, the Hope-Merrill house, is also in this book. Both buildings, Rosalie explains, are "the product of many hours of research into the Victorian period."

Restrictions: Check-in after 3:30 p.m., check-out at 11 a.m. "Children discouraged except by prior arrangement." No smoking.

Beds: The five rooms—three queens and two doubles—share two full and one half-bath.

Breakfast: Fresh orange juice, fresh local fruit in season, homemade breads and coffeecake, muffins, tarts, turnovers, condiments, coffee, tea, and "other specialties of the cook."

Extras: Complimentary wine is served each afternoon at 6 p.m., when guests are "invited to meet one another and the innkeepers." There's a swimming pool across the street, and for $35 guests can tour the vineyards in old stages drawn by draft horses (May through October, picnic lunch and wine included).

Rates: $55 ("cozy," view of Geyser Peak, shared bath) to $70 (wicker furniture, queen bed, attached private bath). Personal checks and credit cards welcome.

5% discount to OHJ members.

Mailing Address: PO Box 42, Geyserville, CA 95441

CALIFORNIA: WINE COUNTRY

GEYSERVILLE

**THE HOPE-MERRILL
HOUSE**
Bob and Rosalie Hope
21253 Geyserville Avenue
Geyserville, CA 95441
(707) 857-3356
Year-round

1885 Eastlake Stick Style

LOCATION: Geyserville, in Sonoma County's premium wine-producing region, is a rural agricultural community. The Russian River, with its renowned canoeing facility, and Lake Sonoma are nearby, as are redwood groves and the Pacific Ocean (45 minutes). Trails for backpacking, hiking, and biking are plentiful.

"We treat guests with the same care and attention that we lavished on this old house."

Rosalie Hope had a fateful meeting with Bruce Bradbury at a conference in 1981. She, an innkeeper and old-house owner, was looking for period wallpapers, and he, a fledgling designer, was seeking places to use his Victorian-inspired wallpaper patterns. The Hopes had just bought their second old house—Rosalie's antique collection had overflowed in the first—and its fine quarter-sawn oak woodwork with odd nooks and alcoves provided Bruce an unusual and elegant backdrop. Some of the custom patterns he produced for the Hopes —a lily-like design in the living room, a garland-with-deer-and-rabbit motif in one of the guest rooms—have gone on to become some of Bradbury & Bradbury's hottest sellers.

The Hopes were in the midst of restoring the Bosworth house (another B&B in this book) across the street when they were first intrigued by the Merrill house. The lawn was overgrown with black-berries, the shades were drawn, and the windows had been greviously remuddled—cut down when the 11-and-a-half-foot ceilings were low-ered to eight. As soon as they signed papers for the house Rosalie and her daughter Randi ran over and pried through the dining room's lowered ceiling to see what size the windows had really been.

The Hopes restored the Merrill house ceilings to their original height, refinished the six-inch-wide redwood floor planks, and in-stalled 15 new redwood-framed windows. They also ornamented the wraparound porch with French doors and stained glass that overlook the vineyard, gazebo, and grape arbor. Above the porch and at the roof peak they replaced the iron railings.

The house is filled with a variety of collections: such as peacock fans, purses (accumulated by Randi, one of five Hope children), and porcelains, along with Rosalie's "Momisms"—poems and other me-morabilia about motherhood.

Restrictions: "Children discouraged except by prior arrangement." Check-in after 3:30 p.m., check-out at 11 a.m. No smoking.
Beds: All of the five rooms (one double and four queens) have private baths.
Breakfast: "Breakfast is very special here," and includes orange juice, fresh fruit with creme fraiche or yogurt, a hot egg or bread main course, meat garnishes; homemade biscuits, muffins, or breads, plus jams, jellies, apple butter, and honey.
Extras: Discount coupons are available for canoeing, and guests are invited to join the innkeepers for wine at 6 p.m. The "Stage-a-Picnic" vineyard tours cost $35; guests ride in old stages drawn by draft horses, and wine and a picnic lunch are included. There's a swimming pool on the property.
Rates: $65 (double or queen upstairs) to $75 (private bath, fireplace). Personal checks and credit cards welcome.
    5% discount to OHJ members.
Mailing Address: PO Box 42, Geyersville, CA 95441

HEALDSBURG

CAMELLIA INN
Del and Ray Le Wands
211 North Street
Healdsburg, CA 95448
(707) 433-8182
Year-round

1869 Italianate

LOCATION: Healdsburg is a small town on the Russian River. There are some 60 wineries in the area, many open to the public. And the town is "a treasure trove of Victorian homes," with countryside "picturesquely reminiscent of France's rolling hills."

The building still looks essentially as it did when this sketch was completed, soon after construction. Only the trees are taller, houses have been built nearby, and women walking past wearing bustles are a somewhat more unusual sight.

Classic Italianate details cover the house: paired and single arched windows, corner quoins, a dentilled cornice resting on brackets. Inside, the double parlors have matching fireplaces. The ceiling brackets and medallions are original, as are the dining room's ornate mahogany fireplace and tiled hearth. The antiques in the rooms include a Queen Anne highboy, a tiger maple bed from Scotland, an Oriental rug in the parlor, and various photos and mementos from the 1880s and 1890s. Bradbury & Bradbury period papers ornament the walls in some rooms. A gross of washers and screws was needed to tighten the ceiling in one room; up to five layers of wallpaper inside and seven layers of paint outside had to be stripped. "And there's many more projects still to come," report the LeWands.

Ransom Powell, the original owner, came to California to seek his fortune during the gold rush. Unlike many others, he did make a fortune, though not in gold: He hauled freight from Sacramento to the gold fields. At various times in his life he owned more land than anyone else in this part of the state.

The landscaped plot features a fish pond where a koi named Leon lives. The hotel is named for the 30 varieties of camellia that grow on the property, reportedly the gift of Luther Burbank, famed plant breeder.

Restrictions: Children by arrangement; no pets; smoking in the parlor only. Check-in between 3 and 6 p.m., check-out at noon.
Beds: Seven rooms, five with private baths.
Breakfast: Full: fresh fruit, juice, coffee, tea, cold cereal, homemade fruit breads, jam, cream cheese, French bread, and soft-boiled egg.
Extras: Wine and cheese in the afternoon are served either in the parlor or by the swimming pool.
Rates: $40 ('cozy,' with double bed and shared bath) to $65 (queen, private bath, former dining room). Personal checks and credit cards welcome.

10% discount to OHJ members Sunday through Thursday.

HEALDSBURG

THE HEALDSBURG INN ON THE PLAZA
Genny Jenkins
116 Matheson Street
Healdsburg, CA 95448
(707) 433-6991
Year-round

1901 Commercial Classical Revival

LOCATION: The inn is set on a town square with trees, a fountain, benches, and a gazebo; most of the buildings date from the turn of the century and have been restored. Shops, restaurants, and a museum are nearby.

"The restoration goes on even now. We love advice and guests can really get involved."

Many famous travellers passed through the Wells Fargo office on the first floor. Those who stayed in Healdsburg may have visited the second floor, which housed the town's first photography studio. Doctors, dentists, and dressmakers also had their offices on the spacious second floor.

For 30 years, until 1965, the building stood empty. Eventually the second floor was used for storage, and later converted into an apartment. Ms. Jenkins began restoring the place in 1982. For one thing, she added bathrooms by dividing the original offices. Her pet project recently has been the photography studio, where she's lined the walls with turn-of-the-century photos of local citizens. She's currently looking for a period camera, backdrops, and props to complete the effect.

There's a Victorian roof garden atop the second storey, bay windows and alcoves in many rooms, and original wooden skylights. The furnishings, all antique, are primarily Eastlake, with iron-and-brass beds, oak rockers, and spindle-leg tables in some rooms. In the baths, brass shower pipes rise from clawfoot tubs; hexagonal tiles cover the floors and the sinks rest on pedestals. Etchings and engravings adorn the walls throughout, and there's pressed-wood panelling in the hallway.

Restrictions: No pets. Smoking in the roof garden only. Children over 12 welcome. Check-in after 4 p.m., check-out at 11 a.m.
Beds: There are six doubles and two two-room suites; the suites have a bath each, and the six doubles have private baths as well.
Breakfast: Full: homemade breads, fresh fruit, juice, egg and meat entree, coffee, and tea.
Extras: Wine and snacks, including local wines, are served at 5:30 in the roof garden.
Rates: $45 (weekdays) to $95 (weekends); off-season 20% to 50% less. Personal checks and credit cards welcome.

10% discount to OHJ members Sunday to Friday only.
Mailing Address: PO Box 1196, Healdsburg, CA 95448

CALIFORNIA: WINE COUNTRY

HEALDSBURG

MADRONA MANOR
John and Carol Muir
1001 Westside Road
Healdsburg, CA 95448
(707) 433-4231

1881 French Second Empire with stick-style ornament

LOCATION: The inn, atop a madrona-tree-studded knoll, is near the Russian River and redwood forests. The coast is 40 minutes away, and the area offers many historic sites.

If you enjoy ghosts, you'll be pleased to know room 201 is supposed to be haunted. And room 101 is probably a good bet too; a San Diego reporter staying there last year claims to have seen the mysterious figure of a woman standing at the foot of the bed, in the middle of the night. When the reporter spoke to it the apparition dissolved. The owners won't deny or verify the rumors, though it seems they did find an odd, closet-like, locked room in the house. And when they cleaned the fireplaces, they uncovered letters addressed in 1880, though the house was built in 1881.

The past owners left behind something more than their letters and spirits—namely, their furniture. Five massive walnut and mahogany bedroom suites grace the guest rooms. Some headboards reach ten feet high, befitting the 14-foot ceilings, and many have matching dressers and armoires.

Other original details abound, like brass hardware on the doors and windows, ten tiled fireplaces, clawfoot tubs, floors of Italian mosaic, and a toilet bowl shaped like an elephant trunk. Floor-to-ceiling windows on the first floor slide up, offering access to the outdoors. Throughout the house are alcoves with arched openings, and some guest rooms open onto balconies. The piano in the parlor is of carved rosewood.

During the past three years the Muirs restored both the main house, which they call the "stately lady," and the carriage house, described as "a frivolous building with lots of cutwork." This outbuilding has been furnished with hand-carved rosewood pieces imported from Nepal.

Restrictions: "Well-supervised" children welcome. Pets accepted with $50 deposit. Smoking allowed in rooms but not in dining and common areas.
Beds: There are 18 rooms and two suites, all with private baths.
Breakfast: Freshly squeezed orange juice, sliced meats and cheeses, soft-boiled eggs, fresh fruit, homemade jams and "churro" (Spanish breakfast pastry), plus coffee and tea.
Extras: Babysitting services are available, as is an outdoor pool. The first floor of the inn houses one of the few three-star restaurants in the greater Bay area.
Rates: $75 (carriage house) to $125 (suite with private deck, four-poster bed). Cots and cribs, $20. Personal checks and credit cards.
Mailing Address: PO Box 818, Healdsburg, CA 95448

LITTLE RIVER

GLENDEVEN
Jan and Janet deVries
8221 North Highway 1
Little River, CA 95456
(707) 937-0083
Year-round

1867 Vernacular farmhouse

LOCATION: Little River is less than two miles south of Mendocino, with its historic buildings and fine restaurants. The inn is adjacent to a state park offering beach walks and swimming.

The deVries have transformed a simple farmhouse into an elegant inn. The old barn and water tower remain, but the house is twice its original size, thanks to a four-room addition that architect Jan designed and Janet decorated. She's also responsible for the period details on the exterior.

The furnishings are a combination of antiques and contemporary art. In the addition, called "Stevenscroft," every room has a fireplace and private bath. The site, a peaceful hilltop spot, is graced with many gardens. Rooms have views of the gardens, the bay below, or both. At night the sounds from the buoys can be heard.

The original house owes its New England character to its first owner, a native of Maine. One long-time owner, known as Aunt Etta, left a more unusual legacy: her diary, years of which were penned in Glendeven's kitchen.

Restrictions: "We take very small babies until they start to crawl and get into things, and then children again over eight—please check with us first." No pets in rooms. Smoking in designated areas. Check-in after 2 p.m., check-out at 11 a.m

Beds: There are ten rooms, six in the farmhouse and four in the addition. Two share a bath, eight have private baths, and all have queen beds (two also have extra beds—in one a single, the other a double).

Breakfast: "Expanded continental"—muffins or coffeecake, freshly squeezed juice, fruit in season or baked apples, hard cooked eggs, tea, and coffee—is offered to most rooms on a tray or in a basket, but "guests are also welcome to dine with others."

Extras: "Just the TLC that comes from enjoying our inn, the beautiful area, and loving sharing it with guests."

Rates: $60 (shared bath) to $200 (spacious, Stevenscroft room with fireplace). Personal checks welcome, Mastercard and Visa by prior arrangement.

10% discount to OHJ members except weekends.

NAPA

THE BEAZLEY HOUSE
Jim and Carol Beazley, and
children Scott and Sonja
1910 First Street
Napa, CA 94559
(707) 257-1649
Year-round

1902 Shingle Style/neo-Colonial

LOCATION: The house, on six-tenths of an acre, is on a tree-lined street with many other distinctive old homes. Restaurants, the quaint downtown, and "vintage Victorian neighborhoods" are close by.

The house has had its share of scandals. The first owners, a surgeon and his wife, divorced in 1910 (gasp!); both soon left town. More recently, socialite Joan Lindburg Hitchcock lived there. She was obsessed, it seems, with John F. Kennedy; she claimed to have had an affair with him, and she was once married to a man who looked just like him. Her San Francisco parties were known as some of the wildest in town (not an easy reputation to achieve in San Francisco!); they frequently lasted all night.

In between the scandalous goings-on, more sedate things happened. One couple owned the house for over 60 years, and the Catholic Church operated a foster home for boys there.

With so few owners the structure remained basically intact. (Still, the Beazleys describe their recent restoration projects as "too numerous to mention.") Inside a variety of woods have been used — redwood for the six-foot-high panelling in the dining room, mahogany insets in the oak floors. The guest rooms are furnished with bedroom sets made of cherry, golden oak, and walnut.

The owners verified the house's original appearance with old photos, and reinstalled striped awnings; the building also has its original color scheme of brown shingles trimmed in white. The Beazleys rebuilt an old barn on the property; they call it the "Carriage House." It stands amid gardens and trees behind the house, and has amenities like private baths and two-person spas. "There are no such modern touches in the mansion!" Jim Beazley assures.

Restrictions: Smoking only in the gardens. No children under 12, and no pets. Check-in between 3:30 and 6 p.m.

Beds: The four rooms in the mansion have private baths. The five carriage house rooms have fireplaces and private baths.

Breakfast: Full breakfast.

Extras: All of the carriage house rooms have spas. Iced or hot tea, coffee, and sherry are available all day on a tea cart in the living room. The hosts can arrange private wine tastings and tours of the 150 wineries in the area.

Rates: $85 to $135, $15 per extra occupant. 10% discount weekdays January through March. Personal checks and credit cards welcome.

10% discount to OHJ members except during August, September, and October.

CALIFORNIA: WINE COUNTRY

NAPA

LA BELLE EPOQUE
Blanca Semmler
1386 Calistoga Avenue
Napa, CA 94558
(707) 257-2161
Year-round

1893 Queen Anne

LOCATION: The inn, close to wineries and a few minutes from Highway 29, is located in a historic section of Napa, with restaurants, theatre, and parks within walking distance.

Herman Schwartz made his fortune in hardware; he owned the largest hardware store in Napa when he had this house built. After his death the place passed to his daughter and from her, in 1903, to one Manuel Silva. Silva was the exclusive distributor of Napa Soda Springs mineral water, and his son Frank became the county's district attorney in 1907.

Some of the extravagant exterior details have been highlighted with polychrome paint; most, though, are so distinctive that they show up even under a single color. Stained glass has been used profusely; the church-quality arched panes in the bay window match the ones in the dormer, and there's more stained glass in the main entrance's double doors and transom. Ms. Semmler's greatest challenge, she says, was making the house conform to city codes without destroying its architectural character.

Restrictions: No smoking in guest rooms, and smoking "discouraged" in common areas. No pets or children under 15. Check-in between 2 and 6 p.m., check-out at 11 a.m.
Beds: Three doubles and one room with twins; two share a bath.
Breakfast: Continental.
Extras: The wine cellar offers wine tasting at no charge.
Rates: $70 (shared shower) to $90 (private bath). Personal or traveler's checks welcome.
    10% discount to OHJ members.

CALIFORNIA: WINE COUNTRY

NAPA

THE GOODMAN HOUSE
Art and June Bowen
1225 Division Street
Napa, CA 94558
(707) 257-1166
Year-round

1880 Stick Style/Queen Anne

LOCATION: This historic section of town is close to the Napa River and features many large old homes. Downtown Napa and its restaurants are close by.

Aptly named, Division Street once separated residential Napa from the business district. Along the tree-lined street a wealthy entrepreneur and philanthropist, George Goodman, built a house for his son Harvey, who at that time was owner of the Napa Goodman Bank.

The Goodmans made several changes to the structure, converting closets and a porch into extra baths; they also added a wing in 1892.

The Goodmans sold the house in 1898; the subsequent owners, the Corletts, lived there until 1951. The house survived the 1906 earthquake, though one fireplace had to be rebuilt. John and Ada Fiske bought the place from the Corletts and carefully restored it. June and Art Bowen have lived there since 1968; "constant general upkeep" has been their major undertaking.

Inside they've combined modern pieces with antique furnishings like lighting fixtures and portraits. In the "Red Room" white contemporary couches stand beside reproduction Victorian flocked red wallpaper. Throughout the house Eastlake details are highlighted by a multi-color paint job.

Restrictions: No children under 15, no pets or smoking. Check-in after 3 p.m., check-out at 11 a.m.
Beds: There's one suite with a king and double bed, and three other rooms that share a bath (a double and two queens).
Breakfast: Continental.
Extras: The kitchenette is stocked with complimentary soda, beer, wine, and hors d'oeuvres. In the afternoon wine and hors d'oeuvres, as well as cake, are served.
Rates: $55 (shared bath) to $75 (suite accommodating four, private bath); cots, $10. Personal and traveler's checks and American Express accepted.

CALIFORNIA: WINE COUNTRY

NAPA

THE OLD WORLD INN
Geoffrey and Janet Villiers
1301 Jefferson Street
Napa, CA 94559
(707) 257-0112
Year-round

1906 Queen Anne

LOCATION: Wineries, horseback riding, a restored grist mill, petrified forest, and Old Faithful geyser are all within driving distance.

Given his customer's profession—the first owner was a contractor—builder Eli Sheppard must have taken extra care with the house. The architect, Luther Terton, also designed the Beazley House, another historic B&B in Napa.

The Villiers cite the lovely room shapes, rare pressed redwood, and the fine staircase as the sights to see; there's also an impressive pair of wood columns surrounding the dining room's wide entrance, as well as leaded glass in the second-storey windows.

Restrictions: No children under 16, no pets, no smoking (because of linens and fabrics). Check-in after 1 p.m., and notify if arriving after 6 p.m.
Beds: Six queens, one double, and one king all have private baths.
Breakfast: "Very substantial continental": fresh fruit, homemade breads and cakes, pancakes, homemade jams, croissants, fresh orange juice plus a hot entree.
Extras: Afternoon tea with cakes and cookies is served "since we innkeepers are English." Complimentary wine is provided in the room. Wine, sherry, and a cheese board is served each night, along with a selection of desserts before bedtime. The outdoor jacuzzi stands under a grapevine.
Rates: $90 to $97 (honeymoon room or room with king bed). Mid-week off-season, $50. Personal checks and credit cards accepted.

10% discount to OHJ members.

CALIFORNIA: WINE COUNTRY

ST. HELENA

AMBROSE BIERCE HOUSE
Tony and Sheila Price
1515 Main Street
St. Helena, CA 94574
(707) 963-3003
Year-round

1870 Vernacular

LOCATION: The Napa Valley's famous wineries are nearby; ballooning, gliding, and partaking of spas and mudbaths are a few of the possible activities.

This modest-looking house boasts two curious features: a winding exterior staircase and a former occupant named Ambrose Bierce. One of America's great short-story writers, Bierce is known for his cynical wit. His famous *Devil's Dictionary* contains entries like "abstainer: a weak person who yields to the temptation of denying himself a pleasure" and "absurdity: a statement of belief manifestly inconsistent with one's own opinion."

His fame was confined to literary circles until 1913, when he left his St. Helena home and disappeared in Mexico. Rumors still abound —did he commit suicide? Was he executed by Pancho Villa? Did he slip away to Europe? The public was intrigued, and interest in his works soared. If he indeed survived, he must have been greatly amused at what his disappearance did for his literary reputation.

The noteworthy interior features in his house include an etched-glass door in the sitting room and the guest rooms packed with memorabilia of Bierce and friends: namely, Lillie Langtry, a beautiful and scandalous actress; Eadweard Muybridge, acclaimed as the father of the motion picture but locally notorious as the confessed, but acquitted, murderer of his wife's lover; and Lillie Hitchcock Coit, "belle of San Francisco," benefactress of the Coit Tower on Telegraph Hill and Bierce's good friend.

Restrictions: No children under 12 or pets. Smoking in common areas only. Check-in after 2 p.m., check-out at noon.
Beds: The two suites each have a queen bed, private bath, and sitting room.
Breakfast: Fresh orange juice, coffee, tea, fruit, Italian and French pastries.
Extras: Sherry is provided in the rooms.
Rates: $85 and up. Personal checks and American Express welcome.
10% discount to OHJ members.

ST. HELENA

THE BALE MILL INN
Tom and Linda Scheibal
3431 North St. Helena Highway
St. Helena, CA 94574
(707) 963-4545
Year-round

1910 Colonial Revival

LOCATION: Wineries, mud baths, spas, and fine restaurants are all within convenient distances. Behind the house lie a log cabin and eight hours of hiking trails that wind past an 1850 cemetery, waterfall, bale mill, and an 1850 waterwheel, part of a state park.

Ernest Hemingway once stayed at the Bale Mill Inn, when it was a roadside tavern. So in his honor the owners furnished one guest room in Hemingway memorabilia; there's a safari helmet hanging on a hat tree, a pair of bull's horns mounted on the wall, and a ceiling fan that evokes the writer's days on Key West. The owners chose four other "legends" for the remaining rooms: Emily Dickinson's has wicker furnishings reminiscent of a New England summer porch; Teddy Roosevelt's is decorated with American flags and has a pair of "his" gold-rimmed glasses on a table; for Jack London, the owners decided upon rough hickory furniture and various pieces of tramp art; and finally to accommodate a collection of yachting-related objects, the owners named a room after an imaginary "Captain Quinn."

Most beds are Victorian, though one dates from 1790. And in case the decorating job inspires you, there's a convenient antique store on the first floor.

Restrictions: No children under eight. Check-in after 2 p.m., check-out at 11 a.m.
Beds: All five rooms have double beds and share two full and one half-bath.
Breakfast: Homemade pastries, fresh juice, Italian coffee, eight types of tea, and fresh fruit.
Rates: $60 to $65, payable in personal checks or credit cards.
   10% discount to OHJ members.

ST. HELENA

THE SUTTER HOME INN
Katie Preger
225 St. Helena Highway
St. Helena, CA 94574
(707) 963-4423
Year-round

1884 Stick Style/Queen Anne

LOCATION: Located in the peaceful Napa Valley (the center of wine country) the inn is close to some 140 wineries, facilities for ballooning, hiking, and picnicking, along with many restaurants.

This complex of three buildings evolved in several stages. First came the winery next door, now called the Sutter Home Winery; a Swiss named John Thomann built it sometime before 1874. He waited about ten years to finish his elaborate residence (now the inn), which is covered in half timber, tiny balconies, unexpected dormers, and gingerbread.

When the Dotys bought the house in 1973 they opened an antique shop on the first floors, and later five guest rooms above. In 1979 they undertook the reconstruction of the property's original water tower, thereby adding four more rooms; all have private baths, fireplaces, and air conditioning. And finally the couple built a carriage house, with a barn-like hipped roof, to accommodate yet more rooms.

Inside the main building "everything is original, as far as we can determine," the new owner says, including wainscotting and plaster walls. Rooms contain a variety of marble-topped tables and dressers, along with handmade quilts on the beds and clawfoot tubs in some baths.

Restrictions: No children, pets, or smoking in the rooms. Check-in from 2 to 11.
Beds: Nine room with private baths and fireplaces.
Breakfast: Homemade breads (muffins, scones, apple and coffee-cakes), a variety of fresh fruit in season, yogurt, juices, coffee, tea.
Extras: After 5 p.m., and all evening long, coffee, tea, homemade

cookies, and wine are available.

Rates: $75 (main house) to $120 (carriage house). Personal checks and credit cards welcome.

ST. HELENA

VILLA ST. HELENA
Ralph and Carolyn Cotton
2727 Sulphur Springs Avenue
St. Helena, CA 94574
(707) 963-2514
Year-round

1939-41 California Mediterranean

LOCATION: The villa is secluded in the hills above St. Helena, overlooking the Napa Valley's vineyards. The 20-acre estate "creates its own private world."

At the end of a three-quarter-mile private drive lies an enormous brick villa. It's partially built into the hillside so that it looks smaller that it is. In fact, the owners say, the building is set in such a way that it's difficult from any point to get a sense of how large it is. The building actually has three levels, two asymmetrical wings, and a courtyard.

Robert M. Carrere, a noted architect of the era, was commissioned to design the structure in 1941. His most famous work is a church in Florence, and he also restored a building in Italy, which may explain the Villa's Mediterranean influences. Because of World War II materials were difficult to obtain; but Carrere managed to find plentiful supplies by buying from the Mexican Exhibit at the World's Fair. The floors are of Mexican tile, the roof is also tiled, and supporting the massive structure are sand-cast bricks and steel beams.

Carrere was known for integrating his creations with the surrounding landscape. Part of the courtyard is carved directly into the hillside. There are also many windows, which afford views of the oak, bay, and madrone woods. The front lawn looks over the town of St. Helena and nearby vineyards.

97

In the 1940s and 1950s various political figures and Hollywood celebrities used the villa as a mountain hideaway. By 1983 both house and grounds were in need of repair, which the Cottons undertook and then began receiving guests that same year.

The innkeepers' eclectic antique furniture is displayed in a environment so elegant that a recent episode of "Falcon Crest" was filmed at the house. The wood-panelled library has a blue Delft tiled fireplace. There's a beamed ceiling in the living room (which is where the show was filmed), along with a massive stone fireplace.

Restrictions: No pets or children under 12. Check-in between 3 and 6 p.m.; check-out at 11 a.m.
Beds: There are two kings and two queens and no rooms share baths.
Breakfast: "Elaborate continental": fresh fruit and juice, homemade pastries and bread, locally produced cheese.
Extras: A complimentary bottle of Villa St. Helena wine is available.
Rates: $115 (wood panelling, sitting area) to $195 (suite with balcony, terrace, and fireplace); 10% to 20% less Monday through Thursday. Personal checks and credit cards welcome.

10% discount to OHJ members.

CALIFORNIA: WINE COUNTRY

ST. HELENA

THE WHITE RANCH
Ruth Davis
707 White Lane
St. Helena, CA 94574
(707) 963-4635
Year-round

1865 Vernacular Gothic Revival

LOCATION: In the area are many older homes, wineries, and restaurants, as well as facilities for ballooning and gliding. The house is near both a river and the Robert Louis Stevenson museum.

After leading a wagon train across this country, Methodist minister Asa White started the first church in the Napa Valley. He lived in this house; he also helped organize Pacific Union College nearby.

The water tower on the property has been used for wine storage. Drop siding covers the main house, where there's also original doors, window panes, and tongue-and-groove redwood siding. Inside you'll find antiques ranging from Queen Anne table and chairs to an Italian marble table and a French clock.

Restrictions: No children, pets, or smoking. Check-in after 2 p.m., check-out at 11 a.m.
Beds: The one suite has a double bed, dressing room, and a private bath.
Breakfast: Orange juice, fresh fruit, homemade breads, jams, plus espresso.
Extras: Sherry is provided in the room; the lawn has a picnic table for guest use.
Rates: $65, payable in personal or traveler's checks.

WESTPORT

1880 Vernacular

DEHAVEN VALLEY FARM
Jack Essex and Wayne Zion
39247 North Highway 1
Westport, CA 95488
(707) 964-5252
March through December

LOCATION: The inn is surrounded by 20 acres of hills, meadows, streams, and woods, sloping to the Pacific Ocean and featuring miles of footpaths, on the Mendocino coast.

Four cottages from the same era, c. 1880, dot the hill around the main house. The cottages have been modernized and re-shingled, but in the main house details like the fireplaces remain. The owners have amassed many period furnishings, including a harpsichord and a spinning wheel, and added period wallpapers. Over the unused well they built a gazebo, and they've also installed a redwood spa.

The wide verandahs and the rooms overlook the ocean, meadow, and mountains. Some guest rooms also have fireplaces.

The owners say they have "an authentic ghost—a suicide resulting from an unhappy love affair."

Restrictions: "We can't accommodate babies." Check-in after 2 p.m.
Beds: There are eight doubles, five of which share a bath. The four cottages have wet bars, baths, and refrigerators.
Breakfast: "Full, hearty, American": ham and eggs, biscuits, and fried potatoes, for example.
Extras: Free aperitifs are served in the evening; coffee, tea, and juices are available at any hour. The inn provides horses and bicycles for guest use. Depending on the season, there's also entertainment in the barn, outdoor picnics, evening campfires, and clambakes on the beach.
Rates: $55 (shared bath in main house) to $125 (three-room suite with wet bar). 20% winter discount. Credit cards welcome.

10% discount to OHJ members.

CALIFORNIA: WINE COUNTRY

WESTPORT

HOWARD CREEK RANCH INN
Charles and Sally Lasselle Grigg
40501 North Highway One
Westport, CA 95488
(707) 964-6725
Year-round

1871 Farmhouse

LOCATION: Rolling hills stretch in all directions from this inn's valley setting. The surrounding area is rural, with beaches and wildlife.

Much of Westport's historic architecture has succumbed to fire and neglect. But this ranch house remains. Once it formed part of a complex with a blacksmith shop, sawmill, and barn; of these outbuildings only the barn and a few cabins still exist. According to the Griggs the enormous barn is the largest, and possibly the oldest, structure of its kind on the Mendocino Coast. A drive-through bisects

100

the first floor, where there's also a tack room and shop. A hayloft and servants' quarters are located upstairs. The Griggs are rehabilitating the structure as their private residence.

The main house was styled after the farmhouses of New England. Once it had a two-tiered porch, and resembled a Southern plantation. Only a partial deck still stands on the second storey. One of the rustic cabins, which has only cold running water, serves as a guest house.

Alfred Howard and his wife Missouri Lavina Cook — both were from the state of Missouri — built the complex after his father sold the land to him. Huge 12-by-12 beams, hewn from first-growth redwoods on the property, were used for construction. Of the couple's seven children, only three survived to adulthood. Lucy, the oldest, etched her name on one of the window panes in the main house, and it's lasted nearly a century.

The Griggs have collected memorabilia and antiques from the 1890s, along with quilts, lace, linens, and Depression glass. The original brick fireplace still stands, along with an upright piano, old harmonium, and a large, stuffed moose head.

Restrictions: Check-in between 2 and 6 p.m. (other times by prior arrangement). Smoking only in specified areas. Children and pets accepted with prior approval.
Beds: There are three suites in the main house, two with private baths; three cabins, two with private baths, one with cold water.
Breakfast: Bacon or sausage with eggs, coffee, juice, fruit, plus assorted "yummies," fresh blackberries in season, local honey, and home-grown mint tea, are all served at 9 a.m.
Extras: There's a wood-fired hot tub and sauna built into the hillside, a horse for petting, and a stable down the road for riding ($18). Massages can be obtained with advance reservations ($25 per hour). The ocean and three-mile beach are free.
Rates: $50 (rustic cabin with wood stove) to $85 (two-room suite with balcony); personal checks welcome.

10% discount to OHJ members except weekends and holidays.
Mailing Address: PO Box 121, Westport, CA 95488

COLORADO

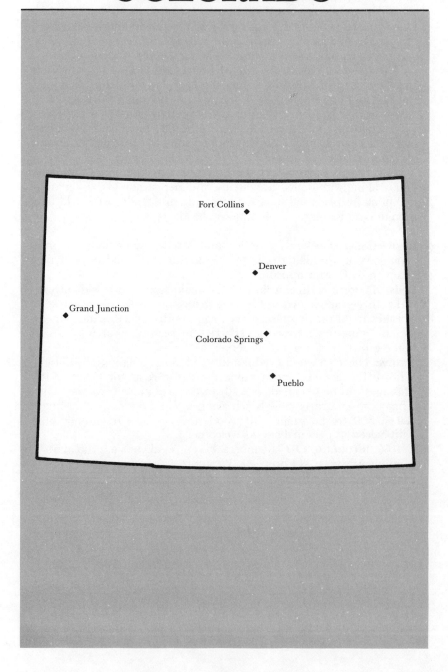

COLORADO SPRINGS

THE HEARTHSTONE INN
Dorothy and Ruth Williams
506 North Cascade
Colorado Springs, CO 80903
(719) 473-4413
Year-round

1885 Queen Anne; C. 1900 neo-Colonial

LOCATION: The inn stands on a residential boulevard, on a large corner lot with lawn, trees, and gardens. Nearby are Pike's Peak, Garden of the Gods, Cave of the Winds, and the Flying W Chuck Wagon diner.

Judson Bemis, the man who "invented" the paper bag, had this house built in the shadow of Pike's Peak in 1885. In 1982, the current owners, Dorothy and Ruth Williams, bought the house next door, and connected the two by moving a carriage house in between them. Both houses have wraparound verandahs and lots of dormers. The mantels are made of carved oak and cherry with tile surrounds. Antiques furnish all 25 guest rooms.

Restrictions: No pets; check-in between 2 and 11 p.m. "Children who show respect for the inn, its guests, and furnishings are welcome."
Beds: Of the 25 rooms, two have two twins, three have kings, ten have queens, and ten are double—two share a bath.
Breakfast: Menu varies—one possibility is country brunch pie with homemade pumpkin bread and fruit salad.
Rates: $45 (under-the-eaves double, shared bath) to $95 (king-sized bed, sitting room, private porch with mountain view). Cots, $10 (includes breakfast); no charge for cribs. Personal checks and credit cards accepted.

COLORADO

FORT COLLINS

**ELIZABETH STREET
GUEST HOUSE
John and Sheryl Clark
202 East Elizabeth
Fort Collins, CO 80524
(303) 493-BEDS
Year-round**

LOCATION: The inn's historic neighborhood is one block from Colorado State University, eight blocks from a restored old-town square. The entrance to Rocky Mountain National Park is 30 miles away.

This sturdy American Foursquare was built by M.G. Conley in 1905. John and Sheryl Clark spent 11 months rewiring, plumbing, and stripping woodwork before they were ready to accommodate guests. The heart pine floors now gleam, and the leaded-glass windows shine. You'll also find antique fixtures in the bathroom (restored by the Clarks as well) and an assortment of antiques throughout the house. Sheryl and her mother are dollmakers, and have their creations on display; Sheryl also collects antique boxes and trunks.

Restrictions: "Not suitable for children under four." No pets, smoking in living room only.
Beds: The three rooms—two doubles, one queen—all have sinks and share one full bath and a half-bath.
Breakfast: Full: coffee, tea, juice, fresh fruit, eggs, muffins, breads, and cold cereals.

Extras: Tea and coffee are always available, and there's a decanter full of sherry provided in the dining room.
Rates: $30 to $38; personal checks and credit cards welcome.
    10% discount to OHJ members.

LA VETA

1899 INN - BED & BREAKFAST
Marilyn Hall
314 South Main
La Veta, CO 81055
(303) 742-3576
Year-round

1909 Tudor Revival

LOCATION: The inn is next door to the Fort Francisco Museum and the library; the town park is one block away. The quiet, rustic town of La Veta, amid the Spanish Peaks and Sangre de Cristo mountains, offers skiing, horseback riding, hiking, and fishing.

Despite its name, this inn was actually built in 1909. Made of massive stone blocks, it has a garage to match out back. There's leaded and bevelled glass, plus false-grained woodwork, that's definitely worth a look.

Restrictions: Smoking limited; no pets.
Beds: A double and a twin/king have private baths; the other rooms —a twin/king, a double, and a double with couch—share a bath; all have lavatories.
Breakfast: The Sunday menu, for instance, features popovers, eggs, fruit. Weekdays the inn offers muffins, eggs, blueberry panc French toast, quiche, or omelettes.
Rates: $22.50 (single) to $27.50 (double) for king with shared bath (children under 14 free) to $25 (single), $32.50 (double) for double with private bath. Cots, $7.50; cribs, free. Personal checks welcome.
    10% discount to OHJ members.
Mailing Address: Box 372, La Veta, CO 81055

MANITOU SPRINGS

GRAY'S AVENUE HOTEL
Tom and Lee Gray
711 Manitou Avenue
Manitou Springs, CO 80829
(303) 685-1277
Year-round

1886 Shingle with neo-Colonial details.

LOCATION: The hotel is located at the edge of Manitou Springs' historic downtown area; to the immediate east is a library funded by the Carnegie Foundation 75 years ago. Most shops and restaurants are within walking distance.

One of the original hotels built in this old resort town, Gray's Avenue Hotel sits 50 feet above Manitou's Main Street. The shingled Victorian, with brackets under its eaves and two large dormers, was built in 1886. The foundation (over nine feet high) and the large, corner fireplace in the library are made of native greenstone from a quarry that closed in the 1920s. Although Tom and Lee Gray purchased the house in 1975, they didn't discover many of the hotel's details until they decided to convert their home into a B&B. The house had been chopped into seven apartments. The Grays had to remove five kitchens, strip walls of paint, wallpaper, and panelling, and open the staircase that had been walled in many years before.

Restrictions: Children 12 and over are welcome; exceptions will be made if group or family rents the entire hotel. Check-in after 2 p.m., check-out at 11 a.m. No pets.
Beds: The ten rooms have either double, king- or queen-sized beds; the three on the second floor share one bath, and the four on the third share another.
Breakfast: Fruit juices, fresh fruit in season, coffee, tea, herbal tea; bacon, ham, or sausage; eggs, quiche, or French toast, homemade pastries or muffins.
Extras: The video store across the street provides the communal VCR with films; soft refreshments are available. The hosts offer a 10%

discount to guests at "the best antique store in the area."
Rates: $40 (shared bath, double bed) to $60 (private bath, king bed) from Memorial to Labor Day, lower the rest of the year. Some personal checks and most credit cards accepted.

10% discount to OHJ members "—absolutely!"

SILVERTON

THE ALMA HOUSE
Don and Jolene Scott
220 East 10th Street
Silverton, CO 81433
(303) 387-5336
June 25 to Labor Day

1898 Vernacular Queen Anne

LOCATION: The mining town of Silverton, elevation 9300 feet, has a population of 800 and is surrounded by 13,000-foot mountains. The famous Durango-to-Silverton railroad ends here. The guest rooms have expansive views of the San Juan Mountains.

The Alma House was built in 1898, constructed of granite and wood. The original wainscotting, pressed tin, brass lights, and leaded glass can be found throughout the building. The Scotts are especially proud of the bay window over the inn's entrance. They've furnished the guest rooms with antique dressers, period wallpapers, plus a collection of "railroadiana" — photos, prints, and paintings.

Restrictions: No smoking (strictly enforced).
Beds: Ten queen rooms share four baths.
Breakfast: Coffee and tea, and occasionally homemade sweet rolls, are served at 8 a.m.
Extras: A large videotape library is available (all rooms have TVs).
Rates: $28 all rooms, regardless of occupancy. No extra beds for children, but "up to two in sleeping bags on the floor is O.K." Personal checks and credit cards welcome.

10% discount to OHJ members.
Mailing Address: Box 780, Silverton, CO 81433

CONNECTICUT

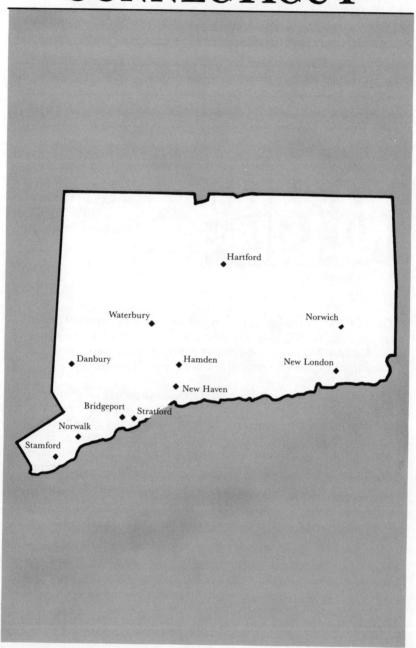

Hartford

Waterbury

Norwich

Danbury

Hamden

New London

New Haven

Bridgeport

Stratford

Norwalk

Stamford

MOODUS

THE FOWLER HOUSE
Barbara Ally, Paul Seals, Penny
& Arnie Davidson
Plains Road
Moodus, CT 06469
(203) 873-8906
Year-round

1890 Queen Anne

LOCATION: The inn stands on Moodus's village green. Nearby you'll find the Goodspeed Opera, Goodspeed at Chester (professional theatre), museums, Gillete Castle, antique shops, fine dining, musical riverboat cruises, state parks, art galleries, craft shows, and beautiful New England countryside.

A highly touted cure for impotence begot this elegant Queen Anne. Dr. Frank Fowler, the man who built it, was a quack physician who made a fortune selling patent medicines, including sugar pills which he claimed cured sexual disorders. At the height of his career, Fowler owned two yachts and several horses, as well as this mansion, and was considered an upstanding member of the community. It wasn't long, however, before people clued in to his antics: At the turn of the century, Fowler was kicked out of town on charges of mail fraud. He died a pauper in New London, where he'd tried, unsuccessfully, to re-build his defunct business.

Fowler may have died poor, but he left behind a rich legacy. His house is equipped with all the most fashionable appointments of his time: stained glass, fish-scale shingles, turret, wraparound porch and, inside, Lincrusta wallcoverings, Italian ceramic fireplaces, and marble

109

sinks. The house is in excellent condition today, thanks to the current innkeepers' elbow grease. You'll find the original gas-electric light fixtures, tin ceilings, clawfoot bathtubs, and even the original carbide gas generator all in smooth working order. They've restored its Victorian color scheme and ornate picket fence, too.

Restrictions: Children over 12 are welcome. No pets. Check-in after 1 p.m., check-out at 11 a.m.

Beds: Six guest rooms. One with queen-sized bed, four with double bed, and one with twin beds. Four rooms have private bath.

Breakfast: Fresh squeezed juice, fresh fruit cup, home-baked muffins, breads, cakes, coffee, tea, cold cereals, and "specials."

Extras: Afternoon tea is served on the wraparound porch or in the library. Bicycles and picnic hampers are available for an extra charge. Guests are free to use the refrigerator.

Rates: $60 to $70. Cots, $10. Credit cards and personal checks welcome.

10% discount to OHJ members.

Mailing Address: PO BOX 432, Moodus, CT 06469

CONNECTICUT

MYSTIC

HARBOUR INNE AND COTTAGE
Charles Lecouras, Jr.
Edgemont Street
Mystic, CT 06355
(203) 572-9253
Year-round

1898 Fisherman's cottage

LOCATION: In the heart of historic Mystic, the inn has over 200 feet of frontage on the Mystic River. Within easy walking distance are all the town's attractions including the Mystic Seaport Museum. Watch the tall ships pass from your room.

Old Clyde, a fisherman, built this rustic, turn-of-the-century cottage. It's built of solid cedar planking, encircled by a stone fence, and adorned with lots of ship memorabilia, including ships' lanterns and, inside, a boat is used for a bookshelf. Next door to the main house is an unusual guest cottage—a renovated World War I Navy housing unit, with a solid cedar interior that looks like the hull of a ship.

Beds: Four rooms plus a three-room cottage. All rooms have a double bed, most have private baths.
Breakfast: Breakfast is not served, but many fine restaurants are nearby.
Extras: Canoes and rowboats are provided for fishing, along with riverside picnic tables, kitchen privileges, and cable TV.
Rates: $20 to $85, depending on room size and bath arrangement. Rates higher on weekends, lower in winter. Cots and cribs, $10 each. Personal checks welcome.

10% discount to OHJ members.
Mailing Address: RFD #1 Box 398, Mystic, CT 06355

NOANK

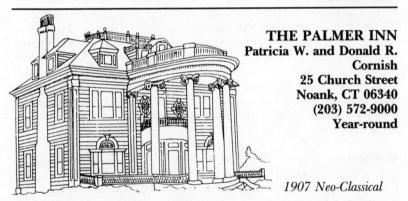

THE PALMER INN
Patricia W. and Donald R.
Cornish
25 Church Street
Noank, CT 06340
(203) 572-9000
Year-round

1907 Neo-Classical

LOCATION: The inn is located in the charming fishing village of Noank. One block away is the water; nearby are charter fishing boats and sailing cruises. Mystic, the Mystic Seaport and Aquarium are two miles away.

"We look forward to having OHJ readers join us as guests. We find that guests who enjoy old houses and their historic significance enjoy their visit to the Palmer Inn the most."

The Palmer Inn towers like a giant over Noank's less ambitious colonials. It's a reminder of one of the nation's most powerful shipping industries that met its demise early in this century.

A century ago, Noank townspeople bowed down before the Palmer family, for whom this palatial dwelling was built. On one typical occasion, Robert Palmer Senior, the family patriarch and a church deacon, decreed his distaste for intoxicants. His fellow citizens promptly voted the town dry, though most of them did not object to an occasional indulgence, and for decades not a trace of spirits could be found anywhere near Noank. It's no surprise that the townsfolk bent to Deacon Palmer's will: He employed just about everyone in town, and those he didn't depended on the ship-builders for business. In its heyday, Palmer and Son was estimated as the nation's largest ship-building industry.

Robert Palmer, Jr., the deacon's son and business partner, built this house as the Palmer fortune reached its climactic crest. He spared no expense to make it the most elegant in the neighborhood. From the outside, it resembles a clapboarded version of the White House, with colossal, 30-foot columns ascending to a circular portico. The wide, marbleized verandah is reminiscent of a southern plantation (not surprising, since the architects hailed from Knoxville, Tennessee). Stained-glass windows, curved-glass windows, and layers upon layers of balconies topped by a widow's walk add to its imposing presence. The interior is no less splendid, with more columns, mahogany woodwork, hardwood floors, and immense fireplaces.

The Palmer shipping industry ground to a halt just seven years after the magnificent house was completed. In 1913, Deacon Palmer died and, a year later, son Robert followed him to the grave. No heir was alive to take over.

Eventually, the younger Palmer's house fell into less fastidious hands. It was allowed to decay for several years, until Patricia and Donald Cornish took on its restoration in 1984, as retold in their photo albums.

Restrictions: No pets. No children under 16. Smoking permitted in parlor only. Check-out at 11 a.m., check-in after 1:30 p.m. and by 9 p.m. unless previous arrangements have been made.
Beds: Six guest chambers. Accommodations range from a room with twin beds and a shared bath to a master suite with queen-sized bed, fireplace, and private bath. Four of the rooms have a private bath.
Breakfast: Continental: herb teas, home-baked muffins and breads served with homemade jams and jellies; coffee.
Extras: Afternoon tea is served, with iced tea, herb tea, or mulled cider, "depending on the season."
Rates: $80 to $125. Personal checks and credit cards welcome.

OLD LYME

OLD LYME INN
Diana Field Atwood
85 Lyme Street
Old Lyme, CT 06371
(203) 434-2600
Year-round

C. 1850 Greek Revival

LOCATION: Old Lyme is a charming town of 5,000 with many old houses; the inn is convenient to Long Island Sound, antique shops, museums in historic buildings, and old seaports, and on the main street of the town's historic district.

"Perfect for old-house owners." Diana Field Atwood

The Old Lyme Inn was lucky for 100 years, from its birth in 1850 until 1950. It stood guard over a prosperous 300-acre farm, and was carefully maintained. Famous American impressionist painters like Willard Metcalfe and Childe Hassam dropped by frequently to use the house, barns, and tree-shaded grounds as backdrops for their artistry. But after 1950, the house fell into bad hands: Inexperienced restauranteurs moved in, set the house accidentally afire several times, and, because their business was not earning much money, never repaired the damage. The structure limped through the next several years scorched and singed.

Diana Atwood rescued it in 1976, completely restoring everything from its ornate iron fence, to its front porch pilasters, to its curly maple staircase. She furnished the house with Victorian and Empire-era antiques, and hung up her collection of early American impressionists' paintings (to complement the house's history).

Among the Inn's interesting features are a large-scale mural in the front hall and two 1870s one-storey wing additions, each with a porch and floor-to-ceiling windows, flanking the house's central section.

Restrictions: Well-behaved pets are permitted, but are not to be left unsupervised in the rooms. Check-in after 1 p.m., check-out at 11 a.m.

Beds: Of the 13 rooms, ten have queen-sized beds, three have twin beds. All have private baths.
Breakfast: Continental.
Extras: The inn's elegant, award-winning restaurant serves lunch and dinner, Tuesday through Sunday.
Rates: $75 to $115. Credit cards and personal checks welcome.
   10% discount to OHJ members on lodging.
Mailing Address: PO Box 787, Old Lyme, CT 06371

CONNECTICUT

OLD MYSTIC

RED BROOK INN
Ruth Keyes
2750 Gold Star Highway
Route 184
Old Mystic, CT 06372
(203) 572-0349
Year-round

1760 & 1761 center-chimney Colonials

LOCATION: Roughly half-way between New York and Boston, the Red Brook Inn is only two miles from the Mystic Seaport Museum. The houses sit on seven-and-a-half acres in a rural area convenient to Connecticut's seacoast attractions.

"These two fine old houses have been restored to museum quality. They offer a chance to study 18th-century architecture first hand." Ruth Keyes

It's rare to find a pre-Revolutionary War house in never-remodelled, mint condition. It's even rarer to find two of them side by side. But that's what you'll see when you visit the Red Brook Inn. Both houses have all their original windows, doors, and hardware. Both have numerous fireplaces and original bake ovens. Both are furnished with antiques of the era, including whale-oil lighting devices (used before kerosene was invented). One, the Nathaniel Creary House, stands on its original site; the other, the Elisha Haley House, was recently moved to Red Brook from its original location two miles away. It would have been demolished had it not found a buyer—the road running by it was about to be widened. A photo album in the Inn documents the entire moving and restoration project.

114

Nathaniel Creary was a sea captain and, coincidentally, Elisha Haley, one of Connecticut's first congressmen, was his son-in-law. (It seems fitting that the houses should be united in this way.) Haley's house served as a stagecoach stop and tavern from the 1760s to the 1880s; the innkeepers have restored the original tap room, and now have it well stocked with board games like chess and backgammon.

Restrictions: No small children. No pets. No smoking. Check-in after 1:30 p.m., check-out at 10:30 a.m.

Beds: Nine double rooms, six of which have original working fireplaces. Also, two rooms with twin beds; one with double and twin.

Breakfast: Full: walnut waffles, fresh fruit, quiche, corn muffins, maple syrup, coffee, tea, and juices.

Extras: Coffee, tea, and ice are always available. The original taproom is now used for board games like chess and backgammon. Firewood is provided for the many fireplaces. November through March, the innkeepers cook Saturday dinner in the old bake ovens and fireplaces as part of "colonial weekends."

Rates: $80 to $125, double occupancy. Rooms without fireplaces are less expensive in the winter. $25 for third person in room. Credit cards and personal checks welcome.

10% discount to OHJ members.

Mailing Address: PO Box 237, Old Mystic, CT 06372

FLORIDA

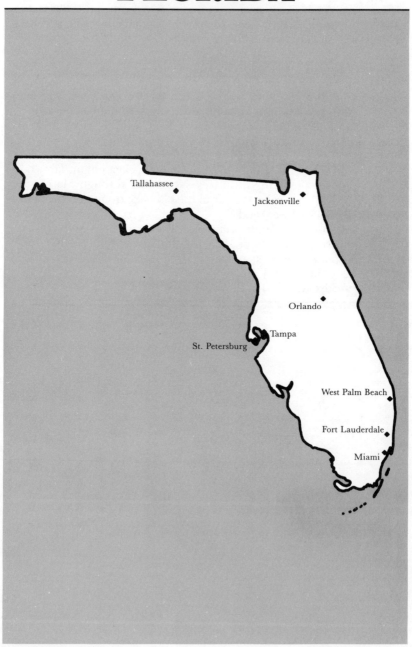

Tallahassee

Jacksonville

Orlando

Tampa

St. Petersburg

West Palm Beach

Fort Lauderdale

Miami

AMELIA ISLAND

1735 HOUSE
David and Susan Caples
584 South Fletcher
Amelia Island, FL 32034
(904) 261-5878
Year-round

1928 Neo-Colonial

LOCATION: Directly on the Atlantic Ocean, the inn is one mile from the historic seaport of Fernandina and near the Georgia-Florida border on a 13-mile long-island.

T he main house's large deck faces the ocean. That marine atmosphere prevails throughout the house, where the innkeepers have hung maritime artifacts on the walls and have an extensive collection of old maritime photographs on display.

Guests can stay in the main house or, for a more unusual experience, in the four-storey lighthouse just down the shore, which sleeps six.

Restrictions: Check-in after 4 p.m., check-out before 11 a.m.
Beds: The rooms accommodate up to four people; each has a double bed and two wooden built-in bunks.
Breakfast: Fresh fruit, juice, fresh baked goods "prepared on the premises," coffee/tea/milk.
Rates: $60 to $65 for rooms with "entertainment areas." Personal checks and credit cards welcome.

10% discount to OHJ members.

CORAL GABLES

HOTEL PLACE ST. MICHEL
Stuart Bornstein and Alan Potamkin
162 Alcazar Avenue
Coral Gables, FL 33134
(305) 444-1666
Year-round

1926 Neo-Mediterranean (Spanish and Moorish)

LOCATION: Located in "one of the most beautiful cities in America," the hotel is within walking distance of a coral-rock swimming pool, beautiful golf courses, jogging paths, and many historical points of interest.

Peter Seralles, founder of the Bacardi Rum Company, converted this building into a fashionable hotel one year after its construction in 1926. The small hotel catered to the well-heeled travelers of the day (Hedda Hopper and other celebrities stayed here), many of whom came to gamble at the famous Tropical Race Track. It was refurbished in Danish Modern in 1969—a real disaster, say current owners Stuart Bornstein and Alan Potamkin who bought the building in 1979 and completely restored it. The building has a magnificent bell tower with a solid nickel church bell dating back to 1890 and a stone facade with an engraved coat of arms. Crown mouldings run throughout the hotel, as do chair rails and stencilling. The curved archway in the hotel arcade is hand-tiled.

More recent notables who've stayed at the St. Michel include Michael Graves, Kurt Vonnegut, and Tom Wolfe. The furnishings are all antique (even the TVs stand on old sewing machine bases).

Plus many of the neighboring buildings are in the same Mediterranean architectural style, both old and new construction — "it's a spirited movement," says Stuart.

Restrictions: No pets.
Beds: Three large suites number among the 28 rooms: 11 doubles, 12 queens, five kings—no twins. All have private baths.
Breakfast: Complimentary continental: freshly squeezed orange juice, freshly baked croissants, marmalade, coffee, tea, or milk. Full break-

fast is available in restaurant, for an extra charge.

Extras: A newspaper is delivered to room door each morning (no charge); there's also no charge for overnight shoeshine, fruit and cheese basket upon arrival, or the turn-down service with Italian chocolates. There's also an established, acclaimed restaurant in the hotel.

Rates: $55 to $110 (suite with deluxe bathroom and sitting area). Cribs at no charge. Credit cards welcome.

FERNANDINA BEACH

THE BAILEY HOUSE
Tom and Diane Hay
28 South 7th Street
Fernandina Beach, FL 32034
(904) 261-5390
Year-round

1895 Queen Anne

LOCATION: The 30 surrounding blocks, on Amelia Island, are all part of a restored historic district. The inn is five minutes from shopping, restaurants, the marina, and the Amelia River. Nearby are tennis courts, the beach, golf courses, and ferries to Cumberland Island.

The Bailey House was a wedding present from Effingham W. Bailey to his wife, Kate McDonnell. Effingham gave Kate two choices: She could have a modest home with elaborate furnishings, or an elaborate home with what furniture they could afford. She chose the latter.

It's believed that Mr. Bailey, an agent for a steamship company, hired boatbuilders to build this Queen Anne. (It was designed by George W. Barber of Knoxville who designed many fine Florida homes at the time.) Their outstanding craftsmanship can be seen in the fish-scale shingles, bay windows, the wraparound porch, turrets, and gables. In the reception hall, the largest of the house's six fireplaces is inscribed "Hearth Hall, Welcome All." Kate Bailey's house was the first in town to come equipped with plumbing, electricity, and a built-in ice box. The house remained in the Bailey family until 1963.

119

Tom and Diane Hay bought the house in 1982. Their restoration wasn't an easy one: They had trouble finding a roofer capable of repairing the variety of turrets, gables, and bays, and had to send the stained-glass windows all the way to New York to be re-leaded and cleaned. Then the Hays furnished their home with an array of antiques: pump organs (guests are welcome to play), brass beds, fringed lamps, and marble-topped tables, and got the place listed in the National Register.

Restrictions: They "discourage" children under ten. Smoking only on the verandah, and no pets. Check-in after 4 p.m.
Beds: One double has a twin roll-away available, another has a 3/4 bed, and one has two twins and a day bed. The queen-bedded room has a 3/4-rollaway available. No rooms share baths.
Breakfast: Choice of juices, fresh fruit compote, homemade muffins, ("special recipe"), and coffee and tea are served in the formal dining room on a marble-topped buffet.
Extras: Guests receive complimentary use of bicycles and beach towels. The turn-down service leaves mints every night, and champagne is provided for special occasions.
Rates: $55 to $85, $7.50 per cot. American Express and personal checks accepted.
Mailing Address: PO Box 805, Fernandina Beach, FL 32034

FLORIDA

LAKE WALES

**CHALET SUZANNE
RESTAURANT AND
COUNTRY INN**
Carl and Vita Hinshaw
U.S. 27 and 17A North
Lake Wales, FL 33853
(813) 676-6011
Year-round, (except Mondays
during May through October)

1920's Eclectic

LOCATION: Orange groves lead to little chalets nestled by a lake amid palm trees. Bok Tower Gardens, Cypress Gardens, and Circus World are nearby; Orlando and Disneyworld are an hour away. There's everything from an air strip to a ceramic studio to a soup-canning plant (open for tours) on the Chalet's grounds.

When asked about the architectural style of their home, Carl and Vita Hinshaw say it's "low and rambling"—and for good reason! After the death of her husband and the loss of the family fortune in the 1930s, Bertha Hinshaw turned her home into an inn and dining room in order to support her two children. Disaster struck again during World War II: the main building burned down. Building materials were in short supply during the war, so the horse stable, rabbit hutches, and chicken coops were put together and added to the circular game room that had not been burned. That was the beginning of the rambling structure that now branches out in every direction on at least 14 different levels. After the war, Bertha's son Carl returned to Florida to help his mother run the chalet. He continued to pursue his flying career (there's a private airstrip within walking distance of the chalet) until he started his soup cannery in the 1960s. (Guests so loved the gourmet food served in the dining room that they began asking for soup they could take home with them. Astronaut Jim Irwin took some with him on the Apollo 16 flight to the moon!)

Restrictions: $3.00 fee per pet; check-in after 2 p.m., check-out at 11 a.m.
Beds: One single, seven twin, nine king and 14 double, none of which share a bath.
Breakfast: Chalet Suzanne Restaurant has an international reputation (breakfast is not included in room rate, unless as part of package deal).
Extras: There's free parking and a reasonable charge for babysitting. Evening wine and cheese are offered for the sampling in the "wine dungeon"; paddle boats and fishing poles are also available. Tee times on nearby golf course are guaranteed for guests. On the property are a cocktail lounge, swimming pool, private lake, gift and antique shops; plus a four-star restaurant.
Rates: $75 to $125 during season; $171 per couple "summer special" includes dinner, room, breakfast, tax, and tip. Personal checks and credit cards accepted.
Mailing Address: PO Drawer AC, Lake Wales, FL 33859

ST. AUGUSTINE

KENWOOD INN
Dick and Judy Smith
38 Marine Street
St. Augustine, FL 32084
(904) 824-2116
Year-round

1865 to 1885 Vernacular Victorian

LOCATION: In the historic district of America's oldest city, the inn is near many historic and tourist attractions.

The Kenwood, built between 1865 and 1885, began taking boarders as early as 1886, and got its name somewhere around 1911. People started restoring it in 1981, and the Smiths took on the project in 1983. Most recently they've added five baths and two showers. Their furnishings run the gamut all the way from Shaker to Victorian.

Restrictions: Children over six, but not pets, are welcome. Prior arrangement requested for arrivals after 9 p.m.
Beds: Two rooms have two doubles, three have kings, one has a queen, and the other nine have one double. None share a bath.
Breakfast: Continental.
Rates: $35 for "small, cozy room" to $60 for "large, spacious room." Cots, $10. Personal checks and credit cards accepted.

GEORGIA

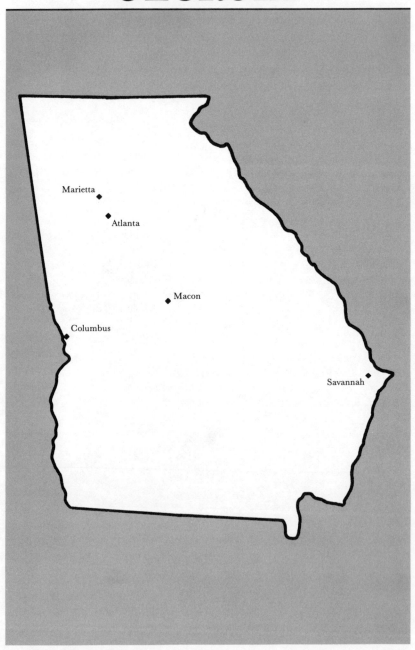

ATLANTA

BEVERLY HILLS INN
Lyle and Bonnie Kleinhans
65 Sheridan Drive NE
Atlanta, GA 30305
(404) 233-8520
Year-round

1929 Neo-classical

LOCATION: One block off Peachtree, the inn is close to the Atlanta Historical Society, Lenox Square, and some 300 elegant stores.

This three-storey building was erected in 1929, in a style similar to Hollywood architecture of the 1920s, hence its name. It's a symmetrical building, with quoins, wrought-iron balconies, and a bridge leading to the front door. Lyle and Bonnie Kleinhans have spent the past five years renovating the place. They retained the original tile and hardwood floors, mouldings, and French doors to the balconies, while giving the walls a fresh coat of paint and fixing up the kitchens and baths. They also added a garden room, as well as a garden.

Restrictions: No pets.
Beds: Twelve rooms, five suites. Some have equipped kitchens.
Breakfast: Coffee, tea, chocolate, hard rolls, sweet rolls, fruit, fresh orange juice.
Rates: $48 single, $57 double to $80 for a suite. Cribs are $5 extra, cots are available at no charge. Credit cards and personal checks welcome.
  10% discount to OHJ members.

ATLANTA

SHELLMONT BED & BREAKFAST LODGE
Ed and Debbie McCord
821 Piedmont Avenue NE
Atlanta, GA 30308
(404) 872-9290
Year-round

1891 Eclectic neo-Colonial

LOCATION: The neighboring houses are of similar character. The area, mid-town Atlanta, is convenient to the historic Fox Theatre, Piedmont Park, Botanical Gardens, shopping and sports facilities, as well as universities.

Architect William T. Downing built this stunning house for Dr. Perrin Nicholson in 1891. Locals claim that Downing trusted Dr. Nicholson to pull him through a serious illness, and when it came time for the doctor to build a home, Nicholson trusted Downing to build it. Downing is famous for designing many Atlanta landmarks including Sacred Heart Church, the Wimbish House, and Trinity Church. Dr. Nicholson's house is ornate and quite beautiful: carved shells, ribbons, and garlands bedeck the exterior.

Restrictions: Families with children can stay in the carriage house. No pets, limited smoking. Check-in after 2 p.m., except by prior arrangement.
Beds: The three rooms in the main house—two singles, one with two doubles—have private baths. The carriage house, with two double beds, also has a private bath.
Breakfast: Freshly ground coffee, orange juice, canteloupe, freshly baked croissants with fillings.
Extras: A morning newspaper, a basket of fruit, fresh flowers, evening chocolates, and beverages are complimentary. "Specialty items" like picnic baskets and chauffeur- driven limousines can be arranged upon request.
Rates: $65 to $95 for the four-person carriage house; cribs at no extra charge. Personal and traveler's checks and credit cards welcome.
   10% discount to OHJ members.

MARIETTA

THE MARLOW HOUSE
Kathleen McDaniel
192 Church Street
Marietta, GA 30060
(404) 426-1887
Year-round

1887 Stick Style

LOCATION: The surrounding historic district offers tree-lined avenues faced with ante-bellum and Victorian homes. Three blocks away is the city square, with restaurants, theatres, galleries, and shops.

This distinctive Victorian resides in the Northwest Marietta Historic District. The Marlow House, originally owned and operated as a boarding house by Idelle Marlow, was built in 1887. Its large verandah and bay window are welcome sights to old-house lovers, as is the spacious central hallway. You will find the house tastefully appointed with Victorian antiques, old photographs, and a player piano.

Restrictions: No pets. Several rooms in the house are set aside for non-smokers. Check-in preferably before 10 p.m., check-out at 2 p.m.
Beds: Of the ten rooms, two two-bedroom suites have a bath and kitchenette; two one-bedroom suites have a bath and kitchenette; all other rooms have private baths.
Breakfast: Full breakfast.
Rates: $49 (double) to $99 (two-bedroom suite that sleeps four or five); cots and cribs are free. Personal or traveler's checks and credit cards welcome.
    10% discount to OHJ members.

MOUNTAIN CITY

THE YORK HOUSE
James and Phyllis Smith
York House Road
Mountain City, GA 30562
(404) 746-2068
Year-round

Pre-Civil War Farmhouse

LOCATION: Amid towering century-old spruce and cedar trees, the inn has a lovely view of the Blue Ridge Mountains.

After the Civil War, William and Mollie York, (known as Papa Bill and Little Mama) added a two-storey farmhouse onto an old log cabin. The Yorks began taking guests in 1896, when surveyors for the Tallula Falls Railroad needed lodging. They soon added a two-storey wing to accommodate their guests. The inn remained open and in the York family until 1979. Ingrid and Philip Sarris purchased the structure in 1983, added private bathrooms, restored the rooms authentically, and furnished the house with turn-of-the-century antiques. The hand-hewn beams and logs of the old cabin, which had been slave quarters before the War, can still be seen. The second floor is appointed with detailed mouldings and reeded casings. Frequent past visitors include Henry Ford and Thomas Edison.

Restrictions: Well-behaved children, but no pets, are welcome. Smoking limited. Check-in after 3 p.m.; check-out at 11 a.m.
Beds: Ten doubles, two with two double beds, and one room with a double and a twin, all have private baths.
Breakfast: Full continental is served to room on a silver tray.
Extras: Guests can prepare their own snacks in the small kitchen.
Rates: $50, weekdays and off-season, for room with one double; room with two doubles costs $70 on a high-season weekend.
   10% discount to OHJ members.
Mailing Address: PO Box 126, Mountain City, GA 30562

SAVANNAH

1872 Italianate townhouse

"417" THE HASLAM
Alan Fort
417 East Charlton Street
Savannah, GA 31401
(912) 233-6380
Year-round

LOCATION: The inn is adjacent to Troup Square (one of Savannah's 22 original squares) and surrounded by 19th-century town houses. "Live oaks dripping with Spanish moss abound," along with azaleas, magnolias, dogwood, and crepe myrtle. The rest of Savannah, including the waterfront, is within 15 minutes away.

The entrance to this 1872 Italianate townhouse is at garden level, an unusual attribute in Savannah. The original woodwork, crown mouldings, medallions, and plaster walls are intact. The floors and window mouldings are heart pine. The garden-level parlor, originally reserved for entertaining visitors, is now part of the guest quarters.

Restrictions: Children of all ages are welcome; pets, too, though there's a charge of $10 each (and no more than two at a time allowed). **Beds:** The single guest suite contains a king-sized bedroom and a den with a set of twins, plus the sofa in the living room converts to a queen-sized bed. There's one full bath for the whole suite, which also includes a living room with working fireplace and an eat-in kitchen. **Breakfast:** "Do-it-yourself" breakfast consists of coffee, tea, Sanka, orange juice, croissants, Danish, English muffins, cereal, and usually eggs, along with the necessary cooking equipment. **Extras:** Soft drinks and a bottle of liqueur are provided. Host will arrange for babysitters. The suite is equipped with a telephone, TV, radio, games, puzzles, and books, and it's accessible for the handicapped. There's private parking and entrances, a garden terrace, and the host speaks German, Norwegian, Spanish, and some French. **Rates:** $65 for one, $80 for two, $125 for three, and $150 for four. From January 1 to March 15, a $400 weekly rate is available. Personal and traveler's checks welcome.

10% discount to OHJ members if mailing label sent with reservation.

SAVANNAH

JESSE MOUNT HOUSE
Howard J. Crawford and Lois
Bannerman
209 West Jones Street
Savannah, GA 31401
(912) 236-1774
Year-round

1854 Greek Revival

LOCATION: On a brick road shaded by live oaks, the inn offers a quiet, residential setting within walking distance of many famous landmarks.

A ttorney and planter Jesse Mount built his home in 1854, during Savannah's heyday as a cotton port. Today, this Greek Revival double house is in the heart of Savannah's Historic District. Innkeepers Howard Crawford and Lois Bannerman have restored the gold-leafed plaster medallions on the 13-foot-high ceilings, and found original mouldings, heart pine flooring, and gas lighting fixtures still in place. All nine fireplaces work, and beautiful antiques abound.

Restrictions: Children "under parental guidance" and smoking permitted; "sometimes we allow pets."
Beds: The two three-bedroom suites have one bath and two fireplaces each; two queens and one double per suite. Single parties of up to six people can be accommodated in each suite.
Breakfast: Continental: freshly squeezed orange juice, two choices of breads or cheesecake, coffee.
Extras: There's complimentary cocktail or sherry, and fresh fruit and candies are available in both suites. One suite has a full kitchen, the other a refrigerator.
Rates: $70 for one or two, $100 for four, $130 for six, $15 each additional person; 15% discount in January. Personal checks welcome.

10% discount to OHJ members except in January, July, and August.

THOMASVILLE

1841 Greek Revival

SUSINA PLANTATION INN
Anne-Marie Walker
Meridian Road
Thomasville, GA 31792
(912) 377-9644
Year-round

LOCATION: The 115 acres of lawns and woodland around the house offer access to quail, deer, turkey, and duck hunting, in the heart of plantation country.

Englishman John Wind built this Greek Revival plantation house for James John Blackshear in 1841. Second owner John T. Metcalfe changed the name from "Cedar Grove" to "Susina," the Italian word for plum, in 1887. He sold the house to A. Heywood Mason four years later. Anne-Marie Walker and her family, the present owners, moved into the guest "cottage," a seven-room house, in 1979, and turned the main house into an inn. Four massive columns support the pediment, on which Wind hand-carved a sunflower. Inside, guests will find heart pine floors and 14-foot ceilings. All the rooms are furnished with antiques.

Restrictions: Check-in after 2 p.m., check-out at noon.
Beds: Some of the seven double rooms offer porches; one room has twin beds.
Breakfast: Eggs Benedict, fruit and cake, orange juice and coffee.
Extras: Dinner is included in the room rate: fish au gratin or soup, meat, vegetables, dessert, coffee, and wine. There's a stocked bass pond, tennis court, and swimming pool on the property.
Rates: $135 to $150, personal checks welcome.
   10% discount to OHJ members.
Mailing Address: Rt. 3, Box 1010, Thomasville, GA 31792

ILLINOIS

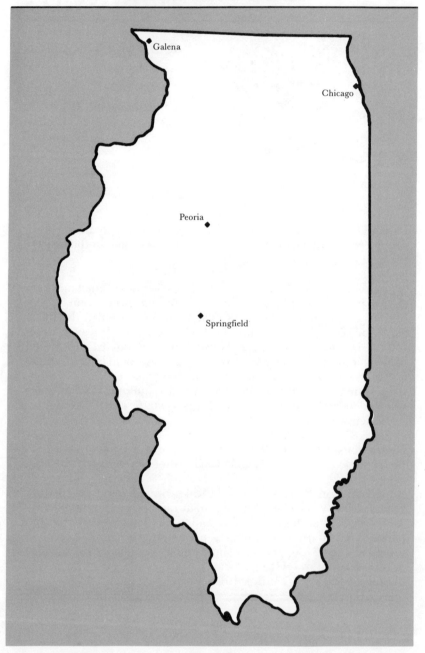

CHICAGO

BURTON HOUSE
Ralph Raby and Glen Hjort
1454 North Dearborn Street at
Burton Place
Chicago, IL 60610
(312) 787-9015
Year-round

1876-77 French Second Empire (exterior); Eastlake (interior)

LOCATION: The inn, in Chicago's Gold Coast, is one block south of Lincoln Park, and near Lake Michigan (two blocks), North Michigan Avenue's shopping district, the Chicago Historical Society, and Art Institute. Major transportation lines are also close by, as are fine restaurants.

Located on Chicago's Gold Coast, this Second Empire house has been in the same family since it was built in 1876! It is constructed of cut brownstone, and it has a mansard roof and several large bays. The carriage house dates back to before the Chicago Fire. The interior is Eastlake. Each room has a different parquet floor, and the original wallpapers, carpeting, and lighting fixtures remain—the gaslights still work. There's a marble fireplace in each bedroom and every room is filled with antiques.

Restrictions: No minors or pets ("we have a house dog"), and "we would rather guests not smoke in the house."
Beds: The double room, with sleigh bed, has a bath and shower; the canopy-bedded (queen) room has a bath without shower, and the twin-bedded room has both bath and shower.
Breakfast: The continental breakfast consists of croissants, sweet but-

ter, fresh juice, coffee, imported jellies and preserves, served in the dining room with antique crystal, china, silver, and linens.

Extras: Afternoon tea and a nightcap are offered at no charge.

Rates: $85 (single) to $115 (double), all rooms. Personal or traveler's checks and credit cards welcome.

10% discount to OHJ members.

GALENA

ALDRICH GUEST HOUSE
Judy Green
900 Third Street
Galena, IL 61036
(815) 777-3323
Year-round

1845, added to in 1853 and 1883; originally Greek Revival

LOCATION: "The hills in town may remind people of San Francisco, while the scenery resembles new England." Galena, near the Galena and Mississippi Rivers, offers old houses and lead mines to explore, as well as antique and craft shops and Civil War-era relics.

A host of Illinois statesmen lived in this house during its 140-year lifetime. Cyrus Aldrich, a state representative, built the original one-and-a-half-storey brick house in 1845 and lived there until J. Russell Jones bought the house. He added a major addition in 1853. Ulysses S. Grant was a frequent visitor when the house was owned by lawyer Robert H. McClellan, who was also an Illinois state senator and bank president. McClellan also added to the building, adopting Italianate details.

The house now has 12 rooms, all carefully restored by Jim and B.J. Crowe, who purchased the house in 1967. They've converted the old summer kitchen and maid's quarters into their living area.

Restrictions: No pets or children under eight; smoking in parlor or on porch only. Check-in usually between 4 to 6 p.m., check-out at 11 a.m.

Beds: One king with private bath, one queen and twin with private bath, one queen with private bath, and one queen and twin with shared bath. A double can be connected with the king to form a two-bedroom suite.

Breakfast: Fresh fruit, coffee, juice, homemade muffins and breads, entrees like quiche, strawberry French toast or eggs Benedict are "served formally, yet unfussily" in the main dining parlor.

Extras: Refrigerator privileges are available throughout guest's stay, and complimentary wine, soda, or tea served during check-in are also available.

Rates: $45 (shared bath) to $60 (private bath). Personal checks and credit cards accepted.

10% discount to OHJ members with minimum two-night stay.

GALENA

FRICKE GUEST HOUSE
Bill and Ginny Hunt
119 South Bench Street
Galena, IL 61036
(815) 777-1193
Year-round

1878 Italianate

LOCATION: "Galena is like a European village"—in the hills a few miles from the Mississippi, the town offers Civil War historic sites and walking tours of its architectural delights. River boat rides are available in Iowa (15 miles away), and Wisconsin's famous "House on a Rock" is less than two hours away.

Henry Fricke was a German-born watchmaker and silversmith. He built this brick Victorian when he retired in 1878. People stop and stare at the magnificent cast-iron fence surrounding the property and the lovely etched glass in the front doors. The house has three fireplaces with marble mantels, two of which are in use. Although innkeepers Bill and Ginny Hunt had to reproduce the graining in the rest of the house, the two parlors retain the original walnut graining. They also restored the original stencilling in the dining room and rebuilt both walnut staircases. The entire house is furnished in Victorian and Empire antiques.

Restrictions: "We welcome babies and well-behaved children." No pets, smoking restricted to parlors. Check-in arranged upon making reservations.

Beds: One Empire-style double and one Victorian double share a bath.

Breakfast: Orange juice, coffee or tea, scrambled eggs, sausage, freshly baked "Fricke Sticky" bran muffins; French toast on second morning of stay.

Rates: $45, with weekday prices generally $5 less (negotiable). Cots, $10; cribs, $5. Personal checks and credit cards welcome.

10% discount to OHJ members.

GALENA

MOTHER'S COUNTRY INN
Patricia J. Laury
349 Spring
Galena, IL 61036
(815) 777-3153
Year-round

1838 Federal

LOCATION: Galena's been called "one of the best-preserved 19th-century towns in America." The inn is one block from its historic main street.

This 1838 Federal building was formerly a two-family house. Patricia Laury has restored the interior, retaining the original fireplaces, wide pine flooring, and staircase. There's an antique shop on the premises that guests can use as a "hospitality room." Decorated with lots of chintz and quilts, the house has a country atmosphere. It's made of brick, like much of Galena's downtown architecture.

Restrictions: No pets.

Beds: Three queens, two doubles, and two twins—only one has a private bath, but all have sinks in the room. One room has a "youth bed."

Breakfast: Continental.

Rates: $35 to $45 (private entrance and bath). Cribs, $5. Mastercard, Visa, and cash welcome.

10% discount to OHJ members.

ILLIOPOLIS

1854 Italianate

OLD ILLIOPOLIS HOTEL
James Browne and Kathleen
Jensen-Browne
608 Mary Street
Illiopolis, IL 62539
(217) 486-6451
Year-round

LOCATION: The town is Illinois' geographical center—midway between Decatur (14 miles) and Springfield (19 miles).

The hotel was built in 1854 as a stopover for passengers and employees of the Great Western Railroad. Local legend says that Abraham Lincoln stayed here when he was a practicing lawyer traveling between Springfield and Decatur. After it passed through many owners' hands, and stood empty for 40 years, James and Kathleen Jensen-Browne bought it and reopened it in 1981.

A previous owner had completed most of the major restoration work. James and Kathleen's toughest task was furnishing the place. They used plenty of period furniture, including pieces inherited from great-grandparents, and added collectibles like old stereopticons, postcards, and photographs.

Restrictions: Arrange check-in times in advance. No smoking inside the building.
Beds: Five doubles share two baths.
Breakfast: Continental: coffee or tea, English muffins, fresh fruit.
Rates: $18 (single), $20 (double). Cots, $2. Personal checks welcome.
10% discount to OHJ members.
Mailing Address: Box 66, Illiopolis, IL 62539

LOUISIANA

BURNSIDE

TEZCUCO PLANTATION
Chuck and Debra Purifoy
Highway 44 River Road
Burnside, LA 70723
(504) 562-3929
Year-round

1855 Greek Revival

LOCATION: One hour from New Orleans, the house sits on the banks of the Mississippi; nearby are six other ante-bellum homes. The grounds (some 20 acres) include a blacksmith shop, chapel, gardens, fountains, restaurant, and shops.

The guest cottages at Tezcuco Plantation are restored slave quarters located behind the main house, a raised cottage. Built in 1855 by Benjamin Tureaud, the house was named after a lake in Mexico: It's an Aztec word meaning "resting place." The house is built of cypress cut on the property and bricks fired in the plantation's own kiln, and has wrought-iron galleries. The interior is appointed with ornate friezes, ceiling medallions, and graining. All of the rooms in the main house are available for touring.

Beds: Fifteen cottages, once the slaves' quarters, stand behind the main house, and range from one bedroom/sitting room to two bedroom, two baths.
Breakfast: Coffee and tea are provided in the room. For $5 extra a full Creole breakfast—eggs, sausage, grits, homemade biscuits—can be served in the cottages on a silver tray.
Extras: Guests are entitled to a free tour of the plantation, as well as

139

a bottle of wine and fresh flowers.

Rates: $50 (bedroom, bath, and porch) to $175 (for suite in the main house). $15 surcharge for extra adult, $7.50 per child. Personal checks and credit cards welcome.

10% discount to OHJ members.

Mailing Address: Rt. 1, Box 157, Convent, LA 70723

NEW IBERIA

MINTMERE PLANTATION
Jane Breaux (curator)
1400 East Main Street
New Iberia, LA 70560
(318) 364-6210
Year-round

1857 Greek Revival

LOCATION: Three acres, including many oak trees, surround the three buildings in the heart of "Cajun Country." Historic Bayou Teche and the old Spanish trail border the property, secluded a mile and a half from town.

Three buildings make up the property known as Mintmere Plantation, but only the main house, overlooking the bayou, is original to the site. Dr. Roy P. Boucvalt saved the Greek Revival structure from demolition in 1976. He restored it and furnished it with period antiques, many of them collected in the Louisiana area. The building sits eight feet off the ground—for both maximum air circulation and flood protection. Iron railings link the wooden porch posts. The front wall, made of Louisiana cypress, has been cut to resemble stone blocks.

During the Civil War, a skirmish was fought on the property. Later, when the North occupied New Iberia, Mintmere was commandeered as a headquarters by Gen. Alfred Lee, the famous "judge-turned-warrior" from Kansas.

The Armand Broussard House, moved to the site by Dr. Boucvalt, is constructed of "bousillage"—mud and moss. Part of the exterior has been stripped to reveal the construction method. Restored and furnished, the house is open only for tours. Broussard's father was a leader of the first Cajuns to flee South when the British destroyed their settlements in Acadia, Nova Scotia.

The West Indies Cottage, used to house guests, was built in 1815.

Restrictions: Children 11 or older only; no pets, smoking permitted. Check-in by "about" 4 p.m.
Beds: There are three suites of one double bedroom, a sitting room, and private bath, and one two-bedroom suite with a sitting room and bath.
Breakfast: A full breakfast is served at 8:30 a.m.: potato quiche, suasage patties, freshly baked banana-nut muffins, fresh fruit platter, freshly squeezed orange juice, and coffee.
Rates: $100 (one-bedroom suite) to $150 (two bedrooms, accommodates up to four). Personal and traveler's checks are accepted.

NEW ORLEANS

THE CORNSTALK HOTEL
David and Debi Spencer
915 Royal Street
New Orleans, LA 70116
(504) 523-1515
Year-round

1890 Queen Anne

LOCATION: The inn is located in the heart of New Orleans' French quarter.

The hotel is named for the famous Cornstalk Fence that surrounds it, a cast-iron concoction of corn ears half-shucked on their stalks; the newel posts rise out of sculpted pumpkins. Local legend has it that an early owner commissioned the fence to remind his young bride of the waving cornfields of her native Iowa.

Built in 1890, this Queen Anne is on the same site as earlier buildings (the land's had structures on it since 1730), where Andrew Jackson stayed while on trial for contempt after the War of 1812, and where Harriet Beecher Stowe is said to have been inspired to write *Uncle Tom's Cabin.*

The house is full of what owners David and Debi Spencer call "Louisiana-plantation workmanship," like ceiling medallions, scroll-work, cherubs, and millwork. They've furnished the house with antiques and reproductions, and it's listed in the National Register.

Restrictions: No pets. Check-in after 1 p.m., check-out at noon.
Beds: The 14 rooms, each with private bath, contain at least one double bed. One has a king, another twins, and another two doubles.
Breakfast: Café au lait, tea, orange juice, croissants or hot biscuits, strawberry jam and butter are served with a newspaper on the balcony, porch, patio, or in guest rooms.
Rates: $60 (single) to $95 (largest double). Cots, $5; cribs available at no charge. Higher rates during Mardi Gras, Sugar Bowl, and other special events. Credit cards welcome.

10% discount to OHJ members based on availability.

LOUISIANA

NEW ORLEANS

TERRELL HOUSE
Stephen F. Young
1441 Magazine Street
New Orleans, LA 70130
(504) 524-9859
Year-round

1858 New Orleans rowhouse

LOCATION: The inn, in the Lower Garden Historic District, is near St. Charles Avenue, Magazine Street's galleries and shops, Canal Street, and the French Quarter.

Cotton merchant Richard Terrell built this elegant house in 1858. Owner Fred Nicaud, who has restored gaslight chandeliers for years, did much of the restoration himself, including the necessary plastering and casting of ceiling medallions. The grillwork along the galleries (all the guest rooms open onto them) is cast in an unusual rose pattern. All the furnishings in the house—from the twin parlors to the guest rooms—are authentic to the period. Several pieces were made by Prudent Mallard, a renowned New Orleans craftsman. There's also a carriage house out back that has been restored as well.

Restrictions: Children welcome, smoking allowed throughout; no pets. Check-in by 9 p.m. (later by prior arrangement).
Beds: Eight doubles, one room with two twins, and one suite (one double bed and a sitting room with a single bed) all have private baths.
Breakfast: Homemade biscuits and muffins, fruits in season, preserves, juice, chicory coffee, tea.
Extras: Complimentary refreshments are served in the afternoons and evenings.
Rates: $30 (former separate servant's quarters) to $75 (original master suite). Cots, $5. Personal checks and credit cards welcome.
   10% discount to OHJ members.

LOUISIANA

OPELOUSAS

ESTORGE HOUSE
Vera Schmitt and Beverly
Soileau
427 North Market Street
Opelousas, LA 70570
(318) 948-4592
Year-round

1827 Greek Revival

LOCATION: The area is rich in history, with a museum commemorating Jim Bowie's childhood spent here and many ante-bellum homes.

All the bricks in this house were made by hand, including the pie-shaped ones in the tapered columns and in the 15-inch-thick walls. Pierre Labyche built his home—with slave labor—in 1827, and it remained in his family for several generations. Roy Boucvalt bought the house from a descendant in 1982. The trompe-l'oeil ceilings in the center hall and the parlor are magnificent. Most of the original hardware and window panes are intact, and the furnishings date from 1820 to 1860. The house is in the National Register.

Restrictions: No pets, children 11 or older only, smoking permitted. Check-in after 4 p.m., check-out at 9:30 a.m.
Beds: The three suites—double bedroom, sitting room and bath—all have private baths.
Breakfast: Ham and cheese omelette, sausage patties, sweet-potato muffins, fresh fruit, freshly squeezed orange juice, and coffee.
Rates: $100 per suite; personal checks accepted.

ST. FRANCISVILLE

**THE MYRTLES
PLANTATION**
Frances Kermeen
Highway 61N
St. Francisville, LA 70775
(504) 635-6277
Year-round

1796 Greek Revival

LOCATION: Many ante-bellum homes and plantations are open for tours in the area; hiking, horseback riding, and antiquing are also possible.

A full 240 feet of galleries surround this 22-room mansion. General David Bradford built it in 1796; he was a leader of the Whiskey Rebellion. Ornaments to look for: fine examples of faux bois, plaster friezes, and even the doorknobs—they're glass lined with mercury, so they look like silver but never need polishing. The wallpaper is hand-screened, and the furnishings, many original to the house, date from the 18th and 19th centuries.

Myrtles has been called "the most haunted house in America." Ask the innkeepers who've been restoring the place since 1980, about the ten murders that have occurred here!

Beds: Of the ten rooms—four in the new wing, five in the plantation, and one suite—none share a bath.

Breakfast: Pork chops, bacon or sausage, eggs, grits, homemade biscuits with strawberry or fig preserves, orange juice, coffee, fresh fruit.

Extras: There's a tavern on the grounds; dinner and lunch (by appointment only) are served. "Mystery weekends" are available for $360 to $430 per couple.

Rates: $65 to $120 (suite); extra persons, $10 each; cribs, no charge. Personal checks and credit cards accepted.

10% discount to OHJ members.

Mailing Address: PO Box 387, St. Francisville, LA 70775

MAINE

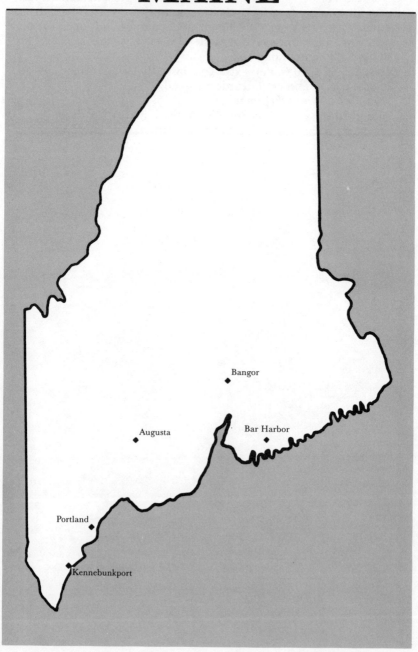

Bangor

Augusta   Bar Harbor

Portland

Kennebunkport

BAR HARBOR

CLEFTSTONE MANOR
The Jackson Family
92 Eden Stret, Route 3
Bar Harbor, ME 04609
(207) 288-4951
Mid-May through Mid-October

1894 English Cottage

LOCATION: The inn stands at the foot of Cadillac Mountain, 500 yards from the "Bluenose" ferry to Nova Scotia. Bar Harbor is known for its quaint shops, fine restaurants, summer theater and concerts, and unrivalled boating and fishing. Nearby Acadia National Park offers 33,000 acres of mountains, carriage paths, hiking trails, swimming, canoeing, hot-air ballooning, and fishing.

W ho can resist the lure of the Cleftstone Manor, with its multi-gabled roof and diamond-paned windows sparkling in the ocean air? Don and Phyllis Jackson couldn't—they came to Bar Harbor for a weekend vacation and ended up buying the house, converting it to an inn, and staying for good.

Cleftstone is a summer "cottage" in the romantic sense of the word. It's patterned after an English country cottage, with simple exterior architectural features blending into the landscape: shingle siding and a noticeable lack of ornament. But in the literal sense, Cleftstone is a palace. Its 33 rooms sprawl languidly over a hill.

Phyllis and Don spent their first months in Cleftstone restoring all the rooms and the gardens. Now guests are greeted in the front hall by a larger-than-life portrait of Queen Victoria and the scent of lavender. Inside, Victoriana abounds: mahogany and velvet furniture, lace curtains, international objets d'art, grandfather clocks, silk valances, and overstuffed chairs.

Restrictions: No smoking. Children over 12 welcome. No pets. Check-in after 2 p.m. Check-out at 11 a.m.

Beds: There are 18 guest rooms, each named after an event, place, or person in English history. All rooms have goose-down comforters, hand-crocheted spreads and table-cloths, and Oriental rugs. Of the 18, 13 have private baths.

Breakfast: Lavish breakfast buffet is served on the sun porch: fresh fruit salad, several varieties of inn-baked muffins (blueberry, bran, strawberry, oatmeal, apple), two coffee-cakes, raisin and cinnamon bread, crumpets, bagels, and English muffins. To drink, there are three types of juices,

Extras: Afternoon tea is served daily from 4 to 5 p.m.: several kinds of tea and home-baked goods (like Scottish shortbread and scones) are presented on a silver tray. Wine and cheese is available nightly between 8 and 10 p.m. Hot-air balloon tours run from the premises.

Rates: $75 to $125 depending primarily on room size. Personal checks, MasterCard and Visa welcome.

MAINE

BAR HARBOR

MANOR HOUSE INN
Jan and Frank Matter
106 West Street
Bar Harbor, ME 04609
(207) 288-3759
May 1 through November 15

1887 Stick Style

LOCATION: The inn is surrounded by the beauty of Acadia National Park and on-grounds garden's. Olympic swimming pool and five clay tennis courts are located directly across the street. Frenchman's Bay and the attractions of the Maine coastline are close by.

Jan and Frank Matter could captivate you for hours with their knowledge of this inn's history and architecture. For instance, they've compiled a chronology of the house's earlier residents, 27 in all! The house, once known as Boscobel, was rented to a different summer vacationer each year until 1950, when it was converted to a guest house. The Matters have written interesting profiles of some residents: One was a Captain Wheeler, who surveyed the Wild West, towed three flat-bottomed boats up 200 miles of Colorado River rapids, killed a few men, and finally settled down to a cushy Washington, D.C., job in the Department of the Army. Another was Robert McCormick, descendant of the man who invented the reaper and cofounded International Harvester. Another was a wealthy socialite who died just as she was packing for her 75th Bar Harbor summer.

The Matters also know Boscobel's architectural features inside and out. They've written an alphabetized glossary which explains the technicalities of everything from the basement (blown out of a granite ledge), to the windows (installed with brass screws in slotted brass cups, so the expanding and contracting window frames can be adjusted with the changing seasons), and all the fascinating features in between. There are original Edison electric lights (Boscobel was electrified from the start), Rumford fireplaces, a three-storey cherry staircase, sunburst-style mouldings, and multitudes of towers, gables, and dormers.

Last but not least, the Matters will be glad to discuss their numerous restoration projects with fellow old-house lovers. They restored the rotting verandah, hiring a local artisan to hand-turn new posts and railing matching the originals. They tracked down the missing top half of one mantel, which had been sold to another family. They fixed the electric bell system, once used to call servants from any room in the house. And recently, they restored the chauffeur's cottage, which had been allowed to deteriorate for years.

Restrictions: Children 12 and over welcome. No pets. Smoking permitted in guest rooms only.
Beds: In all there are 14 rooms and suites; they range from a double with private bath to a suite with king bed, sitting room, fireplace, skylight, full private bath, stained glass windows, and private entrance. All rooms have private baths.
Breakfast: Homemade blueberry muffins and breads, coffee, teas, juices, cereal, fresh fruit, homemade jams.
Extras: Beach towels and blankets are provided. Airport pick-up can be arranged. Swimming and tennis at private club costs $3 per person per day. Box lunches are available for $4.50.
Rates: Rooms from $69 to $99, suites from $79 to $135. Cots, $20. Personal checks and credit cards welcome.

BELFAST

LONDONDERRY INN
Kerry and Sarah Bryant
Star Route 80, Box 3
Belfast, ME 04915
(207) 338-3988
Year-round

1803 Maine Farmhouse with additions in the 1920s

LOCATION: A mile from the Maine coastline, on 50 acres of woods and fields (ideal for hiking and cross-country skiing), the inn features a pond on the property where you can swim in summer and skate in winter. A mile and a half away is Belfast, with its many National Register homes. It's an hour to Bar Harbor, 20 minutes to Camden, and five minutes to Searsport.

> *"Come take day trips along the shore or take a walking tour of the Belfast historic District. Enjoy the waterfront, the windjammers, and of course, the lobster. Witness the renaissance of the entire mainstreet - listed as a commercial historic disrict."*

This inn was built as a tavern, where travelers and frontiersmen could warm their hands before a crackling fire and their insides over a glass of home brew. Later, the house became the hub of a hard-working farm, which produced vegetables, apple cider, and sauerkraut.

The inn had deteriorated much since its prosperous farming days; but after a major restoration project—which included resuscitating the original clapboard siding, refinishing the interior bird's-eye moulding and wide pine floors, and duplicating closely the original paint colors and wallcoverings—it has reclaimed its former character.

Restrictions: Well-behaved children welcome. No pets. Smoking permitted in the three sitting rooms only.

Beds: Seven double rooms share two and one-half baths.
Breakfast: Full breakfast served daily, 8 to 9 a.m. The menu varies, but includes homemade muffins and sweet breads, granola and yogurt parfaits, fruit, eggs, and breakfast meats.
Rates: $32, single; $40, double; additional person in room, $10. Off-season, group, and long-stay rates available. Personal checks welcome.
 10% discount to OHJ members.
Mailing Address: Star Route 80, Box 3, Belfast, ME 04915

BLUE HILL

BLUE HILL INN
Rita and Ted Boytos
Union Street
Blue Hill, ME 04614
(207) 374-2844
Year-round

1830 Federal

LOCATION: At the head of Blue Hill Bay, the inn is surrounded by graceful churches, New England homesteads, and other historic sites. Acadia National Park is nearby, and the immediate locale offers swimming at area beaches in warm weather and cross-country skiing on miles of trails in winter. Fishing, clamming, nature walks, cruises to outer islands, hiking, bicycling, and sailing are all within easy reach.

Time has stood still at the Blue Hill Inn since 1855, the last time it was seriously "remodelled." Hosts Rita and Ted Boytos have 1860 photo of the Inn which proves how well preserved the place is. Outside, the unusual nine-over-six windows, louvered shutters, solid granite foundation, and six 19th-century chimneys are intact. Inside, you can still see the three original staircases, the brass and wrought iron knobs and latches, and the original mouldings. There's even a secret storage nook under the floorboards! The interior floor plan hasn't changed much in the last century, either, because Blue Hill has been a B&B since 1840.
 The Boytoses have furnished the Inn tastefully with antiques. Their collections of vintage clocks, pewter sconces and lamps, antique maps, photos, and paintings are displayed throughout.

151

Restrictions: Children welcome. No pets. Check-in by 6 p.m. Later arrival OK with advance notice. Check-out at 11 a.m.

Beds: Ten rooms: three twins, two doubles, one king, four queens. All have private baths.

Breakfast: No breakfast included, but is available for an additional $1.50 to $3.50.

Extras: Set-up bar is available for mixing your own drinks (BYOB). Dinner, traditional New-England style, can be purchased for $12 to $14, and features homemade bread and popovers, chowder, and fresh seafood.

Rates: All rooms $48. Single rate ($43) available from November 1 through May 31. Personal checks, Visa, and Mastercard welcome. Cots, $10; cribs, $5.

10% discount to OHJ members.

Mailing Address: Box 403, Blue Hill, ME 04614

MAINE

BOOTHBAY HARBOR

CAPTAIN SAWYER'S PLACE
Tom and Binkie Dekker
87 Commercial Street
Boothbay Harbor, ME 04538
(207) 633-2474
May 1 to October 31

C. 1870 Italianate

LOCATION: Proudly overlooking the busy harbor of beautiful Boothbay Harbor, the inn is within steps of restaurants, the wharf, boat trips, dinner theater, etcetera.

The unusual, peak-roofed cupola atop this house had a practical use in its early years. Captain Sawyer, who built the house, used to watch out its windows for ships caught in the clutches of the treacherous, rocky outcroppings surrounding Boothbay Harbor—he was in the ship-salvaging business.

Today, the house is in marvelous shape—nobody has ever tried to "modernize" it. Outside, the intricate, dentilled cornice, the carved brackets, the wraparound porch with its delicate railings and pedimented columns, and the double front doors with arched windows remain. Inside, the old plaster, wood shutters, mouldings, and room arrangement are as they were in 1870.

Restrictions: Children over 12 welcome. No pets. Check-in after 1 p.m.
Beds: Ten rooms. Eight have twin beds put together to form queen-size bed. A two-room suite has a double bed in one room, and twin beds in the other. All rooms have a private bath and quiet sitting area.
Breakfast: Complimentary coffee or tea.
Rates: $40 to $50, July 1 to September 9. Other times, $25 to $40. Cots, $10. Visa and Mastercard welcome.

CAMDEN

EDGECOMBE-COLES HOUSE
Louise and Terry Price
64 High Street
Camden, ME 04843
(207) 236-2336
Year-round

1890 Maine Farmhouse

LOCATION: This small New England town has a fleet of windjammers and a waterfall in the harbor. Camden Hills State Park offers hiking trails in the nearby mountains that command striking ocean views. The area has been compared to England's Lake District. Camden Snow Bowl features Alpine and cross-country skiing. Shops, restaurants, the Camden Shakespeare Theater, and the Bay Chamber Concert Hall are all nearby.

This inn was built as a summer home by a family seeking respite from city heat, humidity, and hustle. It's charmingly decorated with antiques, Oriental rugs, and original art. Surrounded by a stone fence, it was constructed to take maximum advantage of the ocean views. Terry and Louise spent a year at what they call "intensive labor" to restore the house's charms.

Restrictions: Arrangements can be made to accomodate infants and pets with advance notice. No children under eight years of age. Smoking permitted. Check-out at 11 a.m., check-in after noon.
Beds: Six rooms, all with private baths. Most have ocean views; one has a fireplace.
Breakfast: Fruit juice, fresh fruit, home-baked breads, eggs, meat, pancakes or waffles, coffee, tea or milk.
Extras: Afternoon tea or coffee, wine and beer, sherry, and occasionally hors d'oeuvres are provided for no additional charge.
Rates: July through October: $75 to $105; November through June: $60 to $90. Cots, $10. Visa, Mastercard, and personal checks welcome.
    10% discount to OHJ members November through June.
Mailing Address: Star Route Box 3010, Camden, ME 04843

MAINE

CAPE NEDDICK

WOODEN GOOSE INN
Anthony V. Sienicki and Jerry
D. Rippetoe
Route 1
Cape Neddick, ME 03902
(207) 363-5673
February 1 to December 31

1850 Tri-Gabled Ell

LOCATION: In a quiet coastal village 12 miles north of Portsmouth, the inn has five acres of gardens near theatres, antique shops, historic sites, restaurants, hiking trails, and magnificent beaches.

How do you turn a house that's a "complete mess" into a working inn in just 14 days? By working "22 hours a day, seven days a week," like Anthony Sienicki and Jerry Rippetoe did, from mid-June to early July, 1983.

Left untouched on the inside for some 40 years, their typical Maine farmhouse needed a complete overhaul. (The original family, descendants of a schooner captain, had owned it since its construction in 1850 but not kept it up.) So the innkeepers, who restore old houses as a hobby, stripped wallpaper, moved doors and baths around, put in new walls and ceilings, and meanwhile had the outside repainted.

Restrictions: No pets or children under age 12.
Beds: Five doubles and one single, all furnished with antiques, and all with private baths.
Breakfast: Breakfast includes fruit (such as berries in cream, sorbert, or broiled grapefruit), muffins and breads, and an entree (eggs Benedict or Florentine, quiche, omelettes, French toast, or corned beef hash with poached eggs are favorites). Jerry, the chef, can accomodate special diets.
Extras: Afternoon tea, served daily from 4 to 6 p.m. is included in the room rate. The chef's specialties for this daily rite are liver paté and almond croissants.
Rates: From $65 to $75, with one three-person suite for $110. There are also discount packages for weekends for two, dinner included. Personal checks accepted; no credit cards.
Mailing Address: PO Box 195, Cape Neddick, ME 03902

CASTINE

THE MANOR
Paul and Sara Brouillard
Battle Avenue
Castine, ME 04421
(207) 326-4861
Year-round

1895 Shingle style

LOCATION: From a five-acre lawn the house commands a view of Penobscot Bay. The estate borders a 400-acre nature preserve complete with bald eagles and osprey, and Castine Village offers golf, tennis, museums, shops, and restaurants.

"To recreate this place today would cost over four million dollars—it's one of the last great 'cottages.' " Kevin Comeau, Haverhill, Mass.

In the era when John Rockefeller and Andrew Carnegie were scurrying unimpeded up the ladder to the American Dream, and discovering piles of money at the top, Commodore Fuller of the New York Yacht Club built this summer "cottage." Better described as a mansion, it is adorned with numerous gables at odd angles, dormers, bay windows, a portico, and towering fieldstone chimneys. Inside, a breathtaking staircase, accompanied by a row of costly mahogany wainscotting, parades up three flights to the top floor. And in the living room, there's a fireplace that burns five-foot-long logs.

The Fullers, attended to by a squadron of servants, enjoyed lavish summers here, hunting, playing billiards, watching the waves lap the sand at Penobscot Bay, sipping cool drinks on the shaded porch. In their footsteps followed the Eustises, the owners of the *Boston Transcript*, wealthy enough to send their daughter by first-class railroad to San Francisco (where she survived the 1906 earthquake), and to England and back on the Titanic (whose sinking she survived in a rubber life buoy).

But in 1929, the Stock Market crashed and the Depression struck a cold blow to the American Dream. Money no longer grew on trees; the next generations could not afford to maintain this house. When Paul and Sara Brouillard bought it in 1980, just a few months separated it from the cold and destructive blade of the bulldozer.

The Brouillards undertook the area's most complete restoration, fixing everything from the decrepit wiring, to the crumbling stone chimneys, to the pool table and original fixtures in the billiard room, to the green marble and mahogany oyster bar on the front porch. The entire project is documented in an expansive photo album.

Beds: There are 12 rooms: two twin-bedded rooms with private baths, one queen with a private bath, one king with a private bath. Of the eight doubles, six have private baths and two share a bath.
Breakfast: Continental: coffee, tea, juice, fresh fruits, French cheese, pastry, two smoked meats, and "world-famous" bran muffins.
Extras: Babysitting can be arranged with 48-hour notice: guests have golf and tennis privileges at the country club. Also, bicycles are available at the inn.
Rates: $45 (shared bath) to $85 (two-bedroom suite). Varies by season. Cots, $15; cribs, $5. Personal checks, Mastercard, and Visa welcome.
Mailing Address: PO Box 276, Castine, ME 04421

CENTER LOVELL

CENTER LOVELL INN
Bill and Sue Mosca
Route 5
Center Lovell, ME 04016
(207) 925-1575
May 1 to October 31

1805; Mansard roof added in 1865

LOCATION: The inn overlooks Lake Kezar, which, set against the White Mountains, makes for a spectacular view. The town has a population of about 750. A beach, golf and tennis courts, and miles of hiking trails are all within walking distance. There's an old farm museum nearby, and in autumn, there's an old-fashioned, week-long country fair.

> *"The Moscas were the most charming couple. They served Northern Italian cuisine on the screened-in front porch in evenings. In the morning, we ate breakfast on old china in a country kitchen atmosphere. I think of that vacation often." Mary Ann Huls, Jasper, Ind.*

This fancy Mansard was originally a simple, two-storey homestead house. Its original owners were sheep farmers: Their three-storey sheep barn still stands near the Inn, virtually unchanged since it was built in 1805.

In the 1860s, the owner was taken with the Second Empire craze that hit the nation. Eckley T. Stearns, one-time governor of Florida and a man more concerned with fashion than he was with sheep farming, added the stylish mansard roof and the elegant wraparound porch, giving the house a new identity. The house remained in the Stearns family, as a summer residence for Eckley's heirs, until the Moscas bought it in 1974.

The Inn has many features that will fascinate old-house lovers. In addition to the hard-to-miss mansard roof, porch, and cupola, there are wide pine floors and hand-hewn beams left over from the inn's homestead days. In the dining room's fireplace, there's an original Ben Franklin heating fender. Most interesting of all: The Moscas recently hauled an 1830 Cape-style house across four miles of snowy roads to their property. They've restored this house, too, and converted it to a guest annex.

Restrictions: Children are welcome when well supervised; small children must dine early. Check-in after 1 p.m. Check-out at 11 a.m.

Beds: Ten rooms: six have private baths, the other four share two baths.

Breakfast: Strawberries in cream, canteloupe, juices, broccoli-mushroom-cheese omelettes, breakfast meats, blueberry pancakes, toast, and homemade jams. All served with coffee, tea, or Sanka.

Extras: Dinner, featuring Northern Italian cuisine and wine, is included in the room rate.

Rates: $78 to $116 per couple with meals, $27.50 and $42 without. Visa and Mastercard welcome.

10% discount to OHJ members.

MAINE

CHEBEAGUE ISLAND

THE CHEBEAGUE INN-BY-THE-SEA
Russell L. Brown
Chebeague Island, ME 04017
(207) 846-5155
Memorial weekend through Columbus weekend

1926 Shorefront Vernacular

LOCATION: The Chebeague Inn is just a stone's throw from the shore of Casco Bay. The island setting is accessible by boat or ferry only. It is high on a knoll overlooking a golf course and the ocean.

This is a relic of the post-Victorian era, when all ornateness was cast off in favor of nature's simplicity. The clapboarded inn's only exterior adornment is a wraparound porch, devoid of any fancy turnings, primely positioned to capture the invigorating ocean breezes. Inside, the first thing you'll notice is the huge but simple fieldstone hearth, flanked on both sides by bookshelves. Many of the furnishings, but not all, are antiques.

Restrictions: No pets.
Beds: Of the 20 rooms, seven have twins and the rest are full or

queen size. Inland or waterfront views are available, as are private or shared baths.

Extras: Golf, tennis, and the beach are just outside the door. There are bicycles to ride along miles of quiet roads. Babysitting services are available.

Rates: $55 (shared bath and inland view) to $80 (private bath and water view). Cribs are $5 and cots are $10. Checks and credit cards welcome.

10% discount to OHJ members.

CLARK ISLAND

THE CRAIGNAIR INN
Terry and Norman Smith
Clark Island Road
Clark Island, ME 04859
(207) 594-7644
Year-round

1928 Dutch Colonial Revival

LOCATION: Set amid spruce forests and granite outcroppings, Craignair Inn overlooks the ocean and Clark Cove. Ten miles south of Rockland, and ten miles north of Port Clyde, it's convenient to shopping and dining. There's a spectacular view of the lobster boats, shore birds, seals, and windjammers from their wraparound porch.

Scottish and Finnish quarry workers boarded here from the time the house was built until the demise of the profitable granite industry. When the granite industry died, the boarding house was easily converted to an inn: It had 17 built-in guest rooms and three bathrooms on each floor.

Terry and Norman Smith took over Craignair in 1978. They moved a 100-year-old, ten-burner, cast-iron coal-burning stove into the kitchen. They decorated the bedrooms comfortably, with quilt-covered beds, colorful wallpapers, and hooked rugs. And, most recently, they bought an 1890s church next to the inn. They're restoring the church and converting it to an antique shop.

The Smiths have a 150-piece collection of Wedgwood, Delft, and Ming china, which will interest antique collectors.

Restrictions: Well-mannered children and pets welcome. Smoking is permitted.

Beds: Among the 17 rooms, both singles and doubles are available. Two rooms share a bath.

Breakfast: Fruit and juices, eggs, pancakes, French toast, muffins, hot cereals, bacon or sausage, coffee, tea, hot chocolate. Special diets can be accommodated with advance notice.

Extras: Babysitting is available at $2.50 per hour. Taxi service can be arranged for $10 per hour. Dinner is included in the room rate; the menu varies nightly, ranging from a New England clambake (steamers, lobster, chicken, corn, and potatoes) to Italian night (shrimp scampi or lasagne). Vegetables fresh from the garden and homemade breads are always served.

Rates: $38 single, $58 double in July and August, breakfast and dinner included. $34 single and $51 double September through June. Breakfast only and weekly rates are also available. Cots, $10; cribs, $5. Visa, Mastercard, and personal checks welcome.

MAINE

DAMARISCOTTA

BRANNON-BUNKER INN
Jeanne and Joseph Hovance
Route 12A
Damariscotta, ME 04543
(207) 563-5941
Year-round

LOCATION: Damariscotta is four miles to the north of the inn; a lighthouse, fort, and cove are on the same peninsula. Golf and beaches are a short drive away. The inn overlooks a river and is one of many fine 18th- and 19th-century houses in the area.

An eclectic assortment of buildings, each of which has undergone several transformations, makes up the Brannon-Bunker Inn. The earliest structure is an 1820s Cape. Attached is a converted barn, which was moved to the site around the turn of the century.

The barn was used in the 1920s as a notorious dance hall called La Hacienda. In the 1950s another inn in town turned the space into guest rooms to house its overflow. The structure now contains these rooms along with a public space and breakfast area.

160

Across the stream from the barn and cape is a carriage house that has also been converted to rooms.

Furnishings throughout the two structures are equally eclectic. Styles range from Colonial to Mission. A collection of World War I documents and posters is displayed in the barn's upper hallway.

Restrictions: Check-in no later than 10 p.m. except by prior arrangement. Well-behaved pets allowed; children welcome ('we have three!'). No smoking in bedrooms, for safety reasons.
Beds: Of the four doubles and three twins, three share a bath.
Breakfast: Continental: choice of juice, fresh fruit in season, freshly baked muffins, cereal, coffee, tea, milk, various breads for toasting.
Extras: Hors d'oeuvres are served from time to time. Guests can prepare their own meals in the inn's kitchen. "Set-ups" (glasses, mixers) are available (BYOB). Babysitting can be arranged.
Rates: $42 (shared bath) to $50 (private). Single, deduct $7.50; extra person in room, add $10. $10 less, November to May. Credit cards and personal checks welcome.

10% discount to OHJ members.
Mailing Address: HCR 64, Box 045, Damariscotta, ME 04543

MAINE

DENNYSVILLE

**LINCOLN HOUSE
COUNTRY INN
Gerald and Mary Carol
Haggerty
Routes 1 and 86
Dennysville, ME 04628
(207) 726-3953
May through November**

1787 Georgian Colonial

161

LOCATION: "Remote, isolated, and surrounded by nature," the inn overlooks the Dennys River, famous for North Atlantic salmon. The surrounding area includes Moosehorn National Wildlife Refuge, Cobscook Bay State Park, Reversing Falls in Pembroke, and the ferry to Deer Isle.

"The house speaks for itself. If the quiet, remote, and non-commercial area of the most northeastern reaches of the Maine coastline appeals to you, this is a lovely spot."

A braham Lincoln's ancestors built this house. The first owner of the land was General Benjamin Lincoln, to whom General Cornwallis surrendered at the end of the American Revolution. Benjamin's son Theodore, aided by 12 craftsmen from Massachusetts, built the house and developed the town of Dennysville. At that time, Maine was little-explored frontier land, so all the building materials (except wood—there was plenty of that) had to be shipped from Massachusetts.

The Lincoln family lived in the house for 164 years, until 1951. One of their most famous visitors was John James Audubon, who dropped in on his way to Labrador in 1834. The Lincolns' hospitality so moved Mr. Audubon that he named a newly discovered bird the Lincoln Sparrow, in their honor.

The Lincoln home was handed down from generation to generation virtually unaltered. (The only addition was a small side bay window, installed in 1890.) The original granite foundation, doors, latches, enormous brick hearth with kettle set, fireplaces, and even an authentic boot jack are still in place. The Haggertys have done some cosmetic restoration: They've touched up the old horsehair and sand plaster, and copied the original paint in about half of the rooms. They've furnished the place with simple, country antiques. The house is in the National Register.

Restrictions: Well-behaved children welcome. No pets. Smoking permitted. Check-in and check-out times are "pretty casual."
Beds: Six rooms share four baths: three doubles, two twins, and one single.
Breakfast: Full breakfast.
Extras: Tea and coffee are always available; no charge for baby-sitting with advance notice. Hosts will arrange whale-watching cruises ($16). A small rowboat is available at no charge. There's a unique bar in the woodshed. Dinner included in fee: homemade bread, salad, appetizer, dessert, and a different entree every night from lobster to veal to roast strip loin of beef.
Rates: $50 to $55. Cots, $8; cribs, $5. Visa, Mastercard, and personal checks welcome.

10% discount to OHJ members.

ELIOT

**HIGH MEADOWS BED
AND BREAKFAST**
Elaine Raymond
Route 101
Eliot, ME 03903
(207) 439-0590
Year-round

1736 Twin-chimney neo-Colonial

LOCATION: Six miles from historic Portsmouth, New Hampshire —just outside Kittery, Maine—High Meadows B&B has six acres, close to shopping districts, restaurants, recreational areas, and of course, the New England coastline.

"The house was deserted when bought. No heat, no lights, no driveway - nothing! Over the years it has not only been a challenge to restore it to its original state, but also a lot of fun."

Built in 1736 by Eliot Frost, a merchant ship builder and captain, High Meadows B&B retains much of its historic detail. A gravity-flow water system remains intact. Said to be the first running water in Maine, an aqueduct runs from a spring on the grounds to what was once a kitchen. All the rooms are furnished with period antiques. Original exposed beams, wide floor boards, and wood panelling still exist in many of the rooms.

Elaine has been restoring the house since 1961, and has been receiving guests since 1982.

Restrictions: Children 12 and over are welcome. No pets. Smoking is permitted. Check-in after 2 p.m. Check-out at 11 a.m.
Beds: Four rooms: one with queen-size bed, fireplace, and private bath; two with double bed and shared bath, one with twin beds and shared bath.
Breakfast: Fruit juices, fresh fruit compote, homemade muffins, rolls and breads, coffee and tea.
Extras: Tea and wine coolers are served from 4 to 6 p.m.
Rates: $45 to $60. Personal checks accepted.

KENNEBUNKPORT

THE CAPTAIN JEFFERDS INN
Warren C. Fitzsimmons
Pearl Street
Kennebunkport, ME 04046
(207) 967-2311
April through October and winter weekends

1804 Federal

LOCATION: In a well-preserved historic residential neighborhood, near the center of a resort town, the inn is close to many recreational activities, beaches, and the New England coastline.

"Come and enjoy the visual and decorative arts in a warm and friendly atmosphere in a quiet residential section of a beautiful early New England town on the ocean."

Don Kelly and Warren Fitzsimmons bought this old house to display their extraordinary antiques collection, acquired while the two business partners ran a prosperous antique shop. The house was in good shape when they took over: The original fireplaces, mouldings, and unique "captain's bridge" stairwell (so named because it resembles the lookout post of Captain Jefferds, who built the house) were intact. Don and Warren did do lots of cosmetic work, including painting inside and out, wallpapering, and refinishing the floors. They tore down a tacky fence and hired a craftsman to recreate a graceful, finialled, Federal-style fence. And they got in touch with Colonel Jefferds, a descendant of Captain Jefferds, to learn about the house's history. Eleven kids grew up here!

If you like antiques at all, you'll be stunned by this inn's decor, which represents the cream of the crop from several years in the antiques business. The collection ranges from Early American to Victorian, and includes items like an ornate shellwork étagère, an 18th-century American pine corner cupboard, an abundance of polished brass beds, and piles of Majolica earthenware and Staffordshire china. And if the treasures inside don't satisfy your appetite, you can browse through Don and Warren's antique shop in the barn near the inn.

Restrictions: Children 12 and over welcome. No check-in after 9 p.m.

Beds: Of the 11 guest rooms, one has a queen bed, one twin beds, and nine doubles. Two rooms that form a suite share a bath; all other rooms have private bath. There are also three efficiency apartments in the attached carriage house; these must be rented for at least two weeks.

Breakfast: Full breakfast, with a different hot dish each morning: specialties include eggs Benedict, blueberry crepes, ham and cheese quiche, and New England "flannel." Guests are summoned to the morning meal with waltz music, and are introduced around the table.

Extras: Afternoon tea is served in cooler months. Free beach passes are available.

Rates: $65 to $80 depending on room size. Personal or traveler's checks and "everything but charge cards" are accepted.

MAINE

KENNEBUNKPORT

1812 Federal

THE CAPTAIN LORD MANSION
Bev Davis and Rick Litchfield
Corner of Pleasant and Green Streets
Kennebunkport, ME 04046
(207) 967-3141
Year-round

LOCATION: The mansion is located in a picturesque seacoast village that has a large number of stately homes from the 18th and 19th centuries. Many restaurants, recreational and cultural activities, and antique and art galleries are nearby.

Most of this country's shipbuilders were unemployed during the War of 1812, when all trade between Britain and the United States was cut off. But shipwrights in Arundel (now Kennebunkport), Maine, were lucky. Merchant Nathaniel Lord hired them to build this magnificent mansion, and rescued them from the dole.

The artisans built the mansion as sturdily as they would have built a ship. The roof is framed with dowelled and notched beams, fireplaces are of Welsh quarry tiles (used as ship's ballast in those days), and there are blown glass windows and 50-foot-high chimneys rising from a walk-in archway in the basement. One of their real masterpieces was the four-storey spiral staircase winding up to the octagonal cupola, which looks out over the Kennebunk River. (Originally, the staircase had a street entrance so villagers could climb to view inbound ships without disturbing the Lords.) These and endless other architectural delights survive to this day—the house remained with Lord's descendants into this century, and they took good care of it.

When Bev Davis and her husband Rick Litchfield ran across the Lords' house in 1978, it was a home for the elderly. They fell in love with it, recognizing it as their chance to escape the high-pressure world of corporate advertising. They made the down payment, painted, papered, furnished with antiques, and invited their first guests.

If you stay with Bev and Rick, be sure you look for the portraits of Nathaniel Lord's descendants (one of whom haunts the house), the monstrous coal stove which used to heat the Lords' water, and Nathaniel Lord's secret storage vault built from bricks and impermeable railroad ties. And be sure to ask them more about the house's history; they've researched it thoroughly.

Restrictions: Children above age 12 are welcome. No pets. No smoking in public areas. Check-in after 2 p.m. and check-out promptly a 11 a.m.
Beds: There are 16 double rooms: two with two double beds, two with a king-size bed, four with one double bed, and eight with one queen-size bed. All rooms have private baths.
Breakfast: Homemade muffins and sweet breads, fresh croissants and jams, orange juice, Twinings' teas, and coffee.
Extras: The inn serves a free afternoon tea, hot in the fall and winter, iced in the spring and summer. Free beach passes and beach towels are provided.
Rates: $89 (one double bed, third-floor room) to $119 (deluxe corner room with sitting area, fireplace, and oversize bed). January 1 to April 30: $69 to $99. Special packages for three-night stays. Personal checks and credit cards accepted.
Mailing Address: PO Box 527, Kennebunkport, ME 04046

KENNEBUNKPORT

ENGLISH MEADOWS INN
Helene and Gene Kelly
Route 35
Kennebunkport, ME 04046
(207) 967-5766
April 1 to November 1

1860 Victorian Farmhouse

LOCATION: Set at the end of a winding, lilac-lined drive, on six acres of meadow, fruit orchards, and pine groves where deer graze, the inn is a mile from historic Kennebunk Village and a beautiful beach. It's a five-minute walk from shops, restaurants, golf courses, and deep-sea fishing; a wildlife preserve is also nearby.

> *"A model for the inn we hope to have one day. Wonderful!" Melinda and Todd S., Crofton, Md.*

This farmhouse first opened its doors to overnight visitors in 1860, the year it was built. It has been lovingly preserved by the four families who've owned it. The rich interior oak panelling, sliding doors, and staircases are in good shape, and many of the windows still have their original glass. The Kellys, the present owners, have furnished the place with period pieces they've run across in their years as antique dealers: brass and iron beds, hooked rugs, early quilts, and more.

Restrictions: No children under 12 and no pets. Check-in between 2 and 9 p.m., check-out at 11 a.m.
Beds: There are a total of 15 rooms: eight doubles, two singles, and five with twin beds. Four rooms share a bath. Efficiency apartment above the carriage house can be rented by the week or by the month.
Breakfast: Full breakfast, with juice, fresh fruit, eggs, meats, rolls, muffins, and beverage; menu varies each morning.
Extras: Free afternoon tea and beach passes are available.
Rates: $40 (single) to $85 (suite). Rates are $5 less between April 1 and June 1. Cots, $15. Personal checks accepted.
Mailing Address: RFD #1, Route 35, Kennebunkport, ME 04046

KINGFIELD

THE WINTER'S INN
Michael F. Thom
Winter's Hill
Kingfield, ME 04947
(207)265-5421
Year-round

LOCATION: The house sits atop a ten-acre hill in the middle of historic Kingfield—a town of unspoiled beauty. Surrounded by two rivers and the mountain ranges of western Maine, it boasts scenic views.

"Although easily reached from the coast, our inn remains peaceful and remote. The view from the garden and pool area of the mountains to the north and west is unmatched anywhere. The inn is magnificent, unexpected in the area, full of fine antiques and paintings, and the food is four-star, delicious."

The first people to chug their auto up the winding road to this hilltop estate were the Stanley brothers, who invented the Stanley Steamer steam-driven automobile and sold their film plate patent to Kodak and Eastman. Today, at the top of that winding road, you'll see the same storybook-like, orange-and-white Georgian Revival the Stanleys designed, with its statuesque columns, sweeping verandahs, and railed roofs. Inside, a 21-year-old orange tabby cat named Balthazar will greet you and guide you up the rock maple staircase, past the Palladian window, beyond the gallery of 18th- and 19th-century oil paintings, to your room. Later, Balthazar might introduce you to the owner of the house, an architect named Michael Thom, who has his office on the first floor.

Restrictions: No pets, although there is a resident 21-year-old tabby cat. No children or infants in dining area after 7 p.m.
Beds: Of the 14 rooms, eight have private baths. Four rooms have king-sized beds, and there are two two-room suites. The remaining eight rooms have double or twin beds.
Breakfast: Full, all-homemade breakfast: breads, jams, fresh fruit

salads, juices, hot and cold cereals, eggs, omelettes, crepes, meats, potatoes, coffee and tea. On Sunday a more elaborate brunch (included in Saturday's room rate) is served by the poolside.

Extras: Tea is always available. Babysitting can be arranged, at local rates. There are tennis courts on the property.

Rates: $55 to $70, double occupancy. On holidays, add $5 per person per day. Cot available for an extra charge, no charge for cribs. Credit cards, personal checks, and traveler's checks all welcome. Weekly rates and package deals also available.

10% discount to OHJ members with minimum two-day visit.

Mailing Address: PO Box 44, Kingfield, ME 04947

NEWCASTLE

ELFINHILL
Emma Stephenson and Donald Smith
20 River Road
Newcastle, ME 04553
(207) 563-1886
Year-round

C. 1851 Greek Revival

LOCATION: Elfinhill looks out on the Damanscotto River and is convenient to shops, restaurants, and galleries, most of which are open year-round. There are also many old churches and meeting houses in the area, many listed in the National Register.

Nineteenth-century shipwrights turned and sculpted this house's interior woodwork, as well as the ornate carving above the columned entrance portico. Except for the addition of indoor plumbing, the Greek Revival's character hasn't changed since it was built over a century ago. The wide pumpkin pine floors, the etched Bristol glass in the entrance doors, the original attached hand-pegged post-and-beam barn, and the carved millwork are all in fine condition.

Restrictions: The second floor is a non-smoking area. Check-out at 11:30 a.m. Children welcome, though cribs are not available.
Beds: Three rooms: Single, double, or queen-sized beds are available. Guests share one large bath.
Breakfast: Full breakfast includes homemade preserves, coffeecake, and a hot entree. Special diets can be accommodated.
Extras: Tea is served from 4 to 5 p.m., complete with cakes from Don and Emma's specialty cake business.
Rates: Rooms start at $30 for a single and go up to $47.50 for a double with a queen-sized bed. Rates vary during the off-season. Cots are $10; children under 12 are $5 additional.
Mailing Address: PO Box 497, Newcastle, ME 04553

SEARSPORT

CARRIAGE HOUSE INN
**Alden and
Catherine Bradbury
Route #1
Searsport, ME 04974
(207) 548-2289
Year-round**

1874 Mansard

LOCATION: Along the central Maine seacoast, the inn has an ocean view. Nearby attractions include Penobscot Marine Museum, Acadia National Park, Bar Harbor, and local beaches.

Most of this country's Second Empire houses died young; most were badly remuddled, their mansard roofs disguised, their delicate Victorian ornament insensitively obliterated. But this was one of the lucky survivors. It looks now exactly as it did in 1874: The steep mansard roof, carved eave brackets, pedimented dormers, capped chimneys, and verandah are all in fine shape. The unusual, attached carriage house, with cupola and mansard roof matching the house's, is unchanged. And inside, nobody has tried to modernize the magnificent, three-storey bannister, which the innkeepers say was hand-carved aboard a ship. (The house was built by a sea captain.)

The inn has had its share of famous occupants. After World War II (when soldiers in training were garrisoned here), it was the summer retreat of the renowned painter Waldo Peirce. Reportedly, Ernest Hemingway was a frequent guest—Peirce and Hemingway had become close friends during their wartime service in France's ambulance corps.

Alden and Catherine Bradbury, the present innkeepers, have treated the old house with great respect. It's furnished with Second Empire antiques, in keeping with its style. And it's surrounded with Victorian-style flower gardens.

Restrictions: Children welcome. No pets. Smoking on first floor only. Check-in by 8:00 p.m. unless otherwise arranged.
Beds: Six guest rooms. Two rooms have private baths.
Breakfast: Full continental: hot muffins, fresh fruit, and freshly brewed coffee.
Extras: Afternoon tea is served on the porch. And access to the beaches is free.
Rates: Summer: $42 to $49, depending on room size and view. Winter rates are lower. Cribs and cots available for no charge. Credit cards and personal checks accepted.

10% discount to OHJ members.
Mailing Address: PO Box 238, Searsport, ME 04974

SEARSPORT

1860 Mansard

MCGILVERY HOUSE
Stephen Stier and Sue Omness
Route #1
Searsport, ME 04974
(207) 548-6289
Mid-May through mid-October

LOCATION: Searsport is a quaint coastal village with many antique shops and an excellent marine museum. It is centrally locate for easy day trips to Camden, Bar Harbor, and Baxter State Park. The inn overlooks Penobscot Bay.

This house fell on hard times after its distraught first owner, Captain William McGilvery, committed suicide. Captain McGilvery had experienced the American Dream. He'd made a fortune as a shipbuilding entrepreneur, and, confident that his prosperity would last, he poured his wealth into building a home he could be proud of: two-and-a-half storeys with a fashionable, finialled mansard roof outside and a showpiece mahogany stair rail and eight fireplaces inside. But soon after the house was completed, the shipping industry began its rapid plummet. McGilvery lost his fortune and his faith, and shot himself inside this very house.

Stephen and Sue found the house in this sorry condition in 1982. They've undertaken a complete restoration, replacing the rotted porch columns, trim, and plaster cornices, and painting the outside in a period color scheme. They've cleaned the marbleized finish on their slate mantels and the graining on the woodwork. They've furnished most rooms with Victorian antiques, including Captain McGilvery's original parlor chandeliers, salvaged from the cobwebs.

Restrictions: No pets. No smoking. Late-night check-in by special arrangement only.
Beds: Three guest rooms with queen-size beds and private baths.
Breakfast: Full continental: homemade muffins, coffeecake, pastries with homemade jams and jellies, fresh fruit, coffee, and tea.
Rates: $30 to $40. Cots, $5. Personal checks welcome.
  10% discount to OHJ members.
Mailing Address: PO Box 588, Searsport, ME 04974

MAINE

WISCASSET

THE SQUIRE TARBOX INN
Karen and Bill Mitman
Route 144, Westport Island
Wiscasset, ME 04578
(207) 882-7693
Mid-May through the end of October

1825 Federal with 1763 Colonial ell

LOCATION: The 12-acre working farm is surrounded by 100 acres of woods. A pine-needled path leads from the inn to a scenic salt water inlet where beaver, deer, blue heron, egrets, and kingfishers have been sighted. Beaches, shops, and harbors are close by.

Samuel Tarbox, the man who built this house, was Westport's first First Selectman, a position equivalent to that of a modern mayor. Samuel's nickname was the Squire, because he was the wealthiest and most influential man in town. In 1825, the Squire moved the small Colonial which is now the inn's back ell from a hill nearby, and attached it to his new Federal abode.

All the house's original architectural features have survived. There are hand-hewn beams and wide-board pumpkin pine floors in the 1763 section, now a dining area. A few of the old, wavy-glass window panes are still in place, as are the bake ovens and eight original fireplaces. The Mitmans recently painted the carved woodwork in a documentary early American color scheme, and got their house listed in the National Register.

A few more tidbits: The Mitmans have Squire Tarbox's original deed and Bible, as well as several antique photos of the house.

Restrictions: Children 12 and over welcome. No pets. No smoking in dining area, and absolutely no cigars. Check-in after 2 p.m. Check-out at 11 a.m.
Beds: Eleven rooms, all with private baths.
Breakfast: Continental: homemade cakes and breads, juice, tea and coffee, granola and fruit; served buffet style, from 8 until 9 a.m. Special diets can be accommodated with advance notice.
Extras: Soft herbed goat cheese (homemade from the hosts' goats' milk) & sherry are served by the fire before dinner. Blueberries and raspberries are ready for picking nearby. Darts are set up in the barn. Dinner is included in the room rate; specialties include sole stuffed with spinach and Parmesan cheese, and boneless chicken breast stuffed with cheese and baked in a pastry.
Rates: $120 to $140. Personal checks welcome, but "we're not so-phisticated enough to use credit cards."
10% discount to OHJ members in May and June.
Mailing Address: R D 2, Box 2160, Wiscasset, ME 04578

MARYLAND

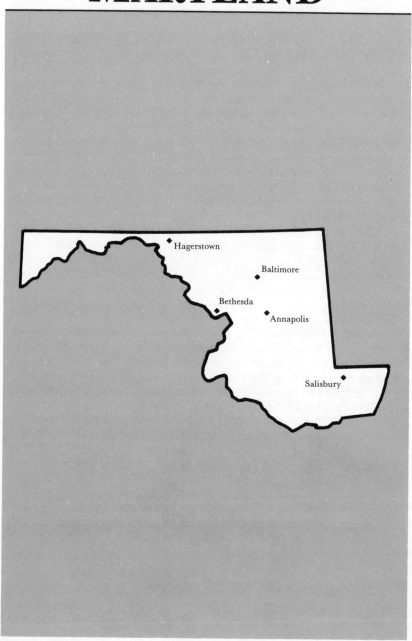

ANNAPOLIS

PRINGE GEORGE INN
B&B
William and Norma
Grovermann
232 Prince George Street
Annapolis, MD 21401
(301) 263-6418
Year-round

1884 Italianate

LOCATION: In a historic district of Maryland's capitol, the inn is one block from the State House, three blocks from the city dock; near 18th-century museum houses, restaurants, and shopping areas.

"We invite you to share our old house—one of a dozen we've restored as a hobby, though we've both worked in the field of historic preservation professionally as well."

Innkeepers William and Norma Grovermann rescue old houses as a hobby. This is their twelfth old house, as exquisitely restored as any you're likely to see. It's built of brick and has an intricate, bracketed cornice, tall narrow windows, and a double-door entry with an etched-glass fanlight. You'll enter through a wide, open stair hall to the parlor, which has 11-and-a-half-foot ceilings and three-tier folding interior shutters. Breakfast is served in a sunny, glassed-in nook at the side of the house, or in the screened-in back porch. All the Grovermanns' furnishings are late 19th-century Victorian, including brass beds, gothic wood beds, wicker settees, fancy carved wardrobes, and antique trunks.

Restrictions: No children under 12, and no pets. Smoking restricted to first floor. Check-out at 12 p.m., check-in after 3 p.m.
Beds: Four rooms: two doubles, one queen, and one with twins, two of which share a bath.
Breakfast: Choice of five juices (or cold soda); cereal, fruit; croissant, muffins; jams, jellies, butter; coffee, tea, chocolate.
Extras: For $4 Mrs. Grovermann's sightseeing service will arrange tours of the naval academy and Annapolis. Ice and mixers are available for guests to make their own cocktails.
Rates: All rooms are $60 double, which includes 5% tax. Cash or personal checks only.
   10% discount to OHJ members.

MARYLAND

EDGEWATER BEACH

CLIFTARA AT CEDAR POINT
Tara and Jack Clifford
124 Park Avenue
Edgewater Beach, MD 21037
(301) 269-2854
Year-round

LOCATION: On a forested cliff at the intersection of two rivers, Cliftara is near the Londontown Publik House (a historic 18th-century ferry stop many notables passed through). Annapolis Harbor is easily accessible by water or car, and Washington and Baltimore are 35 minutes away.

This is a cozy Dutch Colonial Revival, painted beige with matching striped canvas awnings, dormers, and huge casement windows opening out over astounding river views. The living room has an open-beamed ceiling, rich panelled walls, and a built-in corner cupboard full of books. Breakfast is served at an antique table in a glassed-in porch with a view of the river so close you'll think you're in a ship captain's bay. There's a sunny sitting room and a music room with grand piano that guests are also welcome to use. Furnishings are a harmonious combination of old and new: cushioned sofas intermingling with old secretaries, Oriental rugs, and brocaded Victorian chairs. The innkeepers collect stamps and antique ship memorabilia.

Restrictions: Children welcome, but not pets. Smoking in breakfast room only. Check-in after 5 p.m., or later by prior arrangement.
Beds: Two kings and one queen, also a convertible "sleep chair." Two rooms share a bath.
Breakfast: Fresh fruit and juice; whole grain cereal and natural yogurt; soft-cooked egg; sweet rolls, toast, homemade muffins, and jams; coffee and tea.
Extras: The Cliffords serve a complimentary cordial, and also let guests use the pool, rowboats, lawn games, and bicycles, and the guests-only sitting room. Waterskiing boats can be rented, as can a 65-foot yacht, with captain, for longer voyages. (The boat once belonged to Arthur Godfrey and was the official yacht of the governors of Maryland).
Rates: $50 (single, third-floor room) to $65 (double master bedroom). Cash, traveler's and personal checks welcome.
   10% discount to OHJ members.

MARYLAND

FREDERICK

SPRING BANK INN
Beverly and Ray Compton
7945 Worman's Mill Road
(Route 355)
Frederick, MD 21701
(301) 694-0440
Year-round

1880 Gothic and Italianate

LOCATION: Frederick's been called "the prettiest town in America." The inn's setting is rural, with walking paths and farmland adjacent. Both parks and antique shops are nearby, as are Gettysburg, Antietam, Baltimore, Washington, D.C., and Harpers Ferry.

The realtors thought Beverly and Ray Compton were crazy when they decided to buy this grackle-, beehive-, and racoon-infested abandoned farmhouse. Ray and Bev, too, were a little surprised with their own hasty decision. They were cycling along innocently with the Potomac Pedalers Cycle Club, enjoying the scenery, when they ran across this house for sale. They immediately phoned the realtor, asked for a tour, and, despite the lack of electricity and the sprigs of ivy sprouting through broken windows, they left their comfortable home in another part of town and moved in.

Their before and after pictures will show you what a little do-it-yourself elbow grease can do. Ray, who quit his job to tackle the house full-time, has restored the house to its turn-of-the-century elegance: trompe l'oeil, grain-painted woodwork; marbleized slate fireplaces, ceiling medallions, and fancy plasterwork. His latest project is restoring the original, 19th-century ceiling stencilling he found beneath layers of 20th-century wallpaper. In his quest to set the house to rights, Ray has vowed to "not do anything that can't be undone some day." He's made drawings to document all his restoration work. And the new bathrooms he's put in upstairs match the original first floor bathrooms in tile work and fixtures.

Ray and Bev know the house's history like they know their own name. The man who built it was a gentleman farmer named George Houck, who listed his occupation in the 1900 census as "capitalist." He's the one who left the cornerstone that says "Spring Bank Built April 1, 1880—George Houck." After the turn of the century, the Houcks sold the house to a family named Bowers that owned a prosperous local lumber yard. The Bowers were the ones who closed off the second floor for storage in 1925, and left it unoccupied until 1980, when Bev and Ray moved in. Bev and Ray have an artist's 1880s sketch of the house, as well as a large collection of antique books about Frederick County.

Restrictions: No children under 12; no smoking; no pets; check-in after 3 p.m.
Beds: One room with private bath, six others share four baths. All rooms have double beds—"we're still looking for matching Victorian twin beds."
Breakfast: Freshly baked bread, fresh fruit, coffee, tea, etc.; served with antique linens on antique china, and brought to room on request.
Extras: Complimentary sherry or other beverages are provided at almost any time.
Rates: $50 to $75, payable by personal check or American Express. Extra single beds, $10.
10% discount to OHJ members if not paid by credit card.

NEW MARKET

THE STRAWBERRY INN
Jane and Ed Rossig
17 Main Street
New Market, MD 21774
(301) 865-3318
Year-round

Gothic Revival/Italianate 1845, modified c. 1900

LOCATION: All of New Market, surrounded by Maryland country-side, is in the National Register. It's been called "the antiques capital of Maryland." Within an hour's drive are Baltimore, Washington, Gettysburg, and Harper's Ferry.

The Strawberry Inn is in a town where, in the 19th century, west-ward travellers aboard high-wheeled, six-horse Conestoga wagons would stop and get a night's lodging for 25 cents and a glass of whisky for five cents. Innkeeper Ed Rossig, a retired electrical engineer who "always wanted to own an old house," and his wife Jane have restored the house to that era, with painted-grain doors, fancy stencilling, ornate plasterwork, and antique furnishings. Out back, they've got an 1840 log cabin they moved, log by log, from the other end of town. It's completely restored, too, and has a walk-in fireplace, beehive oven, and enough space to hold large private meetings.

Restrictions: No children under seven and no pets, but "smoking is fine."
Beds: Five total: one on the first floor with adjacent porch, two twin beds, and a fold-out sofa; four on the second floor: one double, two queens, and one with two doubles. All have private baths.
Breakfast: Continental: coffee/tea, fresh fruit, butter, jam, served with "whatever Jane bakes that morning," is delivered to the room or served in the dining room.
Extras: "No room phones, no TV, no radios," say the Rossigs with pride.
Rates: $55 to $70. Traveler's and personal checks accepted.
Mailing Address: Box 237, New Market, MD 21774

PRINCESS ANNE

ELMWOOD C. 1770 BED & BREAKFAST
Steve and Helen Monick
Locust Point Road, Route 1
Princess Anne, MD 21853
(301) 651-1066
Year-round

C. 1770, Federal and Colonial

LOCATION: The inn has a tranquil site on the Manokin River, with fields, woods, and water.

At the turn of the 18th century, Arnold Elzey Jones spent ten years building the ostentatious Federal wing of this house. While he was building, perfecting each mantelpiece, each foot of chair rail, each curve of the grand staircase, he housed his family in the simple Colonial wings next door. What finally resulted was this three-wing combination Colonial and Flemish brick Federal, built at ascending levels and interconnected via a series of small staircases. Jones' descendants (among them a Civil War general in the Confederate Army) lived here for 150 years, until a botanist named Norman Taylor moved in in 1947.

Steve and Helen Monick bought the house in 1983, and have undertaken a complete cosmetic restoration. (When they bought it, the house was structurally the same as when Arnold Elzey Jones left it.) Most of the original woodwork, fireplace mantels, and plaster have survived. The Monicks have furnished the house with antiques and Helen's hand-done stitchery.

Restrictions: No children under 12, and no smoking in the bedrooms. Check-in anytime in mid- or late afternoon.
Beds: Of the four rooms, two have queen-sized four-posters; one, a double Victorian bed; and one, twin beds. Four rooms split three baths, with "occasional" sharing.
Breakfast: Fresh fruit in season, or juice, pecan-cream waffles, sausage, plus homebaked breads, coffee, tea.
Extras: Afternoon tea and sweets are served.
Rates: $45 to $65, payable in cash or traveler's checks.

10% discount to OHJ members.
Mailing Address: PO Box 220, Princess Anne, MD 21853

PRINCESS ANNE

WASHINGTON HOTEL INN
Mary A. Murphey
Somerset Avenue
Princess Anne, MD 21853
(301) 651-2525
Year-round

LOCATION: The inn is located in the heart of historic Princess Anne, with its many old homes, on Maryland's eastern shore. Trips to nearby islands are popular.

Out on this inn's wide verandah is a huge bell 18th-century travelers rang to alert the stable boy that they were leaving and needed their horses. Inside, there's a double stairway from the hoopskirt era —one half for the ladies, the other for the gents. The inn's been in continuous operation for two centuries, and these are just two of the relics from its long history.

Innkeeper Mary Murphey has been here since 1956. She's recently redecorated some rooms with period wallpapers and antiques — be sure to ask in advance if you want to stay in one of these.

Restrictions: Only pets are restricted.
Beds: All fourteen rooms—four with two double beds, ten with one double—have private baths.
Breakfast: None is included, but there's a coffee shop.
Extras: Guests can lunch in the inn's coffee shop, and dine in the old dining room.
Rates: $30 to $40; higher in the summer. Cots available at an extra charge. Personal checks and credit cards welcome.

VIENNA

THE GOVERNOR'S ORDINARY

Barbara Fearson
Water and Church Streets
Vienna, MD 21869
(301) 376-3530
Year-round

1791 Federal

LOCATION: The customs house, left over from Vienna's days as a Colonial and Federal port, stands near the inn. Blackwater Wildlife and opportunities for fishing and tennis are also close by. The surrounding town retains much of its Colonial, Federal, and Victorian architecture, and the inn looks out on the Nanticoke River.

This Federal was elegant enough for the governor of Maryland to call home from 1829 to 1841. Today, thanks to William and Barbara Fearson's restoration work, the house looks pretty much as it did in the early 19th century. Outside, the beaded siding, cross-and-Bible panelled front door, dormers and nine-over-six windows are original. Inside, the random-width pine floors, English carpenter door locks, panelled stairway, and chair rails are also original. The Fearsons have furnished the house with antiques from a variety of periods. Their collection includes Empire, Chippendale, and Hepplewhite pieces, as well as Oriental rugs. (The Fearsons also run the neighboring Nanticoke Manor House B&B.)

Restrictions: No pets or children under ten. Smoking only in designated areas.
Beds: Four rooms—one single, the rest double; one has a private bath.
Breakfast: Homemade muffins, breads, juice, fresh grapefruit, butter, cream, coffee or tea.
Extras: Free cheese and wine are served in the double parlors each evening.
Rates: $55 to $75, plus $10 on weekends. Extra charge for cots. Credit cards and personal checks welcome.

10% discount to OHJ members.

VIENNA

NANTICOKE MANOR HOUSE
William and Barbara Fearson
Water and Church Streets
Vienna, MD 21869
(301) 376-3530
Year-round

C. 1740 Colonial in back; main building 1861 Italianate

LOCATION: The town, founded in 1706, served as a port in both Federal and Colonial days. Across from the inn is the original customs house; both it and the inn overlook the water. The natural setting offers opportunities for fishing and tennis, and Blackwater Wildlife Refuge is nearby.

A wealthy seafaring merchant built this Italianate onto a 1740s frame Colonial, now the rear of the house. At the time, the locals called it the "Brick House"—it was the first masonry building in town. The house is tall and symmetrical, and has a partially screened, wraparound verandah, and eight-foot windows that let in lots of sun. Inside, it has original plaster ceiling cornices and medallions, three-storey spiral staircase with a walnut bannister, and five original fireplaces (two in the double parlor) with mantels. All the rooms are authentically furnished with Victorian antiques and antique Persian rugs. In the 18th-century part of the house, you can still see the original, round log sills and joists.

Innkeepers Barbara and Joe Fearson, who also own the neighboring Governor's Ordinary, have invested a substantial amount of their time restoring this house. Their work has included chemically cleaning and re-pointing the exterior brick, replacing 90 percent of the floor joists in the original morticed and pinned style, and salvaging the interior plaster walls.

Restrictions: No smoking, pets, or children under the age of ten.
Beds: Five doubles, one suite, and one efficiency. Three share a bath.
Breakfast: Homemade muffins, bread, juice, fresh grapefruit, butter, cream, coffee or tea.
Extras: Complimentary cheese and wine are served in the early evening in the double parlors.
Rates: $55 to $75, $10 more on weekends. Cots available for an extra charge. Personal checks and credit cards accepted.
10% discount to OHJ members.

MARYLAND

VIENNA

TAVERN HOUSE
Elise and Harvey Altergott
111 Water Street
Vienna, MD 21869
(301) 376-3347
Year-round

1770 Georgian

LOCATION: The town, on the Nanticoke River, was once a port, and the old customs house remains. Within an easy drive are the Blackwater Wildlife Refuge, several museums, as well as many old homes and sites, including some from the 17th century such as the oldest church in the U.S.

"We're not just a B&B, we're real people willing to share our home, our restoration experiences, our interests, our friends."

Harvey Altergott put on hold the airplane he was building when he and his wife Elise, an artist, bird watcher, and avid reader, started restoring this Georgian Colonial. In colonial times, the house was a resting place where southbound travelers could stop and warm their bellies over a mug of hot grog. The tavern owner made an extra profit by operating a ferry across the Nanticoke River, and by running the local post office.

The Altergotts' restoration turned out to be a bigger project than either of them envisioned. They've had to replace the sills, floor joists, and even the posts behind the walls. (They've duplicated the original construction methods wherever possible.) They've also restored the original paint colors in many rooms. The house has its original random-width flooring on the second storey, panelled stairway, interior carved doorways, fireplace mantels, and chair railings. The Altergotts are at present working on furnishing the house in what they call a "comfortable and simple" manner — with a blend of antiques from different periods, family heirlooms, and their own artifacts (like a lamp from a Turkish sailing ship and a handmade Ecuadorian rug) from travels abroad. A carpenter friend of theirs is making all the guest beds in true-to-form, four-poster colonial style. As time passes and the Altergotts pay off their restoration debts, they hope to collect more antiques at local auctions.

Restrictions: No children or pets.

Beds: Four doubles share two baths.

Breakfast: Menu still "under development," but so far includes rolls, fruits, juices, coffee, tea, and cereal.

Extras: Guests can play croquet in the large yard or have afternoon tea or coffee with the Altergotts, or use the bicycles, public boat ramp, and tennis courts less than three blocks away.

Rates: $45 to $50 ($5 less for single occupancy). Personal checks accepted.

10% discount to OHJ members.

Mailing Address: PO Box 98, Vienna, MD 21869

MASSACHUSETTS

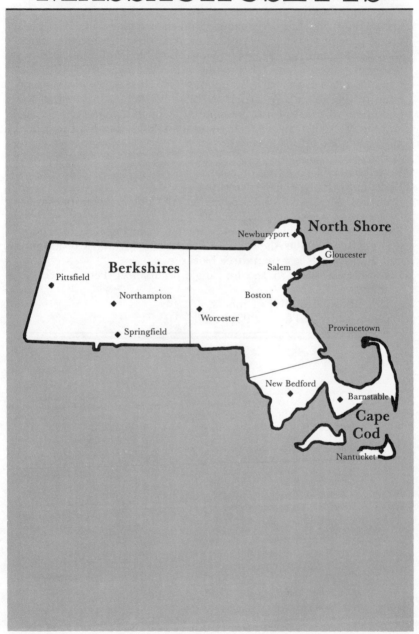

Newburyport

North Shore

Gloucester

Berkshires

Salem

Pittsfield

Boston

Northampton

Worcester

Springfield

Provincetown

New Bedford

Barnstable

Cape Cod

Nantucket

GREAT BARRINGTON

**THE TURNING POINT
INN**
Irving and Shirley Yost
3 Lake Buel Road
Great Barrington, MA 01230
(413) 528-4777
Year-round

1800 Federal

LOCATION: The inn is in the heart of the Berkshires, ten miles from Tanglewood, with its outdoor Boston Symphony Orchestra concerts. Theater festivals, dance concerts, the Norman Rockwell and Clark art museums, and the 18th-century Hancock Shaker Village are all nearby. Outdoor activities include hiking on the Appalachian Trail (across the street from the inn), swimming, horseback riding, golf, tennis, boating, and skiing.

Notable statesman Daniel Webster visited this inn frequently back in the 1800s, when it was a stagecoach stop between capital cities Hartford and Albany.

The inn is typical of the more elegant homes of its era, with marble thresholds, sills, and lintels, and a stone and marble foundation. Inside, the original mouldings, floorboards, and plaster remain. There are also three Rumford fireplaces and a beehive oven original to the house. The Inn is furnished with period antiques, including two-inch-thick chestnut-plank tables in the dining room.

Restrictions: No smoking and no pets. The innkeepers love children and babies.

Beds: One single, two twins, and four doubles. One room has a private bath.

Breakfast: Their bountiful breakfast is a "nutritious delight." Whole grain cereals, fritatas, pancakes, fresh fruit, baked fruit, baked muffins, nut breads, fruit breads, coffee and several teas. They can accommodate special diets.

Extras: A fresh fruit bowl, coffee, tea, and milk are always within reach. Babysitting available (for a fee).

Rates: $40 (single); $60 (double). (Add $5 for one-day stay and $15 for private bath.) Weekdays, $10 less. Off-season, $5 less. Cots, $5 to $10; cribs, $5. Checks accepted; no credit cards.

MASSACHUSETTS: THE BERKSHIRES

LENOX

THE APPLE TREE INN
Greg and Aurora Smith
(owners);
Jake and Lisa Thomas
(managers)
224 West Street
Lenox, MA 01240
(413) 637-1477
April 15 to March 15

1885 Rambling Queen Anne

LOCATION: A 22-acre estate atop Bald Head Mountain, overlooking Tanglewood Estate (the Boston Symphony's summer home), surrounds the inn. There's a splendid view of the Stockbridge Bowl (a lake) and the Berkshires. Apple orchards, extensive flower gardens (with 300 varieties of roses), a heated swimming pool, and clay tennis courts are all on the grounds. Nearby are all the Berkshire attractions: Jacob's Pillow dance theater, Williamstown summer theater, Hancock Shaker Village, outdoor Shakespeare at the Mount, hiking trails, and several ski resorts.

This inn was once a center of 1960s culture, a hangout for famous folk artists like Arlo Guthrie, Pete Seeger, and Tom Lehrer. It was the last and largest place owned by Alice Brook, whose name will go down in history because of Arlo Guthrie's song, "Alice's Restaurant" (as in, "you can get anything you want at ..."). She lived in room 2, by the way.

Underneath the hippie disguise—beads, carpeting on both floors and walls (!), moth-eaten mattresses on the floor, a redwood deck slapped indiscriminately across the front of the house—lay a lovely turn-of-the-century house. The innkeepers redid "virtually every inch of the interiors," in some cases resorting to stripping the walls to bare lath.

Some of the furnishings they've installed have as intriguing a history as the house's: William Fox, of 20th-Century Fox fame, owned the leather-topped desk, and a sea captain used the sea chest in his travels in the early 19th century. All the rooms in the main house are furnished in antiques, including period wallpapers, antique beds, (either four-poster or brass), braided rugs, and lace.

Restrictions: No pets or children under age 12. Check-in after 2 p.m.; check-out at 11:30 a.m.

Beds: In the main house: nine rooms (king, queen, double, and twin), most with private bath. In the guest lodge (built in 1960): 20 air-conditioned rooms, with two full beds in each.

Breakfast: Continental: home-baked goodies, coffee or tea.

Extras: There's a full-service restaurant right in the Inn, which specializes in Northern Italian cuisine: veal scallopine tommaso, fettucine alfredo, chicken alla Venezia, and baked halibut Siciliana, for example. There's also a restored, turn-of-the-century tavern which will delight old-house lovers: oak-panelled walls, carved mantelpieces, an unusual, 13th-century Moslem wall inset, and a beamed ceiling.

Rates: $35 to $245, depending on the season and room—call for more information. Checks and credit cards accepted.

10% discount to OHJ members.

BARNSTABLE

BEECHWOOD INN
Ann and Bob Livermore
2839 Main Street
Barnstable, MA 02630
(617) 362-6618
Year-round

1853 Queen Anne (remodeled in late 19th century)

LOCATION: In the Old King's Highway state historic district, the inn is beside a 40-mile, pre-Revolutionary road winding along Cape Cod's north shore, lined with restored homes. Beaches, museums, antique shops, and quaint villages abound in the area.

"We love to rejoice, sympathize, and complain with others who understand what it's like to live in an old house. We love the Victorian era and enjoy guests who share that enthusiasm."

The Queen Anne style Beechwood Inn is a unique Victorian landmark in a largely colonial neighborhood. While Cape Cod residents boast a long-time record of caring for colonial homes, nobody expressed much interest in the Victorian Beechwood until 1982, when Bea and Jeffrey Goldstein moved in. Victorian lovers and former antique shop owners who left the hustle and bustle of Los Angeles for the serenity of Cape Cod, the Goldsteins spent a year and a half restoring Beechwood's crumbling plaster, rotting joists, peeling paint, decrepit bathrooms, and sagging porch—only to discover the project was more expensive than they had anticipated and the house was much too big for a family of four. The Goldsteins solved both these problems by turning the house into an inn.

Beechwood's five guest rooms (the Rose, Eastlake, Marble, Cottage, and Garret rooms) are furnished with authentic Victorian antiques

190

and papered with reproduction wallpapers. Meals are served on Victorian dinnerware. The Goldsteins delight in explaining their antiques' origins to guests. They're knowledgeable scholars of the Victorian era, and gladly share their learnings with visitors.

Restrictions: No children under 14. No pets. Check-in after 2 p.m.
Beds: One room with queen-size, four-poster bed, three with double beds, and one with double and single beds. All have private baths.
Breakfast: Full breakfast includes fresh-squeezed juice and fresh fruit, quiche or cheese and hardboiled eggs, home-baked muffins, breads or pancakes, and coffee or tea.
Extras: Afternoon tea is served on the porch or in the parlor.
Rates: All seasons: from $85 for Eastlake-style room with colored glass windows overlooking the Cape Cod bay to $105 for room with four-poster bed, working fireplace, and French doors opening onto the verandah. Personal checks and credit cards accepted.
    10% discount to OHJ members.

BARNSTABLE

COBB'S COVE INN
Evelyn and Henri-Jean Chester
Powder Hill Road
Barnstable Village, MA 02630
(617) 362-9356
Year-round

LOCATION: From its 1643 historic site, the colonial-timbered manor commands a 360-degree vista overlooking Barnstable Village, the harbor, and the ocean. National marshlands and bird sanctuaries surround the inn.

This colonial-style Saltbox is built the way it would've been built 300 years ago—but it's new. Innkeepers Evelyn and Henri-Jean Chester fell in love with Cape Cod's historic district, and decided to move here when they found this lovely plot of land for sale. One problem: the only structure on the land was an old stone foundation —no house! So they decided to build, but in the old style, since anything modern would have been an architectural atrocity amongst Cape Cod's colonials. The house is all post-and-beam construction, with

191

exposed Douglas fir timbers throughout. In the keeping room, you can see the 12-by-12 inch ceiling timbers, wide-board flooring, and even a Count Rumford fireplace. Evelyn has furnished the house in what she calls an eclectic style, with some colonial-era antiques, and handwoven fabrics with simple prints. She's planted an authentic herb garden in the yard.

Restrictions: No children, no pets.
Beds: Six suites: double-, queen-, and king-size beds available. All have private baths, whirlpool tubs, and showers.
Breakfast: Full breakfast is served in the "old-time manner, with good food and warm conversation."
Rates: The range, per couple — $119 to $139 — includes breakfast. Personal or traveler's checks welcome.
Mailing Address: PO Box 208, MA 02630

BREWSTER

THE INN OF THE GOLDEN OX
David and Eileen Gibson
1360 Main Street
Brewster, MA 02631
(617) 896-3111
Year-round

1828 Greek Revival

LOCATION: The inn, on historic Old King's Highway on a hill, overlooks the Cape Cod Bay, with one-and-a-half acres of well-kept grounds. Nearby are Cape Cod National Seashore, Museum of Natural History, Rail Trail (21 miles of bike paths), Nickerson State Park, and antique shops, museums, summer playhouses, and tennis courts in the town of Brewster.

The Inn of the Golden Ox has served as a guest house for more than a century. But in its first life, this inn was a church. The Brewster Universalist Society erected the building, complete with steeple, in 1828. As time passed, the Universalist Society incorporated new members and the church began to burst at its seams. Finally, in

1852, the church had to be sold so a larger meeting house could be built. The building's new owner sold the steeple for $1.75, moved the building a mile and a half to its present location, and coverted it to an inn.

When the Gibsons took over in 1983, the building's wide pine floors, hair plaster walls, and original woodwork remained. The Gibsons did, however, restore 12 out of 19 rooms in the inn, furnishing them with simple, colonial-era antiques.

Restrictions: No pets. Children over ten welcome. Check-in after noon.
Beds: Two twin-bedded rooms, one with a queen-size bed, four with double beds. All share four baths.
Breakfast: Continental breakfast includes home-baked breads and muffins, seasonal fruits, country-fresh cream, juices, coffee, and tea.
Extras: Full-service, four-star restaurant features New American cuisine, including specialties such as braised breast of chicken with white grapes and grilled swordfish with tomato fondue. Proprietors David and Eileen, who run the restaurant, are Culinary Institute of America graduates! Wines, imported beers, and other cocktails are served in the lounge.
Rates: May 1 to October 31: all rooms, $48. Off-season: $38. Cots, $15. Personal checks and American Express accepted.

10% discount to OHJ members.

BREWSTER

1860 Federal, with later additions

OLD SEA PINES INN
Stephen and Michele Rowan
2553 Main Street
Brewster, MA 02631
(617) 896-6114
May 1 through November 30;
weekends during April

LOCATION: The inn has three-and-a-half acres of lush grounds on historic Old King's Highway. Quiet beaches, antique and gift shops, bike trails, golf courses, tennis courts, and other historic homes are within walking distance.

For most of this century, the Old Sea Pines Inn was known as the Sea Pines School of Charm and Personality for Young Women — the nation's second Christian Science school. The school was run by Miss Faith Bickford, a descendant of *Mayflower* voyager William Brewster. (The inn, in fact, stands on part of William Brewster's original land holdings.)

Predictably, Sea Pines didn't survive its tenure as a charm school unharmed. The Rowans spent several years restoring its cracking plaster, sagging porches, peeling paint job, and outdated plumbing. They redecorated the inn, too: with Stickley furniture, brass and iron beds, period wallpapers, and their antique clock collection.

The Rowans think their inn's most outstanding architectural feature is its seemingly endless expanse of porches, where visitors can sit and enjoy Cape Cod's refreshing breezes.

Restrictions: No children under eight. No pets. Check-in after 2 p.m.; check-out at 11 a.m.

Beds: There are 15 twin- and double-bedded rooms, including a suite with two bedrooms and a sitting room. Five rooms share baths.

Breakfast: Continental breakfast includes juice, homemade muffins, and coffee or tea. A full breakfast can be purchased in the inn's restaurant.

Extras: The full-service restaurant is open June 15 through September 15, and features Cape Cod's fresh seafoods, seasonal vegetables, homemade breads and muffins, and New England wines. The innkeepers can also arrange bicycle rentals for $8 a day.

Rates: June 15 through September 15: from $32 to $55. Off season: from $29 to $45. Cots, $10. Personal checks and major credit cards accepted.

10% discount to OHJ members.

MASSACHUSETTS: CAPE COD

EAST ORLEANS

THE PARSONAGE
Chris and Lloyd Shand
202 Main Street
East Orleans, MA 02643
(617) 255-8217
Year-round

1770 Cape Cod

LOCATION: The inn is at the "elbow" of Cape Cod, on a street lined with old New England homes, and is accessible to the Atlantic Ocean, Cape Cod Bay, and several freshwater lakes. Charter boat fishing, whale watching, biking on the Cape Cod Rail Trail, and antiquing are popular activities in the area. Fine restaurants, art galleries, and the Academy Playhouse are minutes away in the town of Orleans.

This inn takes its name from its former life as a parsonage, from 1840 to 1881. The inn could just as well be known as The Cobbler's—there's a depression in one upstairs floor where the cobbler who lived there at the turn of this century kept his bench.

The proprietors say their inn's most interesting architectural features are the wavy-glass window panes, the centuries-old plaster, and the traditional Cape Cod wooden fence decorated with handcarved acorns.

In the traditionally unpretentious Cape Cod style, the interior is decorated with colonial-style furnishings, antique quilts, stencilling, and simple floor coverings and lighting.

Restrictions: No pets. Check-in after 1 p.m.; check-out at 11 a.m.
Beds: Three double-bedded rooms, one with a double and a single bed, one with a queen-sized bed, and one efficiency apartment with a queen-sized bed, a sitting area, and a kitchenette. Two rooms have shared bath.
Breakfast: Continental breakfast includes freshly baked goods, fresh fruit, juice, and coffee or tea, served in the courtyard or guest rooms.
Rates: May to October: from $44 for double with shared bath to $55 for efficiency apartment. Off-season: less $10 per room. Cots, $6. Personal checks and credit cards accepted.
   10% discount to OHJ members.
Mailing Address: PO Box 1016, East Orleans, MA 02643

EASTHAM

THE OVER LOOK INN
Ian and Nan Aitchison
Route 6
Eastham, MA 02642
(617) 255-1886
March through December

1850 Queen Anne/Victorian

LOCATION: The Salt Pond Visitor's Centre of the National Seashore is directly across from the inn's one-and-a-half acres of landscaped gardens, in the Cape's oldest town. Nearby are excellent beaches, wildlife trails, and "the Cape Cod Bike Path is at our back door."

Ian and Nan Aitchison moved here because the Cape reminds them of Scotland, their original home. They bought this house because, beneath layers of 1950s congoleum, encrusted brown paint, and harsh floral wallpaper, "we could tell it had potential," Nan says. Their restoration project was a family endeavor: Both sons are artists, and delighted in helping out with everything from stripping peeling layers of wallpaper to selecting authentic color schemes. Right now, they're restoring a 17th-century barn in the backyard, which they'll use as an artists' studio.

The house is elegant, yet not overly ostentatious. Its exterior is pale yellow, with a bay window, delicately turned porch millwork, and wide picture windows (unusual for its era) that look out over 150-year-old oak trees the Captain brought back from Africa. Inside, much of the woodwork is mahogany, also a souvenir from the Captain's voyages to Africa. Ian and Nan have decorated every room Victorian style, with period antiques, wicker, lace curtains, and duvets. They've hung Andrew Wyeth prints in the dining room and Japanese prints in the parlor. Even the bathrooms are authentic, with clawfoot tubs and polished brass hardware. (The Aitchisons didn't add private guest baths—they felt these would've intruded on the house's architectural integrity.)

Restrictions: No children under 12, no pets, and smoking is only permitted in the library.
Beds: Eight rooms, all with private baths.

Breakfast: Full: juice, fruit, cereal, "Kedgeree" or other Scottish breakfast dishes, muffins, and coffee.

Extras: Afternoon tea is served in the parlor.

Rates: $60 to $80. Personal checks and credit cards accepted.

EDGARTOWN

THE CHARLOTTE INN
Gery and Paula Conover
South Summer Street
Edgartown, MA 02539
(617) 627-4751
Year-round

C. 1860 Italianate

LOCATION: The inn is in a cozy garden, surrounded by brick paths, flowerbeds, lawns, and latticework, on shady South Summer Street. On the grounds is a carriage house, and across the street stands the 1705 Garden House, also part of the inn.

Captain Samuel Osborne made his fortune chasing down great whales and selling their booty to Edgartown's thriving whale-oil refinery. From his profits resulted this elegantly embellished, white clapboarded Victorian, with its finialled cupola, arched shutters, paired roof brackets, and bow-windowed conservatory.

The house was home to Osborne and his family, and later to his daughter Charlotte, who opened it to overnight guests in 1920. Today, the hosts are Gery and Paula Conover. They've decorated the excellently preserved house with deep-hued wallpapers, their personal collection of English and French antiques, and a gallery of original paintings and engravings. Gardeners at heart, they've landscaped the grounds English-style, with trellises, vines, shrubberies, and a delightful array of colorful flowers.

Restrictions: No children under 14. Check-out at 11 a.m.; check-in after 1 p.m.

Beds: Of the 24 rooms—eight in the main house, three in the carriage house, six in the 1705 house, and seven in the summer house—22 have private baths.

Breakfast: Continental: homemade rolls, muffins, fresh squeezed orange juice, and coffee/tea.

Extras: The inn's Chez Pierre restaurant combines classical French cuisine with a "crisp and spontaneous style."

Rates: June 7 through October 19: from $100 to $325. Off-season: October 20 through May 9, $48 to $225. Personal checks and credit cards welcome.

FALMOUTH

GLADSTONE INN
Gayle and Jim Carroll
219 Grand Avenue South
Falmouth, MA 02540
(617) 548-9851
May 15 through October 15

1899 Shingle Style

LOCATION: In a quaint Cape Cod town, the Inn overlooks the ocean and Martha's Vineyard.

There's a beautiful set of French doors leading out from the dining room of this peaceful inn. But the doors weren't there when innkeepers Gayle and Jim Carroll moved in in 1970. They'd been walled over in an earlier remuddling. Gayle and Jim ran across the doors accidentally, when they were taking down some sheetrock—the doors were behind it, with curtains still intact.

The Carrolls love telling this and other restoration stories to fellow old-house lovers. They collect antiques, too, and will tell you all about their clock collection. They can also direct you to the area's best, least expensive antique shops.

Restrictions: No children.
Beds: Of the 15 rooms, six have double beds; two have a double and

a single. Five have twin beds and two are singles.

Breakfast: Full: juice, cereals, muffins, quiches, or fluffy casserole. Fresh fruit platter (varies daily) with blueberry cakes or waffles; home-made jams.

Extras: Bikes are available for use on the bike path. Discount tickets can be obtained for the boat to Martha's Vineyard. There are bar-beque grills in the backyard, and the hosts serve happy-hour snacks.

Rates: From $20 for a single to $34 for a double and a single. Personal checks and cash welcome.

10% discount to OHJ members.

NANTUCKET

1834 Greek Revival

FOUR CHIMNEYS
Elizabeth York Gaeta
38 Orange Street
Nantucket, MA 02554
(617) 228-1912
Late April to early December

LOCATION: In Nantucket Island's historic district, the inn is a short walk from the wharves and the cobblestoned Main Street.

This old inn comes complete with ghost. The innkeepers say they've heard her delicate footsteps in the house late at night. But she hasn't hurt anyone, yet...

The mansion was built by a sea captain in 1834 and converted to a guest house called "Bay View" in 1856. The present-day innkeepers say they've tried to recapture the flavor of Nantucket in that year, when the Island thrived on whale oil and trade with China, and Bay View's motto was "No pains will be spared to insure the comforts of its patrons."

The innkeepers have restored the inn's elegant double parlor (the largest on Nantucket) and winding front stairway. They've scattered Chinese rugs and porcelains throughout the house, (recalling the Island's hey-day as home base for the China Clippers). They've furnished six of the original bedrooms with canopied beds and restored their fireplaces to working order.

Restrictions: No children under 16. No pets. Check-in after 1 p.m.
Beds: All 10 rooms have private baths and a double or queen size bed. Almost all beds have canopies.
Breakfast: Continental.
Extras: There's a concierge service; drinks and cocktail snacks are served at 5 p.m.
Rates: From $90 for a room with a double bed and private bath to $145 for a room with a fireplace, queen-size canopy bed, private bath, harbor view, and secluded porch. Personal checks and credit cards welcome.

MASSACHUSETTS: CAPE COD

NANTUCKET

JARED COFFIN HOUSE
Philip and Margaret Read
29 Broad Street
Nantucket, MA 02554
(617) 228-2405
Year-round

1845 Greek Revival

LOCATION: In the heart of Nantucket's old historic district, the inn is a short walk from Main Street's shops and Steamboat Wharf.

This inn has housed guests, including historic figures like President Grant, since 1847. Oil merchant Jared Coffin financed the inn's first building in 1845. Coffin wanted his imposing brick, slate-roofed residence to outdo the stately mansions of Nantucket's other wealthy whale-oil merchants — his home was Nantucket's first three-storey building.

The private home was converted to a hotel in 1847, when Coffin moved to Boston and sold it to the Nantucket Steamboat Company. In 1961, the Nantucket Historical Trust purchased and completely restored the Coffin House. Since then, the inn's owners have restored several nearby historic buildings, increasing the inn's size to 58 rooms.

Restrictions: Check-in anytime. Check-out at 11 a.m. Limited accommodations for children in same room.

Beds: There are single, double, and twin rooms among the 58 total. Many have canopy beds. All have private baths.

Breakfast: Not included in room rate April through December; however, breakfast can be purchased in Jared's Restaurant May through October and on holidays and weekends during November and December.

Extras: Jared's Restaurant, open May through October and on weekends and holidays during November and December, features traditional regional specialties. The Tap Room, open year-round, offers lunch and informal dinners, and features live entertainment nightly all year, and patio dining when weather permits.

Rates: April to December: from $85 for double or twin to $125 for queen, double, or twin with canopy. January to March: 20% discount. Cribs available for $5. Personal checks and credit cards accepted.

OSTERVILLE

OSTERVILLE FAIRWAYS INN
**Bob and Katie Sulzman
105 Parker Road
Osterville, MA 02655
(617) 428-2747
Year-round**

LOCATION: The inn, at the edge of a golf course overlooking Cape Cod Bay, is a short walk from the village center, restaurants, tennis, and boating.

The Cayers say the ghost of this house's original owner, a grizzled sea captain, watches over guests in one particular room. But never fear: The ghost commits minor mischief, but he's also friendly. And he's used to having guests in his home, because the building has always been an inn. The owners believe it may be Cape Cod's oldest continuously operated B&B.

The inn's architecture is simple, in the style typical of Cape Cod. The rooms are furnished with comfortable antiques. A gallery of paintings by the owners and other local artists adds color to the walls.

Restrictions: Check-in after 2 p.m.; check-out at 11 a.m.

Beds: Fifteen rooms, some with twin and some with double beds, all have private baths. One room, the Carriage House, sleeps six and has a fireplace and full kitchen.

Breakfast: Continental breakfast of homemade muffins, juice, and coffee or tea.

Extras: Babysitting and rides to the beach can be arranged. The owners will let you use their bikes free.

Rates: June 15 to September 15: from $53 (for a double room) to $79 (for the Carriage House, which sleeps six). Other times: from $29 to $65. Cots, $9; cribs, $6. Personal checks and credit cards accepted.

10% discount to OHJ members.

MASSACHUSETTS: CAPE COD

PROVINCETOWN

LAND'S END INN
David Schoolman
22 Commercial Street
Provincetown, MA 02657
(617) 487-0706
Year-round

1910 Shingle Style

LOCATION: Perched atop Gull Hill at the very end of Cape Cod, the inn commands a panoramic view of the Cape, the bay, and Provincetown harbor. One mile away is Cape Cod National Seashore, and nearby are beaches and Provincetown's shops, galleries, and restaurants.

This house was conceived of as a dream. It was to be an escape from the fast-paced city life, a place where one could untangle one's nerves and rediscover life's joys. When Boston merchant Charles Higgins built Land's End in 1910, the dream became a reality.

Higgins was a devotee of the Art Nouveau movement, and his love for this era is evident in the inn today. Still displayed in Land's End is his huge collection of art glass, pottery, and Oriental wood carvings. Also remaining are the home's interior beamed ceilings, wide stone hearth, and Oriental-influenced tower — once Higgins' library and now a luxurious guest room.

Restrictions: No pets. Parents are discouraged from bringing children under ten.
Beds: The 15 rooms range from singles and doubles with private or shared baths, to rooms which sleep five, to apartments with kitchenettes.
Breakfast: Continental breakfast of toast and coffee; juice can be purchased.
Rates: $333 to $592, weekly rates. Off-season rates, $49 to $83. Cots, $10. Personal checks welcome.

MASSACHUSETTS: CAPE COD

PROVINCETOWN

**ROSE AND CROWN
GUEST HOUSE**
Preston Babbitt, Jr.
158 Commercial Street
Provincetown, MA 02657
(617) 487-3332
Year-round

1787 Georgian "Square Rigger"

LOCATION: In the heart of Provincetown, where the Pilgrims first landed, the inn is a short walk from the Pilgrim Museum and Monument as well as many historic houses.

Owners Preston Babbitt and Tom Nascembeni had had enough of their pressured lives; they decided to make a break for peaceful Provincetown and open an inn. So they named the place after the 16th-century haven where Queen Elizabeth I, similarly, escaped from the stresses of *her* job.

Somebody in the 19th century tried to make this simple Georgian into a Queen Anne, by pasting courses and triangles of decorative shingles all over the facade. The attempt failed — the structure's straightforward design is still evident under the "frosting," and inside you can even see the exposed beams and posts of the 1787 frame.

The house is full of collectibles, to the point where one delighted guest commented, "It's more like an antique shop than a guest house."

Beds: Three rooms with double, queen-size, or twin beds have private baths; three other rooms (a single, double, and triple) share one bath. There's also an apartment with a sleeping loft, convertible sofa, and kitchenette, and a cottage with similar facilities.

Breakfast: Continental breakfast includes homemade bread or muffins, fruit, and coffee or tea.

Rates: Memorial Day weekend to mid-September and on holiday weekends: from $30 for a single with shared bath to $80 for the cottage. Off-season rates are lower. Personal checks may be used only for advance payments; no credit cards accepted, cash and traveler's checks welcome.

MASSACHUSETTS: CAPE COD

VINEYARD HAVEN

THORNCROFT INN
Karl and Lynn Buder
278 Main Street
Vineyard Haven, MA 02568
(617) 693-3333
Year-round

1918 Craftsman Bungalow

LOCATION: On a lush, three-and-a-half acre estate on Martha's Vineyard, the inn is one mile from the main ferry dock, and just beyond the village of Vineyard Haven.

The inn was known for years as the "little house"—even though it has ten large bedrooms and numerous baths. That's because it was built by Chicago merchant Herbert Ware as a wedding gift for his young son, and the elder Ware's house across the way dwarfs even this immense property.

The Ware family owned the house until 1964, when it was converted to a rest home. The Wares are still around to keep a watchful eye on it. The grandson and great-granddaughter of the original occupant recently visited and expressed delight at the work innkeepers Karl and Lynn Buder have put in. That work has included furnishing each room with antiques from a different period: Styles range from Colonial to Eastlake to Renaissance Revival. The Buders also added six architecturally appropriate bathrooms.

Restrictions: Children over 12 only. No pets allowed. Smoking limited to two rooms only. Check-in after 2 p.m. Check-out at 10 a.m.

Beds: Ten rooms: six have double beds, three have queen beds, and one has twin beds.

Breakfast: The Buders offer a seven-day menu which includes blueberry pancakes and bacon; croissant and omelette sandwich; spinach sausage and cheese pie; almond French toast; quiche lorraine; crustless zucchini and cheese quiche; strawberry pancakes.

Extras: "All the advice on touring and dining any tourist could want (and probably more!). Free of charge, of course!"

Rates: From $135 for a room with a private bath, entrance, and porch (non-smoking) to $95 for a room with private bath (smoking allowed). Personal checks and credit cards accepted.

Mailing Address: Box 1022, Vineyard Haven, MA 02568

VINEYARD HAVEN

THE LOTHROP MERRY HOUSE
John and Mary Clarke
Owen Park
Vineyard Haven, MA 02568
(617) 693-1646
Year-round

1780s Colonial

LOCATION: The inn overlooks Vineyard Haven Harbor, with its own beachfront and a lovely view of the sailboats; the building is a short walk from the ferry dock.

"We feel that anyone who loves old houses will be enchanted by the Merry House (as we were when we first saw it). It is a charming house and we and our many guests who return year after year enjoy it and the lovely setting."

Legend has it that eight yoke of oxen moved the Lothrop Merry House to its present site from a location two miles away. The relocated house was a wedding gift from a loving father to his daughter, say owners John and Mary Clarke.

The Clarkes bought this house in 1980, at which time they restored the home's original 12-over-12 windows (which had been replaced with 6-over-6 panels), stripped the floors, and reshingled part of the exterior. They've furnished the interior with antiques, and decorated the walls with original watercolors by 19th-century Boston portraitist Charles Hopkinson. Six fireplaces, each connected to the large central chimney, warm the house on chilly evenings.

Restrictions: No pets. Children welcome.
Beds: Seven rooms. Four double bedrooms have fireplaces and private baths; one of these has an extra bed. Three double bedrooms have shared baths; two of these have extra beds.
Breakfast: Continental: homemade breakfast breads, fruit juices, coffee, tea, and herb teas, served on outdoor patio overlooking ocean during summer.
Extras: Friendship sloop "Irene" takes up to six passengers for daily or overnight cruises among the Vineyard's coves and harbors. The inn also rent sailboats and skiffs to guests. Babysitting can often be arranged.
Rates: May 10 to October 19: from $60 for double with shared bath to $92 for double with private bath, fireplace, and canopied bed. October 20 to May 9: from $38 to $68. Payment by traveler's checks or credit cards.
10% discount to OHJ members.
Mailing Address: Box 1939, Vineyard Haven, MA 02568

MASSACHUSETTS: CAPE COD

WEST BARNSTABLE

HONEYSUCKLE HILL
Bob and Barbara Rosenthal
591 Main Street
West Barnstable, MA 02668
(617) 362-8418
Year-round

1850 Greek Revival farmhouse, with many later additions

LOCATION: The inn is situated in a quiet village on Old King's Highway, in Cape Cod's historic district, convenient to Hyannis and Sandy Neck Beach.

This house was owned by the same family for four generations! Each generation left its stamp on the Greek Revival farmhouse, adding new wings, bay windows, curving hallways, a screened-in porch, and Victorian decor.

Restrictions: No pets or children under ten. Check-in between 2 and 9 p.m.; check-out at 11 a.m.

Beds: Two rooms with queen-size beds and a third with a king-size bed or two twin beds. All have private baths. The master suite has a fireplace and a chintz-curtained alcove for the bed. Other rooms have stenciled floors.

Breakfast: Summer breakfast is continental, with fresh juice, fruit, homemade breads or muffins, and coffee. In the off-season, waffles, eggs, or pancakes are added to the breakfast menu. Year-round, it's served 8 to 9 a.m.

Extras: Afternoon tea is served, and a complimentary half-bottle of wine, fresh flowers, and down comforters in the guest rooms are provided. Guests can use the inn's tandem bike.

Rates: Memorial Day to Labor Day: from $60 to $75 (for the master suite with fireplace). Off-season: from $50 to $65. Personal checks, VISA, and Mastercard accepted.

10% discount to OHJ members.

MASSACHUSETTS: CAPE COD

WEST FALMOUTH

THE ELMS
Betty and Joe Mazzucchelli
495 West Falmouth Highway
West Falmouth, MA 02574
(617) 540-7232
Year-round

LOCATION: The inn is located in historic West Falmouth Village, near beaches and the Woods Hole Oceanographic Institute.

"The Elms" is an inn that has clung to traditions throughout its history. The original owner of the older building, Lydia Dillingham, was the last Quaker in the U.S. to wear the sect's customary black costume. As early as the 1800s, the tiny 1739 Colonial was called "ye olde homestead." That structure's lines, despite the larger 1850 structure that covers them, are still visible. The newer building was built with lumber taken from a local salt works, and used as an inn from the start, though more recently it became a private residence. It had already been restored by the time the Mazzucchellis bought it.

A mid-19th-century style prevails in the interior, especially on the design of the fireplaces. The Mazzucchellis have added to the atmosphere by filling the place with plants and antiques.

Restrictions: No children under 12. No pets. Check-in after 1 p.m.
Beds: Seven double-bedded rooms and two more with twin beds. Six rooms have private baths; two guest rooms share a bath; the last room shares a bath with the owners.
Breakfast: Full breakfast includes homemade breads and muffins, fresh fruit and juices, eggs Benedict, bananas Foster, crepes, or "the chef's whimsy."
Extras: Sherry is served in the parlor in the afternoon. Beach passes are available for nominal charge.
Rates: From $55 to $60. Personal checks accepted; no credit cards.

MASSACHUSETTS: CAPE COD

WEST HARWICH

LION'S HEAD INN
Bill and Kathleen Lockyear
186 Belmont Road
West Harwich, MA 02671
(617) 432-7766
Year-round

1805 Half-Cape, greatly expanded over the years

LOCATION: On a quiet residential street, a half-mile from Nantucket Sound, the inn is near beaches, Cranberry golf course, summer theater, shops, and restaurants.

Bill and Kathleen Lockyear are thoroughly conversant in the history of their inn. They love sitting by the fireside with guests, telling tales of the home's former occupants.

And there are many tales to tell. The inn is an architectural conversation piece, with its additions from many historic periods. The original stairs, horsehair plaster, wide pine floors, and root cellar remain in the Half-Cape part of the house, built by sea captain Thomas Snow. Later owners added ells at interesting angles, an eight-foot-deep porch which wraps around one of the inn's numerous corners, and a widow's walk.

The house recently underwent a detailed restoration of the exterior clapboards, wooden gutters, and porch. The interior is decorated with period antiques.

Restrictions: No children under 12 in inn (any age allowed in cottages). No pets. Check-in after 2 p.m.
Beds: Captain Snow Suite: three-room suite with bath. Rose Room: double bed, shared bath. Map Room: once Captain Snow's study; two twins, shared bath, plenty of old maps. Morning Room: double bed, sitting area, bath. Two guest cottages with kitchens can be rented on a weekly basis.
Breakfast: Hearty country breakfast: fresh local eggs, home-baked breads or muffins, bacon or sausage, fresh fruit, and juice.
Extras: Complimentary wine or sherry are served in front of the fireplace between 5 and 6 p.m. Croquet can be played in the orchard. Babysitting is available with advance notice.
Rates: From $72 for the Captain Snow Suite to $64 for the Rose or $70 single to $80 double. Personal and traveler's checks accepted.
Mailing Address: PO Box 444, West Harwich, MA 02671

BOSTON

THE LITTLE STONE HOUSE

Maria Paul-Welling
27 Harvard Square
Boston, MA 02129
(617) 242-1799
Year-round

LOCATION: Town Hill, still lit by gas lamps, is within an easy walk of museums, the Bunker Hill monument, and the U.S.S. Constitution. Quincy Market, Paul Revere's home, the Old State House, and the shops, restaurants, and attractions of downtown are nearby. The house overlooks a small, peaceful park dedicated to John Harvard.

This is the oldest house in a very old settlement; the neighborhood dates back to 1630! The builder, General Nathaniel Austin, was a politician-publisher who served as state senator and founded Charlestown's first newspaper. The materials for his house, including granite and bluestone for the 16-inch-thick walls, were quarried on an island he owned in Boston Harbor.

Ask Ms. Paul-Welling, who spent five years restoring the place, to show you the original walls in the kitchen and the oyster-shell mica in the mortar (a technique forbidden in 1812). Hers is one of only two remaining stone houses left in Charlestown, so it's a favorite stop on guided tours. She also has a particular fondness for decorative painting, and the house is filled with marbleizing, graining, stencilling, and spatter finishes — "it's an on-going project." Each room has a fireplace, pumpkin-pine floors, and cheery painted woodwork.

Restrictions: No smoking or pets. Unable to accommodate small children due to steep staircase. Flexible mid-day check-out.
Beds: The one guest room has a double bed and private bath.
Breakfast: Homemade muffins and tea breads, choice of fruits, juices, toast, croissants, plus "the usual breakfast beverages."
Extras: There's a roof deck as well as a fenced patio (for bikes); a color TV can be requested. Seasonal late afternoon refreshments, and, when available, restaurant discounts and museum passes are

offered.
Rates: $70 single to $80 double.
Mailing Address: PO Box 448, Boston, MA 0212

NEWBURYPORT

ESSEX STREET INN
Joseph F. Pearson III
7 Essex Street
Newburyport, MA 01950
(617) 465-3148
Year-round

1880 Vernacular

LOCATION: In the center of historic downtown Newburyport, the inn is just steps away from gracious dining and fine shops. "A short distance away is the ocean and Plum Island, with the exquisite natural beauty of the Parker River Wildlife Reserve."

Down in the cellar of the Essex Street Inn are a some large water cisterns, all that remain of an 1811 horse stable that once stood here. Two Victorian-era real-estate developers, who earned a pretty penny from their many rental properties in town, razed the stable to make way for this house. They built it as a duplex: One half they rented out to a family, the other to bachelors and less permanent boarders, including a sailmaker and bookbinder.

Today, the inn looks as it did when it was built: Two bay windows and bracketed overhangs above the doorways adorn its otherwise simple, clapboarded structure. The inn is furnished with antiques and a large collection of handmade quilts.

Restrictions: Check-in after 2 p.m. Check-out at 11 a.m. No pets.
Beds: Ten rooms with double beds; four rooms with two beds; three suites with queen beds.
Breakfast: Continental breakfast, $3 extra per person.
Rates: $69 to $150. Personal checks, credit cards, and traveler's checks accepted.

NEWBURYPORT

THE WINDSOR HOUSE
Judith Crumb
38 Federal Street
Newburyport, MA 01950
(617) 462-3778
Year-round

1787 Georgian

LOCATION: The inn is located at the south end of Newburyport, two blocks from downtown shopping and fine restaurants. Plum Island and the Parker River Wildlife Refuge are five minutes away, and it's ten minutes to New Hampshire; 45 minutes to Boston.

When clippers and frigates stopped sweeping into Newburyport's harbor, the ship's chandlery that supplied them became obsolete. That section of Windsor House has been converted into a large eat-in kitchen as well as a guest room—appropriately named "Chandler's Suite."

Constructed for his bride by Aaron Pardee, a lieutenant in George Washington's army, the brick structure eventually passed to Pardee's daughter. She was the only surviving child of nine. Her descendants continued to hold the property until the Crumbs purchased it in 1978. The house was never allowed to deteriorate, they report.

The off-street main entrance leads to the largest continuous staircase in Newburyport. Behind the sleigh beds and four-posters can be seen moulding carved with acorn patterns.

Restrictions: "Small pets allowed. If you must smoke, we have ash trays."
Beds: Six rooms: three with private baths (one double, one double and twin, one with two twins), three with shared baths (two double, one with two twins).
Breakfast: "A hearty New England breakfast": coffee, tea, juice, fresh or stewed fruit and cream, sweet bread, eggs or hotcakes, and home-made beef and/or pork sausage—"our own herbs used generously."
Extras: Beach access is free; and "we can find a babysitter for you."
Rates: $72 to $79; $67 to $72, November to April. Personal checks, traveler's checks, and credit cards accepted.

ROCKPORT

THE INN ON COVE HILL
John and Marjorie Pratt
37 Mount Pleasant Street
Rockport, MA 01966
(617) 546-2701
February through October

1791 Federal

LOCATION: The inn is located in a historic New England seaport town, and there's a panoramic view of the dramatic, rocky coastline and the open Atlantic from their third-floor porch. The town's architecture varies from simple 1690s Colonials and 1700s Federal homes, to curious granite structures built when Rockport was a quarry town, to Victorian summer houses. Area activities include whale-watching, biking, and cross-country skiing in the nearby forest.

"It would be a great pleasure to have guests who appreciate the 200-year-old craftsmanship in this fine old home."

According to legend, this home's original owner got the money to build his house from a pirate's treasure trove. Back in 1791, Caleb Norwood was relaxing behind some rocks at a beach near Rockport when a boat pulled in and a bunch of thieves hopped out to bury their hoard. Clever Caleb kept quiet until the coast was clear, and then, whooping and hollering, he unearthed the gold. Presto! The Inn on Cove Hill was born.

The Inn's present owners say they uncover a new treasure in the house each year—in the form of architectural details buried under a series of 1950s remuddlings. Stripping away battleship-gray paint from floors and doors, they found random-width, pumpkin pine flooring and hand-wrought iron hinges. Peeling off acoustical tiles, they revealed 200-year-old horsehair plaster still intact. The best treasure of all is the front hall's spiral staircase with its 13 steps—one to commemorate each of the original colonies. The Pratts have restored one room a year since they moved in, and after seven years they've finally reached the third floor. Says John Pratt, "Marvels of early craftsmanship are still to be discovered!"

The Inn is furnished with colonial antiques and decorated with paintings done by local artists.

Restrictions: No pets. No children under ten.

Beds: Among the 11 rooms are six doubles, two queens, one with two twins, and two with a double and a twin. Three rooms share baths. Most of the rooms have antique beds in varying styles, including a queen-size canopy bed, a Shaker bed, and an 18th-century cannonball bed.

Breakfast: Continental: juice, hot beverage, and hot freshly baked muffins, brought to you on Wedgwood or Royal Doulton English bone china. Served in bed or at an umbrella table in the garden.

Rates: $29 to $57, lower from February to Memorial Day. Personal checks and cash accepted.

10% discount to OHJ members (weekdays, February through May)

MASSACHUSETTS: NORTH SHORE

ROCKPORT

THE SEAFARER
Mary and Gerry Pepin
86 Marmion Way
Rockport, MA 01966
(617) 546-6248
April 15 through October

1893 Dutch Colonial Revival

LOCATION: In 1679, England's Dorchester Company was so impressed by the beauty of this coastal site that they decided to call it home. Three centuries later, Walt Disney named Rockport harbor one of the country's ten most scenic places. The inn overlooks the ocean and is within walking distance of beaches, woods, and the center of Rockport. Whale watching, fishing, boat racing, nature walks, island tours, road racing, golf, tennis, and art-gallery touring in the area.

This inn took its first visitors, who came to escape the hustle and bustle of the city for the serenity of the sea, in 1900. Since then, the inn has housed visitors from Europe, the Far East, Africa, India, Tasmania, the Soviet Union, South America, Canada, and all parts of the U.S.

The Seafarer's large, airy rooms are furnished with antiques and ship paraphernalia, in the manner of a sea captain's home. The walls are decorated with original oil paintings done by area artists. Coffee is served on the old-fashioned, covered porch, which overlooks the sea.

The Pepins bought the Seafarer from a long line of innkeepers in 1975. Their main restoration project was refinishing the interior woodwork.

Restrictions: No pets. Inquire about bringing children, as most guests are adults.
Beds: Nine rooms, all but one with private bath. All have ocean view; two with kitchenettes and dining nooks can be rented on a weekly basis.
Breakfast: Continental: coffee, juice, and pastry. "A social way to start the day with fellow visitors."
Rates: From $42 to $58 for a room with a spectacular ocean view. Cots, $6. Rates are a bit lower from April 15th to June 14th. Personal checks and cash accepted.

10% discount to OHJ members.

MASSACHUSETTS: NORTH SHORE

SALEM

THE SALEM INN
Diane Pabich and Jeanne Jensen
7 Summer Street
Salem, MA 01970
(617) 741-0680
Year-round

Three 1834 Greek Revival townhouses

LOCATION: The inn is surrounded by the museums, shops, and restaurants of Salem's downtown historic district. One block away is Chestnut Street, an avenue lined with buildings recognized in the National Register. A five-minute walk leads to the waterfront.

When Diane Pabich and Jeanne Jensen first set eyes on this build-ing, it was a men's boarding house inhabited by the local derelicts —complete with cracking plaster, peeling paint, leaky plumbing, and frayed electrical wiring. They bought the place in 1983 and trans-formed it to an elegant inn.

Guest rooms in two of the townhouses which make up the Inn are decorated in their original Early American style: period furnishings (many salvaged from the building), fireplaces, and Indian shutters. The rooms in the third house were gutted in 1925 and converted to efficiency apartments—they're now decorated in Victorian style.

Diane and Jeanne are conversant in the Inn's history, for anyone who's interested. For starters: Two of the townhouses were built by Revolutionary War veterans. One was inhabited for a time by Salem's 14th mayor, a man who was later elected to Congress.

Restrictions: Check-in after 3 p.m. Check-out at 11 a.m.

Beds: Of the 23 rooms, three have queen-size beds. Eight have king-size (or twin) beds. Seven rooms have king-size (or twin) beds and kitchenettes. Five suites are available with bedroom, living room, and bath. There are no shared baths.

Breakfast: Continental: coffee, juice, and pastry. They'll serve a full breakfast "as soon as their dining room is finished."

Extras: The secluded brick courtyard and garden offer a serene setting not often found in a city environment.

Rates: From $55 for a double room with a private bath to $70 for a two-room suite with kitchenette. Cots, $7; cribs at no charge. Personal checks and credit cards welcome.

10% discount to OHJ members from November 1 through April 30.

MICHIGAN

HOLLAND

OLD WING INN
Chuck and Chris Lorenz
5298 East 147th Avenue
Holland, MI 49423
(616) 392-7362
Year-round

1844-46 Vernacular with Greek Revival details

LOCATION: The inn sits on two wooded acres, surrounded by fields, in a rural, agricultural area.

Old Wing, named after an early convert, was originally a Congregational mission. Ten Ottawa Indians helped Isaac Fairbanks raise the six 13-foot corner posts and side beams that support the house. (The beams and stringers can still be seen in the root cellar beneath the house.) Fairbanks, a government agricultural agent to the Indians, built the mission for Reverend George N. Smith. After Smith and the Indians moved on, the first Dutch settlers in the area lodged here and in Fairbanks' home, a small cabin near the mission. This event marked the beginning of Holland, Michigan, which was destroyed by fire in 1871. Old Wing, the oldest historic landmark house in the area, is one of three buildings that did not burn in the fire. The mission remained in the Fairbanks family until 1950. Chuck and Chris Lorenz bought the house in 1984. They've furnished it with antiques, and you'll find many old documents, diaries, and books pertaining to the mission. They just got the house listed in the National Register, and have named the rooms after the Smiths' children.

Restrictions: We "prefer children seven or over but have made exceptions." Doghouse and run available for pets. Check-in after 3 p.m., check-out at noon.

Beds: Of the five rooms—four doubles, one with two twins—three share baths.

Breakfast: "Continental plus": fresh fruit and coffee, pastries, orange juice.

Extras: Free sample bottles of wine can be obtained, with the inn's certificates, at a nearby winery.

Rates: $46 on weekdays; $55 on weekends, holidays, or at "tulip time." $40 during off-season. Mastercard and Visa welcome.

10% discount to OHJ members. "You bet!"

LEXINGTON

GOVERNOR'S INN
Bob and Jane MacDonald
7277 Simons
Lexington, MI 48450
(313) 359-5770
Memorial Day to Labor Day

1859 Vernacular with Gothic Revival and Queen Anne details

LOCATION: A quiet, residential area near Lake Huron provides the setting; fresh lake breezes cool every room.

> *"Renovating another old house in Michigan and reading the OHJ gave us both confidence and an appreciation of things old; so we had the nerve to tackle this big old house and restore it to the atmosphere of a turn-of-the-century summer house."*

Charles H. Moore built this Victorian house in 1859 and lived there with his wife and three daughters for many years. His youngest daughter, Mary, married Albert J. Sleeper in 1901, and they eventually inherited the house, and used it as a summer retreat. Albert was elected Governor of Michigan in 1917, hence the current name.

Jane and Bob MacDonald have removed the sheet panelling and suspended ceilings that masked the house's character and returned it to its state at the turn of the century. You'll find lots of wicker, rocking chairs, and iron beds.

Restrictions: "Sorry, no pets." Children over 12 welcome. Check-in after 1 p.m.
Beds: Two doubles and one room with two 3/4 beds all have private baths.
Breakfast: Continental: freshly baked coffeecake, fresh fruit or juice, cereal, milk, coffee or tea.
Extras: "Just intelligent conversation."
Rates: $30 all rooms; cots, $5; personal checks welcome.
   10% discount to OHJ members.

MANISTEE

**E. E. DOUVILLE HOUSE
BED & BREAKFAST**
William C. and Barbara Johnson
111 Pine Street
Manistee, MI 49660
(616) 723-8654
Year-round

1879 Italianate, modified c. 1900

LOCATION: Manistee, on the shore of Lake Michigan, boasts many Victorian buildings in its "Victorian Village." Within walking distance of the inn are a 1903 opera house, an 1892 church with a Tiffany window, plus beaches, breakwaters for fishing, and harbors for boating. Manistee National Forest is also nearby.

"We love to 'show off' and share our home with people; the house, and the whole area, have much appeal to old-house lovers."

Eugene Douville, prominent businessman and former mayor of Manistee, built this Victorian home on the shores of Lake Michigan. The year was 1879, the height of the great lumber era in Michigan, and Douville used lumber from nearby forests. The unusual, ornate woodwork was handcarved by area craftsmen. William and Barbara Johnson, who bought the house in 1978, did all but the rewiring and roofing work by themselves: They scraped six and sometimes ten layers of wallpaper off the walls! They still have a bit of work to do—they'd like to replace the gingerbread that was removed

221

some time ago—but the interior has been completely redecorated. The Johnsons have collected antiques for years; you'll find them throughout the house.

Restrictions: No children under 12, no pets.
Beds: Two doubles and one queen with a love seat share one bath.
Breakfast: Continental.
Extras: Coffee and tea are always available; guests can use the sitting room, TV, refrigerator, and stove. Tours can be arranged of the opera house and historic churches.
Rates: $25 (double) to $35 (queen bed, 16-by-16-foot room). Personal checks accepted.

10% discount to OHJ members.

MARSHALL

THE NATIONAL HOUSE INN
Barbara Bradley
102 South Parkview
Marshall, MI 49068
(616) 781-7374
Year-round except Christmas Eve and Christmas Day

1835 Greek Revival

LOCATION: Marshall, known as "the Williamsburg of the West," features some 1,200 pre-1900 homes, 12 National Register sites, 35 Michigan State Historic Sites, and 15 Historic American Buildings Survey Sites. The inn, on Fountain Circle Park, overlooks the restored downtown.

> *"Why do we like the National House so much? The place has authentic charm. The taste is impeccable. Everything used is top quality. And the people are awfully nice and make us feel at home—we've never been disappointed." Ellie Damm, Sandusky, Ohio*

The National House is not only Michigan's oldest operating inn, but it's the oldest brick structure in Calhoun County. It was built in 1835 by Andrew Mann as a stagecoach stop between Detroit and Chicago. A secret room in the basement indicates that the National House was also a stop on the Underground Railroad. (That room was again used in the 1920s, for the sale and consumption of liquor during Prohibition.) The inn became a windmill and wagon factory for a time, after 1878. The building was later converted into apartments, and finally, in 1976, it was authentically restored. All 16 guest rooms are furnished with antiques.

Restrictions: Smoking allowed, children welcome, no pets. Check-in after 3 p.m., check-out at noon.

Beds: There are 16 rooms in all—nine doubles, four with a twin and double, three with two twins; 14 have private baths, two have private half-baths and share a shower.

Breakfast: Some seven varieties of homebaked goods — hot sticky buns, coffeecake, fruit tarts, breads, muffins, English muffins — as well as applesauce, coffee, teas, juices, fresh fruit in season.

Extras: "Coffee and good conversation are always available." Minges Creek Racquet Club, ten minutes away, can be used by guests at membership rates.

Rates: $50 (shared shower, view of Fountain Circle) to $79 (two-room suite, with bedroom and sitting room). Sundays, $39.95. Cots, $6. Personal checks and credit cards accepted.

MICHIGAN

MECOSTA

BLUE LAKE LODGE
Frank and Elaine Huisgen
9765 Blue Lake Lodge Lane
Mecosta, MI 49332
(616) 972-8391
Year-round

1913 Foursquare

LOCATION: At the north shore of three intersecting lakes—there's excellent swimming—the inn is 65 miles from Grand Rapids, 90 miles from Lansing, and 180 miles from Detroit. "The beach is 50 feet from our door."

A lthough full meals are no longer served at the Blue Lake Lodge, the 75-cent chicken dinner (homemade pie and ice cream included) used to lure tourists from Chicago to this cozy inn. The house, built in 1913 as a fishing hotel, has a cedar-shake roof and a matching gazebo overlooking the lake.

Restrictions: No dogs; well-behaved children welcome; check-in after 1 p.m., check-out at 11 a.m.
Beds: Three doubles and three twins share three baths.
Breakfast: Juice (canned), coffeecake or rolls, and coffee are served in the lounge or, weather permitting, in the gazebo.
Extras: The entire lodge, including the owner's quarters (two kings, one double), can be rented—"nice for family reunions." Horseshoes, fishing and paddle boats are available, as are cooking facilities.
Rates: $30 (double or twins) to $35 (twin and bunks-sleeps three), no charge for cots or cribs. Personal checks and credit cards accepted.
    10% discount to OHJ members.
Mailing Address: Box One, Mecosta, MI 49332

MICHIGAN

MENDON

**THE 1873 MENDON
COUNTRY INN**
Dick and Dolly Buerkley
440 West Main Street
Mendon, MI 49072
(616) 496-8132
Year-round

1873 Italianate

LOCATION: Situated at the point where Little Portage Creek meets the St. Joseph River, the inn has some four acres of rolling fields and woods where guests are welcome to wander. An Amish settlement is nearby, as is a restored grist mill (converted to a private home) and the state's longest covered bridge.

> *"Getting away to our country inn is like staying with a friend of a friend."*

A dams Wakeman rebuilt the Western hotel in 1873 after it burnt to the ground. Not surprisingly, he named the new building after himself. Wakeman House had a number of colorful uses. Travelers by stagecoach, train, and automobile stayed there; some of their initials, carved in the structure's brick surface along with the date, can still be seen. The building was used for storage, as a private home, creamery, bakery, restaurant, and church meeting hall.

Wakeman House sat empty for a year before the Kaisers rescued it. They began with the leaking roof and worked down, stripping stained wallpaper, unbuckling warped floors, replastering walls, replacing windows and frames, installing new plumbing and wiring -- "everything," as Jane puts it. And on top of all the repairs they repainted the interior and repointed the exterior brick.

Restrictions: Children over 12 wlcome. No pets. Check-in after 3 p.m., check-out at 11 a.m.
Beds: Eleven rooms with private baths.
Breakfast: Fresh fruit, assorted pastries, juices, coffee, herbal teas.
Extras: There's no charge for coffee and tea at all times (self-serve), bicycles, badminton, croquet, horseshoes, checkers, etcetera. Canoes rent for $12 each.
Rates: $40 to $72. Personal checks and credit cards welcome.
  10% discount to OHJ members.

MICHIGAN

PETOSKEY

1887 Queen Anne

STAFFORD'S BAY VIEW INN
Stafford C. Smith and Judy C. Honor
613 Woodland Avenue
Petoskey, MI 49770
(616) 347-2771
Year-round

LOCATION: A stand of birches and pine leads from the inn to the nearby bay, where white dunes line the waterfront.

This, the oldest continuously operating resort hotel in northern Michigan, boasts a mansard roof and a Queen Anne turret. It also boasts impressive furniture like a massive mahogany sleigh bed, a cherry cannonball bed, a cabinet from the Governor's Mansion in Vermont and several 100-year-old pieces of wicker. And the hotel even has a miniature iron railroad train, cast in iron to represent the New York Central & Hudson River line. The lobby's recently been redone, but the major restoration work here took place on the outside: The walls and foundation were repaired, and a new full basement dug out of the dirt.

Restrictions: Check-in after 2 p.m., check-out at noon.
Beds: There are 21 rooms, all with private baths.
Breakfast: Full, as selected, from an extensive menu.
Rates: $71 (street view, smaller) to $80 (air-conditioned or bay view, larger). Lower in early summer and late fall. Cots, $22; cribs, free of charge. Personal checks and credit cards welcome.
Mailing Address: PO Box 3, Petoskey, MI 49770

MICHIGAN

PORT SANILAC

RAYMOND HOUSE INN
Shirley Denison
111 South Ridge Street
Port Sanilac, MI 48469
(313) 622-8800
May 1 to September 30

1871 Gothic Revival

LOCATION: The inn's one-plus acre site sits two blocks from the center of Port Sanilac (population 632 in winter). The historic lighthouse still operates. The inn is one block from the Marina, and close to a golf course, museum, and beaches.

Built in 1871 by Uri Raymond, this Victorian home remained in the Raymond family for 112 years. Because the house had been so well taken care of, Shirley Denison had only to update the electricity and plumbing and do some cosmetic work. The sharp peaks of this red brick house are trimmed with contrasting white gingerbread. All the original features remain: classic mouldings, winding staircase, doors, windows — even the antique lighting fixtures! Many of the antiques which furnish the inn belonged to the Raymonds. You'll find the library full of the Raymonds' old books and family portraits. Be sure to ask Shirley about the history of Port Sanilac—she knows lots of local lore, from the steamship era to the bootlegging of the Roaring Twenties.

Restrictions: No smoking, pets, or children under 12. Check-in after 3 p.m., check-out at 11 a.m.
Beds: All six bedrooms have double beds and private baths.
Breakfast: Continental: homemade muffins and nut bread, three fruits (in season), orange juice, coffee or tea.
Extras: There's no charge for using nearby beaches or fishing off the marina. Charter fishing boats — salmon, perch, trout, and whitefish are common — can be arranged, as can horseback riding. Raymond House's bicycles are free for guest's use.
Rates: $45; $10 for cots. Personal checks welcome.
   10% discount to OHJ members.

UNION CITY

**THE VICTORIAN VILLA
GUESTHOUSE**
Ronald Gibson
601 North Broadway Street
Union City, MI 49094
(517) 741-7383
February 1 to December 31

1876 Tuscan Villa

LOCATION: The quaint, river village, c. 1840, of Union City offers proximity to 45 antique shops, six Victorian homes open as museums, restaurants, stock theaters, country auctions, plus fishing and summer festivals.

"If you enjoy Victorian-era restorations and like to talk old houses, we're your kind of guest house."

When Ron Gibson purchased this Italianate villa in 1978, it was a nine-unit tenement with public restrooms. He tore out the flourescent lighting, restored the walnut woodwork, researched the original color scheme, and papered the walls with replica wallpaper. Today the house looks much as it did when William Hurd, a "saddle-bag" doctor until he retired to direct the Union City Bank, built it 1876. The house is made of brick and has not only a two-storey stacked bay, but a fourth-storey tower, bracket eaves, and spacious verandahs. Inside there's a three-storey self-supporting staircase, four fireplaces with marble mantels, cast-plaster cornices, crown mouldings, and ceiling medallions. The Villa is completely furnished with antiques. Each bed chamber, as Mr. Gibson calls them, represents a different style: Empire, Rococo, Eastlake, Edwardian, and Renaissance.

Restrictions: No pets, no smoking, no children.
Beds: Four rooms share two baths, the other four have private baths, including the tower room.
Breakfast: "Continental plus": teas and coffee, fruit juice, Amish and European pastries, toasted crumpets; Amish butter and cheeses; homemade jams, fresh Michigan fruit, hard-boiled eggs.
Extras: A Victorian afternoon "tea for two" is available, as are homemade lemonade and iced tea in the summer. Throughout December the inn offers Victorian Christmas weekends—guests help decorate the tree with period ornaments and partake of hot wassail.
Rates: $50 ("High Renaissance" bedchamber) to $75 (tower suite). Personal checks and credit cards accepted.
   10% discount to OHJ members.

MICHIGAN

UNION PIER

THE INN AT UNION PIER
Madeleine and Bill Reinke
9708 Berrien
Union Pier, MI 49129
(616) 469-4700
Year-round

LOCATION: The inn stands just 200 steps from Lake Michigan, seven miles from Warren Woods Forest (downhill and cross-country skiing), seven miles from New Buffalo's Harbor, and near many restaurants. Fishing, biking, and tobogganing are possible. Wineries are also nearby.

The three buildings of the old Karonsky resort were a shambles when the Reinkes bought them in 1983. Built by Polish immigrants in the '20s, they had fallen on hard times. Not only were there holes in the ceilings and roofs, but the place was in a "time warp": it still had its primitive original plumbing and electrical systems, and it had been sitting abandoned for 15 years.

The Reinkes left the exteriors intact; the clapboard siding only needed some repair and a lot of scraping. But the couple gutted the interiors, leaving just the stairs and pine or maple floors, which they stripped and refinished. The original 24 small rooms are now nine expansive ones, decorated in light colors, lace curtains, and country antiques. There's also a "great room," which has a baby grand piano, more antiques, a 24-bulb chandelier and French doors.

Restrictions: No pets.
Beds: 15 rooms, all with private baths.
Breakfast: Full: fresh fruit, muffins, breads, coffee, teas, plus "whatever the chef fancies."
Extras: An outdoor hot tub is available for guests; in winter "the fireplaces are blazing and a warm cup of cocoa's always on the stove."
Rates: $65 to $85 (room with private deck, oversize bath, wet bar). Cots, $10. Personal checks and credit cards accepted.
10% discount to OHJ members.
Mailing Address: PO Box 222, Union Pier, MI 49129

MISSISSIPPI

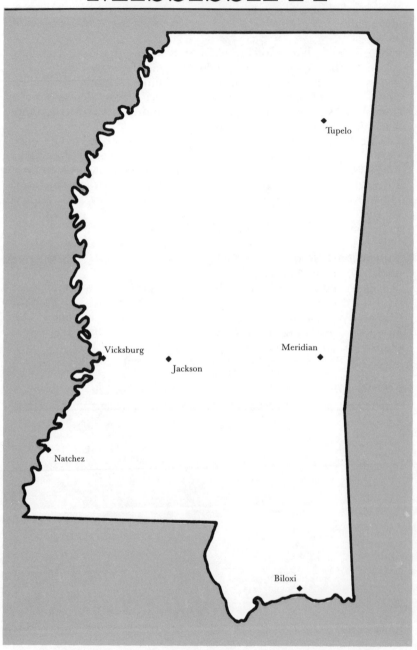

Tupelo

Vicksburg

Meridian

Jackson

Natchez

Biloxi

NATCHEZ

MONMOUTH PLANTATION
Marguerite Guercio
John A. Quitman Parkway
Natchez, MS 39120
(800) 828-4531
Year-round

LOCATION: "We have 26 beautiful acres here." Nearby are many antique shops, fine restaurants, and ante-bellum houses to tour.

Monmouth, named after original owner John Hankinson's hometown of Monmouth, New Jersey, was built in 1818. Hankinson lived in his beautiful Greek Revival home only a short time before he contracted and died of yellow fever. John A. Quitman bought the house in 1826 as a wedding present for his wife, Eliza. Quitman, a congressman, chancellor, governor, and general from Mississippi, received one of six gold swords awarded for valor during the war with Mexico. This gold sword can be seen at Monmouth today, along with other artifacts and furnishings belonging to the Quitmans including their Victorian parlor set and drapes. Mr. and Mrs. Ronald Riches, who bought the house in 1978, have restored it to its original state with the help of partners Mr. and Mrs. Mason Gordon. All the marble mantels are in place, as are the massive cypress doors that were grained to look like oak. The owners also restored the slave quarters, which are open to overnight guests. The house is listed in the National Register.

Restrictions: No pets or children under 12.
Beds: Of the 14 rooms, all with private baths, there's one king, four queens, five doubles, one double with twin, and three rooms with

231

twins.

Breakfast: "Full plantation breakfast."

Extras: At the open bar, guests can mix their own drinks for a nominal fee. All rooms have telephones and TVs.

Rates: $75 (slave quarters) to $135 (main house). Cots are $20. Personal checks and credit cards welcome.

Mailing Address: PO Box 1736, Natchez, MS 39120

MISSISSIPPI

NATCHEZ

PLEASANT HILL
Martha Koon
310 South Pearl Street
Natchez, MS 39120
(601) 442-7674
Year-round

Circa 1835 Greek Revival

LOCATION: The ante-bellum mansions and fall and spring pilgrimages in this area are famous. Natchez, the oldest city on the Mississippi River, offers hunting, fishing, and hiking nearby. The yard around the house is filled with tall trees and tulips that flower in spring.

> *"Not only are the rooms large, period-furnished, neat, and spotless, but the owners are terrific people. They make you feel right at home, they're proud of Natchez and their home, and they know everybody in town!"*
> *Judy and Tom Lee, Glenview, Ill.*

This 18-room Greek Revival, built around 1835, is located in the Natchez Historic District. It was originally owned by John Henderson, a prosperous merchant and book dealer. Martha and Vernon George purchased the house in 1978 and began taking guests in 1982. You'll find the original pocket doors separating the double parlors, black-and-pink marble mantels, and a center-hall staircase that spirals to the third floor. They converted the basement into four bedrooms with private baths, a kitchen, a sitting room, and a garden room. All are furnished with period antiques one guest called "magnificent and tastefully arranged."

Restrictions: Well-behaved children welcome. Smoking permitted. Check-in between noon and 6 p.m.

Beds: Three doubles and one with two twins—none share a bath.

Breakfast: Ham, scrambled eggs, grits, homemade biscuits and preserves—occasionally waffles, bacon, and sausage are also served.

Extras: Guests can swim at the Pilgrimage Garden Club pool nearby. Wine is served, and a film about Natchez can be shown to interested guests.

Rates: $75 to $85; trundles or cribs, $15. Personal checks welcome. 10% discount to OHJ members.

MISSISSIPPI

PORT GIBSON

OAK SQUARE
Mr. and Mrs. William D. Lum
1207 Church Street
Port Gibson, MS 39150
(601) 437-4350
Year-round

C. 1850 Greek Revival

LOCATION: This third oldest town in the state offers "a landmark at every turn"—old homes and churches, old sunken roads; Civil War battlefields, forts, and museums, and the Grand Gulf Military Park. Winder, once one of the South's palatial homes, burned down in 1890 and its ruins remain nearby.

This 1850 Greek Revival is the largest ante-bellum home in Port Gibson, Mississippi, the town General Grant said "was too beautiful to burn" when Union troops passed through on their march to Vicksburg. Originally the home of a cotton planter, the house has six fluted Corinthian columns—each 22 feet tall—supporting the front gallery. The entrance hall has a center stairway with Corinthian columns on the landing. You'll find original pocket doors, ornate millwork, and ceiling medallions throughout the house. The house, which had been remodelled in 1905, was restored by Mr. and Mrs. William

Lum in 1976. They've furnished it with family heirlooms, including 18th- and 19th-century canopied beds. A Confederate sword belonging to Mr. Lum's great-grandfather and other Civil War memorabilia is on display. A courtyard, fountain, and gazebo complement the house.

Restrictions: Kennel nearby for pets, smoking in designated areas. Children welcome.
Beds: Seven rooms: six have canopied doubles, one has antique twins, and all have private baths, television, and air-conditioning.
Breakfast: "Full plantation breakfast": orange juice, in-season fresh fruit, grits, sausage, bacon, cured ham, muffins, homemade biscuits, jelly, preserves, coffee, and tea.
Extras: Wine and cheese are supplied upon arrival.
Rates: $55 to $75; cots $10 to $15, cribs $5 to $10. Personal checks and credit cards welcome.

MISSISSIPPI

VICKSBURG

CHERRY STREET COTTAGE
Don and Betty Barnes
2212 Cherry Street
Vicksburg, MS 39180
(601) 636-7086
Year-round

1925 Vernacular (cottage)

LOCATION: In the surrounding late-Victorian neighborhood, many houses are undergoing restoration. Historic attractions are nearby, and the area is residential and convenient to tennis courts and jogging, walking, and cycling areas.

"We are very proud that we got the (main) house on the National Register. We are trying to restore it as accurately as possible, and will be happy to share our experiences—and the B&B helps support our restoration efforts."

When the Barnes bought the property in 1982, the guest cottage behind the house was a simple garage-turned-apartment. "We completely redid it and made it a lot cuter," says Betty. They added crown moulding and shutters, and planted flowers outside. The circa 1925 structure contains a bedroom, bath, living room and eat-in kitchen, furnished with late-Victorian pieces and turn-of-the-century collectibles.

The 1915 house the Barnes are restoring next door is well worth a visit. A combination of Prairie and Bungalow styles, it features a red-tiled roof with wide eaves and an unusual entry with massive brick piers decorated with stucco. The interior, typical of the early 20th century, winds around wide halls and airy spaces. Its panelled ceilings, colored tiles on the fireplace, walls divided into panels by vertical strips of wood are also typical of the era.

The Barnes say "longevity oozes from the pores of our house." The woman the house was built for is still alive at 100 years of age; the next owner, a bachelor, remained in the house until he died in 1980 at age 103.

Restrictions: "At the risk of sounding tacky, we say only well-behaved children and house-broken pets are welcome." Check-in is flexible.
Beds: The cottage has a bedroom with a double bed and a fold-out sofa in the living room, plus an equipped kitchen and full bath.
Breakfast: An "old South-style" meal: eggs, grits, ham, bacon, sausage, homemade breads, juice, coffee and tea is served in the cottage or on the back porch. Upon request the Barnes will supply the "fixin's" for guests to make their own breakfast.
Rates: $60; $10 for third and/or fourth person, $5 for cribs. Less in winter, November through February. Personal checks and credit cards accepted.

10% discount to OHJ members "with pleasure!"

NEW HAMPSHIRE

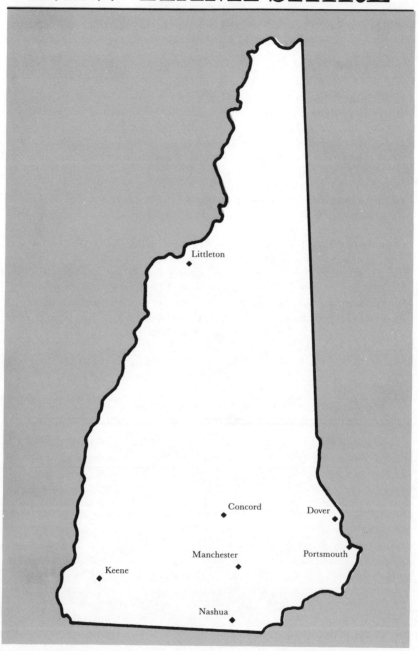

Littleton

Concord   Dover

Manchester   Portsmouth

Keene

Nashua

ANTRIM

THE STEELE HOMESTEAD INN
Barbara and Carl Beehner
Antrim, NH 03440
(603) 588-6772
Year-round

1810 Federal

LOCATION: On four acres of forested countryside, the inn has a landscaped front yard, with flower beds and an expansive lawn, that overlooks a pond. On the property are a stream for fishing and a fruit orchard. Covered bridges, Franklin Pierce homestead, a restored mill town, antique stores, and quaint shopping areas are nearby, as are downhill and cross-country skiing (in winter); water skiing, boating, swimming, and mountain climbing (for warm weather).

Innkeepers Barbara and Carl Beehner recently finished restoring this house. Their immense project involved all the usual old-house horrors: plaster patching, electrical work, plumbing, and massive amounts of paint stripping. Regarding the weeks they spent stripping their ornately carved mantelpiece, the Beehners say "Boy, was that a job!"

One of their more rewarding projects was discovering original Moses Eaton stencilling beneath layers of wallpaper and paint. (The renowned stencil artist actually spent a night in the inn.) Since Barbara and Carl couldn't rescue Eaton's original work (it was too corroded), they hired a local artisan to reproduce the design.

The Beehners say their inn's most outstanding architectural feature is its foundation: It's made of immense, granite boulders. Also, they're fascinated by the home's wooden support beams which are held together by wooden pegs. The Beehners will escort anyone who wants to view these pegs to the attic.

Restrictions: No pets. "Well-behaved children are welcome." Smoking downstairs only. Check-in is normally after 3 p.m. and check-out at noon, but "these hours are flexible."

Beds: Four rooms. The two with private baths have working fireplaces. Two rooms can be combined into a family suite.

Breakfast: A sumptuous, homemade breakfast is served every morning in the dining room, at an hour "voted on by the guests," and includes homemade breads and pastries, meat, an entree ("the cook's choice"), seasonal fruit, juice, and coffee or tea.

Extras: Complimentary wine, juice, or soda and homemade hors d'oeuvres are served in the early evening at a time convenient for guests.

Rates: May 1 to September 2: $42 for room with shared bath; $54 for private bath. Other seasons: $46 to $60. Substantial discounts offered for stays longer than two days. They also have special holiday rates. Personal checks and credit cards accepted.

10% discount to OHJ members except during summer and on holidays.

Mailing Address: RR 1, Box 78, Antrim, NH 03440

BRADFORD

THE BRADFORD INN
Connie Mazol
Main Street
Bradford, NH 03221
(603) 938-5309
Year-round

1898 Dutch Colonial Revival

LOCATION: In this four-season activity area, there's theater, country fairs, outdoor concerts, hay rides, and water sports in summer. In spring and fall are flea markets, auctions, and antique shops.

This inn came into existence at the turn of the century, just before the take-off of the bungalow era, when city dwellers were beginning to appreciate the value of uncluttered nature, and Victorianism was being rapidly outmoded. Two well-known hotel-men caught on with the early tides of the romantic, back-to-nature movement and built the simplistic, nostalgic Colonial Revival out in the woods. Their first guests were Boston writers and artists (like author and actor William Cressy) who were up with the newest trends.

Suiting its inspiration, the three-storey inn has very little exterior ornament: unadorned clapboards (which the current innkeepers recently restored), gently sloping gambrel roof, and wraparound verandah without fancy scrollwork. Inside, the feeling is open and airy, with a wide staircase, wide halls, and two large parlors, one with a fireplace. The current owners have painted and papered the public rooms and guest rooms, and are currently refinishing the woodwork. The Inn is furnished with comfortable, country antiques. A collection of original art and needlework is on display in the public rooms.

Restrictions: Pets welcome with restrictions. Check-in after noon. "Babies and childen welcome."
Beds: There are 12 rooms, all with private baths.
Breakfast: Country breakfast.
Extras: Babysitting can be arranged with advance notice. Dinner and box lunches are available for an extra charge.
Rates: The suites are $72 (for four people). The rooms range in price from $38 (shared bath) to $45 (private bath). Cots, $10; cribs, $5. Personal checks and credit cards accepted.

10% discount to OHJ members.

NEW HAMPSHIRE

CAMPTON VILLAGE

THE CAMPTON INN
Doris Thibeault and Kenneth Martin
Route 175 North
Campton, NH 03223
(603) 726-4449
Year-round

1835 Vernacular with Gothic Revival dormers

LOCATION: Cradled at the foot of the White Mountains lies the Campton Inn. Polar caves, Franconia Notch, skiing facilities, as well as antique shops are nearby; Boston is within some two hours away.

You'll recognize this inn right away by its three steeply pitched gables. The interior is cozy, with wide pine floors, raised hearths, open ceiling beams, and braided rugs. All the furnishings are antique, including one 200-year-old bed and a grandfather clock.

Restrictions: Smoking only in the living and dining rooms. Pets allowed with advance notice.
Beds: The eight rooms range from twin and doubles, to rooms for families or parties of five.
Breakfast: Continental: Choice of eggs or French toast with homemade breads and blueberry buttermilk pancakes; fresh fruit juices; homemade jams and jellies, and coffeecakes.
Extras: The inn offers complimentary passes to Waterville Estates, where guests can use the hot tub, swimming pool, sauna, and tennis courts.
Rates: From $50 to $35, payable with personal checks or Mastercard. 10% discount to OHJ members.

NEW HAMPSHIRE

CENTER OSSIPEE

HITCHING POST VILLAGE INN
Herb and Roberta Lawson
Old Route 16
Center Ossipee, NH 03814
(603) 539-4482
Year-round

1830s Federal

LOCATION: In a quiet town near Whittier and Ossipee Mountains (Mt. Whittier is a 120-million-year-old extinct volcano), the inn is near sporting activities like canoeing, fishing, swimming in lakes, horseback riding, golfing, and downhill and cross-country skiing. There are also plenty of antique shops, country stores, and historic churches in the area.

A century ago, weary wanderers unloaded their trunks from the tops of stagecoaches onto this inn's balcony, to be greeted by New England hospitality and a good night's rest. Of course, the stagecoach balcony has outlived its practical use, since most of the inn's visitors now travel by car. But the balcony is still there for you to see, as are the wide-plank floors, the beamed ceiling, and the inn's original Ben Franklin stove.

Restrictions: No pets. Check-in after noon.
Beds: Eight rooms—all with double beds and some with doubles and twins. All rooms share baths.
Breakfast: Country breakfast of juice, eggs, meat, home-baked goods, coffee or tea, and dessert.
Extras: They serve breakfast in bed. And, there's a full-service restaurant, open for lunch and dinner, right in the inn. The restaurant's specialties are a smorgasbord buffet, homemade soups, steak, and seafood.
Rates: All rooms are $39. Slightly lower rate from January 1 to June 1. Cots and cribs are available at no charge, but there's a $6 fee for extra guests. Mastercard, Visa, and cash welcome.

NEW HAMPSHIRE

EATON CENTER

THE INN AT CRYSTAL LAKE
Walter and Jacqueline Spink
Route 153 at Crystal Lake
Eaton Center, NH 03832
(603) 447-2120
Year-round

C. 1880 Victorian with Greek Revival influences

LOCATION: Amid the scenic White Mountains, the inn overlooks sparkling Crystal Lake.

Nathaniel G. Palmer was a practical Yankee entrepreneur who manufactured ladies' dresses and, with the profits, built this unusual balconied house into the hillside overlooking Crystal Lake.

Never one to miss out on possible gain, he took advantage of the wellspring of city folks who came to Eaton for summer relaxation. He opened his house to guests, and soon it became known as the Palmer House Inn. He also took in one year-round boarder: the city postmaster (and his post office). But in 1937, the Great Depression hit Palmer's inheritors, and the house was transferred out of the family...

When Frank and Mary Gospodarek came across the Palmer Inn in 1975, it was covered in cobwebs. Walls and woodwork were painted pink and blue, its kitchen consisted of one long wooden bench with a few Bunsen burner jets and a lab sink, and there were chalkboards in every bedroom. The house had been used as a school for 20 years (the kitchen was the chemistry lab) until abandoned in 1973.

The Gospodareks were fed up with the high pressure, city-executive life, and were ready to escape to the country. But they asked themselves: Would buying this decrepit house *really* be an escape? "It took lots of imagination to picture the house as it once was or could be," the Gospodareks say. But their imagination proved right. Four intense years of restoration work unmasked an architectural rarity: a Victorian-era split-level, its back half a full storey shorter than its front. Inside, the foyer has a black-and-white marble checkerboard floor and a three-storey, open central stairway.

The Gospodareks have furnished the house with Victorian antiques — lots of marble-topped dressers and tables, oak, wicker, and brass and iron beds. They've converted the attached barn, with its huge granite fireplace, to a guest lounge. On display, they have a collection of "working" antiques which includes a treadle sewing machine, a pump organ, and a Franklin Printing Press.

Restrictions: Children and pets are welcome.
Beds: There are six private rooms and two group rooms. Four private rooms have double beds. The six private rooms share three full baths.
Breakfast: Full: juice, wild blueberry or blackberry pancakes or French toast; with eggs any style, bacon or sausage; freshly ground (in an antique grinder) coffee, and an assortment of herb teas.
Extras: Use of the sailboat, canoes, and town beach are available. Guests also have access to the inn's TV den and refrigerator. A gourmet dinner, limited to 24 persons, is served each evening at 7 p.m. The single entree featured may be roast turkey with oyster-pecan stuffing or coquilles St. Jacques.
Rates: $60 (breakfast included) to $85 (MAP). Dormitory rooms, $13 (breakfast included). Family room, accommodating up to eight is $80 on weekdays, $87.50 Friday and Saturday nights. There are also discounts for longer stays. Checks, Visa, and Mastercard welcome.

10% discount to OHJ members if not paid by credit card.

ETNA

MOOSE MOUNTAIN LODGE
Peter and Kay Shumway
Moose Mountain
Etna, NH 03750
(603) 643-3529
June 1 to November 15;
December 26 to March 31

1938 log ski lodge

LOCATION: High up on Moose Mountain, near Dartmouth College, the inn's porch affords a 100-mile, unobstructed view of the Green Mountains and the wild Connecticut River Valley. Hiking and cross-country ski trails, some connecting with the Appalachian Trail, start right at the front door. The Lodge is one of several inns involved in the "Canoeing Inn to Inn" on the Connecticut River program.

This lodge looks like it sprouted from the land. It's constructed from stones gathered in nearby fields and logs salvaged after a local blizzard uprooted hundreds of trees. Inside, there are wide stone hearths and warm pine panelling. Even the furniture is of the land: It's built from logs, too—some left over from the blizzard and some felled by the present innkeepers.

Restrictions: No pets. Smoking discouraged. Children five and over welcome.
Beds: Twelve rooms with twins, bunks, doubles, queens, and combinations of the above. All rooms share baths.
Breakfast: Hearty country breakfast includes seasonal fruits, juices, homemade granola, eggs from a nearby farm, bacon, sausage, pancakes with the Lodge's own maple syrup, and fresh coffeecake.
Extras: Complimentary coffee, tea, and homemade cookies are served at all times. Dinner and lunch are included in the room rate during the winter. (In summer, there's a $15 charge for dinner, and no lunch is served.) There are two grand pianos and a collection of old books and magazines.
Rates: Summer and fall: from $22 per person (for bunk beds) to $28 per person (for queen-size log bed and great view). Winter: $50

per person—includes three meals. Two-night minimum on weekends; three-night minimum during holidays. Personal checks accepted; no credit cards.

10% discount to OHJ members.

INTERVALE

**RIVERSIDE COUNTRY
INN**
Geoffrey and Anne Cotter
Route 16A
Intervale, NH 03845
(603) 356-9060
Year-round

1906 Colonial Revival

LOCATION: On a riverbank, with breathtaking mountain views, the inn is close to shops and restaurants in Conway and Jackson, and downhill and cross-country ski areas.

Innkeeper Geoffrey Cotter's family has owned this inn since 1906, when it was built as a summer vacation house. Evidence of passing generations is everywhere in the inn. Geoffrey's grandparents left many of the Victorian furnishings and the oak porch furniture. His Uncle Charlie painted the mural in the sunny breakfast room—it colorfully captures the home's mountain view. And photos decorating the inn's walls chronicle the generations who visited the house each summer.

Restrictions: No pets.
Beds: Six double-bedded rooms and one with twin beds. Shared or private baths.
Breakfast: New England, Scottish, French, German, Swedish, and Jewish entrees: The specialties include eggs Benedict, smoked trout, salmon scramble, pork pie, crab Oscar, fruit pancakes, chipped beef, and Welsh rarebit.
Extras: Passes to antique auto museum and a ski mobile ride up a nearby mountain are available.

Rates: In-season (foliage and Christmas/New Year's): $65 for room with river view, shared sitting room and shared bath; $108 for room with brass bed, velvet chaise lounge and walnut armoire. Off-season (April to May): $45 to $75. Personal checks, American Express, and Diners' Club accepted.

10% discount to OHJ members.

Mailing Address: Box 42, Intervale, NH 03845

JACKSON

DANA PLACE INN
The Levine Family
Pinkham Notch Road (Route 16)
Jackson, NH 03846
(603) 383-6822
Year-round

1890 Federal

LOCATION: Five miles north of Jackson, surrounded by the White Mountain National Forest, the inn is set on 300 acres of lawns, gardens, streams, meadows, and woodland trails. Tennis courts, swimming pool, and health club are on the premises. Trails to the top of Mt. Washington (the highest peak in the northeast) and the Appalachian Trail are nearby.

"The peace our inn offers is beyond description."

This inn was built as a wedding gift to Otwin and Fasroni Dana. The young couple decided right away that their property was too beautiful to go unshared: They built guest cottages and opened their home to visitors just a few years after moving in. (The Danas earned extra revenue by running a stagecoach line to the top of nearby Mt. Washington.)

The Levine family found the Inn meticulously preserved when they moved in. Their restoration work was limited to a few small (but nonetheless painstaking) projects, like restoring the aged finish on the dining room wainscotting. The Levines are also pumping the life back into their century-old apple orchard, and plan to make their own apple cider with the fall harvest.

The Inn is furnished with Early American-style antiques. Fasroni Dana's spinning wheel still stands inside for all to view. And anyone who wants to learn more about the Inn's history can consult the current owner, Mr. Eng Chye Low.

Restrictions: Children welcome. No pets.
Beds: Fourteen rooms; eight have shared baths.
Breakfast: Full breakfast: cereal, eggs, pancakes and waffles with pure maple syrup, homemade muffins and breads, and apple cider made from apples grown on the Dana Place Farm.
Extras: Dinner, served in the inn's restaurant, is included in the room rate. House specialties include Chicken L'Oriental, sautéed with snow peas fresh from the garden, and Beef Wellington. They also have a hot tub "to help you relax at night."
Rates: From $45 for a room with shared bath off-season, to $125 for a two-room suite during the peak season. Cots, $10; cribs, free. Personal checks and credit cards accepted.

10% discount to OHJ members.
Mailing Address: PO Box L, Jackson, NH 03846

NEW HAMPSHIRE

JACKSON

NESTLENOOK INN
Tom and Patti Burns
Dinsmore Road
Jackson, NH 03846
(603) 383-9443
Year-round

1890s Farmhouse connected to 1785 Colonial

LOCATION: Jackson Village (150 miles north of Boston) is in the heart of the White Mountains. The inn's grounds encompass 65 acres of rolling pastures and wooded highlands bordering the scenic Ellis River. There are 16 miles of horse trails and 26 miles of cross-country ski trails on the property. Nearby are downhill ski resorts, Mt. Washington, and Jackson's shops and restaurants.

The Burnses rescued Nestlenook from near disaster in 1984. Nestlenook had been well kept for nearly 100 years while it served as a guest house. But in the early 1970s, the building became a private residence under absentee management — with no repairs and no upkeep.

That's where the Burnses stepped in. Their easiest project was restoring the Inn's original name: from Robinwood back to Nestlenook (which describes its location nestled in the crook of a country road at the base of a mountain). After that, their work ran the gamut from repairing the plumbing and heating, to restoring the drooping porch, to hanging period wallpaper and moving in their collection of New England antiques. They spruced up the outbuildings and grounds, too, restoring life to a gazebo, a barn, a carriage house, and an equestrian riding ring. Patti Burns says she'd love to share her experiences with "anyone who will listen," now that the immense project is almost complete.

Architectural features which will interest old-house lovers are the river rock hearth and wide pine floors in the Colonial part of the house, and the tin ceilings and maple floors in the 1890s addition.

Restrictions: Children always welcome (the Burnses have a youngster of their own). Contact the innkeepers in advance if you'd like to bring a pet. (You can board your horse in their stables for a minimal charge.)
Beds: Spring, summer, and fall: 15 rooms plus three housekeeping cottages. Winter: ten rooms and three cottages. Private or shared baths.
Breakfast: Hearty country breakfast: farm-fresh eggs (you can take a basket to the hen house and pick out your own), home-cured pork, New England cheddar cheese, homemade breads, and fresh fruits and juices, plus fresh coffee, or tea from their antique tea chest.
Extras: There's a cross-country ski touring center right on the property, where you can rent and take lessons. Or you can reserve space on one of the inn's horse-drawn sleigh rides (by sunlight or romantic moonlight). They serve a skiers' lunch and complimentary hot cider (always brewing on the wood stove). In summer they have a complete equestrian center, offering shows, races, dressage competitions, and lessons.
Rates: $40 for double room with shared bath mid-week during off-season. $60 for double room with private bath during peak season. Personal checks, Visa, and Mastercard accepted.
10% discount to OHJ members.
Mailing Address: PO Box Q, Jackson Village, NH 03846

LITTLETON

BEAL HOUSE INN
Doug and Brenda Clickenger
247 West Main Street
Littleton, NH 03561
(603) 444-2661
Year-round

1833 Federal

LOCATION: In a quiet town in the White Mountains, the inn is near hiking trails, wild rivers, downhill ski slopes, and cross-country ski trails.

If you fall in love with the four-poster bed you sleep on here, you can probably buy it. Most of the antiques in this inn are for sale! And there's a fully stocked antique store right next door, in the barn.

The Clickengers' most famous recent visitors were Joan Mondale and Lynn Glenn, who stayed at Beal House during the New Hampshire presidential campaign.

Restrictions: Children welcome. No pets. Smoking restricted in the breakfast room. Check-in from 3 to 9 p.m. (unless otherwise arranged); check-out at 11 a.m.
Beds: The 12 units include two two-room suites. There are twin, double, and queen-size beds. Twelve rooms have private baths.
Breakfast: Breakfast is served by candlelight on blue willow china in front of a crackling fire. Complimentary continental breakfast includes hot popovers, homemade bread, juices, and coffee or tea. Scrambled eggs, homemade waffles, ham, bacon, and sausage can be purchased a la carte.
Extras: Tea (35 kinds) is served in the afternoons and evenings, along with cheese and crackers or popcorn or both. In cooler weather, the proprietors provide hot mulled cider.
Rates: From $35 (for shared bath) to $65 (for queen-size bed and private bath). Cots and cribs, $8. Rates increase from September 15 to October 15. Personal checks and credit cards accepted.

10% discount to OHJ members on two-night stay, paid for in cash or by check.

NEW LONDON

PLEASANT LAKE INN
Grant and Margaret Rich
Pleasant Street
New London, NH 03257
(603) 526-6271
Year-round

1790 Farmhouse

LOCATION: The inn stands at the shore of Pleasant Lake, with a view of Mt. Kearsarge on the other side. Hiking trails, tennis, and golf are nearby, and guests can fish, boat, or swim in the lake. Cross-country skiing trails begin at the back door; downhill skiing is five minutes away.

This is the oldest operating inn in the area—it's been welcoming guests for more than 100 years! The innkeepers' old musical instrument, basket, and historic photograph collections will interest antique lovers.

Restrictions: No pets. No children under 12.
Beds: Seven doubles and six twins. Eight rooms share baths.
Breakfast: Full breakfast served, but not included in the room rate: pancakes or French toast and eggs, with sausage or bacon.
Extras: The inn serves dinner, offering everything from seafood to beef, plus an extensive wine list.
Rates: $35 for room with shared bath; $50 for private bath. Cots, $10. Checks and credit cards accepted.
　　10% discount to OHJ members.
Mailing Address: PO Box 1030, New London, NH 03257

ORFORD

WHITE GOOSE INN
Manfred and Karin Wolf
Route 10
Orford, NH 03777
(603) 353-4812
Year-round

1770 Colonial attached to 1833

LOCATION: The inn stands along the main street of historic Orford —a British fort town established in 1765 to control French and Native American uprisings on the Connecticut River. The well-preserved Colonial and Federal homes lining Orford's main street will delight old-house lovers. Nearby are Dartmouth College, hiking trails, bike routes, golfing, and cross-country and downhill skiing.

Orford's first settlers were Thomas Sawyer and his two eldest sons, Edward and Jonathan. Edward Sawyer built this inn's foundation, on a flood plain his father and brother helped him clear.

Edward's house fell into careless hands in 1788. But with its sturdy, hand-pegged mortise-and-tenon joints, it still managed to survive several decades of neglect. In 1833, a well-to-do tanner named Cyrus Cutter rescued the wilting home. Cutter spruced up the house and added new dignity to the property—the Colonial home became the back ell of an imposing Federal mansion.

In 1853, the home's next owner made the place even more elegant. He added an impressive circular porch, which wrapped all the way around the side of the house and reached out to encircle a nearby elm tree. To Orford's old-timers, this inn is known as "the house with the tree growing through the roof." (The diseased tree had to be cut off at the roof line 20 years ago.)

Today, the inn is fascinating to explore. On the back ell, you can see the indentations Edward Sawyer's axe left on the lumber he built his house with. In front, granite Ionic columns support the delicate frieze over the front door. The old elm tree's trunk remains inside the porch. Indoors, there are nine fireplaces with soapstone mantels. And the colonial ell's original staircase and woodbox remain unscathed.

Restrictions: No pets. No children under eight. Smoking in guest rooms only. Check-in after 2 p.m.; check-out at 11 a.m.

Beds: Ten rooms, eight with private baths, two with shared baths.

Breakfast: Home-cooked breakfast includes juices, seasonal fruits, muffins, eggs, French toast, "Dutch-baby pancakes," and coffee or tea.

Extras: Hosts will make dinner reservations at, and supply transportation to, area restaurants.

Rates: From $65 for third-floor room with shared bath, to $95 for large room with stencilled walls and private bath. Personal checks and credit cards except American Express welcome.

10% discount to OHJ members.

Mailing Address: Rt. 10, Box 17, Orford, NH 03777

NEW HAMPSHIRE

RYE

ROCK LEDGE MANOR
Norman and Janice Marineau
1413 Ocean Boulevard (Route 1A)
Rye, NH 03870
(603) 431-1413
Year-round

Mid-19th-century Dutch Colonial Revival

LOCATION: Situated on Concord Point overlooking the Isle of Shoals, Rock Ledge Manor is six minutes from downtown Portsmouth. Its large wraparound porch overlooks the coastlines of Maine, New Hampshire, and Massachusetts. The immediate area abounds with historic homes.

Norman and Janice bought Rock Ledge Manor in 1979 and immediately began a complete restoration. The house was purchased furnished, and many of the house's original furnishings are still used. Eastlake Victorian bed sets, antique brass beds, Paine furnishings, and the Marineaus' own collection of antiques have brought style and elegance to an authentically restored interior. Ongoing restoration projects include reconstruction of the carriage house.

251

Rock Ledge Manor sits on land that was originally acquired through a 'King's grant.' Norman and Janice are the fourth or fifth owners of the property. When the Marineaus opened the inn in 1982, their first guests were in Rye on a genealogy trip. One of these guests (Fanny — now 80 years old) recently discovered she had ancestors who once owned Rock Ledge Manor. Needless to say, she returns often.

Restrictions: Children 11 and over are welcome. No pets. Smoking in designated area only. Check-in between 1 and 5 p.m. (later OK with advance notice).

Beds: Four bedrooms each with double bed. Two rooms have full private bath. The other two rooms each have private half-bath, but share a shower.

Breakfast: Juice, fresh fruit salad, and home baked muffins or breads; then, a combination of home fries and fresh vegetables with home-made sauce. Breakfast meats are served with eggs, omelettes, stuffed crepes, and the "old family recipe" for pancakes. Toast, jams, and coffee are also served.

Extras: Wine and tea get-togethers are available for interested guests —"we all sit and share experiences."

Rates: $45 (half-bath, shared shower) to $50 (full bath). Personal and traveler's checks accepted.

SHELBURNE

**THE PHILBROOK
FARM INN**
Connie Philbrook Leger and
Nancy Philbrook
North Road
Shelburne, NH 03581
(603) 466-3831
May 1 to October 31 and
December 26 to April 1

1834 Farmhouse greatly expanded with later additions

LOCATION: In the Androscoggin River Valley in the shadow of the White Mountains, the inn offers proximity to hiking trails (Philbrook Farm's own trails connect with the Appalachian Trail), cross-country ski trails (starting right at the inn's front door), downhill ski slopes, and swimming in natural swimming holes or the inn's pool.

"Everything here is as it was at the turn of the century—uncomplicated and relaxed. It's a place to get comfortable, to put your feet up." Mike Regnier and Pat Gerrity, Kankakee, Ill.

The Philbrook family began its restoration project way back in 1853. In that year, Susannah and Harvey Philbrook, the first in a five-generation line of innkeepers, bought a rundown farmhouse and its overgrown demesne. They spruced up the deteriorated property, added some extra rooms, and in 1861 welcomed the Philbrook Farm Inn's first visitors.

Since then, demand for the Philbrooks' hospitality has forced the Inn to expand. Guest cottages were built in the late 1890s. Extra wings were added in 1905 and 1934. Today, the Inn's most unique architectural feature is this harmonious blend of additions from several eras.

Inside, too, the Inn represents several eras. Its antique furnishings date from early American to high Victorian. And the heights of the ceilings and the styles of the fireplace mantels vary according to the year they were installed.

Though the Inn has grown with the generations, the way the place is operated remains traditional. Meals, cooked on a turn-of-the-century, ten-burner woodburning stove, are prepared from old family recipes. Many of the vegetables, fruits, jams, and jellies served are grown in the Inn's own gardens and are canned on the spot. (Guests who are around during canning season are invited to join the Philbrooks in the old-fashioned preparations.)

A quote stitched in needlepoint above the register desk sums up the feeling of the place:

Happy to share with you such as we've got
The leaks in the roof, the soup in the pot
You don't have to thank us or laugh at our jokes.
Sit deep and come often—you're one of the folks!

Restrictions: Pets in summer cottages only. Check-in after noon; check-out at 11 a.m.
Beds: Nineteen rooms—single, double, and twin. (You can request a king-size bed for $2 extra per night.) Some rooms have private baths; others share. Five recently renovated turn-of-the-century cottages are available during the summer.
Breakfast: Their country breakfast is home-cooked from old family recipes and served from 8 a.m. (when the bell rings) to 9 a.m. It includes

homemade bread, doughnuts or muffins, cereal, eggs, choice of juices, bacon, and coffee or tea. Sunday breakfast offers traditional codfish balls and corncake.

Extras: Their room rate includes dinner as well as breakfast. (Visitors Mike Regnier and Pat Gerrity said the evening meal is "like Sunday dinners at Grandma's house.") Weekly rates include lunch. Also, coffee and tea are available at all times. And the innkeepers can arrange for a babysitter (rates are determined by the sitter).

Rates: $70 for double with shared bath. $83 for double with bay window, sitting area, and private bath. Cottages are $275 per week. Weekly rates for individual rooms are also available. Cots are free; cribs, $2. Personal and traveler's checks accepted, but no credit cards.

SNOWVILLE

SNOWVILLAGE INN
Peter, Trudy, & Frank
Cutrone
Snowville, NH 03849
(603) 447-2818
Year-round except April

1916 Dutch Colonial Revival

LOCATION: The inn stands high on Foss Mountain, with a spectacular view of the White Mountains and surrounded by rolling lawns, flower gardens, vegetable patches, apple orchards, and miles of hiking and cross-country ski trails. The Inn has its own cross-country ski center, with rentals and instruction, and is near eight downhill ski resorts, lakes, streams, old New England churches, and antique shops.

A harried Washington, D.C., journalist built this house as his summer retreat. It was converted to an inn in 1948, and has been well cared for since then. The present innkeepers bought the house in 1977; their main project has been sprucing up the gardens, which have won several awards.

Restrictions: Children and pets are welcome. No smoking in the dining room.

Beds: Sixteen rooms, with either two double beds, twin beds, a queen, a king, or one double bed. Only two rooms have a shared bath—the rest are private.

Breakfast: Full breakfast varies daily. Specialties are surprise omelettes, chocolate-chip or blueberry pancakes, and French toast. On Sundays, they serve eggs Benedict and champagne.

Extras: A sauna, clay tennis court, beach passes, babysitting, and fresh fruit basket are provided for guests. Dinner — chicken Veronique, veal piccata, coq au vin, followed by strawberry sorbet, apricot Victorian or French silk pie—is also included in the room rate.

Rates: Peak season: $75 per person MAP; $65 per person B&B. Off-season, $20 less. Mid-week package rates available. Checks and credit cards accepted.

10% discount to OHJ members.

NEW JERSEY

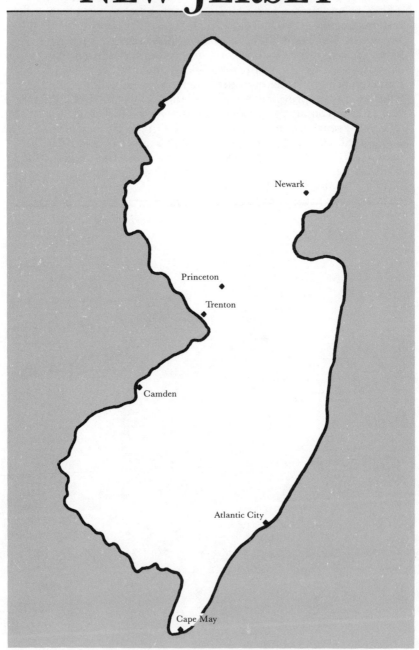

Newark

Princeton

Trenton

Camden

Atlantic City

Cape May

CAPE MAY

THE ABBEY
Jay and Marianne Schatz
Columbia Avenue and
Gurney Street
Cape May, NJ 08204
(609) 884-4506
April to November

1869 Gothic Revival Villa

LOCATION: Cape May offers history, architectural charm, grace, and all the joys of the Atlantic Ocean, including unspoiled beaches. Guided walking and trolley tours are available, with many beautiful homes open to the public. The Abbey is one block from the beach and within easy walking distance of fine shops and restaurants.

If Victoriana is your heart's delight, be sure not to miss out on this inn.

In 1869, a wealthy Pennsylvania coal baron and politician, John B. McCreary, decided to build an elaborate home on the shores of the Atlantic Ocean in Cape May. He contracted a famous architect to design his summer retreat and the result was a beautiful villa with an imposing 60-foot tower, stencilled and ruby-glass arched windows, large comfortable rooms, and shaded verandahs. At that time, Cape May reigned as Queen of the Seaside Resorts, frequented by the highest national and international society, including five U.S. Presidents.

With the advent of the automobile, Cape May's popularity fell as quickly as it had risen—the train to Cape May was forgotten and the fashion-conscious packed up their cars for vacation spots closer to home. This house, along with all the Cape's other opulent Victorians, was left to rot. When Jay and Marianne Schatz moved in in 1979, the roof had been leaking for ten years!

Today, after the Schatzes' detailed restoration, the house is as lavishly Victorian as ever it was during McCreary's time. (Before-and-after pictures displayed inside document their tremendous effort.) It's furnished with elegant Victorian antiques, including 12-foot mirrors, ornate gas chandeliers, a harp, tall walnut beds, and marble-topped dressers. Even the wall decorations and window treatments are high Victorian: dados, friezes, gilded plaster mouldings, and velvet and lace curtains.

Best of all, the hosts love to talk of old houses: they invite you to bring your own restoration photos.

Restrictions: Well-behaved children over 12 welcome. No pets please —"you can use ours." Check-in between 1 and 10 p.m. Check-out at 11 a.m.

Beds: Seven guest rooms. Four with double beds, two with two double beds, and one with a double and a single bed. Four rooms have a private bath.

Breakfast: Full sit-down breakfast is offered in the formal dining room in spring and fall. In summer, continental buffet is served on the verandah.

Extras: Late afternoon refreshments, free beach passes, beach chairs, and on-site parking are available.

Rates: $55 to $85. Visa, Mastercard, and traveler's checks welcome. Personal checks accepted for deposit only.

10% discount to OHJ members for mid-week stays in April, May, and October.

NEW JERSEY

CAPE MAY

ABIGAIL ADAMS
Ed and Donna Misner
12 Jackson Street
Cape May, NJ 08204
(609) 884-1371
Spring and Fall. All week July and August.

1891 Renaissance Revival

LOCATION: The inn stands 100 feet from the beach in Cape May's primary historic district. The porch and many guest rooms overlook the beach. Fine dining and shopping are within easy walking distance.

"After breakfast, settle on the porch and enjoy the morning paper, walk to the beach or mall, or just sit and watch the waves. We look forward to sharing our love of the sea with you."

The Abigail Adams, with its simple, symmetric architectural lines, is perhaps less daunting than the ornate Victorians so abundant in Cape May. Ed and Donna Misner moved in in 1984 and restored all the guest rooms, re-built a period fence, and repaired the rotting lattice- and spindle-work on the delicate porch. Their decor is comfortable, breezy country style: pine and wicker antiques, hand-stitched quilts, hand stencilling, and cheerful chintzes.

Restrictions: Children over 14 welcome. No pets. No smoking at breakfast table. Check-in after 2 p.m. Check-out at 11 a.m.
Beds: Six rooms. Five with double beds, and one with queen bed. Two rooms with private baths.
Breakfast: Varies daily, but usually includes fresh fruit, cereal, or some egg dishes. It always includes fresh-baked muffins or coffeecakes.
Extras: Afternoon tea is served in summer, and beach passes are provided.
Rates: $65 to $89. Cots, $15. Personal checks accepted.
   10% discount to OHJ members.

CAPE MAY

ALBERT G. STEVENS INN
Paul and Alice Linder
127 Myrtle Avenue
Cape May, NJ 08204
(609) 884-4717
Year-round

1900 Queen Anne

LOCATION: Located in Victorian Cape May, the inn is five blocks from the swimming beach and four blocks from the Victorian mall.

It overlooks Wilbraham Park and is right next door to the Wilbraham Mansion. Myrtle Avenue is a quiet, residential street lined with trees.

Dr. Albert Stevens, a local physician, built this house as a wedding gift to his bride. And, indeed, the doctor must have loved her, for this multi-gabled Queen Anne is graced with all the most fashionable architectural elements of its time: a turret with balcony, wraparound verandah, and gingerbread trim.

The house remained in the Stevens family until recently, when it was converted to a B&B by Joe Santoro and Gary O'Neill. They also furnished the inn with antiques (highlighted by the mother-of-pearl-inlaid parlor suite Dr. Stevens presented to his new wife), stripped and repainted the exterior in an authentic color scheme, and re-papered the public rooms using patterns as close to the originals as possible. The current owners, Paul and Alice Linder, will show you many of the house's interesting interior features, such as its floating staircase, which curves all the way up to the turret, and its double parlor with original gas fireplace.

Restrictions: No children. No pets. Smoking on verandah only. Check-in between 1 and 10 p.m. Two-night minimum stay weekends, three-night minimum holidays.
Beds: Five rooms with double beds, three of which have private bath. One two-room suite with private sitting room and private bath.
Breakfast: Coffee/Sanka, tea, juice, eggs, pancakes, French toast, waffles, muffins, coffeecakes, and more.
Extras: Beach tags and off-street parking.
Rates: $70 to $90. Personal and traveler's checks welcome.

NEW JERSEY

CAPE MAY

BARNARD-GOOD HOUSE
Nan and Tom Hawkins
238 Perry Street
Cape May, NJ 08204
(609) 884-5381
April 1 through November

1863 Mansard

LOCATION: In the heart of historic Cape May, the inn is two blocks from the main swimming beach. Historic house tours, state parks, horseback riding, off-shore or back-bay fishing, museums, and fine dining are all nearby.

"We've done all the restoration work ourselves, and we're more than happy to discuss the details with our guests. Many of our previous guests have been OHJ subscribers, and we've learned a lot from them too. We always look forward to meeting other old-house lovers."

Nan and Tom Hawkins are very patient people. Their house was in a dismal state of repair when they moved in in 1980—asbestos siding, rotting roof, faulty wiring. But not once did they resort to a contractor! They've done every bit of the restoration work by themselves, from completely removing the mansard roof and re-shingling it in the original style, to replacing leaky plumbing, to stencilling the walls and refinishing the wainscotting. As you can imagine, they're now experts in the restoration field, and love to advise guests who are facing the same obstacles they overcame.

Nan and Tom have decorated the house with their extensive Victorian antiques collection, including a three-piece, fringed-and-tasseled lounge set in their "Turkish corner." These they've complemented with valanced curtains handmade from antique lace, brocade and velvet.

The house's most outstanding exterior feature is its southern-style, wraparound verandah, completely restored and furnished with white wicker. And you can't possibly overlook Nan and Tom's authentic exterior paint job: cotton-candy pink with maroon shutters and deep purple and white trim.

Restrictions: Well-behaved children over 12 welcome. No pets. "Careful and discreet" smoking is permitted. Check-in after 1 p.m., check-out at 11 a.m.
Beds: Six guest rooms. Four with double beds, one with twin beds, and one with twin beds that can be combined to form king bed. Two rooms have private bath, others share three common bathrooms.
Breakfast: Homemade, gourmet selections include carrot or apple juice, lemon curd with kiwi, homemade bagels, filo and hazlenut pastry, maple sour cream muffins with glaze in summer; in winter the fare consists of fresh strawberry and orange juice, leek-potato flan, and chocolate pastry.
Extras: There's a gathering each evening at 6 p.m. for refreshments. Iced tea is available all day in warm-weather months. Beach passes and bicycles are provided.
Rates: $60 to $80. 10% discount for singles and stays of seven days or longer. Personal and traveler's checks welcome; Mastercard and Visa for deposit only.

CAPE MAY

THE BRASS BED INN
Donna and John Dunwoody
719 Columbia Avenue
Cape May, NJ 08204
(609) 884-8075
Year-round

C. 1872 Gothic Revival with Queen Anne details

LOCATION: The inn is surrounded by large trees and flowers; rooms overlook the quaint street or the chimneys and rooftops of nearby Victorians. Beach is less than three blocks away, shops and restaurants are nearby.

One guest said, "It was nice to get back to the old-fashioned virtues of hospitality, a leisurely pace, and family-style breakfasts!"

Donna and John Dunwoody revealed a bit of history when they decided to strip some dilapidated-looking furniture they found in their house. Beneath layers of encrusted paint, they uncovered the furniture's original, 1872 shipping tags—addressed to the house's original owner! Thanks to their paint-stripping perseverance and furniture restoration efforts, many of the armoires, tables, chairs, and dressers you'll see in the inn today are original to the house. Several brass lighting fixtures, including an ornate gas-electric chandelier, are also original. The Dunwoodys have added their own antiques to those they found in the house, including a Renaissance Revival parlor set, a working gramophone, and a display of early Cape May prints and photographs.

The exterior features are a unique interpretation of Gothic Revival, with fleur-de-lis verge boards, turned finials, and paired brackets. The porch was "modernized" in 1900, its ornate gingerbread trim replaced with then-fashionable Ionic columns.

This inn is especially pleasant at Christmas time, when it's decorated with holly, mistletoe, and a Victorian-style tree with velvet apples, candles, miniature toys, and cornucopias, and family-made popcorn strings.

Restrictions: No pets; smoking on verandah or in public rooms only;

well-behaved children over 12 welcome. Check-in between 1 and 11 p.m., other times by special arrangement.

Beds: A total of eight rooms: two twins, six doubles. Two have private baths, one has a half-bath, others share (two rooms per bath).

Breakfast: Fresh juice, fruit, egg dishes with sausage or bacon; tea, including herbal, or coffee; home-baked goods. House specialty is fruit-filled pancakes with hot cereal; cold cereal substituted for main dish in summer.

Extras: Free beach passes are offered, along with outdoor hot and cold showers and a bathhouse. Complimentary iced tea or lemonade is served on summer afternoons; hot tea and "goodies" in other seasons.

Rates: $48 to $75 in winter, $55 to $90 in summer; cots $20. Personal checks welcome.

10% discount to OHJ members.

NEW JERSEY

CAPE MAY

CAPTAIN MEY'S BED & BREAKFAST INN
Carin Feddermann and
Milly LaCanfora
202 Ocean Street
Cape May, NJ 08204
(609) 884-7793
Year-round

1890 Neo-Colonial

LOCATION: The beach is one-and-a-half blocks away; the Victorian shopping mall is right around the corner (the inn is within the historic district). Trolley rides, walking tours, and carriage rides are a half-block away and many restaurants are within walking distance.

"After all the renovating that has taken place here, OHJ readers will definitely appreciate the place."

Someone moved into this house in the 1940s and decided to "freshen it up a bit" with white paint. Unfortunately, that meant covering over all the beautifully carved, chestnut-oak mouldings, and

263

the costly Eastlake panelling in the dining room. Woe to Carin Feddermann and Milly LaCanfora, who were stuck with the immense project of stripping away all this paint, which by 1979 had been crusted into place with layers of grit.

Carin and Milly persevered, and their efforts were rewarded. The house is once again a marvel of carved wood, Tiffany and leaded glass, and ornate hearths—including one they found behind a 1930s closet. They have before-and-after photos, which will inspire anyone who's undertaking a seemingly-endless seeming stripping project.

Wonder who Captain Mey was? He sailed here from Holland in the 17th century and proclaimed Cape May's climate "just like home." In honor of Mr. Mey, Carin and Milly have scattered Dutch antiques, paintings, and Indonesian artifacts throughout the house.

Restrictions: Smoking only on the verandah. No pets ("we have three of our own"). Children over 12 welcome. Check-in after 2 p.m., check-out at 11 a.m.

Beds: Six of the eight guest rooms are doubles, the other two can accommodate three. Two rooms share a bath.

Breakfast: A full country breakfast is served by candlelight to the sound of classical music. Breads and cakes are home-baked. Quiche dishes, potato casserole, French toast with Grand Marnier may be offered, or the Dutch special: cheeses, breakfast meats, and home-made yogurt.

Extras: Guests receive free beach tags and can park beside the inn. Assorted refreshments are served at afternoon tea.

Rates: $65 (shared bath) to $85 (second floor, private bath). Off-season discounts before Memorial Day or after Victorian week in October. Personal checks are accepted for deposits only; cash or traveler's checks upon arrival.

NEW JERSEY

CAPE MAY

THE DORMER HOUSE
Bill and Peggy Madden
800 Columbia Avenue
Cape May, NJ 08204
(609) 884-7446
Year-round

1899 Neo-Colonial

LOCATION: The house is on a flowered lot, three blocks from the ocean, amid Cape May's densely concentrated Victorian homes.

The man who built this house, John Jacoby, supplied the marble for the famed statue of William Penn atop Philadelphia's Second Empire-style city hall. Remnants of Jacoby's once thriving stone enterprise survive in this house today — fireplace mantels and some bathroom floors are made of marble.

Jacoby's summer cottage was first converted to a guest house during the 1940s. Today, the exterior looks as it did in his time, encircled by Tuscan columns marching around a wide verandah, and framed by many dormers. The interior was divided into eight guest apartments in 1971, and is furnished for family use—with some Victoriana and pieces original to the house, and other, sturdier pieces built to withstand youthful energy.

Restrictions: No pets.
Beds: The eight two- or three-room apartments all have private baths.
Breakfast: Guests can prepare all their own meals.
Extras: Services include a coin-operated washer and dryer, a barbecue, and beach passes for a small fee.
Rates: Weekly rates from $250 (winter) to $620 (summer) depend on size of apartment; daily rates vary from $40 to $102. Cots and cribs free of charge. Personal checks welcome.

NEW JERSEY

CAPE MAY

THE MAINSTAY INN
Tom and Sue Carroll
635 Columbia Avenue
Cape May, NJ 08204
(609) 884-8690
April through October,
November weekends

1872 Italianate

LOCATION: The inn, amid a National Landmark district in Victorian Cape May, is one-and-a-half blocks from the Atlantic Ocean.

"The Mainstay can provide an excellent education to those planning a Victorian restoration. Conversely, it can offer rest and relaxation in a historic environment for those wishing to escape an ongoing restoration project." Tom and Sue

A pair of wealthy gamblers pooled their resources in 1872 and built an elegant, exclusive clubhouse where their friends could devote themselves to gambling and other gentlemanly amusements. They spared no expense and hired a famous architect to design a grand Italianate villa, with 14-foot ceilings, ornate plaster mouldings, elaborate chandeliers, a sweeping verandah, and a cupola to top it off. Luxury was paramount; they selected the most richly ornamented furnishings, 12-foot mirrors, marble-topped sideboards, and graceful loveseats. At the time, the *Cape May Ocean Wave* noted of the house: "In the design on this model building...Mr. S.D. Button, the architect, has won for himself additional honors....It is symmetrical in its proportions, airy and cheerful in its appointments, and finished in that unpretentious elegance so foreign to mansions of the shoddy order."

As you can imagine, public appreciation of this lavish Victorian didn't last, and the building deteriorated. In a leap of faith, Tom and Sue Carroll bought the fallen giant in 1976, restored it, and opened Cape May's first bed and breakfast inn of this century. They recovered many of the house's original furnishings, all its original chandeliers, and added some Victoriana of their own. They hung period wallpapers—probably among the most ornate and authentic in the country today, with Art Movement dados, friezes, and intricate ceiling decoupage.

In all, this is a Victorian delight not to be missed. If you can't stay the night, Tom and Sue give tours of the main floor at 4:00 on Saturdays, Sundays, Tuesdays, and Thursdays. Visitors are invited to stay for tea afterwards.

Restrictions: Children over 12 welcome. Light smoking permitted. Check-in between 2 and 10 p.m.
Beds: There are 12 double rooms, eight with private bath.
Breakfast: Full breakfast is served family style in spring and fall; continental is served on the verandah in the summer.
Extras: Afternoon tea and free beach passes are provided.
Rates: $46 to $87. Lower rates on weekdays in spring and fall. Personal checks welcome.

CAPE MAY

THE MANOR HOUSE ON HUGHES STREET
Mary and Tom Snyder
612 Hughes Street
Cape May, NJ 08204
(609) 884-4710
Year-round

1906 Dutch Colonial Revival

LOCATION: Hughes Street offers an example of practically every major American architectural style of the 19th and early 20th centuries. The beach is two blocks away, shops and restaurants within one block.

A wealthy New York couple presented this gambrel-roofed house to their daughter as a wedding gift, complete with servants. Unlike most Cape May residents, she and her husband lived here year-round, warmed in winter by huge radiators and an unusual iron fireplace, and attended to in all seasons by the five maids who lived upstairs.

Mary and Tom Snyder bought the house in 1984 from a couple who had spent a year tearing down tacky, 1950s panelling and stripping paint that disguised the ornate oak wainscotting and bull's-eye mouldings. (Tom says he and Mary wanted something they could "do together on a small scale.") The Snyders have added their own antiques to the beautifully restored Empire furnishings (probably original to the house) they found when they moved in.

Restrictions: No pets, no smoking inside, no children under 12. Check-in after 1 p.m., check-out at 11 a.m.
Beds: Of the ten rooms—one king, four queens, four doubles, one twin—four have private baths, three have half-baths, and three share a bath but are equipped with sinks.
Breakfast: A four-course full breakfast: juice, fresh fruit, fresh baked goods, choice of egg dishes such as quiche, crepes, pancakes, or French toast.
Extras: Afternoon refreshments are served; beach passes are free, as is parking.

Rates: $70 to $97. Personal checks welcome.
10% discount to OHJ members.

CAPE MAY

THE MASON COTTAGE
Dave and Joan Mason
625 Columbia Avenue
Cape May, NJ 08204
(609) 884-3358
May through October

1871 French Second Empire

LOCATION: Located on a tree-lined street in the heart of Cape May, the inn is one block from the ocean and Victorian mall. Excellent shops and restaurants are within easy walking distance.

The Mason family bought this mansard-roofed house in 1945, and has been running it as a B&B since 1947. Today, the house looks much as it did when Philadelphia entrepreneur Edward Warne built it in 1871. Inside, much of Mr. Warne's mahogany, walnut, oak, and satin wood furniture remains. Outside, the Masons recently restored the house's original color scheme, tin gutters, and roof shingles. All the exterior ornament is still there, too: gingerbread porch millwork, cornice, and peaked dormers. There's even an authentic canvas awning, which shades the porch on bright summer days.

Restrictions: No children or pets, smoking prohibited in guest rooms. Check-in after 1 p.m., check-out at 11 a.m.
Beds: All five have double beds; four rooms have private baths.
Breakfast: Continental: coffee, tea, juice, pastries, jams, cereal, and fresh fruit as available.
Extras: Beach passes are available (for a returnable deposit). There are also bike racks for the convenience of guests.
Rates: Rooms start at $55 to $60 for a small room with shared bath, to $70 to $85 for a large room with private bath and sitting area. 10% discount for visits of four or more nights. Credit cards and checks

welcome.
10% discount to OHJ members except on holiday weekends.

CAPE MAY

1882 Second Empire

THE MOORING GUEST HOUSE
**Carol and Harry
Schaeffer
801 Stockton Avenue
Cape May, NJ 08204
(609) 884-5425
May through October**

LOCATION: Located in a quiet residential section of historic Cape May, this guest house is one block from the ocean and beach and within easy walking distance of fine restaurants, shops, and historic attractions.

"We welcome you to this elegantly restored home. All has been done by our family. We are proud of our daughter who helped with all of the restoration work." Richard and Carolyn Detrick

Richard and Carolyn Detrick have an eye for forecasting fashion. By 1974, when many people still considered the word "Victorian" an architectural insult, the Detricks were restoring their *third* Cape May Victorian. In 1978, before the current B&B craze hit the U.S., they had opened the Mooring as a guest house.

Current owners Carol and Harry Schaeffer have maintained the Mooring's elegant atmosphere, and brought to it a character and feeling unique to themselves.

You should know: Though the Mooring's atmosphere is elegant, it's a "no-frills" establishment—the only food offered is coffee and tea in the morning. But you'll find their rates much lower than those at comparable B&Bs, and the hosts every bit as friendly and excited about discussing the nitty-gritty details of their historic house.

Restrictions: No children or pets. Check-in must be before 10 p.m. Check-out at 11 a.m.

Beds: There are 12 double rooms, two of which have two twins each. There is one single room. Five of the rooms have a private bath, while the eight others share three bathrooms.

Breakfast: No breakfast is offered, but coffee and tea are served from 8 to 11 a.m. each morning.

Extras: Beach passes are available as well as bike racks and off-street parking. There are also refrigerators for guests' use on the second and third floors.

Rates: Doubles from $65 to $70 (shared bath); $70 to $100 (private bath). Cots, $8. 10% discount offered mid-week during off-season. Personal and traveler's checks (or credit cards) accepted.

NEW JERSEY

CAPE MAY

THE QUEEN VICTORIA
Dane and Joan Wells
102 Ocean Street
Cape May, NJ 08204
(609) 884-8702
Year-round

1881 Italianate

LOCATION: Located in the center of Cape May's historic district, The Queen Victoria is within walking distance of some of New Jersey's best restaurants and the beach. This is also one of the most important bird-watching locations in North America.

"Please bring photos of your old house to share with us and other guests! A very large portion of our guests are old-house buffs and love to share stories and solutions."

In October of 1980, Dane and Joan Wells moved into a 1950s-style rooming house, with wall-to-wall beds crowded into tiny, dark rooms. Some 7,000 laborious hours and 350 rolls of wallpaper later, they were living in one of this country's most elegant Victorians. In April, 1981, they invited their first bed-and-breakfast guests.

If anybody is an expert on Victoriana, it's these folks. They've done an absolutely authentic job on their house, restoring everything from the house's original exterior colors (their house was featured on the cover of Sherwin Williams' "Century of Color," the last word on period color schemes), to the marbleized finish on one of their slate mantelpieces, to the shingles on their unusual mansard roof, with its two bevelled, octagonal towers. They have an extensive "Queen Victoria" book collection of art, architecture, and history of the period, as well as 19th-century fiction. Christmas at their place would've made Prince Albert proud: They decorate three trees, each in the style of a different Victorian period, scatter garlands and handmade ornaments all about, and hold Dickens readings by the fireside. To top it all off, Joan is former director of the Victorian Society in America, and a lecturer on old-house restoration. So, if you want to learn more about Victoriana, this place can't be beat. Chances are, many of the Queen Victoria's other guests will be old-house lovers, too!

Restrictions: No pets, no smoking in bedrooms (parlor, porches, and library are OK). "Children usually don't enjoy the Queen Victoria..."; toddlers not allowed. Check-in between 1 and 10:30 p.m.
Beds: Of the 11 rooms, four are large with private baths and beds that range from double to king size. Three are considered "medium" and have double beds and private baths. There are four more medium rooms that have either twin or double beds and share a bath; there is a sink in each.
Breakfast: Full breakfast is served year-round: egg casserole, granola, cereal, fruit, several types of breads, juice, coffee, and tea. "Breakfast is the best time at the inn—guests enjoy sharing conversation."
Extras: There's afternoon tea, concierge services, free set-ups and mixers in library, a full bathhouse with changing rooms, house bicycles, free district/house tour tickets. The Queen Victoria also offers an old-house restoration workshop in October and a Christmas decoration workshop in December. Their Dickens Extravaganza in December has become so popular "it sells out early!"
Rates: The most expensive room is $175; it's one of the large rooms with a private bath. The least expensive room is $69 — a medium room with a sink in the room and a shared hall bath. Personal checks are accepted; Mastercard and VISA for reservations only.

CAPE MAY

WINDWARD HOUSE
Owen and Sandy Miller
24 Jackson Street
Cape May, NJ 08204
(609) 884-3368
Year-round

1905 neo-Colonial

LOCATION: On Jackson Street, the Windward House is in the heart of Cape May's historic district and a half-block from the beach and Cape May's famous Victorian shopping mall.

A certain, conniving Philadelphia lawyer had a practical purpose in mind when he built this summer residence: He stowed away his mistress in the modest cottage he had built next door!

Memories of infidelity aren't all that haunt the Windward. The friendly ghost of an Irish immigrant maid inhabits the third-floor "Summer Suite." The innkeepers say they've never seen her themselves, but two guests have. One visitor was so taken in by the amiable sprite that he returned to the inn on several occasions, and always asked for the same room.

Owen and Sandy Miller, who've lived here since 1977, have expertly restored this marvel of bevelled and stained glass, dormers, balconies, bay windows, and three-inch-thick oak doors. Their most recent project was tearing off the ugly asbestos that was suffocating the cedar shingles, and repairing the trim that the 1940s siding contractor had bastardized. They've furnished the house with primarily Victorian antiques, and have on display Sally's collection of Victorian vintage clothing.

Restrictions: No children under 12. Check-in after noon, check-out at 10 a.m., however, "we do invite our guests to use the outdoor showers, porches, and luggage storage until 2 p.m."
Beds: Eight rooms, each with private baths.
Breakfast: Homemade granola, fresh fruit, juice, coffee, regular and herbal teas, homemade breads, muffins, jams, coffeecakes, and egg casseroles.
Extras: Beach tags and remote parking permits are available to guests.

Rates: $60 ($50 off-season) for a double bed, ocean view, and hand-stencilled walls, $75 ($65 off-season) for two double beds, three bay windows overlooking Jackson St., access to porch, private bath, and small refrigerator. Personal checks and credit cards welcome.

FLEMINGTON

JERICA HILL—A BED & BREAKFAST INN
Judith S. Studer
96 Broad Street
Flemington, NJ 08822
(201) 782-8234
Year-round

1901 Princess Anne

LOCATION: Jerica Hill is located two blocks off Main Street, within walking distance of local shops, outlets, and restaurants. Flemington has been the County Seat of Hunterdon since 1785 and is a well-preserved blend of Colonial, Greek Revival, and Victorian buildings.

This is a quietly restrained Princess Anne, painted two-tone gray and maroon, with an octagonal turret, a bay window, an immense, slate-floored, screened-in porch jutting out one side, and a typically turn-of-the-century lack of ornate exterior ornament. The innkeeper, Judith Studer, is a Flemington native with deep roots in the local history. She's furnished her house with antiques she inherited from her family, Flemington residents for several generations.

Restrictions: No pets—"ours would love your attention." Check-in after 2 p.m. (please advise if arriving after 6 p.m.). Check-out at 11 a.m. Children over 12 welcome. No smoking in the inn.
Beds: One room has a queen, three have doubles, and one has twins. Two have private baths, the other three share.
Breakfast: "Continental plus": fresh squeezed orange juice, fresh fruits, assorted homemade breads, cereal, warm pastries, coffee, assortment of teas.

273

Extras: Coffee and tea are always brewing. Sherry is served in the living room along with snacks and cold drinks to enjoy on the porch. Fresh fruit and flowers are provided in rooms, along with "many little extras."

Rates: $45 for double (shared bath) to $65 for queen bed with private bath. Long-term discounts. Personal checks and credit cards accepted.

NEW JERSEY

MILFORD

CHESTNUT HILL ON THE DELAWARE
Rob and Linda Castagna
63 Church Street
Milford, NJ 08848
(201) 995-9761
Year-round

1860 Gothic Revival

LOCATION: Chestnut Hill's wraparound verandah faces the Delaware River and is surrounded by mountains. New Hope, Penn., is 25 minutes away, and the small town of Milford is around the corner.

"We love what we're doing and feel our guests are the best anywhere!"

Wilson Thomas built this charming house for his bride. Thomas owned nearby grist and saw mills and, innkeepers Rob and Linda Castagna say, "probably the whole town of Milford." The Castagnas are only the house's third residents. (They bought it in 1982 from a family who bought it from the Thomases in 1936.) As a result, all the house's architectural details are in great shape. The Castagnas have done some cosmetic work: scraping the drawing room down to its original colors and reproducing them, including the four tones and gold leaf on the plaster cornice moulding, and hanging 40 rolls of period paper in the Bridal Suite, uncovering an 1878 note trapped behind the old paper in the process. They've also researched the Thomas family history, using 19th-century newspapers.

Furnishings are elegant antiques, including an Eastlake period parlor set and a turn-of-the-century dining arrangement complete with chandelier.

Restrictions: No smoking. No pets.
Beds: Five rooms: one double with a private bath; one double with a semi-private bath; one double with one twin and a semi-private bath. The Bridal Suite has a double bed, private bath, and extra bedroom.
Breakfast: Large country breakfast: fresh eggs, juice, coffee, tea, baked goods, pancakes, and more.
Extras: Coffee and tea can be had anytime. Swimming, tubing, and tennis courts are nearby. And there's cross-country skiing in the winter along the river and canal towpath.
Rates: $55 (bay window with river view) to $75 (the Bridal Suite). Weekly rates are available, as is a bassinet. Personal checks welcome.
Mailing Address: PO Box N, Milford, NJ 08848

OCEAN CITY

LAUREL HALL
Pat and Dick Harris
48 Wesley Road
Ocean City, NJ 08226
(609) 399-0800
Year-round, weekends only
September through May

C. 1900 Vernacular shorefront

LOCATION: Billed as "America's Finest Family Resort Town," Ocean City offers plenty of fine dining, a two-mile boardwalk and many community events. Laurel Hall is in a quiet residential area tucked away from the city's "main drag."

"Visitors to Laurel Hall tend to become friends, who return time and again to enjoy the island and the ambiance of our home. Welcome!"

Here's a house with an unusual look: It's bedecked with a three-storey, Tuscan-columned front porch, shaded at each level by forest-green canvas awnings. The interior is comfortably decorated with antique white wicker, ceiling fans, bright wallpapers, and a parlor stove.

Restrictions: No pets or children under eight. Smoking on balconies only. Check-in after 1 p.m., check-out at 11 a.m.

Beds: Six rooms. One has a double bed, private bath, and separate entrance. Two have a set of twin beds and share a bath. There are two rooms with double beds; they also share a bath and a balcony. The sixth room has two double beds, one twin, a cot, private bath, and a private balcony.

Breakfast: Homemade pastry, fruit, coffee, tea, and juice.

Extras: Beach tags and bicycles are available free of charge.

Rates: $35 to $45. Rates reduced Labor Day to Memorial Day. Personal checks accepted.

NEW JERSEY

OCEAN VIEW

MAJOR GANDY'S
Roseann and Bernard Keenan
180 Shore Road
Ocean View, NJ 08230
(609) 624-1080
Year-round

C. 1815 Gothic Revival

LOCATION: Major Gandy's is centrally located between Atlantic City and Cape May and minutes away from the beaches of Sea Isle City.

"We look forward to having a chat over tea with our OHJ guests and friends, sharing and comparing renovations likes and dislikes, and hearing all about our guests' interests."

Major Gandy was a physician who served in the Spanish-American War, rose to the post of colonel, and eventually became Surgeon General. The house is actually his family home, built before he was born.

There's Victorian trim on everything from the porch to the outhouse. The interior is rich in other original features like window panes, the main staircase, and stained glass around the doorway. The Keenans especially love to show off the stencilled ceiling in the "South Parlor," and they've put antiques and brass and canopy beds in the guest rooms.

Restrictions: No smoking. No pets, and no children under nine.
Beds: There are four rooms: two doubles, one twin, and one single.
Breakfast: Continental: juice, fruit, muffins, preserves, cakes, and coffee.
Extras: Beach passes and afternoon tea are provided.
Rates: $35 (shared bath) to $60 (private bath). Cots, $10. 10% deduction in winter. Personal checks welcome.

10% discount to OHJ members.

SPRING LAKE

ASHLING COTTAGE
Goodi and Jack Stewart
106 Sussex Avenue
Spring Lake, NJ 07762
(201) 449-3553
March 1 through December 31

1877 Victorian "hybrid" cottage

LOCATION: The inn, along the Jersey shore, is one block from the ocean and beach and one block from the spring-fed lake from which the town got its name. Nearby you'll find Allaire State Park, golfing, tennis, camping, canoeing, bird watching, antiquing, and many historic houses.

A particularly innovative builder transported leftover lumber from the 1876 Philadelphia Exposition to Spring Lake and used it on this unusual house. At that time, the farmland that was Spring Lake was being transformed to a fashionable, seaside resort, a vacation spot for Philadelphia and New York gentlefolk. Many of Spring Lake's first investors, builders, and summer residents had donated generously to the 1876 Exposition — thus resulted Ashling Cottage and many houses like it. Some buildings were even moved here whole from Philadelphia!

Though many houses in town are built from Exposition lumber, Ashling is particularly striking. It has a unique roofline—part gambrel and part mansard. Porches jut out from every direction, in every angle, at every height. One glassed-in porch, an entity in itself, serves as a solarium and breakfast room, and looks out over the ocean.

Hosts Goodi and Jack Stewart are friendly folks, and their furnishings are Victorian antiques, mostly made of oak.

Restrictions: Well-mannered children welcome, but keep in mind that "the inn has none of today's 'necessities' (TV, air conditioning, etc.)" No pets.
Beds: Ten guest rooms. Each with queen-sized bed, eight with private bath. Three of the rooms are large enough to accommodate an additional cot.
Breakfast: "Sumptuous" continental: fresh-ground coffee, imported teas, warm croissants, juices, fresh fruit in season, cold cereal, and home-baked "goodies."
Extras: Babysitting can be arranged at local rates. There are impromptu wine get-togethers, beach passes for a one-time $10 charge per room, and "we welcome the challenge to host any private party." Over Labor Day weekend the Stewarts hold a black-tie weenie roast(!).
Rates: $55 to $95. Cots, $15. Off-season rates are 15% lower. A stay of three days or longer is further discounted. Personal checks welcome.

10% discount to OHJ members during off season.

NEW JERSEY

SPRING LAKE BEACH

COLONIAL OCEAN HOUSE
Charles and Virginia Mitchell
102 Sussex Avenue
Spring Lake Beach, NJ 07762
(201) 449-9090
Memorial Day through September

1886 Italianate shorefront hotel

LOCATION: The inn is one block from the ocean and one block from the lake in the heart of Spring Lake, with its many Victorian buildings. Churches, restaurants, and shops are a few blocks away.

Ocean House was built as a resort hotel for wealthy, Victorian-era vacationers from Philadelphia and New York. Like so many houses in Spring Lake, it has its own built-in relic from the 1876 Philadelphia Exposition—a beautiful, winding staircase that leads up from the entrance hall.

The hotel has changed very little in its first century. The old louvered doors still separate guest rooms from the wide hallways; the original, ornate mantelpieces still throw out heat on chilly evenings; and the wraparound verandah, where guests can enjoy refreshing ocean breezes, is as inviting as ever. Best of all, it's still family-run, and so provides the intimacy modern motels lack.

Restrictions: No pets. Check-in after 1 p.m.
Beds: There are 44 rooms total: 12 singles, 32 doubles or twins. Many with private baths.
Breakfast: Continental: coffee, juice, pastries, and fruit in season.
Extras: Beach passes are provided, and there's a "coffee hour" from 8 to 10 p.m.
Rates: $50 to $72 double occupancy. Single rates half as much. Cots available for an additional charge. Rates increase by $5 per person on weekends, $10 per person from July 4th through Labor Day. Credit cards and personal checks welcome. In winter, phone (201) 449-3552.

10% discount to OHJ members.

NEW YORK

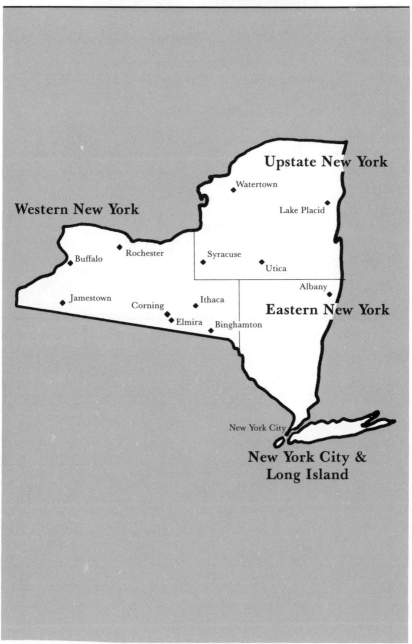

Upstate New York

Watertown

Lake Placid

Western New York

Buffalo

Rochester

Syracuse

Utica

Jamestown

Corning

Ithaca

Elmira

Binghamton

Albany

Eastern New York

New York City

New York City &
Long Island

ALTAMONT

APPEL INN
Laurie and Gerd Beckmann
Route 146
Altamont, NY 12009
(518) 861-8344
Year-round

1765 Late Georgian

LOCATION: Fifteen minutes from Albany, Appel Inn is surrounded by lots of historic homes. There are also many flea markets and auctions in the area. Golf courses and hiking parks are within walking distance.

Several years before the American Revolution, Hendrick Appel built this house and ran a tavern in its front room. More than two centuries later, Laurie and Gerd Beckmann moved in and, always curious to learn more about their house's history, invited Appel's descendants for a family reunion and Christmas celebration.

The imposing, southern-style pillars guarding the front of Appel's tavern are 1908 additions. A man named Osborne added these and the back-side solarium. Osborne was apparently captivated by columns—every home he ever owned had them.

Since 1908, there've been few changes made on the National Register house; its wide pine floors, beamed ceilings, and original fireplaces are in good shape. Laurie and Gerd still use the early 19th-century barns and henhouse out back. And they run an antiques shop on their first floor, specializing in bedroom sets and imported

Victorian bed linens.

Restrictions: Children welcome. No pets. Smoking downstairs only. Check-in by "mutual agreement."
Beds: There are two rooms with fireplaces and access to the porch which have double beds. There is another room with a double bed. One single room is available, and a room with two oversized single beds. Two of the rooms share a bath.
Breakfast: Breakfast is usually what the chef (Laurie) is "in the mood" for, so you could wake up to croissants, fresh fruit, French toast, sausage, eggs Benedict, or pancakes.
Extras: Babysitting arrangements are easily made. Guests can use two nearby pools.
Rates: $35 to $50, single; $45 to $50, double. Personal checks and credit cards welcome.
   10% discount to OHJ members.
Mailing Address: Box 18, RD 3, Altamont, NY 12009

HIGH FALLS

HOUSE ON THE HILL
Shelly and Sharon Glassman
Old Route 213
High Falls, NY 12440
(914) 687-9627
Year-round

LOCATION: The inn is located beside Roundout Creek and its waterfalls, in a hamlet first settled in 1669. Delaware & Hudson Canal, with its locks and museum are nearby, as are acqueducts designed by Roebling of Brooklyn Bridge fame. Streams and rock formations make hiking and nature walks "a memorable event."

The iron, Dutch-oven door to the Rumford fireplace in this inn's keeping room has been missing for over a century. It was turned into ammunition during the Civil War, along with lots of other iron-work from the property. The 19th-century residents who donated their iron were quite generous at heart: They also provided the surrounding village with water from their central well. (Later, these folks had the only running water in town, piped by gravity from the well to the dry sink indoors.)

Behind the ornate, 1856 porch addition, the house retains the basic Roman symmetry of the Federal style, with an equal number of windows on either side of the main entrance and a chimney at each end. Eyebrow windows peeping out under the eaves and the quatrefoil millwork on the front porch make the house distinctive. Inside, the original mouldings, which match the design of the fireplace mantels, and the chair railings are still in place. Innkeepers Shelly and Sharon Glassman have on display their large collections of hand-sewn quilts (there's one on every bed) and antique tools.

Restrictions: Children above six are welcome, but "pets don't work out well with our dog and three cats." Smoking in public rooms. No specific check-out time but approximate arrival time is appreciated.
Beds: Two rooms share a bath, one with double and twin beds, the other a double; both have sitting rooms. One suite with private bath, double bed, and dressing room.
Breakfast: Fresh fruit, home-baked pastries with coffee, tea, or warm cider. Entree can be crepes, blintzes, or eggs, with a meat garnish.
Extras: Complimentary wine, cheese, snacks, fresh fruit, or "a bowl of whatever's cooking in a big pot on the stove" are offered.
Rates: $60 to $65, cots $15 extra. Personal checks welcome.
Mailing Address: Box 86, High Falls, NY 12440

PINE PLAINS

THE PINES
Lorna Mitchell
North Main and Maple Streets
Pine Plains, NY 12567
(518) 398-7677
Year-round

1878 Eclectic, stick-style

LOCATION: This rural setting in a country village in North Dutchess County offers diverse flora, fauna, and geological features, which make for interesting walks. The inn commands a view of its several acres of lawns, within a five-minute walk from town.

Believe it or not, this grand mansion was once a one-family residence. A prominent local lawyer named William S. Eno built it, and his fortune kept it running until 1895, when it was converted into an exclusive boarding house for well-to-do folks like 1920s actors and actresses.

By the time Bruce and Stella Palmer ran across The Pines, the well-to-do were long gone, and it was in a sorry state of disrepair. Nobody had patched the roof for decades; as a result, the interior walls were moldering away due to water damage. Inside was the usual 1950s tasteless decor: loud contact paper, carpeting, and vinyl flooring. Why'd they buy the fallen giant, which they knew would consume a substantial chunk of their life's energy? "Because we're insane," says Stella, only half joking. In truth, they fell in love with its sweeping verandahs, balconies, peaked and dormered tower, asymmetric gables, bay windows and, most of all, its eclectic stick work which, miraculously, had survived the era of anti-Victorianism.

The Palmers' first project, dictated by the necessity of keeping their heads dry during thunder showers, was to repair the roof. They hired a Vermont roofer who specializes in slate and historic preservation. The challenge of the project for him was re-shingling the steep, four-sided tower, the likes of which he'd never before encountered. Eventually, he felt so captivated by that tower he researched a way to duplicate the only piece of missing exterior ornament: the spire atop its pointed roof, illustrated in an early sketch of the house.

After the roof emergency was over, the Palmers tackled the interior: plumbing, wiring, refinishing, restoring the ornamental plaster work, wallpapering, and furnishing with eclectic antiques. The current owner, Lorna Mitchell, can show you through all the work that was done on the house.

Restrictions: No pets. Check-in before 9 p.m.
Beds: Four double rooms with twin beds, also one single. "We limit ourselves to nine guests." Three rooms share a bath.
Breakfast: Full continental breakfast.
Extras: Robes are furnished for the trip to the baths down the hall.
Rates: $55 to $65. Personal checks accepted.
  10% discount to OHJ members.
Mailing Address: RD 1, Box 131, Pine Plains, NY 12567

SARATOGA SPRINGS

1877 Italianate

ADELPHI HOTEL
Gregg Siefker and
Sheila Parkert
365 Broadway
Saratoga Springs, NY 12866
(518) 587-4688
May to November

LOCATION: The small Victorian city of Saratoga Springs off~~, as it did 100 years ago, mineral springs and horse racing. The New York City Ballet and Philadelphia Orchestra make it their summer home, and the fall foliage is colorful.

The Adelphi was part of an era which saw the rise in Saratoga of some of the world's largest and most opulent hotels. Saratoga reigned internationally as Queen of the Spas; all the day's most brilliant luminaries — millionaires, artists, social butterflies, raconteurs — gravitated to the renowned resort.

The Adelphi is one of the last remainders of this grand era. Its spectacular piazza, with its three-storey-high columns and intricate Victorian fretwork, is one of the few left in what was once a dramatic parade of similar facades down Saratoga's main thoroughfare. Inside, the Adelphi has retained its original Victorian splendor, with its grand lobby and staircase, high ceilings, and nine-foot-tall windows. And thanks to innkeepers Greg Siefker and Sheila Parkert, the Adelphi will continue to outlive the others that collapsed before it: They've recently restored the entire hotel, room by room, and decorated it with "truckloads" of Victoriana that will surely last into the next century.

Beds: All 25 rooms—eight twins, 17 doubles—have private baths.
Breakfast: Freshly baked coffeecake, fruit, coffee, and tea are delivered to guest's room, or served in the parlor or outdoor piazza.
Extras: Victorian café and bar with an outdoor courtyard, July and August.
Rates: $55 to $95, rising to $120 to $250 in August. Cots, $15 extra. Personal checks and credit cards welcome.

SOUTH DURHAM

GLEN DURHAM
Dave and Jan Nascimbeni
Morrison Road
South Durham, NY 12413
(518) 622-9878
Year-round

1785 Federal farmhouse

LOCATION: On a farm with a sugar house, the inn is near a fishing preserve, Howe Caverns, Durham Museum, hiking trails, and Catskill Game Farm; it's a two-and-a-half-hour drive from New York City and one hour to Albany.

Stay at this working horsefarm and you'll certainly feel like you've stepped back at least a century. The decor is unpretentious, country-style: candlewick spreads and patchwork quilts Jan Nascimbeni's grandmother made, hand-woven rugs (including a stair carpet her mother and father spun), stencilling, and Early American furnishings, including cannonball and Jenny Lind beds. The 200-year-old maple stairs and floors come from trees on the surrounding property. Just beware of elephants: One was on the run in the Catskills several years ago, and was finally captured right in this glen.

Restrictions: No smoking. Check-in before 10 p.m. Children, but not pets, are welcome.
Beds: Two rooms have 3/4 beds, one has a single—all three share one bath.
Breakfast: Country-fresh eggs, omelettes; buttermilk pancakes and French toast with Glen Durham maple syrup, muffins, homemade pastries, jams, jellies, honey. Full is served from 8 to 9 a.m., then Continental until 10 a.m.
Extras: A full cookie jar is always available for snacks. Serious riders can take lessons from Jan, a certified instructor, for $15. Optional family-style dinner, for $10, includes homemade soup, breads, and dessert. The sugar house is open from mid-February to mid-March.
Rates: Single $45, double $55, payable by personal check.
    10% discount to OHJ members.
Mailing Address: RD 2, Box 816, Cairo, NY 12413

STONE RIDGE

**BAKER'S BED &
BREAKFAST**
Doug Baker and Linda Delgado
Old Kings Highway
Stone Ridge, NY 12484
(914) 687-9795
Year-round

1780 Hudson Valley stone farmhouse

LOCATION: On 16 acres in the Roundout Valley, the house offers a "memorable view": fields, woods, mountains, and the property's pond. Lakes are nearby, as is the art colony of Woodstock. High Falls, settled 1669, is two miles away, with its waterfall and canal museum.

This house is a rare find: It's built with fieldstones gathered in nearby meadows. All the original hand-forged hardware, pine floors and mouldings remain, as well as a Rumford fireplace and part of the beehive oven. Hosts Doug and Linda have furnished it with antiques (some Hepplewhite, some Early American), and Oriental rugs.

Restrictions: Children are welcome Sunday through Thursday. No pets, smoking only by fireside or on porch. Check-in after 2 p.m., check-out before 11 a.m.
Beds: Five rooms with private baths.
Breakfast: Homemade jams, jellies, and pastries; fresh eggs, local meats, choice of juices, vegetables from the garden, freshly ground coffee or herbal teas.
Extras: There are fireplaces in the kitchen, living and dining rooms; a hot tub in the green house, a pond for swimming, and a hammock for two under an old apple tree. Coffee, tea, or wine are offered to arriving guest, Trivial Pursuit and chess games are set up in the living room.
Rates: $58 to $68; cots, $15 extra; cribs at no extra charge. Personal checks accepted.
  10% discount to OHJ members.
Mailing Address: RD 2, Box 80, Stone Ridge, NY 12484

EAST HAMPTON

BASSETT HOUSE INN
Michael Bassett
128 Montauk Highway
East Hampton, NY 11937
(516) 324-6127
Year-round

C. 1830 Federal

LOCATION: Bassett House Inn is surrounded by old estates and the Home Sweet Home Museum. Clinton Academy is not far away. Plus the famous beaches are less than two miles away.

Said recent guests: "Thanks so much for a memorable weekend. . . You have made such a special place out of this house, a real home. We'll be back."

Brothers Talmage and Ezekial Jones probably never dreamed, when they built this simple yet gracious Federal, that in a century-and-a-half their property would be deluged in a sea of tourists—all escaping Manhattan's muggy summer weather for one of the East Coast's most fashionable (and beautiful) vacation spots. Despite the increased number of visitors, their house's original architectural features, including the pilastered doorway and wide pine flooring, are in excellent condition. The friendly innkeeper, Michael Bassett, takes good care of the house. He's in a constant process of refinishing the original mantels, mouldings, and staircase. And he's furnished it in a manner the Joneses would certainly approve of: with a delightful collection of early American antiques, gathered at local auctions and estate sales.

Restrictions: Additional charge for pets. Well-behaved children welcome. Check-in after 2 p.m.; check-out at noon.
Beds: There are ten double rooms and two single rooms. Nine of the rooms share three baths. Three have private baths. A few have fireplaces.
Breakfast: Breakfast is served from 8 to 11 a.m.—"basic, wholesome, and all you want," including eggs, cereal, toast, muffins, pancakes, coffee, tea, and other specialties.

Extras: In need of a babysitter or a cup of tea, perhaps? Michael is more than happy to help you out in any way he can to make your stay pleasant. He also has plenty of beach supplies (towels, blankets, coolers, etc.) for those in need.

Rates: Accommodations can be as low as $45 (for a single) or as high as $135 (master room with private bath and fireplace). Off-season rates are lower. Personal checks and credit cards accepted.

10% discount to OHJ members.

LAUREL

GANDALF HOUSE
Robert Arehart and George
Moravak
Main Road
Laurel, NY 11948
(516) 298-4769
Year-round

1873 Italianate with Mansard wing

LOCATION: Located in the heart of Long Island's vineyards, Gandalf House is one mile away from Peconic Bay; two miles from Long Island Sound; and only 20 minutes from the Hampton beaches.

"We have been running our B&B for the past three years and have had great fun meeting people. We welcome all old-house lovers."

Two parapsychologists who were visiting this inn claimed they chatted with the ghost of the sea captain who built it. The innkeepers themselves have never seen him, but the parapsychologists claim the atmosphere is relaxed yet vibrant, perfect for ghostly wanderings.

The house is excellently preserved both inside and out. Inside, the original woodwork (including chair and plate railings in the dining room) and 11-foot ceilings remain. Outside, the paired roof brackets, delicate porch, and gable-end porthole window are intact. The house is decorated with cheery wallpapers, antiques, and paintings.

Restrictions: No young children. No pets. Check-in is flexible, but arrangements must be made in advance.

Beds: Three rooms—one with a double bed, one with a set of twin beds, and one with a sofa bed—share two baths.

Breakfast: Continental: coffee, tea, juice, fresh Danish or rolls, fresh fruit when available.

Extras: You can arrange to have a gourmet dinner on the premises (arrangements must be made in advance). And there's an in-ground pool.

Rates: The room with a double bed costs $50. Either of the other two rooms are $40. Personal checks accepted.

  10% discount to OHJ members.

Mailing Address: Box 385, Laurel, NY 11948

NEW YORK: NYC & LONG ISLAND

NEW YORK CITY

PENINGTON FRIENDS' HOUSE
Cathi and Dana Belcher
215 East 15th Street
New York, NY 10003
(212) 673-1730
Year-round

LOCATION: In between Gramercy Park and the East Village, Penington Friends' House is 15 minutes from downtown and midtown Manhattan. Stuyvesant Park is adjacent.

"We offer a friendly, homelike atmosphere, and good meals in a big-city environment."

Beaux-Arts school architect Richard Morris Hunt designed this elegant brownstone for the great-grandson of Peter Stuyvesant, one of New York's original colonizers. Since 1897, the building has housed a diverse and ever-changing Quaker community. There are 35 "permanent" residents: students, working professionals, and retirees from a variety of national, religious, and ethnic backgrounds, all sympathizing with the Quaker ethic, all sharing in cooking and housekeeping chores. There's also space to house wayward travellers who want short-term lodgings and meals in a sometimes inhospitable city. (The lodgings have been compared to a country inn in the heart of Manhattan.)

The townhouse's architectural features are every bit as rich as the Stuyvesant fortune: wrought-iron balconies, fences and gates outside; seven marble fireplaces, marble-floored foyer, inlaid cherry parquet floors, mahogany stairway, and 13-foot ceilings inside. Many of the furnishings are antiques donated by Quaker compatriots, including a 1744 grandfather clock and a Chickering grand piano. There's a spacious backyard and garden, where the residents hold summer cookouts and picnics.

Restrictions: Check-out at 11 a.m. Check-in is flexible as long as you make arrangements in advance. Smoking is discouraged.
Beds: The Penington has two double rooms and one single room available for sojourners.
Breakfast: Served from 7:30 to 9 a.m. weekdays and from 9 to 11 a.m. weekends, buffet style: eggs, bacon, sausage, pancakes, French toast, coffeecake, homemade granola, yogurt, fresh fruit, muffins, toast, coffee, and a variety of teas.
Extras: Dinner is served every day at 6 p.m. All food is freshly pre-pared. Meals are buffet and eaten family style at a long wooden table. Vegetarian entrees are available at all times.
Rates: The single room, which has a sink and shared bath, is $30. A double room with a private bath and fireplace is $50. Both include breakfast and dinner. Cots, $15. Personal and traveler's checks accepted.

SOUTHAMPTON

THE OLD POST HOUSE INN
Cecile and Ed Courville
136 Main Street
Southampton, NY 11968
(516) 283-1717
Year-round

1684 Colonial farmhouse with 1705 addition

LOCATION: The Hamptons offer elegant boutiques, restaurants, museums, plus eight miles of beaches. Though most people don't know it, you'll also find the largest collection of windmills in North America here. Sag Harbor, Shelter Island, Montauk Lighthouse, and wineries are also nearby.

As they rehabilitated room after room, Ed and Cecile Courville kept stumbling upon artifacts—a 19th-century medicine bottle, for instance, or a circa 1700 clay tobacco pipe. They realized they had more than just another great old house on their hands, they had an archaeological find. The local archaeological association agreed, and began excavations in the basement.

To date, many interesting things have been found: for example, spoons, scraps of basket and rug, shards of pottery, and part of an early Bible. But by far the most intriguing find is the traces of shellfish, fruit, and vegetable consumption, indicating someone may have cooked and lived down there. This may prove a long-standing rumor —that this house once sheltered slaves escaping via the Underground Railroad.

The Courvilles chose country and antique pieces to furnish the house, and wicker for the porch. In parts of the building, they left sections of structural beams exposed so guests can examine the nail-less construction. Also worth a look are the floorboards, which in some places reach 18 inches wide. And the innkeepers can also show you the "scuttle hole" in the roof; once it provided an ideal vantage point for whale watching.

Restrictions: No children under 12, no pets. Check-in after 2:30 p.m., check-out at 11 a.m.
Beds: One room has twins, the other six have doubles (one room can accommodate three). None share a bath.
Breakfast: Continental.
Extras: The Courvilles offer free transportation to the beach, bus, and train stations.
Rates: $80 ("economy weekends" in off-season) to $150 (summer weekends). Credit cards welcome; personal checks accepted seven days prior to arrival.

10% discount to OHJ members with proof of membership.

BARNEVELD

ROUGHOUSE
Mr. and Mrs. Maitland
Tabb Ijams
Route 28
Barneveld, NY 13304
(315) 896-4441
Year-round

LOCATION: The best part about this inn is its spectacular location, overlooking a fast-moving river and surrounded by towering tamaracks that turn a luminous amber in fall. The 25-acre property is perfect for trout fishing and cross-country skiing, and near Adirondack Park and Hamilton College.

The original part of this house is a charming, white, clapboarded Greek Revival, entered through a pedimented portico that's supported by two Doric columns. Additional wings have been added over the years, including a 1930s library with cathedral ceiling. But the original section, where the guest rooms are, has never been remuddled.

The hosts are local theater producers and dog breeders, and have travelled worldwide to show their dogs. They decided to start taking guests a few years ago, when their kids went off to college. The house is furnished with antiques.

Beds: Two doubles and one single, each with private bath. The first floor has a comfortable sitting room.
Breakfast: Full breakfast; Mrs. Ijams is an accredited chef.
Extras: Afternoon tea is provided, and there's a full bar. Pet sitting is available, and dinner can be served on request. Guests are welcome to use the piano and test the acoustics of the living room's 20-foot ceiling.
Rates: Doubles $45; singles $35. Personal checks accepted; no credit cards.

10% discount to OHJ members.
Mailing Address: Box 33, Rt. 28, Barneveld, NY 13304

CHESTERTOWN

THE FRIENDS LAKE INN
Sharon and Greg Taylor
Friends Lake Road
Chestertown, NY 12817
(518) 494-4751
Year-round

C. 1860 Vernacular

LOCATION: The Inn sits overlooking Friends Lake, in the central Adirondack Mountains. Skiing is ten minutes away at Gore Mountain. Lake Placid and Lake George Village are within driving distance (one hour and 18 minutes respectively).

The Friends Lake Inn was built in the 1860s to accommodate the tanners who worked in the area. Later the Murphy family purchased it to use as a private residence. As more and more of their friends came to visit from Albany, the Murphys did the sensible thing: they opened an inn.

At that time there were about five other inns on the shores of the lake, playing host to the many vacationers who arrived by convenient train. When the train quit stopping here, most of the inns closed. Friends Lake Inn was abandoned in the 1950s and remained vacant until Greg and Sharon Taylor purchased it in 1983 and began restoration.

The dining room still has the original tin ceiling and chestnut woodwork. The large verandah, used for dining, has been screened-in, "to keep out the bugs," explain Sharon and Greg.

Restrictions: No smoking in the bedrooms, no pets.
Breakfast: Full, country-style breakfast.
Extras: Guests are welcome to use the inn's private beach, boats, and sailboat. Picnic lunches are available on request. The restaurant in the inn's dining room offers a dinner menu of homemade pâtés and breads, with entrees ranging from seafood to pasta, vintage wine, and champagne, plus desserts made on the premises daily.
Rates: $40 to $95, single; $55 to $130, double. Personal checks and credit cards welcome.
10% discount to OHJ members.

CLAYTON

GREYSTONE INN
Francis and Gerry Kirkey
Mattis Road
Clayton, NY 13624
(315) 686-2408
May 1 through December 30

Early 19th-century limestone Federal

LOCATION: The inn, in the historic village of Clayton, is three miles from the Saint Lawrence River. Summer activities include boating, hiking, antiquing, and visiting local museums. The setting is quiet, with many dairy farms.

The Greystone Inn sits at the hub of five diverging country roads. What better place for a 19th-century stagecoach stop? Among the weary travelers who rested here before settling nearby were French immigrants fleeing the anti-Bonapartist regime.

The house is built of native limestone, with a wood porch and second-floor gallery extending across the front. Inside are the old wide floor boards, two-foot-deep window sills, and horsehair plaster. The walls in the guest rooms are stencilled; the wallpaper in the upstairs hall was hung in Victorian times.

Restrictions: No pets.
Beds: Three rooms—one with double bed, one with a double and a twin bed, and one with twin beds—share two full baths.
Breakfast: Breakfast varies daily, but always includes fruit juice, coffee, tea, cereal, muffins, and fresh fruit. Entrees include: Pain perdu (special puffed French toast), hot peach or apple gratin, homemade muffins, quiches, and special recipes provided by guests.
Extras: Late afternoon refreshments are served. There are telescopes for star watching. A Coast Guard-approved fishing guide (your host, Francis) is available for an additional charge, and an evening meal can be requested.
Rates: $22.50 per person; double occupancy per night. Personal checks welcome.

10% discount to OHJ members.
Mailing Address: RD 1, Box 341A, Clayton, NY 13624

KEENE

THE BARK EATER
Joe-Pete Wilson and Harley
McDevitt Wilson
Alstead Mill Road
Keene, NY 12942
(518) 576-2221
Year-round

C. 1800 Colonial

LOCATION: The Bark Eater is located on a spacious farm in the heart of the Adirondack mountains. Olympic Village at Lake Placid is five minutes away. There are mountains, lakes, and rivers nearby for hiking or scenic drives.

The Wilson family has been taking guests on their farm since 1930. Theirs is a quintessential farmhouse: dormers and a long porch running across the front; expanded over the years so that the interior floors are at all different levels. The house is furnished with Wilson family heirlooms. Recently, Joe-Pete and Harley McDevitt converted their carriage house into additional guest lodgings.

Restrictions: They prefer a pre-6 p.m. check-in, or notification no later than 9 p.m. No pets; smoking and children permitted.
Beds: Seventeen rooms, thirteen shared baths, four private baths.
Breakfast: Full: hot cereal, homemade granola, and muffins; eggs, French toast, or pancakes; juice, fruit, milk, tea, and coffee.
Rates: Vary according to day of week and season, but range is $52 to $72. Cots are $15 to $21 extra, cribs are free. Personal checks welcome.
   10% discount to OHJ members.

LAKE PLACID

LAKE PLACID MANOR
Jane Reeder,
Carolyn and Robert Hardy
Whiteface Inn Road
Lake Placid, NY 12946
(518) 523-2573
Year-round

1895 Adirondack Rustic

LOCATION: On the banks of Lake Placid, the inn overlooks a golf course with Whiteface Mountain as a backdrop. Water skiing, tennis and golf, hiking, fishing, horseback riding, and of course downhill and cross-country skiing are all nearby.

The Lake Placid Manor is one of those romantic Adirondack camps that artists, writers, and those who craved a break from hectic city life flocked to at the turn of the century. (Damon Runyon, author of *Guys and Dolls*, wrote several short stories while vacationing here.) This camp, like the others of its time, is characterized by a certain truthfulness in architecture—it's built of indigenous wood, with broad overhangs, porches, and multiple levels that blend right into the surrounding forest. Inside, it's just as rustic, with rough-hewn wainscotting, native wood floors, birchwood handrails, and lots of hunting-lodge-size fireplaces.

Unfortunately, Adirondack camp stewards after the 1920s could not afford to maintain buildings so far from "civilization." The Lake Placid Manor went the way of its counterparts, and when Kathi Ransom bought it in 1984, its woodwork was deteriorating. She's recently completed a thorough restoration.

Beds: There are four doubles, 33 twins, and one suite with three beds. Four rooms share baths.
Extras: The innkeepers provide afternoon tea and passes for golf and tennis. Paddleboats, canoes, and rowboats can be rented on the premises.
Rates: $55 to $85; cots, $10. Personal checks and credit cards welcome.
Mailing Address: PO Box 870, Lake Placid, NY 12946

CANDOR

THE EDGE OF THYME
Frank and Eva Mae Musgrave
Six Main Street
Candor, NY 13743
(607) 659-5155
Year-round

1908 Georgian Revival

LOCATION: The inn, located in a quiet town in New York wine country, is close to Cornell University, Ithaca College, Corning Glass, Watkins Glen, wineries, the Finger Lakes, and Binghamton.

Rosa Murphy Canfield wouldn't settle for second class. That's how she got to be John D. Rockefeller's personal secretary. That's why she expected her army of servants to be on call 24 hours a day, why she reprimanded her chauffeur if she sighted a blemish on the chrome of one of her seven automobiles. And that's why she and her husband Amos, a New York City physician, hired a top Madison Avenue architecture firm to design this summer home.

The house represents the epitome of Georgian Revival. Six sets of French doors open to the outdoors. The fireplaces are marble. All the floors are parquet. There's a side porch enclosed with costly leaded glass windows ornamented with elaborate hunting scenes. Even the carriage house is impressive, with its in-house car-wash system. (The plumbing from this clever device is still in place.)

The house was well maintained throughout the years, never modernized. When Frank and Eva Mae Musgrave bought it in 1984, even the original bathroom fixtures were in working order. Only the formal gardens and arbor were unkempt—these they've restored beautifully. They've furnished the house with antiques from the period and before, many of them family heirlooms.

Restrictions: No smoking, no pets (a kennel is located nearby).
Beds: Five rooms with double beds and one with twin beds. Three rooms have a private bath.
Breakfast: Breakfast "as would have been enjoyed in 1908": juice, fruit, homemade breads, muffins, and main dishes such as coddled eggs layered with meat and cheese, sausage pie, or fondue.

Extras: Afternoon tea and an evening snack are provided.
Rates: $30 to $50 double, $25 to $30 single. Personal checks welcome.
10% discount to OHJ members.
Mailing Address: PO Box 48, Candor, NY 13743

CLARENCE

ASA RANSOM HOUSE
Robert and Judy Lenz
10529 (Route 5)
Clarence, NY 14031
(716) 759-2315
February through December

1853 Carpenter Gothic

LOCATION: Clarence abounds with antique shops, many within walking distance of the inn. The town park, a few steps away, offers shaded lawns, a duck pond, and outdoor summer concerts. Tennis and swimming are available to inn guests at the park. The Clarence Center Emporium and Ice Cream Parlour (historic restoration) are nearby. Buffalo is a short drive, and Niagara Falls is 28 miles away.

In 1799, the Holland Land Company offered lots ten miles apart in what is now Clarence to "any proper man who would build and operate a tavern upon it." The first to accept this offer was a young silversmith named Asa Ransom, who'd been plying his trade in the little fur trading post on the shores of Lake Erie. In the hollow of the ledge near a pine grove, Mr. Ransom built a combination log cabin home and tavern. In 1801, he built a sawmill near the creek that now bears his name, and in 1803 he built the first grist mill in Erie County. Trade over the next 50 years proved so successful that Ransom was able to retire in this elegant home, which he built in 1853. (Some stone walls from the grist mill still stand, but the log cabin is nowhere to be found.)

Two of the guest rooms in this inn are in the part of the house Asa Ransom built; the other two are in the two-storey, clapboarded ell innkeepers Robert and Judy Lenz added in 1975. But you probably won't be able to tell the difference between the old and new rooms:

299

They used old building techniques in the new section. The "new" floors are wide plank, held in place with antique nails. One "new" room is stencilled in early American style. And all the rooms are decorated with charming country antiques, including braided rugs, overstuffed chairs, wood stoves, and cannonball, canopy, brass, and iron beds.

The Lenzes run a full-service restaurant and gift shop in the new ell. In the original section are a taproom (decorated Ransom style, with oil lanterns and shuttered windows), and a library with all sorts of books and periodicals.

Restrictions: Children welcome. No pets. No smoking in rooms. Check-in by 10 p.m.
Beds: Four rooms each with private bath and shower: two doubles, one twin, and one room with two double beds.
Breakfast: Fresh fruit, fruit muffins, breakfast egg pie, and beverages.
Extras: Puzzles, chess, and checkers are available in the library. There's a taproom and old radio programs on tape (Jack Benny, Will Rogers, etc.). The full-service, elegant restaurant is open Sunday through Thursday.
Rates: $60 to $70. Cots, $10. Cribs available for no additional charge. Personal checks accepted.

WESTERN NEW YORK

CORNING

THE CECCE GUEST HOUSE
Margaret Cecce and Florence Gaiser
166 Chemung Street
Corning, NY 14830
(607) 962-5682
Year-round

1899 Neo-Colonial

LOCATION: The house is in town, within walking distance of Corning's restored Market Street and many shops and restaurants, the Corning Museum of Glass, the Rockwell Museum of Western Art and the Patterson Museum (built in 1796). A short drive takes you to Watkins Glen race track, the Finger Lakes, or Hammondsport Wineries.

"Our guests are all welcome like relatives."

Margaret Cecce and Florence Gaiser have been taking guests here since 1961. Inside, Margaret says, the decor is "85-percent antique." Their furnishings include a Chippendale couch, an Italian marble table, and an Eastlake bedroom set. The house still has its original terra-cotta fireplace with oak mantel and pillars, oak woodwork, and open stairway.

Beds: Two rooms with queen-size bed and shared bath, two rooms with two twin beds and shared bath. A third-floor kitchen and living room efficiency are available for guests staying for three days or more.
Breakfast: Continental.
Extras: In spring and summer guests may enjoy the water fountain and garden in the backyard.
Rates: Doubles, $30; singles, $25. Cots, $5. Traveler's checks accepted; no credit cards.
10% discount to OHJ members.

CORNING

ROSEWOOD INN
Winnie and Dick Peer
134 East First Street
Corning, NY 14830
(607) 962-3253
Year-round

1855 Greek Revival; remodelled to English Tudor, 1917

LOCATION: First street is lined with shade trees and elegant homes, two blocks from restored Market Street and the Rockwell Museum of Western Art. The Corning Museum, the Patterson Inn, built in 1796, and the Spencer Crest Nature Center are within walking distance.

In 1917, a wealthy town physician converted a Greek Revival with arched windows and two-storey columns into the stuccoed, half-timbered Tudor you'll see here today. Doctors from the nearby Corning Hospital inhabited the house until 1980, when Winnie and Dick Peer (she a retired teacher and he a daily newspaper editor) bought it. They've decorated the house in a whimsical Victorian style, naming each guest room after a 19th-century historical character. The Gibson Room, named for artist Charles Dana Gibson, is decorated with Eastlake furnishings and Gibson prints. The Jenny Lind Room, named for the famed Swedish soprano, is furnished with a Jenny Lind bedroom set. The Frederick Carder Room (Carder's glass artistry led to the formation of Corning's Steuben Glass Works) has a cozy solarium with wicker furnishings and antique stained-glass windows. The Herman Melville Room, furnished with walnut, has an interesting collection of whaling memorabilia.

Restrictions: Babies and children welcome. Smoking permitted. Check-in after noon.
Beds: Six rooms. Two two-room suites, one with private entrance, double beds and fully-equipped kitchen and one with twin beds and a sitting room; three double-bedded rooms; one room with twin beds. Four of these rooms have private bath; two share.
Breakfast: Continental: fresh fruit and juice, hot cereal, homemade granola, breads, and muffins are served in an elegant Victorian dining room.
Extras: The hosts can meet planes or buses. A welcome basket of fruit, candy and nuts awaits guests. Babysitting, for a fee, is available.
Rates: Doubles, $55 to $75; singles, $50 to $70. Cots, $5 and $10. Personal checks, MasterCard, and Visa accepted.

WESTERN NEW YORK

CORNING

VICTORIA HOUSE
Ron and Billie Jean Housel
222 Pine Street
Corning, NY 14830
(607) 962-3413
Year-round

1904 Tudor Revival

LOCATION: The house is situated on three city lots in the heart of Corning's historic south side and surrounded by formal and informal flower and rose gardens. Within walking distance are restored Market Street's shops and restaurants, the Corning Museum of Glass, and the Rockwell Museum of Western Art. New York Finger Lakes and local wineries are within a 30-mile radius.

The mayor of Corning built this high-style Tudor Revival for his newly wed son. (The mayor's mansion, a flamboyant Second Empire, is just across the street.) The house is a combination brick and half-timbered structure with tall chimneys and leaded-glass windows. It looks like something you'd find in the English countryside, except for one unusual feature: the classical columns supporting the portico.

Its interior features are grand. The foyer is 33 feet long, panelled in Spanish oak, and has massive open beams on the ceiling. The wide staircase leading up from the foyer winds alongside a two-storey stained-glass window. And every room on the main floor except the kitchen has a fireplace — 12 in all. Curiously, the living room was designed in Victorian style, with Second Empire mouldings and plaster work. (Tudor Revival is normally considered the antithesis of Victorianism, a reaction against Victorian ornateness.)

Hosts Ron and Billie Jean Housel bought the house in 1984, and completely restored it. They stripped eight layers of wallpaper from the music room, repainted in three shades of rose, and moved in their piano and harpsichord, which guests are welcome to play. They scraped generations of encrusted paint from the dining room panelling, restored all the plaster ceilings, and, in a feat of strength, moved the house's original "chambers" stove from the servants' quarters downstairs to their kitchen upstairs, a task completed only with the aid of 12 people. Last we heard, they were refurbishing the old wine cellar, repainting the exterior trim, and planting an English garden.

Restrictions: Babies and children welcome. Smoking restricted to portico and solarium. Check-in should be coordinated with hosts at time of reservation.
Beds: Two rooms with queen-size beds; one room with twin beds; one room with a double bed; plus a two-room suite with fireplace and private bath.
Breakfast: Continental is served 8 to 9:30 a.m. weekdays, 8 to 10 a.m. weekends and holidays; fresh fruit, cereals, homemade rolls or muffins, homemade jellies and jams, and tea or coffee.
Extras: Complimentary wine and cheese are served in the early evening.
Rates: Doubles, $40 to $50; singles, $35 to $40. Personal and traveler's checks accepted, but no credit cards.
   10% discount to OHJ members.

EAST AURORA

ROYCROFT INN
Kitty Turgeon and Robert Rust
40 South Grove Street
East Aurora, NY 14052
(716) 652-9030
Year-round

1895 - 1903 Arts and Crafts/Prairie School

LOCATION: East Aurora is a restful village 19 miles southeast of Buffalo, with charming architecture and a historic Main Street. The inn stands amid ten National Register buildings that once formed the "Roycroft Campus," a community for craftspeople established in the early 20th century.

Elbert Hubbard shed his worldly life as a soap executive in 1894. Inspired by the crafts center William Morris created in England, Hubbard set up an American counterpart in East Aurora. He was apparently a man of great charisma, because he attracted artisans of all kinds to his utopia. He and the Roycrofters, as his followers were known, built a campus to house their numerous activities: among them making jewelry, furniture, stained glass, fabrics, books and more.

In 1895 Hubbard constructed a one-room print shop adjacent to his house. He based his plan in part on Wordsworth's church in Grasmere, England, but he was also undoubtedly influenced by the low, sweeping rooflines characteristic of the works of his friend, Frank Lloyd Wright. Added to several times, the structure became an inn in 1903. Hubbard's wife ran it, while he supervised the shops across the street.

Much of the Roycrofters' artistry remains, especially in this inn: you'll find paintings and murals by Alex Fournier, stained and leaded glass by Dard Hunter, along with tongue-in-groove yellow pine matchstick wainscoting and the original Roycroft furniture. And part of the massive peristyle still stands, surrounding a courtyard with an untamed Japanese garden.

The innkeepers have put a lot of wallpaper, paint, and elbow grease into the place, and are awaiting a large grant before commencing more large-scale renovations.

Restrictions: Anything done in "good taste and with respect for others" is acceptable. Check-in after 2 p.m., check-out at 11 a.m.

Beds: Of the 16 rooms, there are two queens, one king, seven doubles and six twins. Most have a private bath.

Breakfast: Hard-boiled eggs, blueberry muffins, juice, and coffee.

Extras: Museum, swimming, golf, and riding passes can be arranged for a modest charge.

Rates: $45 to $100. Cots, $12. Personal checks and credit cards welcome.

10% discount to OHJ members.

FREDONIA

THE WHITE INN
David Palmer and David Bryant
52 East Main Street
Fredonia, NY 14063
(716) 672-2103
Year-round

1868 and 1919 Classical Revival

LOCATION: Historic Fredonia is a small college town between the Allegheny foothills and Lake Erie that boasts many 19th-century houses. Antique shops, wineries, daily concerts, and lectures at the college and at nearby Chautauqua Institution are available.

The first White Inn guest room David Palmer set his eyes on alarmed him so that he grabbed his suitcases and fled to the nearest motel. Now, years later, Mr. Palmer is the inn's proprietor. What changed his mind?

A bank loan. Simple as that. It wasn't the cost of the rooms that deterred Mr. Palmer on his first visit, when he was looking for lodgings on his first day as a philosophy professor at Fredonia State University. What offended him were the seedy accommodations: dark black woodwork, dusty bare lightbulbs, acoustical tile ceilings, disintegrated panelling, and bricked-over windows. Years after that first encounter, a bank officer approached Mr. Palmer and business partner David Bryant, and asked if they'd like to buy the bankrupted inn at a reduced rate. Palmer and Bryant had already transformed a crumbling fire hall into a profitable office building now listed in the National Register, and resuscitated a long-forgotten 40-unit apartment building. Encouraged by these successes, they decided to accept the bank officer's challenge.

Bryant quit the philosophy department and Palmer cut his teaching job to part-time. They took off the neon sign; unbricked fireplaces and windows; tore down an inappropriate formstone addition; restored original plaster ornament; replaced dangling lightbulbs with elegant brass chandeliers, and green burlap wallcoverings with rich Victorian papers; hung curtains and valances; and bought truckloads of Victorian bedroom sets at local auctions. The White Inn today is hardly the same place David Palmer fled on his first visit to Fredonia.

The hotel is named in memory of Squire White, who built the first house on this property in 1811. The Squire's son replaced that house with a huge, Second-Empire mansion in 1868. In 1919, a new owner enclosed the original mansion with the Classical Revival facade that stands today: a symmetrical white body marked by a 100-foot-long verandah, a three-storey pillared portico, and dozens of forest green shutters.

Restrictions: Children welcome. No pets. Smoking permitted. Check-in after 2 p.m., check-out at 11 a.m.
Beds: There are 18 rooms with a variety of bed arrangements, all with private baths.
Breakfast: Continental: fruit juices, herbal tea, homemade muffins, toast, jams, and coffee. Full hot breakfast is available for an additional charge.
Extras: Babysitting can be arranged at modest rates.
Rates: $39 to $69. Cots, $5 or $10. Credit cards and personal checks welcome.

10% discount to OHJ members.

HOMER

DAVID HARUM HOUSE
Ed and Connie Stone
80 South Main Street
Homer, NY 13077
(607) 749-3548
Year-round

1815 Victorian-ized Federal

LOCATION: Surrounded by historic homes in the Old Homer Village historic district, the house is one block from the village green.

Who was David Harum? If you'd asked that question at the turn of the century, you would've been laughed out of town, for he was quite famous in his day. His dealings as a wheeler-dealer banker, farmer, horse trader, and keeper of the so-called Cardiff Giant (a famous hoax that fooled many), were chronicled in two popular Victorian-era novels (*David Harum*, and *The Real David Harum*), a 1930s radio serial, and a 1934 movie starring Will Rogers. In the 1930s this house, where Harum once lived, became a mecca for his devotees, and was pictured on many postcards.

But when Ed and Connie Stone came across the house in 1981, David Harum was forgotten, and the house had stood vacant for eight years. The restaurant that occupied it for 20 years had gone bankrupt; the house was sealed shut; and all its accoutrements had been auctioned off.

Despite its sad and neglected appearance, Ed and Connie fell in love with the house. They could see beneath the cobwebs to its Moorish-style exterior porticoes and its graceful interior spiral staircase. They've done all the restoration work themselves, including stripping woodwork inside and out, repainting in the original color scheme, and refinishing the plank floors (a remnant from the Federal period, before the house was Victorian-ized). They've decorated with Empire-style furnishings, period print wallpapers, and Oriental rugs.

If you're curious about the inn's namesake, Ed and Connie have both David Harum novels, as well as a substantial collection of Harum memorabilia.

Restrictions: Children welcome. No pets. Restricted smoking. Check-out at 11 a.m. Check-in by 10 p.m., unless previously arranged.

Beds: Two rooms each have double bed and private bath.

Breakfast: Danish, fresh fruit and juice, bacon and eggs, toast, cereals, coffee.

Extras: Low-cost babysitting, coffee, tea, or soft drinks are always available; complimentary wine is served from time to time.

Rates: $28 to $42. Cots: $4 for child, $8 adult, when more than three in room. Cribs available at no additional charge. Personal and traveler's checks welcome.

10% discount to OHJ members for Lenox room, 5% for Westcott room.

ITHACA

ROSE INN
Sherry and Charles Rosemann
813 Auburn Road, Route 34
North
Ithaca, NY 14851
(607) 533-4202
Year-round

1851 Italianate Villa

LOCATION: In the heart of the Finger Lakes region on 20 landscaped acres, which include a stocked fishing pond, stands of spruce, birch, and maples, and an apple orchard, the inn is within minutes of Cornell University, Ithaca College, and Wells College. Three state parks, 30 wineries, and many antique shops are all a short drive away.

> *"A home such as this, with its attention to detail and craftsmanship, is a real treasure. It gives us great joy to be able to share it and give delight to so many other people."*

Guaranteed, this house has the most amazing staircase you've ever seen. It's built of solid mahogany and loops in three full circles on its upward spiral to the third floor cupola. Unfortunately, neither the man who designed the staircase nor his son ever lived to see it completed.

Abraham Osmun conceived of the plan early in the 19th century, when he began construction of this Italianate farmhouse. He was a millwright, and built his house with heavy timbers, hand-carved chestnut doors, and quarter-sawn oak floors inlaid in parquet. The house's showpiece was to be the circular staircase, and he devoted his full attention to it as soon as the rest was completed. Osmun died unexpectedly before the staircase was finished; the door at its base remained shut for years.

One day, his son Charles decided it was time his father's wishes were concluded. He bought hundreds of feet of Honduras mahogany in New York City, and searched high and low for a craftsman to give it shape. But his search ended in disappointment—nobody dared take on the daunting project, and the priceless mahogany was stored in the hog shed for half a century.

Out of the blue in 1922, a man named Will Houser drove up to the old Osmun homestead in a battered truck. He unpacked his tool kit, unlocked the hog shed, threw open the dusty staircase door, and started to work. Two years later, the stairway was built exactly as Osmun had planned—solid mahogany in a triple arc, with a railing so exquisitely fashioned it gives the illusion of being one solid piece. His work completed, Houser disappeared from whence he came, and nobody heard from him again.

Restrictions: No children under the age of ten. No pets (there is a kennel nearby). No smoking. Check-in after 3 p.m. Check-out at eleven.
Beds: Ten rooms, nine with private baths. Honeymoon suite has two-person jacuzzi. Most rooms have private entrances.
Breakfast: Continental: fresh juice, cider from orchard, croissants, sweet muffins, homemade jams and jellies. A full breakfast (additional charge) may include German apple pancakes with local syrup, eggs Benedict, lox and bagels.
Extras: A prix-fixe dinner can be arranged in advance.
Rates: Ranges from $95 to $175. From December 1 to April 30, rates are $10 less. Cots, $15. Personal checks and most credit cards accepted.

10% discount to OHJ members except weekends, May through November.
Mailing Address: PO Box 6576, Ithaca, NY 14851

PENFIELD

STRAWBERRY CASTLE
BED & BREAKFAST
Cynthia and Charles Whited
1883 Penfield Road (Route 441)
Penfield, NY 14526
(716) 385-3266
Year-round

1875 Italianate

LOCATION: The inn is located right outside of Rochester, convenient to many restaurants, golf courses, The Eastman House of Photography, Strong Museum, and Lake Ontario. There are three acres of land with gardens and a pool surrounding the building.

This house's first owners raised strawberries and grapes and sold them in decorative gift packages — thence comes the unusual name, known to area residents for generations. The house's original design is today virtually unaltered. On the outside, it has its original belvedere with finial, carved eave brackets, rear porch with delicately turned wood pillars, and tall, arched windows with louvered shutters. Inside, the sculptured plaster ceilings, Italian marble fireplace, hardwood floors, and three-room parlor remain. Its three-acre grounds, too, look as they might have 100 years ago: sweeping lawns punctuated by hardwoods, dogwoods, and garden benches.

Innkeepers Cynthia and Charles Whited have decorated the interior in a romantic interpretation of Victorianism: all the furnishings, wallcoverings, throw rugs, and chandeliers are from the period, but rooms are uncluttered and airy. The Whiteds have hand-stencilled ceiling borders in some rooms. Their antiques collection includes a player piano, pier mirror, fainting couch, Empire chairs, and brass beds. *Upstate* magazine recently nominated Strawberry Castle as the area's most romantic small inn.

Restrictions: Children under 12 restricted unless part of one group or family reserving entire guest accommodations. No pets. Check-in after 3 p.m., check-out at 11 a.m.
Beds: One two-room suite; two single rooms; three rooms share two baths.

Breakfast: Continental: hot croissants and coffee. Longer stays entitle guests to quiche, eggs, and other entrees.

Extras: The innkeepers provide tickets for free wine or beer at nearby restaurants. They also serve refreshments at poolside and special amenities for anniversaries and honeymoons.

Rates: $55. Personal checks and credit cards accepted.

10% discount to OHJ members.

ROCHESTER

**ROSE MANSION &
GARDENS**
Jeanne and Stephen Ferranti
265 Mt. Hope Avenue
Rochester, NY 14620
(716) 546-5426
Year-round

1837; remodelled to Tudor style, 1910

LOCATION: Located in the historic district of Mt. Hope Avenue, the Rose Mansion & Gardens are on five acres within walking distance of Highland Park, the site of the world-famous Lilac Festival and the Victorian Mount Cemetery. Minutes away are Rochester's cultural district, museums, art galleries, GEVA Theater; and Restaurant Row.

Here lived renowned horticulturalist George Ellwanger of Ellwanger-Barry Nurseries, the world's largest nurseries in the 19th century. The Ellwangers bought the property from a farmer in 1867 and remodelled the original farmstead twice to come up with this elaborate Tudor. On the south side of their property, inside a grey stone wall, they planted a magnificent garden, with fruit trees, boxwood-edged paths, varieties upon varieties of roses, flowering shrubs and perennials. Generations of Ellwangers cared for this garden, while the boxwoods grew to be 100 years old, until 1980, when George Ellwanger's granddaughter bequeathed the estate to the Landmark Society of Western New York, which three years later handed the property over to Stephen and Jeanne Ferranti. That makes the Ferrantis only the third family to own the property (the Ellwangers were the second); they're dedicated to preserving both the mansion and the gardens.

The mansion is one of those grand Tudors so popular among this country's wealthiest citizens at the turn of the century. It's reminiscent of a 16th-century English nobleman's house, with heavy beamed ceilings, immense fireplaces, and a Great Room and Grand Hall framed by Corinthian columns. From the Grand Hall rises a carved oak staircase, where you can almost imagine a medieval sword fight taking place. On the landing above is an 1883 Hooks and Hastings pipe organ. There's a glass-enclosed conservatory on the sunny side of the house; it overlooks a cobblestone patio, where pheasants sometimes wander.

The Ferrantis recently finished restoring the 20-plus rooms in the mansion, and now they're working on the turn-of-the-century carriage house. It's an architectural masterpiece in its own right, with Palladian windows, wainscotting, and oak-lined horse stalls. The Ferrantis have decorated the house period style, and named each guest room after a rose. Their collection of Ellwanger memorabilia includes four books the Ellwanger sons wrote, one entitled "This is My House."

Restrictions: No pets. No accommodations for children under 12. Smoking is not permitted in certain areas; smoking is permitted in guest rooms, but not encouraged.
Beds: There are ten guest rooms: four queen size, five double and two twin beds, each with reproduction wallpaper, imported lace draperies, color-coordinated linens, firm mattresses.
Breakfast: Continental: fresh juices, coffee, and teas, fresh fruits and melons, home-baked breads, pastries.
Extras: The special weekend packages include complimentary chilled champagne, breakfast in bed, free passes to Rochester Museum & Science Center. There are no telephones or TVs in the rooms, but guests can use the common telephones and TVs.
Rates: $72 to $100; personal checks and credit cards welcome.
   10% discount to OHJ members.

SENECA FALLS

LOCUSTWOOD COUNTRY INN
Nancy and Bob Hill
3563 Route 89
Seneca Falls, NY 13148
(315) 549-7132
Year-round

1820 Federal

LOCATION: In the heart of New York State wine country, the Locustwood Country Inn is within an hour's drive of Sonnenberg Gardens, Corning Glass Center, legendary vineyards and wineries, fishing in famous lakes and streams, thoroughbred racing, and many concert, dance, theater, and museum offerings.

The original exterior and interior architectural features of this Federal-style brick house are well preserved. On the exterior: original dentilled cornice, front door sidelights, window heads, and chimney pots. Inside: wide plank floors, hand-hewn beams, five fireplaces, and a winding central stairway with delicate balusters. The house is charmingly decorated with braided rugs, antique trunks, rockers, dust ruffles, and simple, unimposing wallpapers.

Restrictions: Children over 13 welcome. No pets. Smoking in designated areas only.
Beds: Four rooms. One with king-sized bed, one with twin beds, and two with double bed. Two rooms have private bath.
Breakfast: Full breakfast.
Extras: There's a large common room for guests' use, equipped with games and television.
Rates: $35 (twin) to $50 (large with king bed).
  10% discount to OHJ members.

NORTH CAROLINA

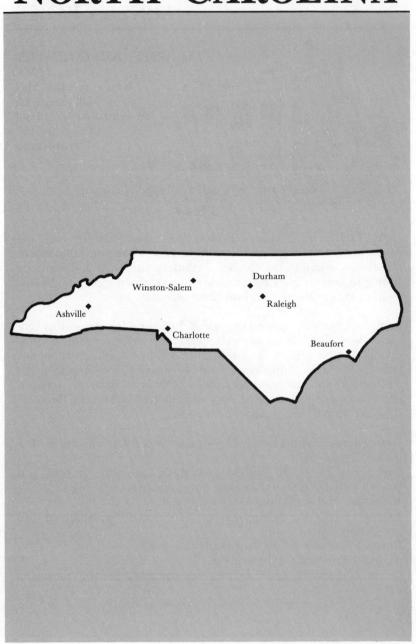

Durham

Winston-Salem

Raleigh

Ashville

Charlotte

Beaufort

ASHEVILLE

FLINT STREET INN
Rick and Lynne Vogel
116 Flint Street
Asheville, NC 28801
(704) 253-6723
Year-round

1915 Prairie-style Foursquare

LOCATION: The house, complete with an acre of dogwood, oak, and rhododendron, is part of Asheville's oldest neighborhood, the Montford Historic District. Located just north of the city, the inn offers easy access to Civic Center, shops, and restaurants. Nearby are mountains, hillside villages, the Biltmore Mansion, and the homes of Thomas Wolfe and Carl Sandburg.

"Come and share our lovely old family home."

This 1915 Foursquare is sided with cedar shingles and traditional lap siding. A wide Montford bracket marks the 50-foot front porch, a feature attributed to (or maybe just influenced by) the famed architect Richard Morris Hunt, who also designed the Biltmore House. Owners Rick and Lynne Vogel, who bought the house in 1981, say that it required little restoration. The original owners, the Clark family, loved their home and took good care of it. Guests will find heart pine woodwork and flooring throughout the house. Brick fireplaces are the main features in the two parlors and the dining room. The bevelled glass in the massive front door and sidelights is also worth a look. The furnishings are in keeping with the period: Art Nouveau and Art Deco prevail.

315

Restrictions: No children under 12, and no pets.
Beds: Eight double rooms all with private baths.
Breakfast: "Southern style": orange juice, coffee, tea, homemade biscuits, muffins, toast, choice of eggs, sausage or bacon, assorted jellies —and the morning paper.
Extras: Coffee, tea, and wine are complimentary. Asheville outings, an "old-fashioned touring company" specializing in historic Asheville, has its office in the inn.
Rates: $60 (double) to $50 (single). Cots furnished for $10. Personal checks and credit cards accepted.

10% discount to OHJ members.

NORTH CAROLINA

ASHEVILLE

**THE RAY HOUSE BED &
BREAKFAST**
Alice and Will Curtis
83 Hillside Street
Asheville, NC 28801
(704) 252-0106
Year-round

1891 Colonial Revival/Craftsman

LOCATION: On a prominent site in one of Asheville's older neighborhoods, the inn overlooks downtown; the University of North Carolina at Asheville and University Botanical Gardens are nearby. Spruces and a Japanese maple surround the building.

Captain John Edwin Ray owned this house first, in 1891. A large porch wraps around the two-storey structure with its mullioned windows, exposed beams, and dark woodwork. Every room has a fireplace and most are furnished with antiques. The owners, Will and Alice Curtis, have a fine collection of antique culinary equipment in the kitchen. There's a grand piano in the library/music room, which opens onto the porch. F. Scott Fitzgerald, a one-time resident of Asheville, was a visitor here, and bought a Packard touring car from a former owner.

Restrictions: Babies and children welcome, though pets are discouraged. No specific check-in or check-out times.

Beds: Four rooms—two with private baths, two share baths.

Breakfast: Continental: coffee or tea, orange juice; homemade breads including their noted "Lemon Loaf," jams, and jellies. The meal is served in the formal dining room, though in spring or summer guests may prefer to bring it out to the large porch.

Rates: $37 to $42; free night for stays of a week or more. $5 for cots, cribs free of charge. Traveler's or personal checks accepted.

10% discount to OHJ members.

BALSAM

BALSAM LODGE B&B
Marie and Gordon Pike
Valley Drive
Balsam, NC 28707
(704) 456-6528
June 1 to October 31

1904-8 Vernacular, railroad depot

LOCATION: The inn, one mile off the Blue Ridge Parkway, is located in the Great Smoky Mountain "high country." Nearby attractions include whitewater rafting, hiking, antique and craft shops, country dancing, and horseback riding.

"Sit on the porch, listen to the water rushing over the water wheel, watch the hummingbirds, and rejuvenate both mind and body."

The original owner and his wife, related to Lady Astor, called this house "The Virginia Cottage" when it was built by Aaron Bryson in 1904. The house still has a large porch that wraps around two sides, as well as the original baseboards, wainscotting, and arched fireplaces inside. The depot behind the yellow house is also part of the lodge. It was built in 1908, the year the railroad between Balsam and Murphy was completed. The depot was moved up the hill in 1960, when it was first used as a guest house. It's the highest elevation passenger depot east of the Rockies. Owners Marie and Gordon Pike, who bought the house in 1983, are collecting antiques and railroad memorabilia with which to furnish the two buildings. They have an old Victrola and a 1936 vacuum-tube radio in the living room that guests can listen to when they're not out exploring the Great Smoky Mountains.

Restrictions: In the main house no smoking or pets. Check-in after 1 p.m., check-out at 11 a.m.
Beds: Three doubles, one with twins, and one single twin in the main house share one-and-a-half baths. Two twins, one double, and one double with trundle in the depot all have private baths.
Breakfast: Continental: "made-this-morning" biscuits, muffins, or breads "hot from the oven"; juice; fresh fruit in season, homemade jams and jellies, coffee, tea.
Extras: Coffee and tea are available all day, usually with baked goods, along with roast chestnuts in the fall and ice cream from time to time.
Rates: $25 in main house, $35 in depot. Cribs are available free of charge; cots cost $7 for adults, $5 for children. Traveler's and personal checks welcome.
Mailing Address: PO Box 279, Balsam, NC 28707

NORTH CAROLINA

BEAUFORT

THE SHOTGUN HOUSE
Victor and Muriel Jackson,
Clara Finch
406 Ann Street
Beaufort, NC 28516
(919) 728-6248
Year-round

1854 Greek Revival

LOCATION: The seaside town of Beaufort, with its many 18th-century houses and old shop fronts, offers a quaint harbor where shrimp boats pass, pelicans dive, and wild ponies wander the shoals. Antique shops, an old burying ground, restored homes, and restaurants serving fresh seafood are among the other attractions. The inn's garden is planted with magnolia, wisteria, camellias, grape vines, and bamboo.

"See what can be done with a house Beaufort was about to bulldoze."

This 1854 Greek Revival is called the Shotgun House because "a man could stand in his front door and shoot a gun down the hall and out the back door." Victor and Muriel Jackson, New Yorkers who fell in love with Beaufort after a brief visit, bought the house in 1981. Deemed an eyesore and a dangerous nuisance by the city and scheduled for demolition, the house had no roof and was littered with garbage. But the Jacksons saw through the debris and, after several months of commuting from New York to oversee the restoration, outfitted the house with family antiques and down comforters, hired Clara Finch to manage the inn, and began taking guests.

They met Clara, by the way, because she was the receptionist at the motel they stayed at while the restoration was in progress—and hired her because she seemed so friendly and "not completely happy" working at the motel. "Lord, you have smiled upon this child," she said upon accepting the job.

Restrictions: No children or pets.
Beds: One double with a brass bed, one twin with verandah and private bath, one queen with verandah. The double and the queen share a single bath.
Breakfast: Freshly squeezed orange juice, homemade bread, fresh eggs from free-ranging chickens, sausage, homemade jams and marmalade, coffee, all served in "unlimited portions."
Extras: Soft drinks, lemonade, peanuts, mixers, et cetera are provided.
Rates: $55 to $85 (highest during the April 15 to November 15 season). Credit cards welcome.
Mailing Address: PO Box 833, Beaufort, NC 28516

NORTH CAROLINA

BLOWING ROCK

GIDEON RIDGE INN
Cobb and Jane Milner
6148 Gideon Ridge Road
Blowing Rock, NC 28605
(704) 295-3644
Year-round

1939 English Cottage

LOCATION: Two miles south of the village of Blowing Rock, the house sits on a ridge overlooking the Blue Ridge Mountains. The site, which is surrounded by rhododendron and mountain laurel, offers a stone terrace for enjoying the view. The Blue Ridge Parkway is nearby.

The stonemasons who erected the Duke University Chapel built this native stone house for a nephew of Moses Cone, owner of a textile mill in Greensboro, North Carolina, in 1939. It has an extremely well-constructed slate roof with lightning rods, dormers, and large casement windows. Inside, the walls are plastered and the beams are exposed. There are fireplaces in eight rooms—including one in a bathroom. Five sets of French doors open onto a massive stone terrace that locals say was built over a bomb shelter at the height of World War II. (There are 14-inch concrete walls in the space under the terrace to support this theory.) The furnishings are eclectic— family antiques, Oriental rugs, rag rugs, Victorian bedsteads—but elegantly comfortable. Owners Cobb and Jane Milner have been welcoming guests since 1982.

Restrictions: Pets and children under 12 are not permitted; smoking is restricted; check-in after 3 p.m.; check-out at noon.
Beds: Eight rooms all with private baths.
Breakfast: Coffee, juice, fruit; eggs, omelettes, pancakes, or French toast; bacon or sausage; jam; English muffins, homemade scones or biscuits; grits or sauteed apples are also available from time to time.
Extras: "Ice, tea, et cetera" are free of charge in the afternoons. Thursday through Sunday night's dinner, by reservation, is served for both guests and non-guests.
Rates: $65 to $125. Personal and traveler's checks and credit cards are all welcome.
  10% discount to OHJ members.
Mailing Address: PO Box 1929, Blowing Rock, NC 28605

DURHAM

ARROWHEAD INN
Jerry and Barbara Ryan
106 Mason Road
Durham, NC 27712
(919) 477-8430
January 15 to December 15

1775 Greek Revival

LOCATION: The inn stands on what was once an Indian trading path from Virginia to points west. Nearby are Duke University, Research Triangle Park, Stagville Restoration Center, the site of the Civil War surrender, and the North Carolina Botanical Gardens.

"One of Durham's oldest and best-loved buildings, as well as the town's first B&B" Jerry and Barbara

Many traces of the past have turned up on the Ryan's property: for instance, a headstone from the original owner's tiny family graveyard. In the attic, the marks of the builder's tools can be seen on the hand-hewn, peg-jointed beams. The Ryans have also been told that slaves made the bricks in the portico and "keeping room."

Two-hundred-year-old trees, a fishpond, and grape arbors grace the property. The house retains its original woodwork and wainscotting, and the Ryans, who have also restored a Victorian mansion in New Jersey, furnished the guest rooms in different periods ranging from Southern Colonial to Victorian.

Restrictions: Designated areas for smoking; no pets; check-in by 6 p.m., check-out at noon.
Beds: One room has twins, four have doubles, and one has a queen-size; two share a bath.
Breakfast: Juice and fruit, meat, eggs, homemade bread, rolls, preserves, and coffee are served in the dining room or keeping room. A smaller breakfast can be brought to the guest's room.
Extras: Tea and sherry in the afternoon; babysitting can be arranged with sufficient notice.
Rates: $45 (shared bath) to $75 (private bath and garden access, seating area). Cots, $10; cribs, $5. Personal checks and American

Express welcome.
10% discount to OHJ members.

EDENTON

THE LORDS PROPRIETORS' INN
Arch B. and Jane F. Edwards
300 North Broad Street
Edenton, NC 27932
(919) 482-3641
Year-round

1783, 1890, and 1901; predominantly Queen Anne

LOCATION: Edenton, 90 miles south of Norfolk, Virginia, was once North Carolina's colonial capital. It retains its quaint charm with 18th- and 19th-century homes flanking tree-lined streets. Old homes, an 18th-century courthouse, and an 18th-century church are open to the public for tours.

This inn is composed of three adjacent restored houses: one an 1890 Queen Anne, one a 1901 Georgian Revival, and the third a 1783 house Georgian-turned-Georgian Revival (in 1906). The Queen Anne and the Georgian Revival have their original mahogany mantels and woodwork intact; the third was abandoned when innkeepers Arch and Jane Edwards bought it, and had been stripped of its details. (Townsfolk had lost track of how old that derelict house was until the Edwards uncovered its 18th-century framing, floors, and hearths during restoration.) All the houses are furnished with antiques and each is named after some historical occupant, like the South White House, in memory of one-time resident Miss South Carolina White, whose sister was called North Carolina. (What patriotic parents they must've had!)

Restrictions: No pets, no smoking in the dining room.
Beds: Two suites of bedroom, sitting room and bath; five twins; four

kings; and eight queens. None share a bath, and all have cable TV.

Breakfast: Homemade bread and muffins, fresh fruit, homemade preserves, coffee, tea.

Extras: Tea, any time, is served at no charge. In winter the inn offers tours of four 18th-century private homes that range from a rural millhouse to a fine plantation—"fascinating for people interested in restoration."

Rates: $60 for rooms, $75 for suites. $8 for cots, $5 for cribs. Personal checks accepted; guests can also request to be billed.

HENDERSONVILLE

1911 Neo-Colonial

REVERIE BED & BREAKFAST
Michael Abriola and Kathy Price
1197 Greenville Highway
Hendersonville, NC 28739
(704) 687-0534
March to December

LOCATION: Halfway between Hendersonville and Flat Rock, the inn is convenient to Flat Rock Playhouse, Carl Sandburg home, and the Biltmore House and Gardens. The Blue Ridge Parkway is also nearby.

According to innkeepers Michael Abriola and Kathy Price, this 1911 structure was originally a boarding house. It has an interesting floor plan, and lots of eight-over-eight windows. The most striking feature of the facade is a fan-lit entrance. The furnishings range from Victorian to Art Deco.

Restrictions: No pets, smoking, or children under 12.

Beds: Of the eight rooms—one with twins on the first floor, seven doubles on the second floor—two have private baths. There's a sink in every room.

Breakfast: Continental: croissants, fruit, jams, fresh juices, freshly ground coffee.
Rates: $45 (shared bath) to $60. Credit cards and personal checks welcome.
10% discount to OHJ members.

NORTH CAROLINA

HENDERSONVILLE

THE WAVERLY
Steve and Judy Zebos
783 North Main Street
Hendersonville, NC 28739
(704) 693-9193
Year-round

LOCATION: The 1863 St. James Episcopal Church is across the street; the town's quaint shopping park, theatres, tennis, and other churches are within a short walk.

"Many of our bed-and-breakfast guests are interested in old inns—and our permanent guests, mostly retirees, look forward to meeting them. No one finds a stranger here."

The owners love to tell about the famous and not-so-famous people that have stayed at the Waverly. Kay Kyser "dined there many times"; Mrs. Jane Smith, an original Florodora girl, once lived there. Miss Ingersol Minge, the 1903 Mardi Gras queen, stayed there as did one Mrs. Hewson, the daughter of General Custer's second-in-command at Little Big Horn, Captain Yates.

Some of the curious items the inn contains: a red velvet "courting" sofa, said to be 250 years old and to come from a chateau in Scotland; portraits of family ancestors; a cup collection including several used by former Presidents—"a topic of conversation among the guests," we're told.

324

Most of the building—built as an inn—needed little restoration. The owners just re-papered the lobbies, halls, and some rooms with period papers. On the front porch are rocking chairs that offer a view of the 1863 church across the street.

Restrictions: No pets.
Beds: Double or twin beds in all 22 rooms; private baths on first and second floor, while the eight third-floor rooms share baths. All rooms have basins with running water.
Breakfast: Cereal, fruit or juice, beverage of choice, and choice of: eggs with bacon or sausage, or pancakes with sausage or bacon.
Rates: $30 (shared bath) to $45 (private bath). Slightly lower from November 1 to April 1. Mastercard, Visa, and traveler's checks welcome.

MURFREESBORO

THE WINBORNE HOUSE
Edna Hammel
333 Jay Trail
Murfreesboro, NC 27855
(919) 398-5224
Year-round

1818 and 1850 Greek Revival/Italianate

LOCATION: Murfreesboro is a small, rural, college town with an active historical society. Four buildings are open to the public, plus there are many private restorations. Williamsburg and Outer Banks are two hours away.

"Old-house people are never strangers here!" That's what host Edna Hammel says about her B&B. She and her husband finally settled down into this early Greek Revival in 1975 after having moved 28 times (her husband is in the military). She says the house is furnished with family heirlooms and "traveling buys" collected at the many places they've called home. The house has many original features intact, including wavy glass windows, pine floors, and several original gas lighting fixtures (this was the first house in town equipped with such a luxury). It's called Winborne after a Judge Winborne who lived here, and who wrote a family and county history that researchers still use.

Beds: One room has two twins, one has a double bed, and the two rooms share one bath.
Breakfast: Continental.
Extras: Coffee and tea are available anytime; a glass of wine is offered before dinner.
Rates: $20 to $25; rooms furnished with teddy bears, dolls, and miniature books. Cots, $5; cribs, $1. Personal checks and American Express accepted.

NORTH CAROLINA

NEW BERN

HARMONY HOUSE INN
A. E. and Diane Hansen
215 Pollock Street
New Bern, NC 28560
(919) 636-3810
Year-round

1850 Greek Revival

LOCATION: Within walking distance of this historic district are the Tryon Palace, two rivers, many fine restaurants, and the Royal Governor's residence.

Back in 1851, Harmony House was a four-room, two-storey house owned by Benjamin and Elizabeth Ellis. As their family grew, they added rooms and porches on to the house. Around the turn of the century, the house was sawed in half. The west side was moved over nine feet, a new hallway and stairs were built, and a wall was installed to divide what had essentially become two homes. A front porch that stretches the width of the building was also added. A.E. and Diane Hansen purchased the house in February, 1985, and by May had installed ten bathrooms, rewired, painted, and furnished the entire house. The house still has much of its original Greek Revival wood-work and the original staircase. The Hansens have retained the changes that occurred over the years and present "all of its blended parts" to their guests, hence the name "Harmony House."

Restrictions: Smoking only in guest rooms, no pets. Check-in after 3 p.m., and check-out at 11 a.m.
Beds: Nine rooms, all with private baths.
Breakfast: Full: strata, coffeecake, fruit, coffee, and juice.
Extras: Soft drinks and juices are provided.
Rates: $65 (double), $45 (single); $10 each for both cribs and cots. Personal checks and credit cards accepted.

NEW BERN

KINGS ARMS—A COLONIAL INN
David and Diana Parks

212 Pollock Street
New Bern, NC 28560
(919) 638-4409
Year-round

1847-48, 1898, and 1905 with mansard roof

LOCATION: In the heart of a historic district, the inn is within walking distance of Tryon Palace (an 18th-century Georgian mansion where the royal governor of the colony once lived).

Carpenter John A. Meadows built Kings Arms, then a two-storey house only one room deep, in 1847. The rear rooms were added on in 1898, the same time the stairway, identical to those at Christ Church, was installed. Not long afterward, the front porch was enlarged to the entire width of the house and a mansard roof was added on, providing four more rooms. In 1978, Sarah Bradbury bought the property and returned the porch to its original size and renovated the rear of the house which had fallen into disrepair. She converted part of the house into an antique shop until 1980 when the current owners, Walter and Bettye Paramore, Uzie and John Thomas, and Evelyn and John Peterson, bought the house and turned it into an inn. The house is decorated in a combination of Federalist and Empire styles with a "dash of Williamsburg." Each room has a fireplace and a canopy, poster, or brass bed.

Restrictions: No pets.
Beds: All eight rooms—two queens, two with two doubles, two with one double, and two with twins—have a private bath.
Breakfast: Ham or sausage biscuits, sweet roll or muffin, juice, coffee or tea. Cereal and milk are available for children.
Extras: Champagne, for newlyweds, can be arranged. A local newspaper is delivered to guests' rooms each morning.
Rates: $52 to $58; cribs are free; cots, for extra persons over 12, cost $5. They accept personal and traveler's checks and credit cards.
Mailing Address: PO Box 1085, New Bern, NC 28560

NORTH CAROLINA

RALEIGH

THE OAKWOOD INN
Diana Newton
411 North Bloodworth Street
Raleigh, NC 27604
(919) 832-9712
Year-round

1871 Italianate

LOCATION: The Oakwood Historic District is a Victorian neighborhood; nearby sites include Andrew Johnson's birthplace in Mordecai Historic Park.

"This is the nicest and most elegant inn we have stayed in. What elegant furnishings and comfort! Plus the hospitality was just great!" Bette Downs, East Lansing, Mich.

Five friends and fellow historic preservation enthusiasts got together to rescue this old house, which, when they ran across it, was in a state of rapid decline. The house would've been too costly for one of them to buy and restore alone—turning it into a single family residence was out of the question. But with the aid of five pairs of hands and five pocketbooks, the house with nine fireplaces was exquisitely restored and converted to an ostentatious B&B.

They've equipped it with all the authentic Victorian accoutrements. The exterior is painted lavender, with grey and cream trim and canvas awnings. Interior colors and wallpapers are Victorian jewel tones—rose, emerald green, wine, taupe, and deep blue. The hardwood floors are clothed with Oriental throw rugs only—no wall-to-wall carpeting here (except in the hallway, where a sound barrier was needed). And all the windows are outfitted with heavy, valanced curtains with as much shirring and as many flounces as Queen Victoria's ball gown.

But all this decor is just the backdrop for Oakwood's impressive antiques collection, so comprehensive it extends right down to the high-tank toilets, brass wall sconces, and even the tall, spindled plant stands. Some of the more notable items you'll find are a wardrobe with sterling silver pulls, an oval walnut dining table, a marble-topped sideboard, a mahogany four-poster bed, and a unique collection of chandeliers, both crystal and brass.

Restrictions: No pets or children under 12. Check-in after 3 p.m.; check-out at noon.
Beds: All six rooms—four doubles, two queens—have private baths.
Breakfast: Fresh fruit and juice, egg dish with side orders of meat; fresh breads and rolls, coffee and tea.
Extras: The inn offers free newspapers and walking tour guides of the area. Fresh fruit and flowers, imported Belgian chocolates, imported soaps and other toiletries are also provided.
Rates: $55 to $80. Personal checks and credit cards welcome.
10% discount to OHJ members.
Mailing Address: Oakwood Inn c/o Preservation Inc., PO Box 11001, Raleigh, NC 27604

WILMINGTON

ANDERSON GUEST HOUSE
Landon and Connie Anderson
520 Orange Street
Wilmington, NC 28401
(919) 343-8128
Year-round

1851 Italianate

LOCATION: The 200 surrounding blocks are all part of a historic district whose diverse architecture "represents the changing life of this vibrant North Carolina port over the last 250 years." Nearby sites include the gardens of Orton, the battleship U.S.S.N.C., Thalian Hall, an 1850s theatre, the Confederate Fort Fisher, and many beaches.

Before Landon and Connie Anderson moved into this house, the same family had lived in it for 100 years! The house looks like a Mediterranean country villa: a stucco facade, a front piazza with flowery cast-iron grillework and tent roof, and a wide balcony. The house has an 1895 addition that's also Italianate style, except for the bay windows.

Restrictions: Smoking in guest rooms only. No set check-in times. Babies and children can sometimes be accommodated — "we have three small children of our own."
Beds: Two rooms have private baths—one queen, one double. Pallets can be brought in for a third person per room, but "if more than three people are in your party, we would strongly suggest taking both rooms."
Breakfast: Coffee and juice, plus some "specialty" dish like crepes with cream sauce, eggs Florentine, or blueberry cobbler with whipped cream. Special food problems can be accommodated.
Extras: Drinks are available upon guest's arrival or in the afternoon. Babysitting can be arranged.
Rates: $55; $10 charge for third adult in room. Personal checks welcome.
    10% discount to OHJ members.

WINSTON-SALEM

1887 Queen Anne

THE COLONEL LUDLOW HOUSE
Terri Jones and Ken Land
Summit and West Fifth Streets
Winston-Salem, NC 27101
(919) 777-1887
Year-round

LOCATION: The area around the inn is known as the West End Community, a historic district. The restored 18th-century Moravian village of Old Salem is one mile away. Cultural centers are within walking distance.

Proprietor Ken Land has been restoring houses full-time since 1972. This particular house was divided into four shabby apartments when he got hold of it. It's now one of his masterpieces, a high-style Queen Anne with stained glass in every window, sawn wood ornament, large porches, and intricately decorated gable ends. Inside, many of the mouldings, in a variety of hardwoods, have their original finishes. Ken has furnished the house with 100% authentic Victorian antiques, including brass beds, ornately carved high-backed beds, a gas-electric gold-plated chandelier, tall mirrors, and wing-backed chairs. Ken lives next door, in another exquisitely restored house.

Restrictions: Children over ten permitted, but no pets. Check-in after 3 p.m.; check-out at noon.
Beds: Nine rooms all with private baths.
Breakfast: Freshly squeezed orange juice, fresh fruit cup topped with yogurt and granola; choice of pastries and bread; cheese, preserves, butter; coffee/tea/milk.
Extras: Guests receive complimentary cheese, crackers, and bottle of wine; a two-person whirlpool is available for some rooms.
Rates: $55 any day for smaller rooms; larger rooms have whirlpools and range from $72 on weekdays to $125 on weekends. Cots cost $5. Personal checks and credit cards welcome.

OREGON

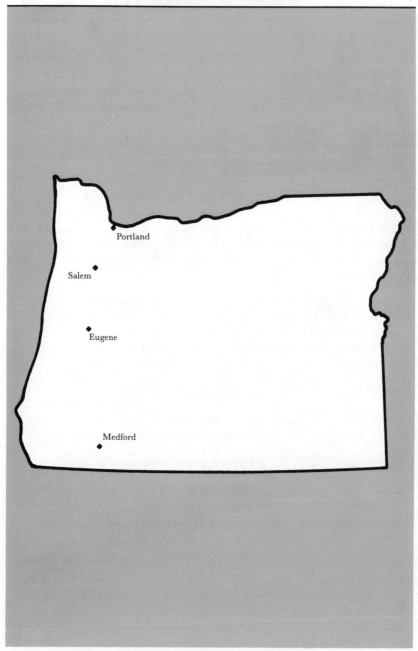

Portland

Salem

Eugene

Medford

MCMINNVILLE

MATTEY HOUSE INN
Gene and Susan Irvin
Mattey Lane
McMinnville, OR 97128
(503) 434-5058
February to December

LOCATION: Ten acres of evergreens, fruit trees, and a one-acre vineyard surround the house. Willamette Valley's many wineries and tasting rooms are nearby.

Guests can look out from a hooded balcony on the second floor, from stained-glass windows on any floor, through a half-moon window in the attic, or even from the widow's walk that crowns the house (but that's only for the truly adventurous).

Built by dry-goods storekeeper Joseph Mattey, the house is in the National Register. Mattey was a fair businessman, at least according to his own ads in the *Oregon Register*: "highest prices paid for farm produce. When the Irvins bought the house they removed simulated wood panelling in the hallways, only to discover damaged plaster underneath. These walls have been restored and painted, and they're capped with an ornamental wallpaper border. There are also turn-of-the-century wallpapers on the first floor.

Restrictions: No smoking or children under 12. No pets ("we supply them"). Check-in after 3 p.m., check-out at noon.
Beds: Four rooms, one with private bath; suite available.
Breakfast: Fruit, rolls and/or bread, juice, coffee, and a hot egg dish.

333

Extras: Afternoon tea and refreshments are served. From time to time there's live classical music.
Rates: $35 to $50 ($5 discount for singles). Personal checks welcome.
Mailing Address: Route 2, Box 53, McMinnville, OR 97128

OREGON

OAKLAND

THE PRINGLE HOUSE
Jim and Demay Pringle
114 Northeast 7th Street
Oakland, OR 97462
(503) 459-5038
Year-round

1893 Vernacular Queen Anne

LOCATION: The house sits on a rise overlooking this small, hidden-away city of 850 with many Victorian buildings, all in the National Register. There are tree-lined streets, rolling hills, plus a museum, dinner house, and a carriage works that still makes horse-drawn carriages by hand.

> *"When we began as innkeepers we didn't realize so many of the strangers we'd meet at our door would later be saying 'good-bye' as friends—and most of them love this old house as we do. It's been wonderful!"*

"It's not all done yet," says Jim Pringle modestly. But a lot has been done, and many things undone, during the five years he and Demay have been working on the house.

In the 1930s somebody tacked on a modern garage to the side of the house. The Pringles took it off in order to restore the building as a 1904 photo shows it: with four porches, three on the first storey and one on the second. Jim then built another garage, this one designed to resemble a carriage house, with style and trim to match the main building. They've also reversed much of what they call "the unnecessary 'modernizing' inside the house."

If Oakland had beaten nearby Roseburg in the competition for county seat, this inn would have served as temporary courthouse. That's one of the reasons it, like many other buildings in town, is in the National Register. Several past owners were involved in the commercial development of Oakland, and more famous folk have visited since—including, in the Pringles' first year in business, a U.S. senator on the day after his election victory.

Lit by bay windows and a stained-glass keyhole window, the interior boasts its original nine-foot pocket doors, a curved wall at the end of the upstairs hall, and a "pass-through" for food that connects the dining and living rooms.

Jim gives this partial listing of the antiques and heirlooms in the house: a circa 1850 bedroom set, a hutch, sideboard, tables, china cabinet, clocks, quilts, linens, samplers, and a fainting couch. In the kitchen there's an old cooking stove, butcher block, and dough box. Plus Demay has a large collection of dolls on display. And tucked at the end of Jim's list is one curious entry: "wife."

Restrictions: No pets; older children only, smoking on outside porches only.
Beds: One room has an 1850 extra-long double bed, and the other a queen and a single. The two share a bath.
Breakfast: Coffee, tea, milk, or cocoa; freshly squeezed orange juice, croissants (freshly baked), fresh fruit and melon, homemade jams and jellies, creme caramel, and oatmeal on chilly mornings. Special diets can be accommodated with advance notice.
Extras: Coffee and 14 varieties of tea are available all day. An afternoon glass of sherry is offered in the parlor or beside the fireplace.
Rates: $35 both rooms; cots, $10. Personal checks welcome.

PENNSYLVANIA

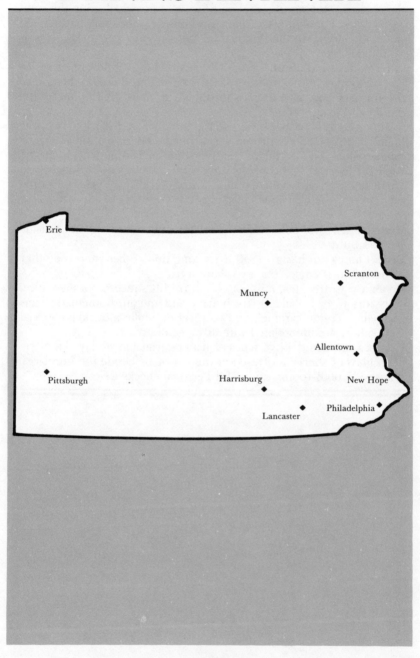

AIRVILLE

SPRING HOUSE
Ray Constance Hearne
Muddy Creek Forks
Airville, PA 17302
(717) 927-6906
Year-round

1798 Colonial with Victorian details

LOCATION: The inn is in a wooded valley cut by Muddy Creek with a waterway (seldom muddy) for swimming, canoeing and trout fishing. The Susquehanna Valley offers museums, winery tours, antique shops, farmer's markets and agricultural shows, hiking, birdwatching, and auctions. Historic Lancaster and York are a short drive away.

Innkeeper Ray Hearne believes in doing things the old way. Each spring, she whitewashes the interior of her 1798 Colonial with the real, old-fashioned stuff made of limestone. She heats the inn with a wood-burning stove. She's stencilled several rooms Colonial style —copying the idea from the original, 18th-century stencilwork that survived in many other rooms. And, need I add, all her furnishings are antique, collected at local country auctions. The newest additions to Ray's house are the Victorian front porch, and the bay window in the music room.

Spring House has lots of delightful amenities, like handmade quilts, featherbeds, and paintings of the neighborhood. And Ray has a copy of the 18th-century land grant for the property: William Penn's family bequeathed the plot to a Pennsylvania legislator named Robert Turner, who subsequently built the house from local fieldstones.

337

Restrictions: Well-behaved children welcome. No pets. No smoking. Check-in between 5 and 9 p.m. Check-out at 11 a.m.
Beds: Five rooms. One large double-bedded room with grand piano, bay window and private bath; three rooms with a double-bed each; one room with a double bed and small adjoining room with 19th-century child's bed. Four rooms share a bath.
Breakfast: Full breakfast is cooked on an antique woodburning stove. Fresh eggs, scrapple or hickory-smoked sausage or ham, frittata, spoonbread, kugelhopf, fresh fruit, herb tea (from the garden), coffee with fresh cream, hot-cross buns, and homemade preserves.
Extras: Late afternoon tea is served, complimentary wine (from local winery) and cheese are available, and "Hadrian, the English setter, gives tours of the nearby country lanes."
Rates: Rooms with shared bath, $50; large room with private bath, $75. One-night stays on either Friday or Saturday in room with private bath, $80; $60 for room with shared bath. Cots, $15. Personal or traveler's checks and money orders accepted, no credit cards.

PENNSYLVANIA

BIRD-IN-HAND

GREYSTONE MOTOR LODGE
Phyllis Reed
2658 Old Philadelphia Pike
Bird-In-Hand, PA 17505
(717) 393-4233
Year-round

C. 1850 French Second Empire

LOCATION: The inn stands on two acres in Pennsylvania Dutch country. Amish farms, restaurants, craft shops, antiques and railroad museum are all within a short distance.

The Greystone is a far cry from your typical motor lodge. It's a beautiful, brick, Second-Empire building with tall arched windows, carved eave brackets, and a slate mansard roof. The lobby is furnished with Victorian antiques and has leaded, bevelled-glass doors and fancy plasterwork. Some of the guest rooms have stained-glass

338

windows, cut-crystal doors, original woodwork and antique bath fixtures—just be sure to ask in advance if you want one of these, and not one of the modern rooms in the carriage house out back.

Restrictions: Children welcome, but no pets. No smoking in lobby or crafts shop. Check-in between 2 and 9 p.m.
Beds: The 12 rooms all have private baths. Four single rooms with double bed; one single room with two double beds; six two-room suites with two double beds (three rooms have kitchens); one two-room suite with three double beds.
Breakfast: Coffee and donuts are served in the Victorian lobby.
Extras: There's a quilt and crafts shop in the basement, and Amish farmland bus tour tickets are sold in the lobby.
Rates: $24 (single with double bed) to $52 (two-room suite with three double beds and a kitchen). Rates vary according to the season. $4 per night for each additional person occupying a room. Personal checks and most credit cards accepted.
Mailing Address: PO Box 270, Bird-in-Hand, PA 17505

CANADENSIS

PINE KNOB INN
Dick and Charlotte Dorrich
Route 447
Canadensis, PA 18325
(717) 595-2532
Year-round

1840 Gothic Revival

LOCATION: Two acres of landscaped grounds and 13 acres of woodland surround the inn. An excellent trout stream is across the road (season runs April 15 to September 4). The nearby Pocono Playhouse offers professional summer theater. There are good antique and craft shops in town and "even some nightclubs." Good skiing is within a half hour, and the Delaware Water Gap is 45 minutes away.

> *"This old house has seen so many years of happy times that it seems to radiate good vibes."*

In 1976, Jim Belfie abandoned his corporate post at an insurance agency, packed up his house in suburban New Jersey, moved out to the woods, and went into business with his wife, June. Since then, they've made a name for themselves as the friendliest innkeepers in Pennsylvania's Pocono mountains. Many guests — such as one lady who planned to stay for a week, ended up spending six weeks, and when she finally left, reserved "her room" for the next entire summer season—are repeat visitors.

Their house, a high-style, board-and-batten Victorian Gothic, was built by a wealthy tanner named Dr. Gilbert Palen. His business partner built a house next door, and the two men re-named the town (once known as Frogtown) Canadensis—Latin for the type of hemlock tree whose bark is used in tanning. In 1886, Palen sold the house and the next owner converted it to an inn. Inside, it's warm and cozy, with a huge stone hearth in the living room, antique furnishings, country quilts, and a gallery of original art, much of which is for sale.

Many of Pine Knob's guests are artists who come to paint in the quiet serenity of the surrounding woods, or to attend one of the 12 artists' workshops June has organized, each led by a well-known contemporary artist. June herself is an accomplished painter.

Restrictions: No pets. Children over five welcome. Check-in after 2 p.m.; check-out at 11 a.m.
Beds: Two single-bedded rooms; 22 with doubles; three with twin beds. Six rooms share a bath.
Breakfast: Full breakfast is served 8:30 to 10 a.m., and may include eggs, muffins or blueberry pancakes, Swedish pancakes, Pennsylvania scrapple, sausages, ham or bacon, fruit, coffee or tea.
Extras: There are an outdoor swimming pool and tennis courts. Discounts for some golf courses or ski resorts are available for guests. A full dinner—choice of some ten entrees, homemade soups, breads, cakes, and pies—is also included in the room rate.
Rates: Ranges from $50 to $60 per person, and includes breakfast and dinner (MAP). Personal checks and most credit cards accepted.
10% discount to OHJ members except holidays and summer weekends.
Mailing Address: PO Box 275 H, Canadensis, PA 18325

COOKSBURG

GATEWAY LODGE
Joseph and Linda Burney
Route 36
Cooksburg, PA 16217
(814) 744-8017
Year-round

1934 Log Cabin

LOCATION: Towering pine and hemlock surround the inn. Within an easy drive is Cook Forest State Park, 8,000 acres of virgin woodlands. Miles of scenic roadways wind into the interior which includes 12 miles of maintained cross-country ski trails (ski trails also surround the Lodge) and 27 miles of hiking trails.

Ray and Beth Griscom built this log cabin inn in 1934 as a family-style getaway camp. While the children romped in the woods, parents were supposed to relax in the rustic atmosphere of log ceilings, knot-holed panelling and hand-split chestnut furnishings.

Today the Gateway's atmosphere is similar. Except for an added stairway and unobtrusive front porch, the exterior looks the same as it originally did, with unpainted logs, a fieldstone foundation, and an immense fieldstone chimney. The hand-split chestnut beds are the ones the Griscoms had. The dining room is as rustic as ever, furnished with colonial chairs and tables, kerosene lanterns, and a chandelier made from a wagon wheel. And there are lots of antique knick-knacks in the lounge, including a spinning wheel, a rag rug, and some old hunting rifles. (Some furnishings, like the cushioned sofas in the lounge, are new.) Innkeepers Joseph and Linda Burney (Gateway's third owners) cook all the meals.

Restrictions: No pets. Only children old enough to have their own room. Check-in after 3 p.m. Check-out at 11 a.m.
Beds: Seven rooms with a double; one with two twins; five rooms share two baths. Nine cabins with two or more beds, a fireplace or woodburning stove, living room, kitchen, and bath. Guests must bring linens, towels, dishes, and utensils. (Blankets, pillows provided.)
Breakfast: There's an extra charge for breakfast, served daily, 8 to 9 a.m.

Extras: Lunch is served, June through November, for an extra charge, 11:30 a.m. to 1:30 p.m. Dinner is available every day but Monday. The cabins are supplied with free firewood.

Rates: Rooms with shared bath, $50; rooms with private bath, $60; log cabins range from $65 to $97. Checks and most credit cards accepted.

10% discount to OHJ members.

CRESCO (LA ANNA)

LA ANNA GUEST HOUSE
Kay and Julie Swingle
Route 191
Cresco, PA 18326
(717) 676-4225
Year-round

1879 Tri-gabled Ell

LOCATION: Cresco, designated as a Pike County Historical Site, is in the Pocono Mountains surrounded by woods and waterfalls. State parks nearby invite hikers and other sports enthusiasts. Lake Wallenpaupack offers swimming, boating, and other water sports.

Mrs. Gilpin slept with a silver pistol under her pillow when her husband was away. Which was often: He was a lumberman, and spent his days galloping over hundreds of miles of Pennsylvania territory, urging his steed on with a cherished pair of brass spurs, in search of unclaimed timber groves.

The brass spurs are still there, and so is the silver pistol. And so, for that matter, is Mr. and Mrs. Gilpin's granddaughter. She's Kay Swingle, who in 1974 opened the house her grandfather built to guests.

The house is built of sturdy hemlock clapboards from the Gilpin mill, and has an ornate, wraparound verandah with all its original trim. Kay, who grew up and raised her own family here, has kept the house in excellent repair. She's decorated it with her grandparents' Victorian and Empire furnishings, Oriental rugs, and Victorian reproduction wallpapers that closely match those her grandfather hung more than a century ago.

Beds: Five rooms: two with twin beds; two with double beds; one with a double bed and a single bed. Two rooms share a bath.
Breakfast: Continental.
Rates: All rooms $12 per night per person. Cots and cribs, no charge. Personal checks accepted; no credit cards.
    10% discount to OHJ members.
Mailing Address: RD 2, Box 1051, Cresco, PA 18326

DANVILLE

**THE PINE BARN INN AND
GUEST HOUSE**
Martin and Barbara Walzer
One Pine Barn Place
Danville, PA 17821
(717) 275-2071
Year-round

1860 Pennsylvania German Bank Barn

LOCATION: The inn is set in a secluded residential section of Danville, at one time an Indian settlement and later an important mining center. A few original log cabins remain, as well as some 30 covered bridges. It's ten miles from the Susquehanna River.

> *"Important plans, as well as conspiracies, were first concocted in our country inns, and many a memorable and provocative discussion transpired before the open fire of the tavern. Pine Barn Inn carries on this tradition of early innkeeping."*

The immense barn that houses this inn was once the center of a prosperous 19th-century farm that raised apple trees, corn, barley, wheat, horses and cows. Later, when the town began to encroach on the farmland, the barn was converted to a riding stable. It was converted to a private home, complete with a solar glass roof and second-floor swimming pool, in the 1940s, and to an inn in 1950. Many of the guest rooms are furnished with antiques. In the dining rooms, you can see the barn's post-and-beam construction, as well as a display of early photographs of local mansions.

Restrictions: Some rooms reserved for guests with pets. Check-out at 1 p.m.
Beds: There are 33 singles and 18 rooms with twin beds. All have private baths.
Extras: Wake-up service, laundry service, as well as dining in the inn's cocktail lounge and four dining rooms, are available.
Rates: Double room, $28 to $36; single, $26 to $32. Each additional adult occupant, $2. Cribs, $2 and cots, $2. Personal checks and credit cards accepted.

PENNSYLVANIA

EAST BERLIN

THE LEAS-BECHTEL MANSION INN
Charles and Mariam Bechtel,
Ruth Spangler
400 West King Street
East Berlin, PA 17316
(717) 259-7760
Year-round

1897 Queen Anne

LOCATION: In an 18th-century village in Pennsylvania Dutch country, the Mansion itself as well as the entire block have been recommended as an historic district. A walking tour of the town includes excellent examples of colonial and Victorian architecture, and local stone, brick and weatherboard German-style bank barns. Superb antiquing is available in nearby Abbotstown and New Oxford. Historic Gettysburg is 18 miles away.

William Leas, a wealthy entrepreneur who dabbled in just about every business in town, including banking, wagon building, saw milling, and farming, built this house. It's an asymmetrical mass of shapes that's a delight to explore, and every bit as multi-faceted as the man who built it. A turret, an arched balcony, a wide-capped chimney, shingles, porches, a winding verandah, dormers, bay windows, gables projecting at odd angles, and mismatching levels—this house can't decide what architectural form to take. The entire house, inside and out, right down to the Victorian barn with original hay mow, chicken house, horse stalls and granary, is excellently preserved, a few added baths the only changes made in the last century.

Inside, most of the brass chandeliers, bedroom curtains, and several carpets are original to the house. Many guest rooms have built-in wardrobes and full-length mirrors; all are furnished with antiques and Pennsylvania Dutch handmade quilts; one connects to the original Victorian bathroom. The family room (with the original Leas family cookstove and built-in oak cupboards), the living room (with oak woodwork and a burgundy Bokhara rug), and the dining room (with etched glass windows, a large window seat and a built-in corner cupboard), are all authentically furnished and for public use. But the showstopper is the Victorian parlor, which you can rent as part of a honeymoon suite.

Restrictions: No pets. Children over age eight welcome. Smoking restricted to private balconies and porches. Check-in by 11 p.m.
Beds: Seven guest rooms. Four with private baths. Three rooms share one full bath. A private "special occasion" suite has private bath and its own Victorian parlor. A limited number of rooms in the rustic Carriage House (shared bath in Mansion) are available.
Breakfast: Continental: fresh fruits and juice, homemade biscuits, buns and hot breads, apple butter, Amish preserves, coffee and tea.
Extras: Tea in the afternoon with homemade buns, pies, or cookies is served, and a complimentary glass of wine is offered.
Rates: Mansion rooms, $45 to $85; carriage house, $50; private suite, $100. (All rooms 10-15% less during winter months.) Cots, $15. Checks and most credit cards accepted.

10% discount to OHJ members.

PENNSYLVANIA

EPHRATA

HISTORIC SMITHTON
Dorothy Graybill
900 West Main Street
Ephrata, PA 17522
(717) 733-6094
Year-round

C. 1762 German Colonial

LOCATION: The inn stands on a hill overlooking the Ephrata Cloister, one of Pennsylvania's major historic sites, in Northern Lancaster County—home of the Pennsylvania Dutch.

Reclusive religious groups have always been attracted to this part of Pennsylvania. Along with the Amish and Old Order Mennonite, in the 18th century came the Seventh Day Baptists. They built a Germanic, medieval-looking cloister as their headquarters, and it rapidly became a tourist attraction. One member of the sect, Henry Miller, was a particularly skilled stonemason. To house tourists he built this inn on a hill overlooking the cloister, and flaunted his skills by creating a checkerboard facade out of light and dark sandstone.

Henry and his wife Susana came to a rather tragic end. When the wounded from the Battle of Brandywine were brought to the cloister for treatment, Henry and Susana volunteered their services. Both soon succumbed, as did many of the soldiers, to an epidemic of camp fever.

The inn remained in the hands of Henry and Susana's descendants until the late 1970s. The current owner, an architect and restoration professional, has restored most of the building, though work continues on the west and south wings. Only closets, bathrooms, and a modern kitchen have been added.

There are corner fireplaces in every room. A massive domed storage cellar lies just a few steps below the kitchen. Some of the ceilings are beamed, in keeping with Henry's German ancestry. And the furnishings include antiques and handmade reproductions, some of them copies of pieces made by the artisans of the cloister.

Restrictions: "Children are welcome if mannerly." Check-out at noon; check-in after 3:30 p.m.
Beds: The six rooms and one suite have either a king, queen, or double, plus a trundle or roll-away. The suite sleeps four in its king canopy bed, trundle, and cupboard bed. No rooms share a bath.
Breakfast: The "all-you-can-eat Pennsylvania Dutch country breakfast" usually consists of beverage, fruit, juice, and waffles with fruit, whipped cream, and syrup topping.
Extras: Afternoon tea and bedtime snacks are free of charge. Dinner for inn guests is available only with advance reservations; there's an additional charge. Night shirts and candles are provided in some rooms.
Rates: $45 to $120 (for the suite); $10 to $20 more on Fridays and Saturdays. $15 charge for extra person. Personal checks and credit cards welcome.

HAWLEY

**ACADEMY STREET BED &
BREAKFAST**
Judith and Sheldon Lazan
528 Academy Street
Hawley, PA 18428
(717) 226-3430
June to October

1863-5 Italianate

LOCATION: The inn is located on a quiet street in town, with a large lawn near the Lackawaxen River. A five-minute ride away is Lake Wallenpaupack, with its boat ramps, picnic grounds, fishing, swimming, boating, and scuba diving. Theater, golf, horseback riding, and a railroad museum are close by. Good restaurants and good blueberry picking are also available.

This house, built by a Civil War veteran, survived a 19th-century flood that wiped out almost every building for miles around. Innkeepers Judith and Sheldon Lazan, who'd dreamed about owning an old house for years, bought it in 1983. They've continued the restoration work begun by artist Dennis Corrigan, who owned the house before them, and rescued it from its state of 1950s neglect (acoustical tile ceilings, fake panelling, the works). Corrigan painted the exterior in an eye-catching, authentic, three-tone color scheme that accents the paired eave brackets, ornate window heads, and porch detail. The Lazans have decorated the interior with antiques from a variety of periods, reproduction wallpapers, and hand-made country curtains. The house has several fireplaces and two very beautiful mantelpieces: one cast-iron with a marbleized finish; the other beautifully carved wood with a tile inset.

Restrictions: No pets or children. "Discretionary" smoking requested.
Beds: Seven rooms with double or queen-size beds. Six rooms share two baths; one room with private bath.
Breakfast: Full "gourmet" breakfast.
Extras: The afternoon tea, 2 to 4 p.m., includes homemade cheesecake and pastries; high tea is available for $3. Host is a gourmet cook and baker.

347

Rates: Rooms with shared bath, $45 on Friday and Saturday, $35 Sunday to Thursday; room with private bath, $55. Cots available at minimal charge. Personal check, MasterCard, and VISA accepted.

10% discount to OHJ members (in winter)

Mailing Address: 1330 15th Street, Fort Lee, NJ 07024 (201) 224-2276

PENNSYLVANIA

JIM THORPE

THE HARRY PACKER MANSION
Robert and Patricia Handwerk
Packer Hill
Jim Thorpe, PA 18229
(717) 325-8566
Year-round

1874 French Second Empire

LOCATION: The inn is situated in a National Historic District of a once bustling coal and shipping port on the Lehigh River. A walking tour begins next door at the fully restored, 20-room Victorian mansion of the inn's original builder and goes on to include more than 25 restored buildings and churches as well as cemeteries, markers, and parks.

Asa Packer, president of the prosperous Lehigh Valley Railroad, built this house as a wedding gift for his son Harry. But poor Harry didn't live long to enjoy it—he died of a liver ailment at age 34. The house is a magnificent example of Second Empire, with slate mansard roof, porthole dormers, and hand-carved sandstone porches. It has one unusual feature: a tower that looks like a belfry. Inside, there's a library with solid mahogany bookshelves and mouldings and three stained-glass windows that depict the era's famous writers.

The Handwerks bought the house in 1984 and have spent a year restoring it. They were lucky to acquire all the original chandeliers with it.

Restrictions: No pets. No smoking in guest rooms. Check-in after 5 p.m., check-out at 11 a.m.

Beds: Three rooms with two double beds, two of which share a bath. One suite with sitting room and private bath.

Breakfast: Continental: fresh juice and fruits, pastry, bread and homemade preserves, coffee or tea. Meals served on the verandah, weather permitting, or in the elegant formal dining room under the original chandelier.

Extras: High tea is served on weekends ($3.50). Sightseeing and walking tours are arranged by the hosts.

Rates: Ranges from $150 for the suite to $65 for a room with double beds and a shared bath. Cots, $10; cribs, $10. Personal checks and American Express accepted.

10% discount to OHJ members.

LANCASTER

WITMER'S TAVERN - HISTORIC 1725 INN
Brant E. Hartung
2014 Old Philadelphia Pike
Lancaster, PA 17602
(717) 299-5305
Year-round

Pre-Revolutionary Colonial

LOCATION: On the old Philadelphia turnpike, the inn stands between the seaport of Philadelphia and the city of Lancaster with its specialty antique and craft shops and whole blocks of restored colonial homes. Within easy reach are dozens of restaurants and taverns with a colonial atmosphere and Pennsylvania Dutch fare. A few miles away are the Amish Homestead; Dutch Wonderland, an amusement park and wax museum; and Pennsylvania German Gardens.

Legend has it that George Washington, the Marquis De Lafayette, and other illustrious colonials slept here. Around the time of the Revolutionary War, Witmer's was one of the most popular of 62 taverns that lined the Philadelphia-to-Lancaster turnpike, frequented by stagecoach travellers and Conestoga wagon men. Witmer's served as an inn and boarding house for two centuries until, gradually, it was forgotten.

The Tavern stood vacant for a year, collecting dust and decay, before Brant Hartung took it under his wing in 1969. He used it as office space while saving money to undertake its restoration. He began in 1974 and, last we heard, was still at it. One of Brant's first projects was chiselling the clingy stucco off the blue limestone walls and re-pointing them. Inside, he stripped seven layers of paint off the heavy, panelled doors, chair rails and trim, and repainted them in their original colonial colors. He's still working on the ground-floor tavern, a great vantage point for looking at the mortise-and-tenon floor joists above. Along the way, he's uncovered some unusual artifacts, including centuries-old crocks beneath the floors and between partitions.

Brant has tried to keep the decor as authentic as possible. That's why you'll be awakened at the crack of dawn by King Tut the rooster and his clucking Banty chickens—after all, all old inns had their own livestock.

Restrictions: No pets. Children welcome. Check-in after 2 p.m.; check-out at 11 a.m.
Beds: Five fully restored rooms with fireplaces (and popcorn poppers) share two baths.
Breakfast: Continental is served in the communal sitting room.
Extras: Pandora's Quilt, an antique shop, is open between 9 and 6 p.m., selling quilts, textiles and collectibles. Guests receive a complimentary rose daily and, for those staying three days or more, a bottle of champagne.
Rates: From $45 to $75, depending on the season and whether fireplaces are in use. Cribs and cots, $10. Personal checks accepted; no credit cards.

PENNSYLVANIA

LITITZ

THE HISTORIC GENERAL SUTTER INN
Joan and Richard Vetter
14 East Main Street
Lititz, PA 17543
(717) 626-2115
Year-round

Early 19th-century Federal

LOCATION: On the square in town, the inn is the perfect starting point for a walking tour of the historic district that includes the Moravian Church Square, the Sturgis Pretzel factory (the oldest pretzel factory in the country), Linden Hall School for Girls, and other 18th-century buildings. Many quaint antique and crafts shops, as well as the Wilbur Chocolate Factory, are nearby.

The General Sutter has operated as an inn since 1764. Founded by the Moravian Church and originally known as Zum Anker (Sign of the Anchor), it was well known in the 18th century for its feather beds, heated rooms, good food—and prohibition of dancing, cursing, gossip, and bawdy songs. The inn underwent significant structural changes in 1803, 1848, and 1930, and finally evolved into the expansive brick, semi-Federal structure it is today. All the guest rooms are decorated with country and Victorian antiques. The lobby is high Victorian, done up with Empire sofas, marble-topped tables and brass and crystal parlor lamps. And in the center of their outdoor patio, there's a cast-iron fountain that was given to the town in 1895.

Beds: Thirteen rooms all have private baths. Cots and cribs available at minimal charge.
Breakfast: Breakfast is served in the inn's informal coffee shop (cost not included in room rate).
Extras: The inn's more formal Gaslight Dining Room serves lunch, dinner, and a happy hour from 4 to 6 p.m.
Rates: $50 to $60. Personal checks and most credit cards accepted.

MERTZTOWN

**LONGSWAMP BED &
BREAKFAST**
Elsa and Dean Dimick
Route 2
Mertztown, PA 19539
(215) 682-6197
Year-round

1740 - added to in 1790, 1820, and 1863

LOCATION: Next door is a dairy farm, nearby are ski areas and antique shops, as well as the Amish country. Fifty acres of oak forest stretch behind the house.

"Though we did our best on this great old place, most of the work—as I'm sure you know—doesn't show! Still, we think you'll like it."

As the Trexler family's fortune grew, so did this house. The Trexlers were early occupants of the house who owned the prosperous iron foundry across the road, and had their money invested in several other mercantile interests. With each new profit, they added to their house—a total of three expansions, the last the mansard roof in 1863. But no amount of expanding, redecorating, or covering the old walls in new paper could rid the house of its age-old ghost. Colonel Trexler, one of the earliest family members who lived here, murdered his daughter's lover in a fit of paternal jealousy. His punishment was decreed: he was to sweep the foundry's floor for eternity. When the Colonel died, his ghost returned to the old house after each day's sweeping to haunt its inhabitants, and send a common chill up their spines. Finally in the late 19th century, the occupants hired a priest to exorcise the ghost—and, word has it, never heard from it again.

Elsa and Dean Dimick moved into Longswamp in 1983, and completely restored it. Their only concessions to modernity were the new kitchen—Elsa was a professional caterer before she went into this business—and two new guest bathrooms. Today the house looks pretty much as it did in 1863, the last time it was modified. Inside, there's a three-storey, curving staircase of what Elsa calls "considerable consequence." Floors on the first and second storeys are pegged oak; on the top floor they're pine. There's a summer kitchen (where guests are welcomed with wine and appetizers) with its original, 18th-century woodwork and fireplace. The furnishings are all antiques, and every guest room is decorated uniquely, with an antique or Amish quilt the room's centerpiece.

Restrictions: No smoking in bedrooms, no pets; check-in time is flexible, check-out at 1 p.m.
Beds: Nine rooms—five with private baths, two with fireplaces.
Breakfast: The full country features "everything homemade": berries and cream, wheat germ waffles with maple syrup or jam; bacon; coffee and tea.
Extras: There's complimentary wine and cheese, coffee and tea, use of the bikes and an indoor basketball/handball court in barn.
Rates: $50 single, $60 double. Credit cards and personal checks accepted.
10% discount to OHJ members.
Mailing Address: RD 2, Box 26, Mertztown, PA 19539

MUNCY

THE BODINE HOUSE
David and Marie Louise Smith
307 South Main Street
Muncy, PA 17756
(717) 546-8949
Year-round

1805 Federal Townhouse

LOCATION: Set on a tree-lined street surrounded by other restored 19th-century homes, the inn is within the Registered National Historic District of Muncy. The area offers many summer and winter activities such as hiking, fishing, boating, swimming, auctions, antique shops, summer theater, cross-country skiing, tobogganing, and skating.

The same family lived in this house from 1805 until 1976! The house was restored in 1976, before David and Marie Louise Smith bought it in 1978. All its original exterior features are intact, including the pedimented front doorway, attic fanlight, and a carriage house in the rear. The Smiths even hang a reproduction colonial flag out front. The sidewalk running in front of it is brick.

Inside, there are wide plank floors, some original plaster and hardware, and four working fireplaces — one with its original cooking crane.

Restrictions: No pets. Children over six welcome. Smoking areas provided.
Beds: Four rooms: one with antique 3/4 bed, two with double beds, one with twin beds and fireplace. Three rooms with private baths.
Breakfast: Full breakfast is served 7:30 to 8:30 a.m. around the main fireplace.
Extras: Complimentary wine and cheese are served, 5 to 7 p.m. Bicycles are available for town tours. Second-floor library and sitting room are open to guests, and the baby grand in the living room welcomes players.
Rates: Single, $25; double, $30; double with half-bath, $35; twin with fireplace, $35. Cots ($5). Personal checks accepted; no credit cards.
10% discount to OHJ members.

NEW HOPE

HOTEL DU VILLAGE
Barbara and Omar Arbani
North River Road
New Hope, PA 18938
(215) 862-9911
Year-round

1907 Tudor Revival

LOCATION: In the heart of Bucks County countryside, the inn is five minutes from the Delaware River and a half-mile north of the town of New Hope with its many restaurants, theaters, and craft and antique shops. The building's ten acres of landscaped grounds include a pond and Primrose Creek.

In the 17th century, William Penn gave the tract of land this house sits on to the Ely family. Two hundred years later, in 1895, an Ohio physician bought the land from Ely's descendants, and his sister built this rambling Tudor Revival mansion. But the house didn't stay long in her hands. In 1917, she sold it to the exclusive Holmquist School for Girls, a white-gloves institution for "the academic and social preparation of young ladies." (Margaret Mead was one of the young ladies Holmquist turned out.) A school it remained until 1976, when Barbara and Omar Arbani bought it, opened their elegant French restaurant, and, two years later, started taking overnight guests.

Restrictions: No pets. Well-behaved children welcome. Check-in after 2 p.m.; check-out at 11 a.m.
Beds: There are 19 rooms with private baths: doubles, queens, kings, and twins.
Breakfast: Continental
Extras: An outdoor swimming pool and two tennis courts are open Memorial Day to September. The restaurant specializes in French country cuisine, including duckling, rabbit, and sweetbreads (open evenings except Monday and Tuesday).
Rates: $70 for large room with king-size bed and sitting area to $55 for room with double bed and private bath (tub but no shower). Cots, $10. Personal checks and American Express accepted.

NEW HOPE

LOGAN INN
Carl Lutz and Arthur Sanders
10 West Ferry Street
New Hope, PA 18938
(215) 862-5134
February 12 through January 3

1727 Federal

LOCATION: The inn is located in the center of picturesque New Hope, "mecca for antique collectors." Old houses and shops predominate. A mule barge still travels the Delaware Canal, and an antique train makes journeys through the countryside nearby.

The night before George Washington defeated the British at Trenton, before his famed Christmas, 1776, crossing of the Delaware, he and his highest ranking officers plotted their attack at this very inn. The Logan is the oldest building in New Hope.

The inn has expanded over the years. Today, it's a pleasing combination of Colonial and Victorian. From the Victorian era: the main dining room in the fern-, orchid-, and cast-iron-filled conservatory; and an authentic 1838 portrait of Prince Albert, painted the year before he married Victoria. From Colonial times: the bell stagecoach drivers rang to alert the innkeeper; and a taproom chock-full of old clocks and ale steins. All the guest rooms have antique beds (brass or carved wood) and huge wardrobes. The innkeeper is Carl Lutz, mayor of New Hope.

Restrictions: No pets. "Well-behaved children are welcome, but rooms have no TVs."
Beds: Four rooms have double beds and private baths; one room with twin beds also has a private bath. Three doubles share one bath, two doubles share another.
Extras: The full-service gourmet restaurant features old standards like chicken Kiev and filet mignon, and specialties like shrimp with dill butter and wine sauce.
Rates: $85, private bath; $75, shared bath. Cots, $10 extra. Personal checks and credit cards are welcome.

NEW HOPE

PINEAPPLE HILL B&B
Suzie and Randy Leslie
River Road
New Hope, PA 18938
(215) 862-9608
Year-round

1780 Federal; Gothic Revival addition

LOCATION: The inn stands some four miles south of New Hope, with its galleries and antique shops. Nearby are many historic sites, including William Penn's 17th-century estate. Philadelphia is an hour's drive away.

"Readers of OHJ are interested in the same things as we innkeepers —let's get together!"

Pineapple Hill is a unique blend of three architectural periods: early Federal, Greek Revival, and Victorian. The original clapboarded, Federal farmhouse was built in 1780; it was expanded in 1810 with a stone, also Federal-style addition; in 1840 the parlor was "remodelled" Greek Revival-style; and the front-end, Victorian Gothic-style gable was added in 1870. Two of the second-floor bedrooms have their original, early Federal woodwork, and several rooms have the original, random-width flooring. There's an old cold cellar in the basement. And on the property are stone ruins from two early barns, a smoke house, and a carriage house. Innkeepers Suzie and Randy Leslie have used these ruins artfully, planting an herb garden in one, a sunken garden in another, and setting their pool amongst the old stone foundation on the 1850 barn. Inside the house, they've stencilled several rooms, and decorated with country primitive antiques, antique quilts, and American folk art. Suzie and Randy will welcome you to their house with a historical tour of the property.

Restrictions: No smoking, please. Small children only during the week. No pets. Check-in after 2 p.m., check-out at noon.
Beds: There are five rooms, all double beds; one of the five adjoins a room with twin beds, making a suite—"nice for families." Three rooms have private baths.
Breakfast: Fresh fruit salad topped with yogurt, coconut, etc.; gen-

erously sized croissants with homemade jams and jellies, tea, coffee, juice, and milk.

Extras: Various afternoon refreshments and evening after-dinner drinks are complimentary.

Rates: $50 to $80, weekdays; $60 to $90, weekends. One crib and one cot available, no charge. Personal or traveler's checks and American Express accepted.

Mailing Address: RD 3, Box 34C, New Hope, PA 18938

TOWANDA

VICTORIAN GUEST HOUSE
Barb Mower
118 York Avenue
Towanda, PA 18848
(717) 265-6972
Year-round

1897 Queen Anne

LOCATION: The inn is a stone's throw from the Susquehanna River, ideal for fishing and white-water canoeing. (There's a canoe rental shop not far away.) It's also near several state and county parks (one with 35 waterfalls), where you can swim, hike, or cross-country ski. Steamtown USA (a steam engine museum with a working antique locomotive) and the Corning Glass Works are nearby, and there are also plenty of road races and triathalons in the area.

The lumber dealer who built this house had five rambunctious sons who used the top floor ballroom as a basketball court. Unfortunately, the ballroom isn't there anymore. The house's second owner was a baker who had a case of permanent bad luck: First, the top floor of the house caught fire. Later, the baker lost his fortune in the stock market crash of 1929, and had to convert his home to a guest house to make up for his lost profits.

Barb Mower has lived here since 1946. She has a copy of the

newspaper article about the 1920s fire in the house, which tells how the whole neighborhood helped to douse the flames and rescue the furniture from the smoldering mansion. She also has the original blueprints, which show that, despite the fire, the house looks almost the same as it did when it was built—all that's missing is the widow's walk atop the flat-roofed turret. Most of the house's original, lavish interior millwork is also in excellent condition. Mouldings are cut from a variety of woods, including curly oak, quarter-sawn oak, cherry, birch, and pine, all the best pieces from the stock of the lumberman who built the house.

Barb has furnished the house with her diverse collection of antiques. She has stories about many of the items — like one rocker which she brought home in a paper bag, all in pieces, and put back together. Her decor is authentic, too, with lots of period wallpapers she hung herself. (The three-storey entry hall took 74 rolls of paper!)

Restrictions: No pets.
Beds: Of the ten rooms, six have private baths.
Breakfast: Free coffee is available.
Rates: $28 to $38, all rooms with telephone, color TV, and air conditioning. Personal checks and credit cards welcome.

10% discount to OHJ members if stay is more than one night.

PENNSYLVANIA

UPPER BLACK EDDY

BRIDGETON HOUSE
Beatrice and Charles Briggs
River Road
Upper Black Eddy, PA 18972
(215) 982-5856
Year-round

1836 Federal

LOCATION: The historic Delaware River runs right through the backyard; Roosevelt State Park, with 60 miles of paths for hiking, biking, and picnics, is a half-block away.

"Our guests enjoy the restoration and appreciate the love that's gone into it—they especially like the before and after pictures!"

This building survived two floods, life as a bakery and candy store, and a host of careless apartment dwellers before Beatrice and Charles Briggs rescued it in 1981. When they came across it, the house was hardly a sight to behold: boarded-up windows, bricked-in fireplaces, layers of linoleum, flimsy partitions, and asphalt shingles. They immersed themselves in restoration for a year, and completely changed the house's shabby character—back to its original Federal charm. They replaced the original front doors and windows that had been removed and blocked; excavated the original fireplace from behind a closet; re-created wood mouldings to match the few originals that had survived; uncovered the wide board flooring; and added French doors at the rear to capture the picturesque view of the Delaware River. The Briggses have decorated the Inn with country antiques (all rooms have four-poster beds), rag rugs, Oriental rugs, simple Federal-era chandeliers, and a collection of pottery and copper pots.

Restrictions: No pets. Smoking "not encouraged." No children on weekends. Check-in between 1 and 9 p.m.
Beds: The seven guest rooms all have private baths: One with a twin bed, five with doubles, and one with queen.
Breakfast: Fresh fruit, followed by eggs, (asparagus and cheddar cheese omelettes, for example), homemade baked goods; coffee, including decaffeinated; tea, including herbal; fresh juice.
Extras: Complimentary sherry is served. Fresh flowers, fruit, and "special amenities" are provided in each room. Guests can swim or tube on the river.
Rates: $50 mid-week, $75 on weekends. Personal checks are welcome, as are credit cards.
Mailing Address: PO Box 167, Upper Black Eddy, PA 18972

TEXAS

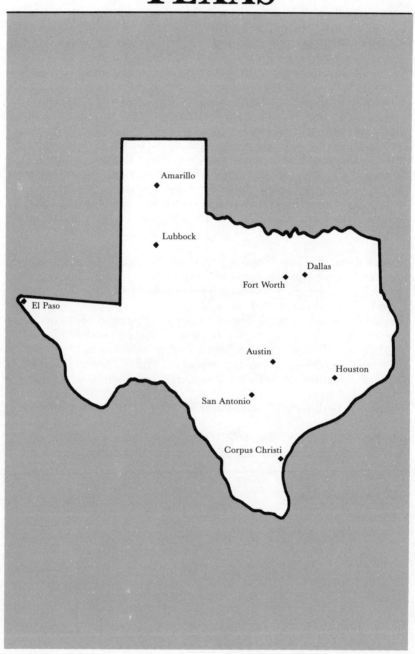

AUSTIN

THE McCALLUM HOUSE
Roger and Nancy Danley
613 West 32nd Street
Austin, TX 78705
(512) 451-6744
Year-round

1907 Princess Anne

LOCATION: The University of Texas/Austin is one mile away, downtown Austin is two miles. Three lakes are in Austin and "hill country" borders it. LBJ's ranch is 50 miles; San Antonio, 70 miles.

Roger and Nancy Danley must love old houses. First they took on this challenging Princess Anne—all the stained glass and woodwork were sorely in need of restoration, the walls were damaged, the structure wasn't even level. Then they put up a garage in the back and are now working on a greenhouse. But the piéce de résistance is another old house they've built and furnished—this one's a miniature Victorian, on display for all to see (and, if they're careful, maybe even play with).

A.N. McCallum, who was Austin's superintendent of schools for 39 years(!), and his wife Jane, an active suffragette who eventually served as Texas' secretary of state, built the house in 1907. It was their heirs who sold it to the Danleys.

Restrictions: No pets or smoking. "Set-up for children is very limited, but we have had them occasionally."
Beds: The one double suite has a private bath, screened porch, and foyer/dining area adjacent.

Breakfast: Full: egg dish, fruit, coffeecake, rolls, sometimes bacon, ham, or sausage is normally served in the dining room, but can be brought up to the foyer near guest room.

Extras: Drinks are available to guests arriving in late afternoon, plus a possible picnic lunch "now and then." "These are spontaneous gestures—neither guaranteed nor charged for!"

Rates: $50; personal and traveler's checks welcome.

10% discount to OHJ members.

BIG SANDY

ANNIE'S BED & BREAKFAST
Anita Gentry
Les and Martha Lane
106 North Tyler
Big Sandy, TX 75755
(214) 636-4355
Year-round

1901 Queen Anne

LOCATION: The decorative porches of Annie's, surrounded by a white picket fence, are located in the heart of the "stately pines" of northeast Texas. The Tyler Rose Gardens are a half-hour away, and there's a gift and antique shop across the street.

W.B. Mask and his wife, Annie, built a 20-by-50-foot cottage on this lot in 1901. Several years later, Wylie and Virginia Kay, who bought the house in 1913, remodelled the house. They doubled it in size, added two fireplaces, and reroofed the entire thing. Although the house was built in the early 1900s, it looks very much like a Victorian cottage: Gingerbread and gables abound. Anita Gentry, the current owner, can give you the history of the house and its many occupants. She's adorned the house, which has 13 guest rooms, with antiques and imported rugs.

Restrictions: Children welcome; no pets; smoking not allowed in the house. Check-in after 3 p.m. on weekdays, and before 6 p.m. on weekends.

Beds: Of the eight doubles, two twins, and three queens, five share a bath.

Breakfast: Guests may have gourmet: Strawberry soup, freshly squeezed orange juice, stuffed French toast, strawberry crepes, eggs Benedict; or southern-style: grits, eggs, and sausage.

Rates: $48 (double or twins, shared bath) to $115 (private bath, spiral staircase, queen bed). Special weekend rates of 25% off. Personal checks and credit cards welcome.

Mailing Address: BOX 928, Big Sandy, TX 75755

TEXAS

GALVESTON

THE MATALI, AN HISTORIC INN
Dan Dyer
1727 Sealy
Galveston, TX 77550
(409) 763-4526
Year-round

1886 Queen Anne with Stick Style and Eastlake details

LOCATION: The Galveston Trolley stops at the inn's front door and guests board free; nearby attractions include museums, shopping on the Strand, and beaches, all within a half-mile. The surrounding area, the East End Historic District, has many distinctive homes.

An elaborate Queen Anne with Eastlake and Stick Style features, the Matali is one of the most photographed houses in Galveston. Isabella Offenbach Maas, daughter of the Rabbi of Cologne and sister to the famous composer, was a pioneer of the island and known for her benevolence. She married Samuel Maas, a Galveston business-man, whom she had met during one of his trips to Germany. They settled in Galveston after their marriage in 1844. The house is named after the last person to own it before innkeeper Dan Dyer purchased it in 1983. Amadeo Matali bought the home in 1928, though it was in poor condition. He upgraded the house, installing a new kitchen and large first-floor bathroom. The cement benches and ornaments in the carefully landscaped gardens were commissioned by Matali in

1932. They were a gift to his wife and bear her nickname, "Neni." Mr. Dyer has spent 15 months restoring the woodwork, wainscotting, and the jeweled stained-glass windows. (The four elaborate cherry and mahogany fireplaces are exquisite.) In 1984 the Galveston Historical Homes Tour featured this as a house "in process"; by 1986, they declared it officially restored.

Restrictions: Check-in after 2 p.m. Check-out at noon. No children under 12; smoking allowed; kennel arrangements can be made for pets.
Beds: There's one king, one double, and one twin; two share a bath. Each room has a private porch overlooking the historic district.
Breakfast: "Hearty continental": coffee, juice, fresh-fruit compote, cheese quiche, hot croissants or muffins, all served family style in the dining room.
Extras: Evening cheese tray and trolley transportation (stops at the inn's front door) are included. Private tours via horse and carriage of the nearby historic districts, at sunset, can be arranged for an extra charge. Wine and cheese tray can be served on board.
Rates: $75 to $95 (discounts for two nights or more), $75 between Labor Day and April 1 except for holidays and special events. Cots, $25. Personal checks and credit cards welcome.

TEXAS

GALVESTON

THE VIRGINIA POINT INN
Tom and Eleanor Catlow
2327 Avenue K
Galveston, TX 77550
(409) 763-2450
Year-round

1907 Mediterranean

LOCATION: Galveston, Texas's oldest major city, offers the Strand restored shopping district, beaches, fishing, boating, and a pleasant, pervasive "sea aroma." The surrounding area is known as the Silk Stocking Historic District.

Harry Hawley built this 1907 Mediterranean-style stucco house on three city lots. The house remained in the family until 1984, when Tom and Eleanor Catlow purchased it and converted it into an inn. They've restored the house inside and out, including the spacious, landscaped gardens. A large part of the antiques that furnish the house belonged to Hawley and his descendants. Everything from the plumbing fixtures to the ceiling fans are original to the house, but the 12 old clocks came from Tom's great-grandfather.

Restrictions: Children over 12 only. No pets, smoking only on porches or downstairs. Check-in after 3 p.m., check-out at noon.
Beds: One single has a 3/4 bed, there are four doubles (two with twins, one with a king). Two rooms share a bath.
Breakfast: "Hearty continental": ham, cheese, fruit salad, juices, hot bread, rolls, croissants, coffee, tea, and "other tasty treats," are served from 8 to 10 a.m.
Extras: Afternoon wine and cheese, badminton or croquet on the lawn, sight-seeing train tickets, and use of bicycles are all complimentary.
Rates: $75 (single) to $125 (master suite with twins or king, private bath). Cots, $20. Personal checks and credit cards accepted.
  10% discount to OHJ members.

JEFFERSON

MCKAY HOUSE
Tom and Peggy Taylor
306 East Delta Street
Jefferson, TX 75657
(214) 665-7322
Year-round

1851 Greek Revival

LOCATION: Once a busy port on the Texas frontier, Jefferson has historic districts in both commercial and residential areas. Thirty antique shops are within walking distance of the inn, a canoeing river flows through downtown, and Texas's only natural lake is 15 miles downstream.

This house has virtually not changed since 1851. The original exterior shutters are still operable, and throughout the house you'll find the original hardware, gas/electric lights, red heart pine floors, and a fireplace in each bedroom. The house first belonged to Antonio Glover, a prosperous builder and cabinetmaker. Tom and Peggy Taylor purchased the house in 1984 and spent a year preparing to take guests.

The house is listed in the National Register.

Restrictions: Limited accommodations for babies and children. Outdoor pets only, smoking outside only. Check-in after 2 p.m., check-out at 11 a.m.
Beds: Of the four bedrooms—three doubles, one with twins—two share a bath (and can be used as a suite) and two have private baths.
Breakfast: "Wake up to the aroma of coffee being brewed," followed by (menu varies) homemade biscuits, honey-cured ham, fresh fruit, homemade strawberry bread, muffins, whole grain breads, fruit juice, and herbal teas.
Extras: For newlyweds and anniversaries, breakfast is served in bed. Upon arrival guests can partake of fresh lemonade or hot tea on the front porch. The hosts can arrange for canoe rentals, buggy rides, and tours of museums and historic homes.
Rates: $50 ("primitive-style" furnishings) to $70 (large double, private bath). 10% discount for stays of more than two days. Cots (roll-away twin), cribs, $15. Personal checks and credit cards welcome.

10% discount to OHJ members.
Mailing Address: 9659 Broken Bow Road, Dallas, TX 75238

TEXAS

NAVASOTA

CASTLE INN
Helen and Tim Urquhart
1403 East Washington
Navasota, TX 77868
(409) 825-8051
Year-round

1893 Queen Anne modified to Prairie/Mission Style

LOCATION: Houston is 70 miles from this small town full of Victorian mansions. Rolling farmland, the Brazos River, fishing lakes, and the birthplace of Texas's government are all nearby.

"In all modesty ours is the most elegant old house in private hands in Texas—it's really one of a kind."

Built of blonde brick and cypress, the Castle (and it's big enough to warrant the name) is a century-old Queen Anne with an incredible array of fine appointments. The turret is topped with copper and the wraparound porch has 110 panes of bevelled glass. The entry hall is parquet and from the 14-foot ceiling hangs a Tiffany light fixture. The staircase leads past a 20-foot stained-glass window to a large hall and balcony. The wainscotting is made from now-extinct curly pine. The pocket doors are curly pine on one side, tiger oak on the other. The house was a wedding present from Ward Birrell Templeton to his new bride, Annie Foster. Using local craftsmen of German origin, Templeton had every modern convenience installed, including a built-in porcelain ice box and a cast-iron garbage receptacle. Both are still in the house today.

Owners Helen and Tim Urquhart love their house. The antiques that furnish the mansion are from a collection they've been amassing for more than thirty years. Weather permitting, the Urquharts will give guests a tour of town in their Model A.

Restrictions: No children under 12, no pets; check-in and check-out flexible.
Beds: All four double rooms have private baths.
Breakfast: Homemade muffins, fruit, orange juice, and coffee are served buffet style on a table near the rooms.
Extras: Evening wine and cheese are complimentary. Plus "if our guests want we'll talk with them as long as they like—or we'll leave them alone—at no charge."
Rates: $50 all rooms; personal checks welcome.
10% discount to OHJ members.

UTAH

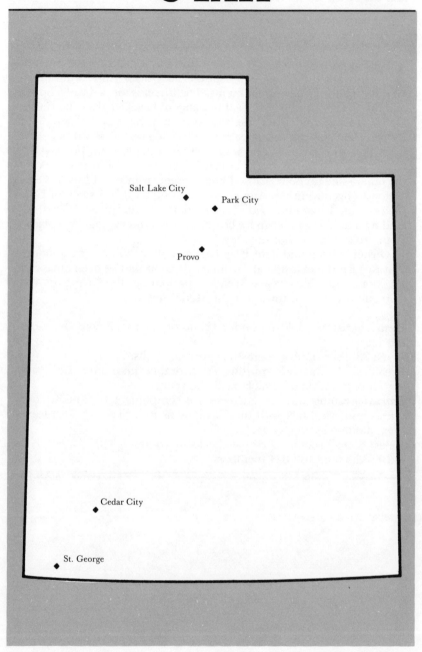

MANTI

MANTI HOUSE INN
Jim and Sonya Burnidge, Alan
and T.K. Plant
401 North Main Street
Manti, UT 84642
(801) 835-0161
Year-round

1860-1880 Vernacular

LOCATION: Manti, bordered by national forests, has many streams, lakes and mountains in the surrounding valley. Settled by Mormons, it also has many historic buildings and hosts, each July, the Mormon Miracle Pageant.

This house is built of oolitic limestone, a stone quarried in only two places on earth: Greece and Manti, Utah. The inn was built in 1860 by Andrew Van Buren, who ran a hotel. The Mormon Church purchased it in 1884, to house craftsmen working on the magnificent Mormon Temple during the 11 years it took to build it. John D.T. McAllister, third president of the Mormon Temple, who had nine wives, bought the house in 1897 and used it as his personal residence. Many of the men who built the temple worked on the inn's 1880 addition; the temple's staircase is a copy of the one in this house— the workmen practiced here first. The stone walls are 18 inches thick, and much of the window glass is original. The doors, both interior and exterior, are called Mormon doors because of their simplistic design, and all have original locks and knobs.

Jim and Sonya Burnidge and Alan and T.K. Plant restored the house, which had been vacant for 15 years, in 1984. They stripped no less than five layers of asphalt shingles from the roof and replaced them with cedar shingles. They completely rewired and plumbed the inn, and chased away the pigeons and bats that had roosted in the attic. Antiques and reproductions furnish the house, which is a Utah Registered Historical Site.

Restrictions: No smoking in the building, check-in after 3 p.m.
Beds: The wedding suite has a queen bed; the other rooms have either doubles or queens with trundles, or one double bed. All have private baths.
Breakfast: The "hearty country breakfast" menu varies, but can include German apple pancakes, creamy scrambled eggs with muffins, southern pancakes with homemade strawberry jam. Farm-fresh milk and homemade butter are served each day.
Extras: The gazebo offers a spa, and guests can take complimentary horse-drawn carriage rides. Dinners, lunches, and ice cream are served in the hotel.
Rates: $35 (four-poster bed) to $75 (wedding suite with jacuzzi, balcony, and fireplace). Cots, $5; cribs free for children under two. Personal checks and credit cards accepted.
   10% discount to OHJ members.

PARK CITY

THE OLD MINERS' LODGE - A BED & BREAKFAST INN
Hugh Daniels, Jeff Sadowsky, and Susan Wynne
615 Woodside Avenue
Park City, UT 84060
(801) 645-8068
Year-round

1893 Vernacular

LOCATION: Park City, founded in the 1850s as a silver-mining town, is known for golf in summer and skiing in winter. Historic Park City is in the National Register, and it's 25 miles from Salt Lake City.

This lodge was established in 1893 to house miners working in the two local silver mines. It's been added to twice, once in 1898 and again in 1960, but it still has shiplap clapboards, balloon-style framing, and decorative mouldings and corbels. The building was in serious disrepair when its current owners purchased it in 1983. The restoration is ongoing, but a lot of the major jobs are done. The lodge has a new roof, repaired siding and mouldings, and a new coat of paint. The innkeepers have furnished it with antiques, and all the rooms are named after important people in Park City's history.

Restrictions: "Children are O.K., but the young ones find us boring." Smoking in the parlor only; no cigars. No pets. Check-in between 2 and 6 p.m., check-out at noon.
Beds: Two doubles, two queens, one double and queen, one room with two doubles, and one room ("with a great view!") has a king and two twins. Six rooms with private baths; one with shared.
Breakfast: "Full gourmet": main dish (omelette, waffles, quiche), fresh fruit, juice, meat side dish, beverage.
Extras: Complimentary wine and cider before the fireplace are served each evening; an outdoor hot tub is available. There's also a turn-down service, ski/golf locker, and kitchen and laundry privileges.
Rates: $40 (shares bath with innkeepers) to $80 (suite with sunporch and view) in summer, $65 to $125 in winter, except during some "value times." Personal checks and credit cards accepted.
    10% discount to OHJ members limited in winter.
Mailing Address: PO Box 2639, Park City, UT 84060

UTAH

PARK CITY

1889 Schoolhouse

**WASHINGTON SCHOOL
INN**
**Donna & Frank
O'Bryan**
**543 Park Avenue
Park City, UT 84060
(800) 824-1672
Year-round**

LOCATION: Located in historic "Old Town" in Park City, the inn is convenient to entertainment, dining, shopping, and is between Park City Ski Area and Deer Valley Resort. Historic Main Street is one block away, and the Old Town ski lift is two blocks away.

The Washington School opened its doors to students in 1889. Built of hammered limestone from a quarry in Peoa, Utah, the structure cost $13,000 to build. The school served the educational needs of the community until 1931, when it was purchased by the Veterans of Foreign Wars for a mere $200. The VFW used it for social events up until the 1950s; it then stood empty for 30 years until the current owners bought it and converted it into an inn. Now listed in the National Register, the school retains many of its original features, including a bell tower, dormers, large classroom windows, and three chimneys. The rooms are furnished with antiques and reproductions, as well as Park City memorabilia from the town's colorful mining days.

Restrictions: No smoking in guest rooms, no pets, no children under 12. Check-out at 10 a.m.
Beds: Twelve rooms with private baths include nine queens, three with twins. The three suites have queen beds, sitting areas, baths; two suites have fireplaces.
Breakfast: From 7:30 to 9:30 a.m. an "Americana" breakfast—consisting of hot and cold entrees, fruit, muffins, rolls, juice, coffee, and tea—is served in the dining room, which seats 15.
Extras: Afternoon refreshments are served in the parlor and spa; there's morning beverage service to the rooms and daily maid service. The innkeepers can arrange theatre and event tickets, passes to private clubs, and ski passes.
Rates: $75 (spring, summer, and fall) for room; $145 in ski season, $170 from December 21 to January 3. Suites range from $110 to $225. Personal checks and credit cards welcome.
Mailing Address: PO Box 1806, Park City, UT 84060

SALT LAKE CITY

SALTAIR BED &
BREAKFAST
Jan Bartlett and Nancy Saxon
164 South 900 East
Salt Lake City, UT 84102
(801) 533-8184
Year-round

LOCATION: Historic Temple Square and the Mormon Genealogy Library are ten blocks away; canyons and glorious winter skiing are within a short drive.

An old swing on the front porch of this 1903 Foursquare welcomes guests. The windows are glazed with etched, leaded glass; antiques, both from the Eller family and years of collecting, give the house a home-away-from-home feeling. You'll find three sets of solid oak pocket doors as well as the original oak woodwork on the first floor. The second floor has five guest rooms. The house once belonged to Fortunato Anselmo, the Utah and Wyoming Vice Consul to Italy, who entertained many celebrities and dignitaries between 1920 and 1950, including Pope Pius XII and, rumor has it, even Mussolini's mistress.

Restrictions: No smoking or pets. Check-in is flexible.
Beds: One single, one double, three queens.
Breakfast: Buffet: fruit, muffins, pastry, juice, variety of cereals, coffee, tea.
Extras: Cold lemonade and iced tea, with cookies, are served.
Rates: $29 (single), $35 (double), $39 (queen). Cots, $5. Personal and traveler's checks welcome.

ST. GEORGE

SEVEN WIVES INN
Donna and Jay Curtis
Alison and Jon Bowcutt
217 North 100 West
St. George, UT 84770
(801) 628-3737
Year-round

C. 1873 Gothic Revival

LOCATION: Utah's "Dixie" area is near Zion National Park, Bryce Canyon, and the north rim of the Grand Canyon.

The unusual features of this 1873 house, listed in the National Register, include the balconies and "Dixie dormers," dormers that cut through the roof line. The massive woodwork in the interior still has the original graining. The house is completely furnished with European and American antiques. The many guest rooms are named after the seven wives of the innkeeper's great-grandfather.

Restrictions: No smoking, but well-behaved children and pets accepted. Check-in after 3 p.m., check-out at 11 a.m.
Beds: One room has two doubles, another a queen and a fold-out bed; there are two queens, two doubles, and two queens with added singles. All have private baths.
Breakfast: Full is served 8 to 9 a.m.; choices include sausage pastry with scrambled eggs and apple muffins, German apple pancakes with bacon and scrambled eggs, blueberry soufflé with croissants.
Extras: Complimentary homemade candy is provided in the rooms, along with seasonal fresh fruit and flowers. There's a new swimming pool and a hot tub ("not appropriate to an old house, but oh well...").
Rates: $25 (small room with private bath across hall) to $50 (larger room with canopied bed, fireplace, old tub). Personal checks and credit cards welcome.
   10% discount to OHJ members.

VERMONT

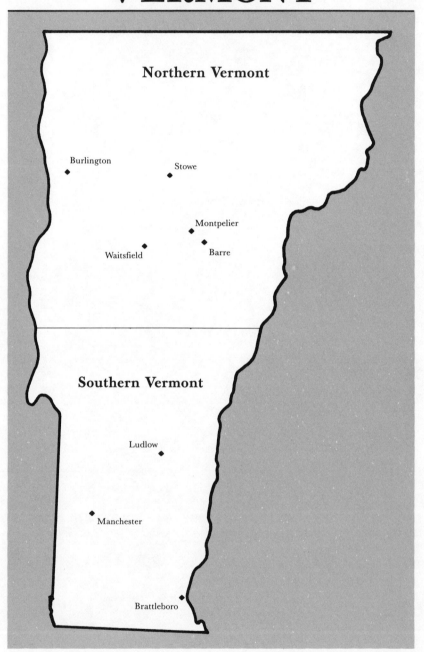

Northern Vermont

Burlington

Stowe

Montpelier

Waitsfield

Barre

Southern Vermont

Ludlow

Manchester

Brattleboro

BARRE

WOODRUFF HOUSE
Robert and Terry Somaini and
daughter Katie
13 East Street
Barre, VT 05641
(802) 476-7745
Year-round

1883 Queen Anne

LOCATION: The inn is located on a quiet, scenic park within walking distance of downtown Barre. Barre is in central Vermont with rolling hills, mountain views, and gorgeous fall foliage. Ski areas are a short distance away.

The Somainis' restoration of this Queen Anne is an ongoing project. Already, they've duplicated the original, three-tone exterior color scheme: blueberry with vanilla trim and cranberry shutters. They've refinished the golden oak woodwork and parquet floors. They've redecorated several rooms, including a second-floor sitting room in Art Movement style, with navy blue floral wallpaper, a dark green ceiling, and Oriental rugs. They've furnished the house in Edwardian style, with antiques, plants, and lots of mirrors.

Except for a missing front porch, the exterior now looks exactly as it did in 1883, with fish-scale shingles, bay window, and an arched breezeway leading to the barn. The Somainis are planning to rebuild the pilfered porch, going by an early photo of the house.

Restrictions: Well-behaved children welcome. No facilities for infants. No pets and no smoking. Check-in early evening.
Beds: Two guest rooms, one with twin beds and one with a double bed, share a common bath.
Breakfast: Light continental or large full breakfast, "whichever you like." Specialties in season, always home-baked breads.
Extras: Anything that comes out of Robert and Terry's oven is graciously shared with their guests. "Friends are always dropping in, we're busy people — we encourage guests to become part of what's happening."
Rates: $35, double occupancy. Personal checks welcome.
  10% discount to OHJ members.

NORTHERN VERMONT

GOSHEN

BLUEBERRY HILL FARM
Tony Clark
Ripton Road
Goshen, VT 05733
(802) 247-6735
Year-round

1813 Colonial

LOCATION: Tucked into the Green Mountains, the inn is surrounded by beautiful scenery. It's a cross-country ski touring center in the winter, and only one-and-a-half miles away from the Long Trail. In summer, Lake Dunmore (just down the road) offers swimming, windsurfing, and boating. There is also trout fishing in local mountain streams.

This house, originally a farm and a logger's home, has been an inn for a long time. Tony Clark has owned it since 1968, and before that it was run by a woman named Elsie Masterton, who published three Blueberry Hill cookbooks. Many of its classic features are preserved, including some original stencilling (there's also new stencilling), mouldings, mantelpieces, and wide plank floors. The furnishings are antique, and there's a collection of original American and Eu-

378

ropean paintings hanging in the public rooms. Tony and his staff recently restored one of the outbuildings: an early 1800s blacksmith shop with the original bellows intact.

Restrictions: Children welcome. No pets. Smoking in one designated room only. Check-in after noon.
Beds: Twelve rooms, all with private baths.
Breakfast: Three courses: fresh fruit, muffins, a main course (usually eggs). And, yes, they serve lots of blueberries!
Extras: Tea and coffee are always available, as well as an "endless supply" of chocolate chip cookies and fresh fruit. Babysitting can be arranged for an additional fee. Dinner is also included in the room rate.
Rates: Winter, $72 per person per night. $56, May and June. $60, July through September 12. $68, September 13 through October 31. Children not eating meals stay free, cribs provided free of charge. Personal checks and credit cards welcome.

RIPTON

THE CHIPMAN INN
Bill Pierce and Joyce Henderson
Route 125
Ripton, VT 05766
(802) 388-2390
May through March
(closed April)

1823 Federal

LOCATION: This quiet village setting is in the midst of the Green Mountains, eight minutes from Middlebury and its cultural attractions and antique and crafts shops. Four miles away are the Long Trail and Middlebury Snow Bowl.

A sign outside the door lists road tolls for carriages and ox carts. No, this isn't Amish country — it's the former home of Daniel Chipman, toll collector for the ante-bellum Center Turnpike, now called the Robert Frost Memorial Highway in honor of Ripton's most distinguished native. But this inn is more than the home of a former toll collector: Chipman was also a prominent legislator and founder of Middlebury College. The house's present occupants are quite fascinating, too. Bill and Joyce Pierce have travelled to exotic places all around the world, and have on display a rare collection of artifacts from stays in Egypt and East Africa. The inn is comfortably furnished with antiques, warmed by an original Dutch fireplace with baking ovens and a Franklin stove, and graced with authentically reproduced stencilling in the dining room.

Restrictions: No pets.
Beds: Eight rooms with a double bed. Some of these have twin beds also. One two-room suite is also available.
Breakfast: A full, hot breakfast is included in room rate.
Extras: Afternoon tea, "as appropriate," is served at no charge.
Rates: $75 to $95 per person (highest in foliage season). Credit cards and personal checks welcome.
Mailing Address: PO Box 37, Ripton, VT 05766

NORTHERN VERMONT

SHOREHAM

SHOREHAM INN AND COUNTRY STORE
Cleo and Fred Alter
Route 74 West
Shoreham, VT 05770
(802) 897-5081
Year-round

1799 Federal

LOCATION: In the historic village of Shoreham, the inn is five miles from Lake Champlain with views of the Adirondacks to the west and the Green Mountains to the east. It's also near Fort Ticonderoga.

Built circa 1790 as a "publick house" and way station for the floating railroad bridge and ferry across Lake Champlain, the inn was and still is the center of town. Despite various additions over time, like the peculiarly angled staircase balustrade from an old town church, the building's lines remain pure and simple, true to New

England form, with white pine clapboards and a standing-seam roof. Fireplaces installed not long after the house was built and made of hand-moulded bricks still heat the interior on chilly evenings.

If you fall in love with the inn's country auction antique furnishings, there's a chance you'll find similar items for sale in the Alters' antiques shop, right inside. The Alters also run the Shoreham Country Store next door. It's been a fixture in town for over 150 years, and sells local Vermont crafts, wines, cheeses, and maple syrup.

By the way, Fred loves discussing his weekend restoration projects with anyone who will listen. He's forever occupied fixing the cracks, leaks, creaks, lumps and bumps that are a given in any old house. Meanwhile, "Cleo talks about other things!"

Restrictions: No pets. Smoking allowed only in first-floor sitting rooms.
Beds: Of the 11 guest rooms, five have double beds. Guests share three full baths, two shower rooms, and two half-baths.
Breakfast: Juice, fresh fruit, granola, plus homemade apple butter preserves served with home-baked muffins and breads; eggs, cheese, and croissants; coffee, tea, or hot chocolate.
Extras: Sunday tea is served November through April. Champagne for guests can be arranged with advance reservations. The innkeepers also provide apples from local orchards.
Rates: $35 single, $50 double. Personal checks welcome.

NORTHERN VERMONT

STOWE

1860 HOUSE
Rick Hubbard and Rose Marie
Matulionis
School Street
Stowe, VT 05672
(802) 253-7351
Year-round

1860 Gothic Revival

LOCATION: Stowe Village is located by Mt. Mansfield, Vermont's tallest peak. Skiing, hiking, tennis, golf, swimming, and many other recreational activities are all nearby.

Rick Hubbard and Rose Marie Matulionis take pride not only in the intimacy of their cozy inn, but also in the painstaking care they take in preserving it. Recently, they took out all the deteriorating window frames, stripped them, repaired the rotting wood, refinished and re-installed them — quite an involved project! They also hand-turned spindles for their stairrail to replace some that were missing, being careful to duplicate precisely the old pattern.

The house, listed in the National Register, is a good example of free-form Gothic Revival style, with a steeply pitched central gable, tall, narrow windows, and paired scroll brackets adorning the eaves. Inside, the original barnboard trim in the living room, solid brass hardware, and wide pine flooring are in mint condition. It's furnished with antiques (including a beautiful, playable Briggs upright piano), Oriental rugs, and a healthy dose of greenery.

Restrictions: Non-smokers only please. Pets with advance permission.
Beds: Five guest rooms. Two with queen beds, and three with king or two twins. Three rooms have private bath.
Breakfast: Light breakfast with fresh fruit, home-baked breads, fresh orange juice, coffee, and tea, is served buffet style in the living room.
Extras: Coffee and tea, apples, and kitchen privileges are offered. Bicyclists will find indoor storage for their mounts, as well as a work-room for repairs and maintenance.
Rates: $34 to $38 regular season, $45 to $50 during fall foliage, $40 to $50 in winter. Weekly and monthly rates also available. Cots, $10. Credit cards and personal checks welcome.

10% discount to OHJ members.
Mailing Address: PO Box 276, Stowe, VT 05672

NORTHERN VERMONT

WAITSFIELD

**LAREAU FARM
COUNTRY INN
Dan and Susan Easley
Route 100
Waitsfield, VT 05673
(802) 496-4949
Year-round**

C. 1802 with 1838 Greek Revival addition

LOCATION: The farm is situated in a wide meadow along the banks of the Mad River. The river valley offers fine dining and shopping. Three major ski area's are within five minutes of the inn. The immediate vicinity offers all of the outdoor activities and beautiful scenery that Vermont is famous for.

Waitsfield's first physician built this house, and he and his family are buried on a nearby knoll. Sometime in the late 19th century, the house's occupants took to dairy farming. Their original dairy barn stands today, in virtually unaltered condition, with the original milking parlor intact. The house was converted to an inn in 1983, when the family Lareau sold it after more than 40 years of farming.

The Inn's most outstanding architectural feature, besides the barn, is its set of wraparound porches—one in front and one in back. There are wide plank floors inside, and in the recently restored woodshed (converted to guest lodgings) you can see the original, hand-hewn beams. All furnishings are antique, beds are covered with hand-stitched quilts, and walls are stencilled or papered with period prints.

Restrictions: Well-supervised children welcome. No pets. No smoking in the bedrooms.
Beds: Ten rooms, each with double bed. One room also has two additional single beds. Six rooms have private bath.
Breakfast: Full country breakfast is cooked on Mrs. Lareau's old-fashioned wood cookstove: raspberry pancakes with home-grown fruit, home-baked goods, meats, and egg dishes.
Extras: Optional Saturday evening dinner is $15 to $18 per person, with wine. Bicycles are available for rental and hors d'oeuvres are served in the fall.
Rates: In season: $80 to $90. Off-season: $60 to $70 (spring, summer, and late fall). Weekend and weekday package rates also available. Cots are available for an additional charge. Cribs can be rented for $5 nightly. Credit cards and personal checks welcome.

10% discount to OHJ members except during holidays.
Mailing Address: PO Box 563, Waitsfield, VT 05673

BELMONT

THE PARMENTER HOUSE
Cynthia and Lester Firschein
Church Street
Belmont, VT 05730
(802) 259-2009
Year-round

1874 Greek Revival

LOCATION: Located in the scenic lakeside village of Belmont, The Parmenter House is in close proximity to most of Vermont's famed ski trails. In summer you can swim in Star Lake, just a few steps away.

Lester and Cynthia Firschein fell in love with this town and this house when they were passing through in 1982. They dropped everything—including Lester's job as a Hunter College professor— to buy it, and started immediately on an authentic restoration.

The house is filled with cabinetry, more than usual for its time. Turns out the man who built it, Frank Parmenter, owned a wood- turning factory, and, in fact, had his own woodworking shop attached to the house. (The Firscheins have turned this shop into an efficiency suite, converting Mr. Parmenter's tool cabinets to kitchen cabinets.) Frank's son Charles lived here after retiring from his post as director of Boston's Mechanic Arts High School. Charles's daughter lived here after that, until her recent death at age 90.

All the house's original hardware, much of its original wood grain- ing (which makes softwoods look like hardwoods), original butler's pantries, peaked mouldings, and curved plaster walls are intact. The Firscheins have decorated the interior beautifully, in true-to-form Victorian country style. The parlor is papered with Bradbury and Bradbury's Anglo-Japanese room set, its pocket doors polychromed in a matching color scheme. Curtains are lace filigree; furnishings are Victorian (Cynthia's grandfather made some of the pieces); bed quilts are family heirlooms (her mother made these). The best thing about this inn is Lester and Cynthia's never-ceasing hospitality. They're willing to share literally everything with you, from their heirloom antiques to detailed and sometimes funny restoration stories.

Restrictions: No smoking. No pets ("we have cats and dogs of our own"). Children must respect the house and its furnishings.
Beds: There are five double rooms. Two also have a twin bed. All have private baths.
Breakfast: Full, served outdoors when weather permits (otherwise in the dining room).
Extras: A canoe is available, free, for "those who know how." There are occasional Saturday barbecues (price varies with menu). Mountain bikes are available with a box lunch for $25 per person. Bikes are also available for a half day (without lunch) for $10.
Rates: From $65 to $80. Cots are available. Personal checks and credit cards accepted.

   10% discount to OHJ members.
Mailing Address: PO Box 106, Belmont, VT 05730

BETHEL

GREENHURST INN
Lyle and Barbara Wolf
River Street
Bethel, VT 05032
(802) 234-9474
Year-round

1891 Queen Anne

LOCATION: The inn is located in central Vermont, midway between Montreal and Boston. Cross-country and downhill skiing, hiking on the Appalachian trail, golfing, boating, fishing, hunting, and many other activities are nearby.

"The Inn is as close to living in Victorian times as I could have hoped."
R.B., Quincy, Mass.

Lyle and Barbara Wolf hit upon the idea for this inn when they were traveling in Europe, staying at B&Bs. At the time, both were feeling disillusioned with their more traditional careers (Barbara was a nursing supervisor and Lyle was a high-school social studies teacher), and were looking for a life change. When they heard Greenhurst was up for grabs, they dropped everything in California and transplanted themselves to Vermont.

The lucky old house had survived its first century unremuddled, with turret, bays, and wraparound porch intact. Still, Lyle and Barbara had restoration work to do: Greenhurst had been an inn since the '30s, and had been subjected to lots of everyday wear and tear. The Wolfs cleaned the thick oxide crust off the floral-embossed brass doorknobs, refinished the worn floors, and revived the cracked finish on the woodwork. They moved in their collection of Queen Anne antiques and picked up more period pieces at nearby auctions.

Restrictions: Well-behaved children and pets are welcome. Smoking permitted.
Beds: There are 13 rooms: seven have private baths; six share baths.
Breakfast: Full continental, with fresh fruit, fresh muffins or biscuits, tea or fresh-ground coffee, is served in the period-decorated dining room to the sounds of a crackling fire and Mozart.
Extras: Light refreshments are served in the evenings. Babysitting is available with prior notice. There's a tennis court on the grounds and a 3500-book library. Perrier is provided in every room, and mints are left on the pillows.
Rates: $40 to $60. Cribs available for no additional fee. Cots, $10.50. Single occupancy, $10 discount. 15% discount for stays of seven days or longer. Credit cards and personal checks accepted.

10% discount to OHJ members Monday through Thursday only.

BROWNSVILLE

BROOKSIDE BED & BREAKFAST
Patricia Gavin Wenz
Route 44
Brownsville, VT 05037
(802) 484-5072
Year-round

Mid-19th-century barn

LOCATION: At the base of Mt. Ascutney, the B&B is a short drive from Killington, Pico, and Okemo ski areas.

The Brookside Bed & Breakfast was once a horse barn. The house it belonged to burned down many years ago, the owner, Patricia Gavin Wenz, reports. Ms. Wenz has also heard that an old woman used to sit on the back porch of that house and smoke a clay pipe, a scandal in those days.

The beams and stone foundation are original, while the spiral staircases are a more recent addition.

Restrictions: No children or pets. Check-in anytime; check-out at 11 a.m.
Beds: Three doubles (two with sitting rooms and separate entrances), two singles; two rooms share a bath.
Breakfast: The "generous continental" includes fresh fruit in season and homemade donuts.
Extras: Afternoon tea is served at no charge.
Rates: $25 for a single in a loft, $40 for a double. Cots, but no cribs, available for an extra charge. Personal checks welcome.

10% discount to OHJ members.

SOUTHERN VERMONT

CHESTER

THE HUGGING BEAR INN & SHOPPE
Georgette and Paul Thomas
Main Street
Chester, VT 05143
(802) 875-2412
Year-round

C. 1850 Italianate with Queen Anne & Colonial Revival addition

LOCATION: The inn stands on historic Chester's village green. The entire Main Street area is in the National Register. (The Thomases moved to Chester because of its historic charm.) The rear of the inn looks out over fields, brooks, and wooded hills with plenty of hiking trails. Summer theater, antique and other shops, restaurants, and plenty of recreational activities are nearby.

This house displays features from three stylistic periods: the original Italianate followed by Queen Anne and Colonial Revival additions. The Fullertons, who built the house, had an eye for architectural fashion; when one style fell from public grace they were quick to change their house to match the newest trend. The last additions were the slate-shingled, octagonal Queen Anne tower and the Colonial Revival verandah, built in 1910. (Be sure to inquire about the tower guest room if you make reservations here. It's a fantastic place to stay, with four windows viewing the town at four different angles.)

The Fullertons owned this house for 102 years! It was sold to a neighboring elementary school when Grace Fullerton, born here in 1851, died in the tower room at age 101. Georgette and Paul Thomas moved in in 1982, and found the house in excellent repair.

Inside, there are many well-preserved architectural features which will interest old-house lovers. The living room is panelled in quarter-sawn oak and has a large bay window. There's hand-painted Victorian wallpaper on one wall of the dining room. And the graceful main stairway has red cherry railings, carved walnut posts, and hickory and maple treads.

Restrictions: Children are "most welcome!" No smoking except on porches. Pets only by prior arrangement. Check-in after 2 p.m., check-out at 11 a.m.
Beds: Six guest rooms. Three doubles with private bath. Two rooms have a single and a double bed with private bath. The other room has twin beds, a fold-out double couch, and a private bath. A den with daybed and shared bath is available to groups reserving entire inn.
Breakfast: Complete, all-you-can-eat breakfast: eggs any style, French toast or buckwheat pancakes, breakfast meats, large variety of teas, cereals, breads, etc., plus self-serve coffee and fruit juices.
Extras: When the skiers return on winter afternoons, they'll find hot cider, cheese and crackers; hot coffee, tea, or hot chocolate waiting for them. In summer, iced tea, cold cider, or fruit juices are provided. Babysitting can be arranged at local rates. The innkeepers provide passes to a local fitness center. The town tennis courts, playing fields, and swimming pool are all within a half-mile.
Rates: Single $45, double $60. Third adult in room costs an additional $20. Children under 14, additional $10 for cot. Cribs, one-time charge of $5. Off-season discounts: 10% to 20%. Credit cards and personal

checks welcome.
Mailing Address: Box 32, Main St., Chester, VT 05143

CHESTER

STONE HEARTH INN
The Stroameyers
Route 11
Chester, VT 05143
(802) 875-2525
Year-round

1810 Georgian Colonial with attached buildings

LOCATION: Located in the historic town of Chester, The Stone Hearth Inn is close to many ski areas and other recreational attractions. Horseback riding, golf, hiking, shopping, antiquing, swimming, and fishing can be enjoyed nearby. Weston is nearby with its summer theater, famous stores, the Weston Bowl Mill, and historic atmosphere.

Most of the original features in this cozy farmhouse have survived the 20th century, including open-beamed ceilings, wide pine floors, and fieldstone fireplaces. The owners recently stripped off some unsightly modern siding to unmask the house's original clapboards. They also converted the attached barn to a comfortable common room. The house is furnished with period antiques.

Restrictions: Children welcome. No pets.
Beds: Ten guest rooms, eight with private baths.
Breakfast: Full country breakfast: fresh baked pastries and muffins, bacon or sausage, eggs, French toast, pancakes or waffles, juice, coffee and tea.
Extras: There's a well-equipped game room, with table tennis, pool table, and board games. The fully stocked pub serves drinks and

389

sandwiches.
Rates: $28 to $30 single, $56 to $60 double. Third person in room for half the single rate. Personal checks accepted.
Mailing Address: PO Box 422, Chester, VT 05143

SOUTHERN VERMONT

DORSET

THE LITTLE LODGE AT DORSET
Allan and Nancy Norris
Route 30
Dorset, VT 05251
(802) 867-4040
Year-round, closed for part of November and April

1810 Federal, with later additions

LOCATION: In a historic district, the inn overlooks a pond and the picturesque Green Mountains. The Dorset Summer Theater, the southern Vermont Art Center, and Robert Todd Lincoln's house are all nearby. Area recreational activities include skiing, trout fishing, biking, hiking, boating, and golfing.

This old house was rescued from a flood in 1928. It was transported, board by board, from a Massachusetts town about to be swallowed up by a federal dam. Many of the original architectural features survived the move, including wide board floors, elephant-ear mouldings, and 12-over-12 windows. The Norrises bought the house in 1981 and have furnished it mostly with antiques.

Restrictions: No pets.
Beds: Five rooms with either king-sized or twin beds. All rooms have private baths.
Breakfast: Choice of juices and cereals, homemade breads or muffins, and beverage.
Extras: Guests can ice skate on the inn's pond. Crackers and Vermont cheese are served every afternoon. Tea, coffee, and hot chocolate are always on hand. The innkeepers can arrange for a local babysitter.

Rates: $75 to $85, depending on room size; $25 extra per person. American Express and personal checks accepted. "we prefer checks 10% discount to OHJ members.
Mailing Address: Box 673, Dorset, VT 05251

DORSET

MAPLEWOOD GUEST HOUSE
Marge and Leon Edgerton
Route 30
Dorset, VT 05251
(802) 867-4470
Year-round

1770s Federal

LOCATION: The inn's surrounded by the beautiful Green Mountains and shaded by 200-year-old maples. (The Edgertons have won prizes for their maple syrup!) Bromley and Stratton ski areas and many cross-country ski trails are nearby, and America's oldest nine-hole golf course, an abandoned marble quarry for swimming, and the Dorset Playhouse are all within walking distance.

Marge and Leon Edgerton have lived in Maplewood since the 1930s, and have taken guests since 1960. Their spacious Colonial is well preserved, with slate roofs, old weathervanes, original glass in some windows, and hand-hewn beams still visible. Old red barns, remnants from Maplewood's farming days, still stand on the grounds. The Edgertons have furnished the home with heirloom antiques, such as a pre-Civil War carved mahogany dining table, a spinning wheel, roll-top desks, and marble-topped bedroom sets. Hand-stitched quilts and artifacts from their worldly travels (such as a Chinese screen) decorate the walls. The Edgertons recently restored two inscribed stone posts that frame their driveway. The inscriptions read: "Agriculture — oldest occupation" and "Agriculture — greatest science."

Restrictions: No smoking. Trained, well-mannered pets may be accepted when the inn isn't crowded.

Beds: Five guest rooms. One with three twin beds, two with queen-sized bed, and two with double beds. The five rooms share three baths.

Breakfast: Juice, eggs, english muffins, homemade muffins, pancakes or French toast served with the inn's own prize-winning maple syrup, plus coffee, tea, milk, and hot chocolate.

Extras: Afternoon tea and cheese and crackers are served daily. Babysitting can be arranged.

Rates: $40 to $65. Personal checks welcome.

Mailing Address: RD 1 Box 1019, Dorset, VT 05251

SOUTHERN VERMONT

FAIR HAVEN

THE VERMONT MARBLE INN
Shirley Stein,
Beatrice and Richard Taube
12 West Park Place
Fair Haven, VT 05743
(802) 265-8383
Year-round

1867 Italianate with
  Mansard roof

LOCATION: On the green in Fair Haven, the inn is near Lake Champlain and several major ski areas. Boating, fishing, swimming, sailing, antiquing, and skiing are all nearby.

Descendants of Ethan Allen's brother Ira built this unusual, mansarded Italianate from locally quarried golden marble blocks. You heard it right—marble! The roof is slate, also quarried locally, from the same pits where slate for the White House was unearthed. Outside, the marble house is an excellently preserved work of art, with delicately turned porch posts, carriage port, arched eyebrow windows, and a belvedere with a fine view. Its interior details are just as elaborate: eight hand-carved Italian marble fireplaces, etched window panes, intricate wood and plaster mouldings, and a three-storey central staircase.

392

Restrictions: No pets.
Beds: 12 bedrooms with private baths.
Breakfast: Full six-course breakfast.
Rates: $60 to $90. Cots, $20. Credit cards welcome.
  10% discount to OHJ members.

GUILFORD

THE CAPTAIN HENRY
CHASE HOUSE
Pat and Lorraine Ryan
West Guilford Road
Guilford, VT 05301
(802) 254-4114
Year-round (closed for
Thanksgiving and Christmas)

C. 1798 Colonial Vermont Farmhouse

LOCATION: In "one of Vermont's prettiest valleys," on 25 acres of woodland and pasture, the inn borders the Green River, "a trout fisherman's dream." A few miles down the road is Green River Village, complete with a covered bridge and old-fashioned swimming hole. A short drive away are several major ski resorts.

"We have heard our guests say, more times than we can remember, how much they love our home and how comfortable they feel in it."

It's rare to find a 200-year-old Colonial in mint condition. "We know," says innkeeper Lorraine Ryan, "because we looked for years to find this one." The Ryans long search was certainly worth the effort —they ended up with a gem. The house's original slate roof, large central chimney, 12-over-12 windows (some with original glass), ten-foot-wide hearth with beehive oven, wide board floors, and colonial hardware are all intact. The old barn is there, too, with an arched breezeway connecting it to the house. The Ryans have furnished their rooms with a comfortable mixture of antiques and period reproductions.

Restrictions: No pets.

Beds: Three guest rooms, each with double bed. There are no private baths, but the house does have three bathrooms.

Breakfast: All-you-can-eat pancakes served with pure Vermont maple syrup made from the Inn's own sugar maples; juice, coffee, and tea.

Extras: Guests are invited to indulge in Lorraine's home-baked goodies, or to help themselves to tea and coffee. Babysitting, for a fee, can be arranged with advance notice.

Rates: $35 double, $25 single. Cots (third person) $10. Personal checks welcome.

Mailing Address: RFD 4, Box 788, West Brattleboro, VT 05301

SOUTHERN VERMONT

LUDLOW

BLACK RIVER INN
Marilyn and Tom Neunan
100 Main Street
Ludlow, VT 05149
(802) 228-5585
Year-round

1835 Federal

LOCATION: On a shaded bank of the Black River, at the foot of the Okemo Mountain ski area, the inn is 20 minutes from both Killington and Bromley. Green Mountain National Forest, Calvin Coolidge's birthplace, excellent trout fishing, and canoeing are all nearby.

You might be lucky enough to sleep in Abe Lincoln's bed if you visit this inn. Honestly! The bed, built in 1793 in Collinsville, Illinois, is the highlight of a diverse antiques collection that ranges from Colonial to Victorian Eastlake and is displayed in the inn.

The original owners put lots of elbow grease into restoring their inn. They've polished the marble mantels, grained the sitting room woodwork, spruced up 1859 bath fixtures to use in five added baths, freed the beautiful black cherry and maple floors from suffocating layers of carpet, tile, and tarpaper. They've decorated with rich period wallpapers, feather pillows, grandmother quilts, and 1893 hand-blown etched-glass lighting fixtures. They'd certainly love to discuss their many projects and the house's history with a fellow old-house enthusiast.

Restrictions: No children. No pets. Check-in after 2 p.m. Check-out at 11:30 a.m.
Beds: Ten rooms, eight have private bath.
Breakfast: A romantic breakfast is served in bed. Home-baked popovers, muffins, and assorted breads are included. Served 7 a.m. "till whenever."
Extras: Dinner every night (MAP or not).
Rates: $125 per couple (MAP); $89, B&B. Credit cards and personal checks accepted.

LUDLOW

THE COMBES FAMILY INN
Ruth and Bill Combes
Lake Rescue
Ludlow, VT 05149
(802) 228-8799
May 15 to April 15

1835 New England Farmhouse

LOCATION: The inn stands on 50 acres of fields and meadows, with a spectacular view of Okemo Mountain. Nearby are playhouses, quaint towns, maple syrup and cheese factories, and Calvin Coolidge's birthplace. In winter there's cross-country skiing on the property and downhill skiing at nearby resorts, and in summer, swimming and canoeing in local lakes.

The Ellison family owned this farmhouse for 125 years. They built the house from lumber gathered on the land, and for the next century supplied Ludlow with milk, maple syrup, and Saturday-night barn dances. Ruth and Bill Combes bought the house in 1978. They've decorated it with antiques and wallpaper, and refinished some of the wide pine floors in the guest rooms. Ruth and Bill do some farming in the Ellison tradition: They keep two goats and a healthy garden where, during summer, you can help pick vegetables for dinner.

Restrictions: Pets in the attached motel only. Check-in after 2 p.m., check-out at 11 a.m.
Beds: Seven guest rooms, three with private baths. One room can accommodate five.
Breakfast: Full: coffee, tea, fruit juice, cereal, choice of eggs, omelettes or pancakes, bacon, sausage or ham. Two-meal plan also available.
Extras: Refrigerator space, coffee, and soft drinks are always available.
Rates: Summer, for two: $90, MAP; $66, B&B. Fall/winter, for two: $98, MAP; $72, B&B. Credit cards and personal checks accepted.
Mailing Address: RFD 1, Box 275, Ludlow, VT 05149

LUDLOW

THE GOVERNOR'S INN
Charlie and Deedy Marble
86 Main Street
Ludlow, VT 05149
(802) 228-8830
Open eleven months. Closed in April.

1890 Queen Anne Carpenter Gothic

LOCATION: Okemo Mountain ski area (one mile away) is visible from most of the inn's rooms. Antique shops, crafts, country fairs, summer band concerts on the green, summer theater, golf and tennis, and numerous lakes are all in close proximity.

William Wallace Stickney, one-time governor of Vermont, built this house to please his high-minded Victorian wife. When Stickney became prominent in Vermont politics, his wife decided the farm where they were living was inappropriate for their social standing. Up went what is now the Governor's Inn, all in the highest style, with stained-glass windows, a delicate porch, golden oak mouldings, huge pocket doors, and hand-painted slate fireplaces.

Charlie and Deedy Marble bought the house in 1982 and carefully restored it, refinishing the woodwork and hanging period wallpapers.

They furnished the entire inn with family heirlooms, including a collection of antique photographs that lines the stairwell and a brass bed that the Marble family has owned for over 100 years.

Restrictions: No small children, no pets.
Beds: Eight guest rooms. One with twin beds, seven with double beds. Each room has private bath.
Breakfast: An award-winning, four-course breakfast is served by staff clad in Edwardian bloomers and mop caps, and includes juice, home-made coffeecake, hot cereal, and an entree which changes daily. (One favorite is rum-raisin French toast with ice cream and maple syrup.)
Extras: Afternoon tea is served on English china. Cocktails and hors d'oeuvres are served in the parlor before dinner. You can also order the Governor's luncheon picnic a day in advance: It comes in a wicker picnic basket with wine, sandwiches, dessert, and cut flowers.
Rates: All rooms, $160, meals included. Credit cards and personal checks welcome.
   10% discount to OHJ members.

SOUTHERN VERMONT

MANCHESTER

1790 Colonial

BIRCH HILL INN
Jim and Pat Lee
West Road
Manchester, VT 05254
(802) 362-2761
Late May through October,
December through early April

LOCATION: On a quiet knoll two miles from Manchester, with mountain views on all sides, the inn is close to ski slopes, white-water canoeing areas, the Appalachian Trail, summer theaters, the three-generation home of President Lincoln's descendants (open for tours), and the Southern Vermont Art Center (for art exhibits and classes, chamber music, and old movies).

Innkeepers Pat and Jim Lee were on familiar ground when they moved here in 1980 — Pat's family has lived in the house since 1917! The much expanded Colonial is sunny and spacious, with large rooms. It's furnished with antiques, including a spinning wheel and oval dining table with colonial chairs. In the oldest part of the house, you can see the original, hand-axed beams. Pat has stencilled the walls in some rooms.

Restrictions: Children over six welcome. No smoking in dining area. Check-in after 2 p.m., check-out at 11 a.m. No pets.

Beds: Five rooms. Two have twins, one has a king, one has a double, and one has a queen-sized bed. All have private baths. There's also a cottage out back, with queen-sized bed, sitting room, terrace, and private bath.

Breakfast: Served 8 to 9 a.m., the full breakfast includes juice, fruit, cereal, homemade muffins, and a main dish (eggs and bacon, French toast, or pancakes).

Extras: Eight miles of cross-country ski trails wind through their woods. There's also a swimming pool and trout fishing pond on the property. Tea is served in the afternoons; soft drinks are available. Dinner, served family style around the oval dining table, is also included in the room rate.

Rates: Per person, double: $58 to $60, MAP; $46 to $48, B&B. Single, $70 (MAP), $58 (B&B). Third person in room costs an additional $37. Personal checks accepted; Mastercard and Visa accepted for deposits on short notice.

Mailing Address: PO Box 346, Manchester, VT 05254

SOUTHERN VERMONT

MANCHESTER

**THE INN AT
MANCHESTER**
Harriet and Stan Rosenberg
Route 7A
Manchester, VT 05254
(802) 362-1793
Year-round

1890 Victorian with three-bay front

LOCATION: The inn is located in historic Manchester, surrounded by mountains and old houses. Ski areas, the Southern Vermont Art Center, Robert Todd Lincoln's home, and warm-weather recreational activities are all nearby.

Before Harriet and Stan Rosenberg could invite any guests to this inn, they had to spend a year restoring it. Nobody had bothered to care for the house for 40 years: plaster ceilings sagged, corroded paint covered the wood floors, and there were holes in the crumbling plaster walls. Why, you might ask, did Harriet and Stan dare to move into such a crumbling wreck? Simply, they were attracted by the house's delicate Queen Anne features, still beautiful despite years of mistreatment: a wraparound front porch, lots of bay windows, dormers, wooden sunbursts, marble patio, and, out back, a barn complete with cupola.

The Rosenbergs went at their house with a fervor. They patched, stripped, painted, papered. They moved in their collection of (mostly) Victorian antiques. Now, the house is as beautiful as it was when it was built as a summer retreat for a family called Shephard (for whom the side street next to the house is named). The Inn is listed in the National Register.

Restrictions: Children over five welcome. No pets. No smoking in bedrooms. Check-in after noon.

Beds: There are 21 rooms, 13 with private baths.

Breakfast: "Full country": Specialties include cottage cheese pancakes with apricot sauce, "farmer's breakfast," and waffles.

Extras: Inquire about their mid-week package rate, which includes theater tickets, dinner at a local restaurant, and free admission to Robert Todd Lincoln's house.

Rates: $50 to $80, depending on room size and bath arrangement. Rates increase from mid-September through late October (foliage season). Credit cards and personal checks welcome.

10% discount to OHJ members except during foliage season and on summer weekends.

Mailing Address: Box 41, Manchester, VT 05254

MANCHESTER

**MANCHESTER
HIGHLANDS INN**
Harry and Donna Williams,
Marge and Connie Bellestri
Highland Avenue
Manchester, VT 05255
(802) 362-4565
Year-round

1898 Queen Anne

LOCATION: On a residential side street on "Fowler Hill" (named for the man who built the house), the inn affords a view of Manchester and Mount Equinox. Downhill ski slopes are 15 minutes away.

"Many of our guests remark that they feel they are staying in a lovely old home of a friend. The building is beautiful."

Joseph Fowler, a prosperous insurance agent whose one-time client was Abe Lincoln's son, built this house. Joseph's 90-year-old son Earle still lives next door. His insurance company, now headed by his great-grandson, is still in town.

The house stayed in the Fowler family until 1954, and hasn't changed much over the years. Original tin ceilings, stained-glass windows, woodwork, oak panelling, hardwood floors, and wide staircase all survived the century. The old carriage house is still out back; it's been converted to a guest house, connected to the main building via an underground tunnel. One corner of the wraparound porch has been enclosed for dining space, but otherwise the exterior looks the same, with three-storey turret, peaked roof, and tall chimneys. The present innkeepers have furnished the inn with antiques and family heirlooms.

Restrictions: No pets. Check-in after 2 p.m.
Beds: Of the 13 guest chambers, four have king-sized beds and 11 have private baths.
Breakfast: Donna Williams and her mom do all the cooking themselves. Breakfast is homemade muffins, fruit and juice, cereal selection, eggs, pancakes with maple syrup, bacon, sausage, and sometimes

quiche.

Extras: Coffee, cider, and snacks are served in the library; iced tea in summer. There's a licensed bar, lounge with fireplace, putting green, and large game room with pool table and shuffleboard. A candlelight dinner is served Wednesday through Sunday at 7 p.m. by reservation only ($11.50 to $15.75 price range), and includes nightly entree, homemade soups and bread, salad bar, vegetable, and dessert.

Rates: All rooms, $76. Cots, $18 per extra person in room. Credit cards and personal checks welcome.

10% discount to OHJ members.

Mailing Address: Box 1754, Manchester Center, VT 05255

SOUTHERN VERMONT

MANCHESTER VILLAGE

1811 HOUSE
Mary and Jack Hirst
Pat and Jeremy David
Route 7A
Manchester Village, VT 05254
(802) 362-1811
Year-round

1811 Federal, with 1770 Colonial wing and 1870 addition

LOCATION: In the center of historic Manchester Village, the inn is set on three acres of grounds landscaped in the manner of an English garden, with rock, herb, rose, and other flower gardens. It overlooks a golf course and, beyond that, the Green Mountains. Nearby are several ski areas; the area's summer recreational activities are also easily accessible.

"If you demand the very finest, join us at the 1811 House. It is not just another Early American inn."

Abraham Lincoln's granddaughter, Mary Lincoln Isham, lived here for 30 years at the turn of the century. But for that brief interlude, the house has been an inn since 1811. The house has all the typical appointments of the Federal era: pilastered doorways with sidelights, dentilled cornice, 12-over-12 windows, hand-hewn beams, wide floor boards, and numerous fireplaces. The current owners have restored the house to its 1811 look, and have furnished all rooms with English and American antiques and paintings. The house is listed in the National Register.

Restrictions: No children under 16. No pets. Check-in after 2 p.m.
Beds: 14 rooms, each with private bath, range from fairly small with double bed to a suite with four-poster bed, fireplace, and sitting room.
Breakfast: Full: orange juice and seasonal fruit, eggs Benedict, pancakes, omelettes, French toast, or English breakfast (eggs and bacon, bread sautéed with apples and mushroom tomato and home fries).
Rates: $65 to $100, plus 6% sales tax and 14% gratuity. Credit cards and personal checks accepted.
Mailing Address: Box 39, Manchester Village, VT 05254

MANCHESTER VILLAGE

RELUCTANT PANTHER INN
Loretta and Ed Friihauf
West Road
Manchester Village, VT 05254
(802) 362-2568
Closed November 1
to December 7,
April 7 to Memorial Day

C. 1850 Georgian

LOCATION: This is a small, New England village at the base of Mt. Equinox, the highest mountain in southwestern Vermont.

"For couples only—quiet, romantic, clean, unusual." Loretta and Ed

Loretta and Ed Friihauf enjoyed their first two years of innkeeping so much that they decided to expand. They bought a private home that neighbored the Panther in the rear, and connected it with a clapboarded walkway that's barely visible from the street, and matches the architectural style of both houses. They painted the whole exterior in a color scheme perhaps not 100% authentic, but a pleasure to behold nevertheless: a soothing lavender-gray, with amber shutters and black trim. The main house has several unique architectural features, including a marble-faced foundation and marble terrace, and a solarium Ed says is "very old."

Restrictions: No children or pets (couples only).
Beds: There are 13 rooms, 8 with working fireplaces, all with private baths and cable TV; two with whirlpool tubs.
Breakfast: Continental (coffee, croissants); full (pancakes, French toast, eggs, meats) is served at extra cost.
Extras: The innkeepers' membership in a private country club (offering tennis and golf) includes their guests.
Rates: $90 to $160 during Christmas week, Presidents' week, and foliage season; $79 to $149 other times. Personal checks and credit cards accepted.
Mailing Address: Box 678, Manchester Village, VT 05254

SOUTHERN VERMONT

PERU

THE WILEY INN
Patrick and Toni Smith
Route 11
Peru, VT 05152
(802) 824-6600
Year-round

1835 Federal Farmhouse

LOCATION: On Bromley Mountain, with spectacular mountain views, the inn is surrounded by Green Mountain National Forest, with trails, ponds, brooks, meadow, and woods right on the property. Antique shops and historic homes are nearby in Peru village, and there are plenty of outdoor activities in the area; skiing, fishing, horseback riding, water rafting, hiking on the Appalachian Trail. Also nearby are Weston Summer Theater and maple syrup houses.

This inn has been lodging guests since 1943, and it was a stagecoach stop and tea house even before that. Patrick and Toni Smith bought it in 1983; they've undertaken a complete restoration. Their most recent project was painting the exterior in a Colonial Williamsburg color scheme. They've also hung period reproduction lighting fixtures throughout, are slowly furnishing the rooms with antiques, and plan to uncover the wide board floors. Many original architectural features are still intact, including 12-over-12 windows, a hearth with original bricks and mantel, the open main staircase, mouldings, and wavy window glass.

Restrictions: Children welcome. No pets. Check-in after 2 p.m., check-out at 11 a.m.
Beds: The 17 rooms have a variety of bed arrangements. Nine rooms have private baths and there are four two-room family suites with private baths.
Breakfast: Full country breakfast with homemade breads and pastries.
Extras: There's an outdoor pool, children's play area, BYOB lounge, game room, and library. If you really love gardening, you can help them hoe in their summer vegetable patch, or pick apples in their orchard. In winter dinner is included in the room rate.
Rates: Summer: $60 for double with private bath. $100 for four-person, two-room suite with private bath. Rates increase in fall and winter: $110 to $120 (MAP) for double; $190 to $200 (MAP) for suite. Credit cards and personal checks accepted.
Mailing Address: PO Box 37, Peru, VT 05152

SOUTHERN VERMONT

PITTSFIELD

PITTSFIELD INN
Tom and Sue Yennerell
Route 100
Pittsfield, VT 05762
(802) 746-8943
Year-round

1903 Reproduction of 1835 vernacular

LOCATION: Picturesque clapboard houses surround the inn of the village green, located in the Green Mountains near cross-country and Killington downhill ski trails, as well as two fishing rivers.

"We've worked very hard at restoring it for four years, and we're very proud of the result. One of our greatest joys is sharing it with guests.

Tom and Sue consider Pittsfield one of Vermont's best-kept secrets. Their inn overlooks a peaceful village green, where little seems to have changed since 1781.

Though it looks much older, the structure dates from 1903, when the original circa 1830 inn burnt to the ground. The Yennerells think the newer building is a fairly exact reproduction of its predecessor. Both buildings once served the Rutland to Montpelier stagecoach route.

Much original detail remains, such as hardwood floors, butternut panelling in the dining room, a pot-belly stove, and several light fixtures. The clawfoot bathtub was reportedly the first of its kind installed in Pittsfield.

The innkeepers have restored the two-storey porches to near-original condition, and refinished the parlor and tavern areas. All guest rooms evoke a pre-Victorian country style: They're decorated with cheery period wallpapers and fabrics, with quilts on top of antique beds.

Restrictions: No pets.
Beds: Ten rooms, six with private baths.
Breakfast: In winter: full breakfast of eggs, fruit, pancakes with sausage, coffee, and juice. Continental in summer, with Danish, fruit, cereal, coffee, and juice.
Extras: The inn has its own guide service, offering programs in backpacking, orienteering, rock and ice climbing.
Rates: From $45 to $60; cots for extra charge. Mastercard and Visa welcome.
Mailing Address: PO Box 526, Pittsfield, VT 05762

SOUTHERN VERMONT

PROCTORSVILLE

CASTLE INN
Michael and Sheryl Fratino
Junction of Routes 103 & 131
Proctorsville, VT 05153
(802) 226-7222
Memorial Day through October,
Mid-December through March

LOCATION: High on a hill overlooking the Green Mountains, the inn is some three miles south of Ludlow and Okemo ski area.

The Castle Inn is English Revival at its finest. It's a rambling stone expanse, complete with gables and diamond-paned windows, which looks like it was modelled after an English gentleman's country castle. It's built from granite quarried right on the property. Inside, there's a great hall with a huge, carved-stone fireplace and an ornamental plaster ceiling. The dining room is oval, with an original Louis XIV chandelier handing from an elaborate plaster ceiling medallion. One of the guest rooms is furnished with a heavy, carved cherry set original to the house.

Restrictions: Children over six are welcome. No pets. Check-in noon to midnight. Check-out at 11 a.m.
Beds: Thirteen rooms. Four with queen-sized bed and private bath. Four with two double beds and private bath. A two-room suite with private bath is also available.
Breakfast: Full: eggs, bacon, sausage, French toast, buttermilk pancakes, and Vermont maple syrup.
Extras: Pool, hot tub, sauna, and game room are open year-round. Six championship clay tennis courts with a professional instructor are open during the summer. And a choice from the dinner menu is included in the room rate.
Rates: $70 off-peak (MAP), $90 peak (MAP). Higher during fall foliage, winter weekends, and holidays. Cots, $10. Credit cards accepted, though you can pay with cash and save 5%.
   10% discount to OHJ members.
Mailing Address: Box 157, Junction Rts. 103 & 131, Proctorsville, VT 05153

SOUTHERN VERMONT

ROYALTON

THE FOX STAND INN
Jean and Gary Curley
Route 14
Royalton, VT 05068
(802) 763-8437
Year-round

1818 Federal

LOCATION: Along scenic Route 14 and the White River, the Fox Stand Inn offers canoeing, tubing, swimming, bicycling, or fishing nearby.

Built in 1818 to service the Montreal-to-Boston stagecoach traffic, the Fox Stand Inn flourished until the coming of the railroad. From the 1860s until 1978, the building functioned as a private residence and once stood abandoned.

Its builder, Jacob Fox, also constructed the two brick buildings across the street. One, though now used as a private home, still bears a sign reading "Foxville General Store."

Restored and re-opened, the inn once again welcomes visitors through its elegant fan-lit doorway. The imposing Federal brick structure has ten fireplaces, two with beehive ovens—some of which are now used as convenient places to store firewood. Six guest rooms divide what was once the second-floor ballroom.

Restrictions: No pets; check-in flexible, "sometime around noon."
Beds: Six total, including two with twins, three with doubles, one with a double and a single. All six share two baths.
Breakfast: Eggs, bacon, sausage, or French toast comes with potatoes, toast, juice, and coffee.
Rates: $25 single, $35 double. They accept personal checks, credit cards, and traveler's checks.

SOUTHERN VERMONT

SHREWSBURY

1808 Federal with Victorian porches

MAPLE CREST FARM
William and Donna Smith
Lincoln Hill Road
Shrewsbury, VT 05738
(802) 492-3367
Year-round

LOCATION: In the heart of the Green Mountains, Maple Crest Farm sits high above the surrounding countryside, offering sweeping views of surrounding valleys. It's in the Rutland area, and close to ski areas.

Innkeeper William Smith's family has lived in this 27-room farmhouse for five generations. Many original architectural features are intact, including the old plaster, wood floors, mouldings and marble fireplace mantels. (William's 92-year-old grandfather, who grew up in the house, is intact, too.) The house is furnished with the Smiths' fifth-generation antiques. It's still a working farm, complete with sugar maples.

Restrictions: No pets. Minimum two-day stay.
Beds: Four B&B rooms, each with double and single bed. One room has a half-bath. Two apartments are also available by the weekend or week. Families with children encouraged to use apartment.
Breakfast: The full breakfast is served daily, and always includes "special pancakes" with the Smith's own maple syrup.
Extras: Tea is served.
Rates: $35 per couple; cots and cribs available for an additional $5. Personal checks welcome.
Mailing Address: PO Box 120, Cuttingsville, VT 05738

SIMONSVILLE

ROWELL'S INN
Lee and Beth Davis
Route 11
Simonsville, VT 05143
(802) 875-3658
Year-round

1820 Greek Revival

LOCATION: Near a village offering museums, summer theatre, and the Weston Priory, Rowell's Inn is also accessible to Bromley, Stratton, Okemo, and Magic Skiing mountains.

Major Edward Simons built this inn as a stagecoach stop between Manchester, Vermont, and New Hampshire. Along with the inn, Simons founded a town which, not coincidentally, he named Simonsville. Simon held many civil offices and represented Simonsville in the legislature, until his indulgent lifestyle outpaced his earnings and he died a pauper.

The Inn passed through several hands, always providing lodgings and, at times, operating as a post office and general store. In 1900, F.A. Rowell bought it and added elegant tin ceilings, cherry and maple flooring, central heating, and indoor plumbing. Today, the interior is decorated as Rowell had it, with delicate print wallpapers, country antiques, brass beds, and turn-of-the-century brass lighting fixtures. Rowell's well-preserved tavern is now a BYOB pub for guests. The exterior is as it was in 1820: red brick with a three-tiered front porch crowned with a unique, enclosed arch. The Inn is in the National Register.

Restrictions: Children six and over are welcome, but no pets.
Beds: Five rooms, all with private baths: two with double beds, two with a double and twin, one with two twins.
Breakfast: "Full country repast," with bacon and eggs, ham-and-cheese soufflé, omelettes, pancakes; baked goods made fresh each morning include buns, bread, or muffins.
Rates: M.A.P. $100 to $140 on Fridays and Saturdays (other nights, dinner by reservation in advance only); B&B only, $55 to $65. They accept personal checks.

SOUTH WALLINGFORD

GREEN MOUNTAIN TEA ROOM & GUEST HOUSE
Tracy and Ed Creline
Route 7
South Wallingford, VT 05773
(802) 446-2611
Year-round

1792 Colonial

LOCATION: On eight acres in a rural, quiet setting bordering Green Mountain Forest, the inn is near Otter Creek (perfect for canoeing, fishing and swimming) and the Appalachian Trail (they border the property as well).

Back when this nation was just testing its newfound independence, stagecoach drivers would stop at this house to trade in weary horses for fresh ones. Inside in the tavern, they'd warm their innards with the local brew and catch up on some gossip before continuing their rugged journey from Bennington to Rutland. Fifty years later, when the frontier moved westward away from Vermont, the house became a gathering place for more refined socialites. A ballroom was built and invitations were sent to area influentials to join in opulent extravaganzas. Some of these invitations, dated July 4, 1865, are framed and hanging in the inn today.

The inn has stood the test of time. Its slate roof, stone foundation, original 12-over-8 windows, Indian shutters, wide board flooring, and even original wrought iron latches are no worse for two centuries of wear.

Restrictions: No pets. Check-in after 2 p.m., check-out at 11 a.m.
Beds: Five guest rooms. Two with twin beds, two with double beds, and one with two double beds.
Breakfast: Full breakfast and lunch are available for an extra charge.
Extras: Plenteous afternoon tea is served daily: 15 varieties of tea, homemade desserts, and Vermont cheese and crackers.
Rates: $18 to $22, double occupancy. Cots, $10. Personal and traveler's checks welcome.
Mailing Address: PO Box 400, South Wallingford, VT 05773

SOUTHERN VERMONT

TYSON

ECHO LAKE INN
Phil and Kathy Cocco
Route 100
Tyson, VT 05149
(802)228-8602
Closed April

LOCATION: Adjacent to three lakes, across the street from a river, and located amid the Black River Mountains, the inn is a half-hour from Woodstock and several summer theatres, minutes from Killington and Okemo ski areas.

President Calvin Coolidge used to dine at the Echo Lake Inn with cronies Andrew Carnegie, Andrew Mellon, and Thomas Edison. An inn since it was built, it's the blueprint for many country inns that followed it: white clapboards, a two-tiered front porch with simple railings, and (an unusual feature) three steeply pitched dormers. You'll find many original interior features intact, including a hand-carved mantelpiece, a cherry banister, and hardwood floors. In one corner, there's an old Tyson stove, manufactured in the 19th century by the company for whom this town was named. Furnishings are antique, and include brass beds and grained dressers.

Restrictions: No pets or smoking in guest rooms; check-in after 2 p.m., check-out at 11 a.m.
Beds: There are 26 rooms—seven with twin beds, the rest doubles. Nine have private baths, 16 share, and there's one large suite.
Breakfast: Breakfast is available in the restaurant downstairs; price is included in room rate.
Extras: Babysitting, golf discounts, and boats are available. The restaurant's menu varies daily but may include fish terrine, duck and mushroom cream soup, native lamb chops with garlic hollandaise, and poached pears in orange zabaglione.
Rates: $33 for family unit, minimum four people; up to $72, for suite. Cots and cribs for extra charge. 10% increase during Christmas and Presidents' week; 10% discount mid-week in any season. Personal checks and credit cards welcome.
   10% discount to OHJ members off room rate only.
Mailing Address: PO Box 154, Ludlow, VT 05149

SOUTHERN VERMONT

WALLINGFORD

THE WALLINGFORD INN
Dan Stevens
9 North Main Street
Wallingford, VT 05773
(802) 446-2849
Year-round

1876 French Second Empire

LOCATION: In a valley in central Vermont, the inn is 30 minutes

411

from the Killington ski area and near both museums and Manchester.

"...it's a beautifully preserved piece of Americana..." Dan Stevens

Themes The Wallingford Inn couldn't be a more typical French Second Empire house. Fortunately much of the original detail remains, especially the interior woodwork: including the wainscotting, made of oak, cherry, maple, and walnut, as well as sliding doors and parquet floors. And the old outbuildings, a gazebo and carriage house, still stand.

The furnishings, besides the original marble fireplaces, include Victorian bedroom and parlor sets and brass and iron beds. The entire interior was recently redecorated with period wallpaper and paint colors.

Birney Bachler, the last member of the original family to own the house, was an inventor. Among other interesting items his patents included a vacuum tube system.

Restrictions: No infants (under two), no pets; smoking permitted in rooms.
Beds: Ten rooms, eight with private baths.
Breakfast: Full, with juice, eggs, French toast or pancakes, sourdough, Vermont maple syrup, coffee, tea (not all items available every day).
Extras: Coffee and tea are available all day.
Rates: $65 to $70, depending on season. Personal checks and credit cards welcome.
Mailing Address: PO Box 404, Wallingford, VT 05773

SOUTHERN VERMONT

WEST DOVER

SNOW DEN INN
Andrew and Marjorie Trautwein
Route 100
West Dover, VT 05356
(802) 464-9355
Year-round

1885 New England Farmhouse

LOCATION: The inn stands two miles south of Mount Snow Ski Area, and is close to numerous lakes and streams. Recreational facilities include Mt. Snow Country Club, open to the inn's guests. Summer playhouses, antique shops, museums, craft shows, and fairs are all nearby.

"Inns are delightful alternatives to this all-too-plastic world in which travelers are assured that every motel is absolutely identical to every other motel. So look for places like our where the floors creak, vegetable are fresh, windows are old, and room numbers are unnecessary . . ."

This family farmhouse was converted to an inn in 1952 to lodge skiers from Mt. Snow. Milt and Jean Cummings took over its proprietorship in 1977, and found it in nearly mint condition. Restoration projects were limited to refinishing a few floors, redecorating and furnishing with antiques, and, of course, keeping up with the never-ending repairs familiar to every old-house owner. (They also added extra guest baths.)

Snow Den's most outstanding architectural feature is its floors. They're made of maple, oak, and wide pine—the farmer who built the house owned a sawmill across the road, and so had his pick of the area's best lumber. The marble fireplace mantels are another striking feature.

Anyone who wants to know more about the inn's history will be delighted to know that descendants of Mr. Davis, who built the house, are still living in town. They stop by the inn frequently to express their satisfaction with its maintenance.

Restrictions: No pets. Check-in after 1 p.m., check-out at 11 a.m.
Beds: Eight guest rooms, most with a double and single. All the beds except one (a canopy) are antique, and all are covered with hand-stitched quilts. You might sleep on a brass bed, a four-poster, a 200-year-old sleigh bed, or a high oak bed. Every room has a private bath; some have fireplaces.

Breakfast: Full: French toast, pancakes, sausage, bacon, juice, coffee, and toast.
Rates: $65 to $75, summer double; $80 to $110, winter double; $180 to $220, weekend package. Weekly rates also available. $10 for third person sharing room. Personal checks accepted.
  10% discount to OHJ members.
Mailing Address: PO Box 615, West Dover, VT 05356

WESTON

1830 INN ON THE GREEN
Sandy and Dave Granger
Main Street (Route 100)
Weston, VT 05161
(802) 824-6789
Memorial Day through October
31, December 1 through Easter

1830 Colonial

LOCATION: The inn is located on the village green, in a historic district. The Weston Playhouse (Vermont's oldest summer theater) and the Farrar-Mansur Historical Museum are across the green. Country stores, antique shops, restaurants, and the Weston Priory are within walking distance. Outdoor activities in the area include: skiing, hiking, biking, golfing, tennis, fishing, and canoeing. Four major ski areas are located within a 15-mile radius.

"We love to talk about our home's architecture and history with anyone who will listen, and we especially appreciate guests who share our interest in both."

This inn has changed careers several times since its conception. It started life as a blacksmith shop with living quarters above, and later ran the gamut from being town hall, to an undertaking parlor, to a bawdy house, and finally a private home, before the Burkes bought it in 1984. Its most beautiful architectural feature is certainly the indoor spiral staircase, so magnificent it was dismantled and moved twice: first into the home of 19th-century multi-millionaire and financial wizard Hetty Green (once known as the "witch of Wall

414

Street"), and later into this house. Its furnishings are antique (Burke family heirlooms); its floors wide board and maple; its roof, slate; its windows and doors shuttered; its proprietors genuine old-house enthusiasts!

Restrictions: Children over 14 are welcome. No pets. Check-in after 3 p.m. Check-out at 11 a.m.
Beds: Four rooms. One with queen-sized bed and half-bath. One with double bed and semi-private bath. Other two rooms have twin beds, one has private bath. All rooms have rocking chairs, fluffy comforters, and lots of flowers.
Breakfast: Full: juice, fresh fruit, homemade bread, and a "chef's choice" main dish that changes daily.
Extras: Cheese and crackers are served from 5 to 7 p.m.; there's a bedtime snack (fresh cookies and tea or hot cider) and bowls of fruit and nuts to munch on at all times. OHJ subscribers will receive a free pass to the Farrar-Mansur Museum.
Rates: $60 to $70. Personal checks accepted.
Mailing Address: PO Box 104, Weston, VT 05161

WILMINGTON

NUTMEG INN
Del and Charlotte Lawrence
Route 9W
Wilmington, VT 05363
(802) 464-3351
Year-round

1777 Colonial

LOCATION: This rural Vermont mountain valley is in the heart of the Mount Snow recreational area, near skiing, hiking trails, golf, tennis, swimming, fishing, antique shops, craft fairs, summer theater, music festivals—or just relaxing in the cool mountain air.

This is a typical Vermont farmhouse: multiple wings added to a tiny colonial cottage, transforming it to a spacious rambling structure large enough for a farm family. The dining room is in the original colonial section: there are ax marks on the exposed ceiling beams. There's a pressed tin ceiling in the foyer, a remnant of a later addition. And at one point, a carriage house was attached to the side of the house—it's still there and is now used as a guest lounge, with a large fireplace.

The additions stopped after 1890. Del and Charlotte have an antique picture collection you can browse through; one shot shows the exterior a century ago, looking almost the same as it looks today. The house has been an inn since 1957, and the Lawrences have operated it since 1984. Most of their furnishings are antique.

Restrictions: Children over eight welcome. No pets. No smoking in dining room. Check-in after 2 p.m.
Beds: Among the 11 rooms there is a variety of bed arrangements. All rooms have private baths.
Breakfast: Bountiful country breakfast: eggs any style, French toast, pancakes, bacon, sausage, toast, muffins, cereal, coffee, tea, or milk, plus a "special of the week."
Extras: Full dinner is included in winter rate. On weekends in summer and fall, dinner is provided for an additional $10 to $15.
Rates: $60 to $93 summer, $73 to $150 winter. American Express and personal checks accepted.
Mailing Address: Box 818, Wilmington, VT 05363

SOUTHERN VERMONT

WILMINGTON

THE WHITE HOUSE OF WILMINGTON
Robert B. Grinold
Route 9
Wilmington, VT 05363
(802) 464-2135
Year-round

1915 Colonial Revival

LOCATION: Atop a hill, with a panoramic view of Wilmington and the Green Mountains, the inn is surrounded by towering hardwoods and formal flower gardens. Haystack and Mount Snow ski areas, miles of national forest trails, numerous historic sites, and quaint shops are all nearby.

"The White House is a fine example of turn-of-the-century elegance. We like to share its intricate detailing with those who appreciate it."

New England lumber baron Martin Brown didn't cut any corners when he built this palatial mansion. Its exterior is breathtaking, with two-storey porticoes supported by soaring pillars, and French doors crowned with elliptical fanlights. Inside, there are eight fireplaces and a hidden staircase modelled after that in Nathaniel Hawthorne's famed House of Seven Gables. Mr. Brown even had built a private nine-hole golf course and a bowling alley.

Years of everyday wear had left the house fallen from its once-glorious state. When Robert Grinold bought it in 1978, he faced a large-scale restoration project. He stripped the exterior to the bare wood and repainted it. He refinished the beautiful hardwood floors upstairs and down, and replaced the crumbling ceilings. He restored the gallery's original wallpaper, printed in France in 1912, and hung period reproductions in other rooms. He got hold of some of Mr. Brown's original furnishings, supplemented those with period antiques (including wrought-iron patio furniture), hung brass and crystal chandeliers, and laid down Oriental throw rugs. The White House of Wilmington is now as elegant as it ever was when Martin Brown occupied it.

Restrictions: Children over ten welcome. No pets. Check-in after 2 p.m., check-out at 11 a.m.
Beds: All of the 12 rooms have private baths. Accommodations range from twin beds with shared bath to a two-room balcony suite with fireplace, two double beds, sofa bed, and private bath.
Breakfast: Full country breakfast with choice of menu.
Extras: There's a complete health spa on the basement level, with whirlpool, sauna, heated swimming pool, and masseuse. There's also a 60-foot outdoor pool surrounded by a formal flower garden. And the inn has its own cross-country ski touring center, with rentals, instructors, and 22 kilometers of trails. Dinner menu features chicken cordon bleu, filet mignon, sole amandine, homemade desserts.
Rates: $160 to $200 per couple (MAP). Extra persons in room, $45. Variety of special package and holiday rates available. Personal checks accepted. 5% surcharge for credit-card payment.
10% discount to OHJ members.

WINDSOR

JUNIPER HILL INN
Jim and Krisha Pennino
Juniper Hill Road
Windsor, VT 05089
(802) 674-5273
May 1 to October 31, December
15 to March 15

1901 Colonial Revival

LOCATION: In Vermont's Connecticut River Valley, Juniper Hill Inn, on 14 wooded acres, is three miles from St. Gaudens National Historic Site and seven miles from Mt. Ascutney. There's skiing in winter and breathtaking colors in fall.

This palatial mansion was the private residence of Maxwell Evart, a man with deep roots in the nation's history. Evart's ancestor, Roger Sherman, signed the Declaration of Independence. His father served as U.S. Attorney General for President Andrew Johnson, and Secretary of State for President Rutherford B. Hayes. Evart himself was a friend of Teddy Roosevelt (who visited here in 1902), a Vermont state legislator, a bank president, and Union Pacific Railroad's chief legal counsel. That Evart raised his children in a Colonial Revival seems fitting.

Juniper Hill's architectural features are classic. The huge portico resembles a Greek temple, with massive Ionic columns raised on a high foundation. The portico leads into a 30-by-40-foot, oak-panelled great hall, with a hunting lodge-sized fireplace and an imposing staircase. Another staircase rises up to a Palladian window. The dining room and parlor fireplaces are hand-carved with turn-of-the-century scenes.

Jim and Krisha Pennino bought the mansion in 1984 from a religious organization. (It had been used for several years as a spiritual retreat center.) They've furnished it with antiques collected in Europe and the U.S., and are restoring the grounds to their original splendor.

Restrictions: Children over 12 welcome. No pets. Check-in after 2 p.m.
Beds: Fifteen guest rooms, some with queen-size beds, some with

418

doubles, and some with singles. All rooms have private baths.

Breakfast: Full: eggs, bacon or sausage, French toast or pancakes, and coffee or tea. It's served from 7:30 to 9 a.m. Breakfast in bed available for extra charge.

Extras: The innkeepers will prepare four-course dinners for $13.50 to $16.50 per person.

Rates: $65 to $75. Third person in room costs an additional $13.50. Credit cards and personal checks accepted.

10% discount to OHJ members with minimum two-night stay.

Mailing Address: R R 1, Box 79, Windsor, VT 05089

VIRGINIA

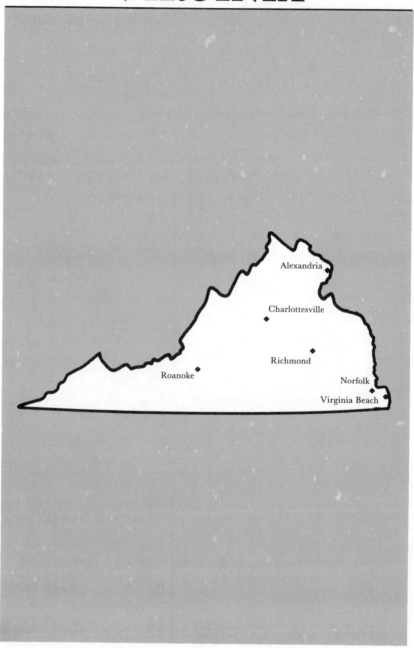

BOWLING GREEN

THE OLD MANSION
Peter Larson and Ruth Curlee
State Route 2
Bowling Green, VA 22427
(804) 633-6873
Year-round

1670 Pre-Georgian

LOCATION: The inn sits on 126 acres, still landscaped as they were centuries ago, complete with 300-year-old trees, fields, pasture, and woodland. The birthplaces of Robert E. Lee and George Washington are nearby, as are many Civil War sites, Richmond, and an 18th-century tavern-turned-dinner theatre.

In 320 years a house can gather in a lot of ghosts, and this one certainly has its share: ghostly hoofbeats warning of impending doom, a spurned wife returning to haunt her adulterous husband; it's enough to send chills up the spine of the bravest old-house devotee.

Fortunately, this fascinating old house has many other things going for it. Nothing's been added since 1770, and the place has been entirely preserved, thanks in part to a live-in curator, Peter Larson (his co-proprietor and wife, Ruth Curlee, does the cooking), and also to steady ownership — the Carys, who currently own the property, are descendants of Major Hoomes, who built the house on a royal land grant in about 1670.

Modern conveniences have been added without major structural changes. The original floors remain; they've never even been sanded. The furnishings, all heirlooms, reflect the changing tastes of the passing generations, and run the gamut from colonial to Victorian.

Restrictions: Smoking and pets not permitted in the house "for obvious reasons!"

Beds: There are two baths for the three rooms—two with fireplaces, two with one double and one with two double beds.

Breakfast: "Full country": homemade bread, homemade sausage, local eggs, all ingredients fresh. "I'm told I am a great cook," Ruth says modestly.

Extras: Guests get discounts on visits to the Barksdale Dinner Theater and nearby King's Dominion. And they're offered a glass of wine or tea upon arrival.

Rates: $40 (one double bed) to $50 (two doubles). Personal and traveler's checks accepted.

10% discount to OHJ members.

Mailing Address: PO Box 835, Bowling Green, VA 22427. (804) 633-5781.

VIRGINIA

CHATHAM

THE SIMS-MITCHELL HOUSE
Henry and Tricia Mitchell
242 Whittle Street SW
Chatham, VA 24531
(804) 432-0595
Year-round

C. 1870 Italianate

LOCATION: Located in the tranquil town of Chatham, the inn is a half-block from saddlemaker Paul Shelton's shop, three blocks from the "genealogical treasures" of the county courthouse, and a short drive from many of North Carolina's and Virginia's historic and scenic attractions.

Around the time of the Civil War, Chatham lawyer and Virginia State Senator James M. Whittle set out to have a grand house built for his daughter Matoaka and her husband, Colonel William E. Sims. When completed, the house was a showplace, a fine Italianate with raised English basement, bay window, 11 fireplaces, and 15 rooms including an upstairs ballroom.

By the time Henry and Tricia Mitchell bought the house in 1975, years of neglect and vandalism had brought it to the brink of demolition. Despite this, the Mitchells say the architectural integrity of the house was never significantly altered. It still has its original tongue-and-groove pine siding, decorative interior cornices and medallions, and all 11 fireplaces with their original mantels. The Mitchells have spent the last ten years reclaiming all these beautiful details. They've furnished the house with antiques, many of them generations-old family heirlooms.

Restrictions: No pets or smoking. Check-out at 11 a.m.; check-in between 3 and 9 p.m. (later by special arrangement "so one of us will be here to welcome you").
Beds: Two bedrooms, each with a double bed, share a sitting room and bathroom. There's a private street-level entrance to both.
Breakfast: Juice or fresh fruit, eggs, homemade whole-grain bread are served in "stately dining room"—beginning at 7:15 a.m. weekdays, and at 8 a.m. weekends.
Extras: Guests are given a complimentary packet of local travel and historical information, including post cards and walking-tour guide. Fresh fruit is provided in the rooms. Dinner, family style, can be served for $8.50 per guest with 48-hour notice.
Rates: $35 each room; personal and traveler's checks and credit cards welcome.
10% discount to OHJ members with mailing label.
Mailing Address: PO Box 846, Chatham, VA 24531

VIRGINIA

CHINCOTEAGUE

1886 Queen Anne

MISS MOLLY'S INN
Dr. and Mrs. James Stam
113 North Main Street
Chincoteague, VA 23336
(804) 336-6686
April 1 to December 1

LOCATION: The inn is minutes from Assateague National Seashore and Chincoteague National Wildlife Refuge, and overlooks the water.

The man who built this house was known in his day as the Clam King of the World. Miss Molly was his daughter, and she lived here for eighty-four years.

The house is a dreamy sort of place, with five porches and a gazebo that capture the misty ocean air. Writer Marguerite Henry stayed here with Miss Molly for a time, and dreamed up the plot for her well-known children's book *Misty of Chincoteague* (about a horse that survives a shipwreck) while rocking on the front porch.

Hosts Dr. and Mrs. James Stam have been here since 1982, and have completely restored the house. They've furnished it with antiques, many original to the house. They have a display of photographs of Miss Molly and her family.

Restrictions: Children over 12 and smoking permitted; no pets; check-in after 2 p.m.; check-out at 11 a.m.
Beds: Fifteen guest rooms, some with queen-size beds, some with doubles, and some with singles. All rooms have private baths.
Breakfast: Choice of three kinds of juice, fresh melon stuffed with strawberries and topped with honey-rum sauce, crab quiche with sliced tomatoes and avocadoes; coffee, tea, and milk.
Extras: Complimentary afternoon tea is available.
Rates: $59 to $95, all seasons; add $10 for each additional person. Personal checks welcome.

VIRGINIA

EDINBURG

MARY'S COUNTRY INN
Mary and Jim Clarke
218 South Main Street
Edinburg, VA 22824
(703) 984-8286
Year-round

C. 1850 Vernacular Victorian

LOCATION: Edinburg, in the Shenandoah Valley, celebrates "Ole Time Days" each September with craft sales, battle re-enactments, and townspeople in costume. Nearby are the Shenandoah River, vineyards, caverns to explore, antique shops, and New Market Civil War battlefield, plus hiking in George Washington Forest and skiing on Bryce Mountain.

For decades, Edinburg's main industry was the mill right next to this house. Not surprisingly, the house was home to millers from the time it was built until 1983.

Mary has restored the house room by room, in the process uncovering walnut pocket doors that had been hidden behind walls for half a century. The doors match the walnut trim and bannister. She's furnished the house with antiques the last miller's family left behind, and has on display a set of 19th-century catalogs, photographs, and lithographs she found in the house.

The house's outstanding architectural features are its wraparound verandah with Victorian millwork, massive Jeffersonian French doors, and bay windows.

Beds: Six doubles, one with private bath; the rest share, two to a bath.
Breakfast: "Country": freshly baked muffins, fruits, juices, coffee or tea, cereals.
Extras: Croquet on the green and lemonade in the afternoon on the porch are complimentary.
Rates: $40 to $45; cots $7.50, including breakfast for the additional guest. Personal checks accepted.

10% discount to OHJ members.
Mailing Address: Route 2, Box 4, Edinburg, VA 22824

VIRGINIA

MASSAPONAX

LA VISTA PLANTATION
Edward and Michele Schiesser
Route 607
Massaponax, VA 22401
(703) 898-8444
Year-round

1838 Georgian

LOCATION: Ten country acres, plus 300 acres more of cropland

and forest, surround the house. The grounds include many tall trees, flowering shrubs, and a pond stocked with bass and sunfish. Nearby historic sites are numerous: Fredericksburg, Monticello, Mount Vernon, Robert E. Lee's Stratford Hall, along with several wineries.

During the Civil War, a group of Yankee stragglers were approaching this house, which was inhabited by Confederate sympathizers named the Boulewares. Mrs. Bouleware, afraid the Yanks would make off with her family heirloom, a silver cake platter, dashed out to the barn and hid the plate in some hay under a sitting hen. The Yanks found and killed the hen, but the plate remained safe, and today you can see it at the Fredericksburg Battlefield Museum. After the war was lost, the bed Stonewall Jackson died in was entrusted to Mrs. Bouleware, then the president of an organization dedicated to establishing a Confederate cemetery. The bed is now on display at the Stonewall Jackson shrine just a few miles down the road.

Today, the plantation house looks much the same as when the Boulewares built it—with the exception that the innkeepers "joined the 20th century" by having a new electrical system installed. The house is a restrained interpretation of Southern Greek Revival, with a two-storey front portico with fluted columns that are elegant but not overbearing. Inside it has high ceilings, wide door and window mouldings with acorn and oak leaf corner pieces, random-width pine floors, and a gracious staircase with mahogany handrail that ascends to a large window on the landing. The house is furnished with antiques and comfortable country furniture. The host is a sculptor who works in limestone, and his pieces are displayed throughout the house.

Restrictions: Children and well-behaved pets are welcome. Smoking permitted. Noon check-out time is flexible.
Beds: The one 1200-square-foot suite has a bedroom, living room, sitting room, kitchen, two fireplaces, a double bed and a queen sofa bed. Private bath is in the suite.
Breakfast: Fresh farm eggs, any style; toast, Danish, choice of jams, bacon, coffee/tea, orange juice, milk. Guests staying longer than one night can substitute French toast or pancakes for eggs on subsequent days.
Extras: There's no extra charge for the radio, TV, phone, bicycling, fishing in a stocked pond, a fire (in season) laid in the hearth, sodas, ice; and laundry for extended stays.
Rates: $55, cribs at no extra cost. Personal checks welcome.
   10% discount to OHJ members.
Mailing Address: Rt. 3, Box 1255 A, Fredericksburg, VA 22401

ORANGE

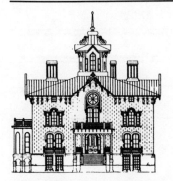

MAYHURST INN
Stephen and Shirley Ramsey
Route 15 South
Orange, VA 22960
(703) 672-5597
Year-round

1859 Italianate

LOCATION: In the foothills of the Blue Ridge Mountains, Orange stands at the crossroads of two historic highways and near the site of Wilderness Battlefield. Wineries, Charlottesville, and Fredericksburg are all within easy driving distance.

John Willis, James and Dolley Madison's great-nephew, wasn't constrained by lack of funds when he built this house. It's a fanciful piece of architecture, like something most people would only see in a dream. It's built of wood that masquerades as stone, a technique called rustication. The windows take all different forms: single-and double-hung arched windows, a sort of Palladian window, and round windows that peek out from the third floor. The scrolled brackets under the eaves and the elaborate finials atop each of four gables look like decorations from a fancy wedding cake. Topping it all off is the cupola, a miniature replica of the house, complete with four mini-gables.

Inside, you'll find a large entry hall with a marble-mantled fireplace and an oval staircase that spirals up four floors to the cupola. To the right of this is a library with old portraits, Oriental rugs, and antebellum books and furnishings. All the guest rooms are named for people affiliated with Mayhurst (like Stonewall Jackson, who spent a night here, and Dolley Madison). All the furnishings are pre-Civil War.

Restrictions: Well-behaved pets and children welcome; no smoking.
Beds: The six rooms plus a cottage all have private baths.
Breakfast: Full country: Virginia ham or sausage, eggs, baked apples, pumpkin muffins, and homemade marmalade, are served in the sunny dining room, facing south.
Extras: They serve an afternoon English tea (with scones, sandwiches,

and cookies). There's a pond for fishing or swimming, fields for picnicking and strolling, and a barn full of antiques for sale.

Rates: $72 to $85 weekdays, $78 to $95 weekends. Cots and cribs, $8 extra. Personal checks accepted.

10% discount to OHJ members.

Mailing Address: PO Box 707, Orange, VA 22960

VIRGINIA

RICHMOND

THE CATLIN-ABBOTT HOUSE
Dr. and Mrs. James L. Abbott
2304 East Broad Street
Richmond, VA 23223
(804) 780-3746
Year-round

LOCATION: Within one mile are the White House of the Confederacy, Edgar Allan Poe Shrine, John Marshall House, Virginia State Capitol, Shockoe Slip, the financial district, and downtown Richmond.

Though he was held in bondage, and never received even a penny for his labor, the slave who built this house was known in his day as one of the finest masons around. He was named William Mitchell, and he built this house for his owner, William Catlin. There are several examples of Mitchell's fine craftsmanship in town: Catlin turned an extra profit by hiring his slave out to do brick work for other Virginia gentry.

After the South lost the War, the house ran on hard times. In 1870, financial constraints forced the family that lived here to turn it into a boarding house, adding six boarders' rooms at the back.

Years and decades passed, boarders moved in and out, and eventually the once lavish mansion was abandoned, gutted, and condemned by the Health Department. That's how the Abbotts found it in 1980. They hired a restoration expert to bring the house back to life. His project involved, among other painstaking tasks, duplicating the sparse few surviving original mouldings to replace all those that had been pilfered.

Mrs. Abbott did all the interior decoration. She's furnished the house entirely with period antiques; some are heirlooms handed down through her family. Her valuable collection includes Czechoslovakian crystal chandeliers, Chippendale and Queen Anne wing-back chairs, a pink Chippendale sofa, and several Oriental rugs. One of the guest rooms has a four-poster, canopied bed so tall you need a step-stool to get under the covers. There are lots of 19th-century portraits hanging around the house, as well as some of Mrs. Abbott's needlework samplers.

Restrictions: No children or pets. Check-in after 2 p.m.
Beds: Three doubles, two suites (one with twin beds, one double). All rooms have private baths.
Breakfast: Coffee, Sanka, or tea are served in room at wake-up time. Breakfast is served either in the room or dining room on fine china: bacon, eggs, and potato pancakes.
Extras: The Abbotts provide transportation to airport, financial district, or Medical College of Virginia. There's an evening turn-down service, with sherry and mints left at bedside.
Rates: $67.50, single; $77.50, double; $120 to $140, suites. Credit cards and personal and traveler's checks accepted.

10% discount to OHJ members for rooms with private bath only.

SPERRYVILLE

THE CONYERS HOUSE
Sandra and Norman
Cartwright-Brown
Slate Mills Road (Route 707)
Sperryville, VA 22740
(703) 987-8025
Year-round

1777 Colonial, added to in 1810 and 1979

LOCATION: This inn is located in a particularly scenic part of Virginia. The only other signs of civilization in this mountain valley are a nearby 1815 church and the lights of a single neighbor. A fine nouvelle cuisine restaurant is 15 minutes away.

O
n the wall behind the grandfather clock in the living room are two notes: "Put pigs in pen to fatten—October 14, 1864" and "Mrs. Thornton owes 86 cents." The notes are left over from the house's 19th-century term as a general store.

The oldest part of the house was built in 1777 by German soldiers who lent their services to the Revolution and stuck around when the battles were over. In 1810, a man named Bartholomew Conyers moved the house to its present site, attached it to his Federal farmhouse, and started what was known as Conyers' Old Store.

Guest rooms are furnished with antiques like an authentic rope bed, a 1793 winding clock once used to count off skeins of wool, and a seven-generations-old family heirloom rocker.

Restrictions: "We do not encourage young children"—a mid-week visit, though, may be possible. No smoking in the bedrooms—porches and common rooms available for that. Pets must stay in outbuildings or cellar kitchen.

Beds: Five doubles (some with waist-high beds!), two queens and a king; two share a bath.

Breakfast: "Hearty, to say the least": fresh fruit platter, homemade cider, English muffins slathered with cream cheese and red pepper jelly, cheese strata, bread pudding, fresh bread, fresh cream. Menu varies for second and third mornings.

Extras: Afternoon tea—a piece of "our famous parsnip cake" with wine, homemade cider, coffee, or tea—is complimentary.

Rates: $80 to $100, singles deduct $10. Cribs and cots loaned free of charge. Personal checks welcome.

Mailing Address: Rt. 1, Box 157, Sperryville, VA 22740

VIRGINIA

STANLEY

JORDAN HOLLOW FARM INN
Marley and Jetze Beers
Route 626
Stanley, VA 22851
(703) 778-2209
Year-round

1790 Colonial surrounded by 1882 vernacular Victorian

LOCATION: In the foothills of the Blue Ridge Mountains, near Shenandoah National Park, the inn offers a rural setting with mountain views, a few miles from the Luray Caverns and the George Washington National Forest.

The 19th-century, clapboarded farmhouse with the huge, two-storey verandah that's here today was built around a 1790 log cabin. Inside the farmhouse, you can still see the log cabin's old stone chimney, blown-glass windows, weathered and worn steps, and hand-planed woodwork.

Overnight accommodations are in two guest lodges: a restored and converted former horse stable and machine shed, and a new, clapboarded building that matches the architectural style of the other buildings on the property. Guest rooms are decorated rustically. Some, but not all, have antique furnishings.

Restrictions: Children are welcome, and pets can be boarded at a kennel a few houses away.
Beds: There are 16 rooms; each has both a single and double bed. All have private baths.
Breakfast: Not included, but full-service restaurant in the farmhouse serves a "country French" menu.
Extras: Horseback riding and lessons are $10 per hour. Swimming, ping pong, volley ball, as well as a pool table and board games are available. The lounge with TV and bar has an extensive selection of beers and wines.
Rates: $65, with cots available for $10. Personal checks and credit cards welcome.

10% discount to OHJ members on weekdays only.
Mailing Address: Rt. 2, Box 375, Stanley, VA 22851

VIRGINIA

STAUNTON

FREDERICK HOUSE
Joe and Evy Harman
18 East Frederick Street
Staunton, VA 24401
(703) 885-4220
Year-round

1810 Greek Revival, with later additions

LOCATION: Woodrow Wilson's birthplace is two blocks away, Mary Baldwin College is across the street. The area, known as the Beverley Historic District, has most of Staunton's principal stores.

This house has been everything from a doctor's office (which housed Staunton's first x-ray machine), to a dance studio, to a knitting shop, to a beauty salon. By the time Joe and Evy Harman got to it in 1983, it had been remodelled so many times that the original floor plan was completely reversed. During restoration, they rebuilt old walls that had been knocked down and took out newer partitions.

The B&B is actually three houses: Two are connected from the outside but not the inside; the third stands on its own plot. The earliest house is the eye-catching Greek Revival that dates from 1810. The newest was built in 1910. Rooms are furnished with antiques and art from the Harmans' collection.

Restrictions: No smoking, and no pets.
Beds: Eleven rooms, all with private baths.
Breakfast: Continental: fruit, juice, roll, coffee. Also full breakfast, not included in room rate.
Extras: Guests can purchase $5 guest passes to the restored athletic club, complete with pool, next door. Shenandoah Valley spring water is available on request.
Rates: $30 to $45, lower between December and April. Credit cards and personal checks all accepted. Cot, $5.
Mailing Address: PO Box 1387, Staunton, VA 24401

STAUNTON

**LAMBSGATE BED &
BREAKFAST**
Dan and Elizabeth Fannon
Route 254W and Route 833
Staunton, VA 24479
(703) 885-8798
Year-round

1816 Farmhouse: Victorian porch and 20th-century wing

LOCATION: The inn stands on a seven-acre sheep farm — "lambs frolic February through June" — in the Shenandoah Valley, five miles from Virginia's second highest mountain.

This house, like most of Virginia's other historic homes, has its own slice of Civil War history: At one time, a Confederate Army major who fought at Gettysburg lived here. The house is built from hand-made bricks. Its long Victorian verandah has two different balustrades — it was built at two different times. On the top floor is a curious set of permanently closed blinds — not a window at all, but an optical illusion meant to create symmetry. Inside the house, two large down-stairs rooms and three upper-floor bedrooms still have their original woodwork, doors, simple fireplace mantels, and pine floors. If you make a trip to the attic, you'll see the original, pegged roof rafters, pencilled with Roman numerals left by a 19th-century carpenter who liked to keep his work organized.

Restrictions: No pets or smoking; children are welcome.
Beds: Three rooms—two doubles, one with twins—share one bath.
Breakfast: Full "Southern" breakfast: juice, fruit, or melon in season, eggs "as you like them," bacon or country ham, toast or muffins, grits with butter or red-eye gravy, coffee or tea.
Rates: All rooms $25 year-round, with reduced rates for stays of over seven nights. Personal and traveler's checks welcome.
Mailing Address: Rt. 1, Box 63, Swoope, VA 24479

WARM SPRINGS

THE ANDERSON COTTAGE
**Jean Randolph Bruns
Old Germantown Road
Warm Springs, VA 24484
(703) 839-2975
April 1 to mid-November**

Late 18th-century Colonial, with additions

LOCATION: The town's warm springs (98°) flow through the inn's two-acre property. The picturesque mountain village has many other period homes. Restaurants, shops, walking trails, and recreational areas are nearby.

The original four rooms of this farmhouse are log. Pencilled on the chinking between two of the logs is a melancholy, two-line poem dated 1837, probably composed by some lonely traveller who stopped at this one-time tavern for a cup of ale. The rest of the house is clapboarded—white with green trim, a tall verandah, and windows that let in lots of sun. You can tell how old the house is by its rustic construction methods: as innkeeper Jean Bruns puts it, "No straight lines and no right angles!"

The house has original pine floors and several original fireplace mantels. Some of the furnishings are left over from the house's term as a summer inn, from the 1870s until the 1950s.

Restrictions: Not recommended for small children, no smoking in bedrooms.
Beds: One double has a private parlor, bath, and entrance; two doubles share a bath, one queen has a private bath, one single shares a bath. In all, three rooms share two baths.
Breakfast: Full country: sausage, fried apples, biscuits, homemade preserves, fruit, coffee, etc. or bacon, eggs ("a special recipe"), Sally Lunn, fruit, coffee, etcetera.
Extras: Guests can use the nearby tennis and bath facilities and the inn's kitchen to prepare snacks, tea, or coffee; there are open fires in the dining room and two parlors on chilly days. Plus there's lots of books, games, and puzzles.
Rates: $40 to $50; $25 for a single, $5 extra for cots. Personal checks welcome.
   10% discount to OHJ members.
Mailing Address: Box 176, Warm Springs VA 24484

VIRGINIA

WOODSTOCK

**THE INN AT NARROW
PASSAGE**
Ellen and Ed Markel, Jr.
Route 11 South and Route 672
Woodstock, VA 22664
(703) 459-8000
Year-round

LOCATION: The inn overlooks a small boat landing on the Shenandoah River. The nearby George Washington Forest links up with the Appalachian Trail. Nearby attractions include the Luray Caverns, New Market Battlefield, Wayside Theater, vineyards and antique shops, as well as Bryce ski resort.

"We think you and your children will find the Inn a perfect place to relive history in a personal way—imagine Indians lurking outside the sturdy log walls, or soldiers camped in the yard!"

This log colonial was built as part of a small German settlement on the Virginia frontier. In the limestone cellar, there's evidence of a tunnel leading toward the river—where the house's occupants could go to escape hostile intruders. More than a century after the house was built, Stonewall Jackson used it as headquarters for one of his campaigns, and camped his soldiers on the surrounding property.

Innkeepers Ellen and Ed Markel found the house in 1983 and, though it had been abandoned for several years and was rapidly deteriorating, they fell in love with its log architecture and its river-bank setting. They began a massive restoration in the spring of 1984, re-chinking the log walls, replacing unsafe porches on the clap-boarded, Federal-era addition, and installing modern plumbing and electrical systems. The house has its original limestone foundation, blown-glass windows, pine floors, and several old doors—one with the original wrought-iron strap hinges. The fireplaces are floor-to-ceiling limestone, with arched openings. Furnishings include colonial wardrobes and canopy beds.

Restrictions: Babies and well-behaved children are welcome, but no pets. No smoking in the guest rooms; check-in after 2 p.m.
Beds: Twelve rooms, eight with private baths.
Breakfast: Full country breakfast includes juices, fruits, homemade muffins and pastries, cereal, eggs, ham or sausage, plus "seasonal surprises."
Extras: Cookies and hot cider are served around the fireplace in winter; lemonade is offered on the porches overlooking the river in summer. Bikes (free) and box lunches ($2.50) can be obtained for picnics. There's swimming, fishing, and canoeing off the inn's boat landing. A nominal fee is charged for dinner-time babysitting in summer. Horses can be boarded at modern facility nearby.
Rates: $50 to $60, with trundle beds for $4. Credit cards or personal checks accepted.
10% discount to OHJ members.

WASHINGTON

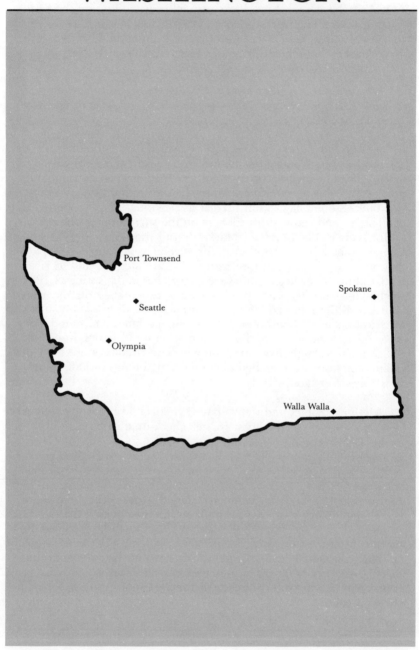

Port Townsend

Spokane

Seattle

Olympia

Walla Walla

LANGLEY

THE ORCHARD B&B
Martha Murphy
619 Third Street
Langley, WA 98260
(206) 221-7880
Year-round

1901 Farmhouse

LOCATION: The inn is on the east side of Whidbey Island (in Puget Sound) in the village of Langley. Fruit and nut trees, firs and hemlocks surround the house, and there's a large play yard. Beaches and the shops of Langley are a short walk away.

Martha Murphy loves plants. Not only is her inn surrounded by them—lilac bushes, fruit and nut trees, firs and hemlocks—but she also added a greenhouse to the house to take advantage of a southern exposure.

The kitchen she describes as "quaint and cozy"; there and in the living room she's displayed her collection of baskets. The sitting room comes equipped with a fireplace, and the two guest rooms are located upstairs. The swing on the wraparound porch offers a view of the Cascade Mountains.

Restrictions: Children welcome. No smoking or pets.
Beds: There are two doubles that share a bath.
Breakfast: Freshly ground coffee, choice of teas including herbal, fresh fruit, juice; cereals, eggs; and bran muffins, baked daily.
Extras: Tea is always available. Childcare in the large, safe yard is $2 per hour, and bikes are $2 as well per hour. Horseback riding,

with lessons, is $10 per hour.

Rates: Both double rooms rent, together, for $70 and can accomodate a family of four. Cots and cribs available at no charge. Personal checks welcome.

10% discount to OHJ members.

LEAVENWORTH

EDEL HAUS
Mark and Betsy Montgomery
320 Ninth Street
Leavenworth, WA 98826
(509) 548-4412
Year-round

1930 English Revival

LOCATION: Located in the center of a "Bavarian" village in the Cascades, the inn is near every outdoor sport "except ocean-oriented ones." Mountains and a park surround the site.

While not the oldest B&B included in this book (built in 1930), Edel Haus certainly has many old-world charms: for one, the view of the neo-Bavarian village of Leavenworth, tucked into the Washington Cascades.

The building was constructed to house doctors for the former hospital across the street. The physician who built the house later lived there with his family, and then sold it to the current owners. With minor alterations the Montgomerys converted the house to a licensed B&B and turned the garage into a guest cottage — that "matches the house very well," they say.

The exterior white stucco walls and built-in dressers inside are all original; the Montgomerys have furnished the interior with 1930s furniture, other antiques, and some Pennsylvania Dutch pieces.

Restrictions: No pets, smoking only in the living room. Check-in between 1 and 11 p.m.

Beds: Three rooms share a bath; there's also a family room and cottage.

438

Breakfast: "Full": coffee, tea, juice, fresh fruits, French toast with cinnamon butter, apple sauce, and sausage, and another main course: baked eggs with cream and cheese, plus muffins and sausage "unforgettable," say Mark and Betty.

Extras: There's an indoor/outdoor cafe, and an outdoor hot tub, popular with the many skiers who stay in winter.

Rates: $44 (double, shared bath) to $60 (cottage with private entrance and bath). Holiday and festival rates $10 higher. Personal checks welcome. Discount for Canadian money.

10% discount to OHJ members.

PORT ANGELES

TUDOR INN
Jane and Jerry Glass
1108 South Oak
Port Angeles, WA 98362
(206) 452-3138
Year-round

1910 Tudor Revival

LOCATION: The inn is in the old residential area of Port Angeles, headquarters of Olympic National Park and the largest city on the Olympic peninsula. The ferry to Victoria, British Columbia, docks 12 blocks away.

Rumors abound about the house's eccentric original owner, James Jackson. What's known is that he was an Englishman with a German wife, and that they lived in the house from 1910 to 1961. He reportedly went to a local rain forest to choose a tree with which to build his own coffin, and then did so on the third floor of the house.

The building retains its original interior panelling and woodwork, all made of local fir. Especially attractive are the brown frames of the sitting room windows that contrast with the room's light color scheme. The owners spent eight years in England, and have furnished the house with turn-of-the-century English antiques. Guest rooms look out on either the Olympic Mountains or the Strait of Juan de Fuca.

Restrictions: No children under 12 ("with exceptions"), no pets, no smoking in the inn.
Beds: Five rooms, one with private bath.
Breakfast: The menu varies, but usually consists of bacon, eggs, bran muffins, English muffins, melon, juice, berries, and freshly ground coffee. Granola is also available.
Extras: Afternoon tea and cookies are served, and late-arriving guests are offered a glass of complimentary wine.
Rates: $45 (small, mountain view) to $68 (king bed, mountain view); $40 to $65 in winter. Personal and traveler's checks accepted; there's a 5% surcharge for Mastercard and Visa.

WASHINGTON

PORT TOWNSEND

ARCADIA COUNTRY INN
Michael Newbaur
1891 South Jacob Miller Road
Port Townsend, WA 98368
(206) 385-5245
Year-round

1908 Shingle Style

LOCATION: The inn is situated on a hill looking south toward the Olympic Mountains and surrounded by 70 acres of woods and pasture, as well as orchard. Salt water is two miles away in three directions.

Rumor has it that the first owner, a local attorney named Snyder, had the Arcadia built to house his mistress. That was just the first in a whole series of, well, "dubious" uses the building has had.

The building once served as a chicken ranch: when Prohibition passed, the owners began selling bootleg alcohol along with chicken dinners. By this point—the 1920s—the name Arcadia Inn had stuck and travelers along the only road to Port Townsend were staying there. It was during this period that the building spent its most scandalous days. A still bubbled in the basement; liquor bottles were stored in a concrete room with barred windows that still exists today.

The Shrouts have kept the place basically intact, though they installed an oak bar, a modern kitchen, and three exterior decks. The hipped-roof dormers, though they look perfectly original, are actually compatible recent additions.

The exterior brickwork is said to be made of ballast bricks, once used to weight the clipper ships that returned empty to Port Townsend from overseas. The barn was built in 1926 as a dance hall, and its hardwood floor is still the largest dance floor in Jefferson County. In the back pasture lies a horse racing track (Snyder expected the area to become a fashionable racing district, which it never did).

The spacious, airy interior is furnished with an eclectic mixture of antiques.

Restrictions: No pets or smoking indoors. Children allowed "if specific rooms are available." Check-in and check-out times are very flexible.
Beds: Five rooms, all with private baths.
Breakfast: Various freshly baked items, fresh fruit, juice, coffee, and teas, "all you can eat."
Extras: Use of the hot tub and swimming pond are free.
Rates: $39 to $65, winter; $44 to $70, summer. Cots, $5; cribs, free. Personal checks and credit cards accepted.
Mailing Address: 186-35th Avenue East, Seattle, WA 98112

PORT TOWNSEND

1878 Italianate

HERITAGE HOUSE
Bob and Carolyn Ellis,
Jim and Pat Broughton
305 Pierce Street
Port Townsend, WA 98368
(206) 385-6800
Year-round

LOCATION: Built on a bluff overlooking Port Townsend Bay, the house has a view of the Olympic Mountains. Fort Warden State Park (where "An Officer and a Gentleman" was filmed) is a 5-minute drive away.

At Heritage House, guests can wander through French doors onto a balcony that overlooks Port Townsend, the bay, and the snow-capped mountains beyond. In the rooms are an intriguing variety of antiques, from false-grained pine beds to a tin and oak clawfoot tub that folds into the wall like a Murphy bed. There are also eight-foot-high cedar sliding doors. Period papers cover the walls, and the exterior—minus a few trees and a picket fence—looks just as it did in an 1880 photo that the owners have turned up.

Restrictions: No smoking, pets, or children under eight. Check-in after 2 p.m.
Beds: Of the five doubles and one room with two doubles, three share a bath.
Breakfast: "Continental plus": Fruit/melon in season, juice, coffee, tea, plus three or more varieties of homemade breads and pastries —"all you can eat."
Extras: Tea, coffee, cookies, and fresh fruit are available all day.
Rates: $40 ("cozy and cute") to $76 (two-room suite with private bath); discounts on weekdays November to February. Personal check and credit cards accepted.
10% discount to OHJ members.

WASHINGTON

PORT TOWNSEND

PALACE HOTEL
Ruth and Les Skogman
1004 Water Street
Port Townsend, WA 98368
(206) 385-0773
Year-round

1889 Richardsonian Romanesque

LOCATION: The inn is located in the downtown center of this historic 19th-century seaport, close to shops and restaurants and affording views of the bay and mountains. There are many historic buildings and homes in town, and Olympic National Park is 50 miles away.

The previous owners restored this National Register structure from foundation to sheet-metal cornice, aided by Federal and state grants. All of Port Townsend, in fact, has undergone a similar rebirth in the past two decades. Once expected to become a major seaport, the city was heavily built up in the mid- to late-19th century. When the Union Pacific Railroad passed it by in the early 1890s, the city began to decline. Much of its original architecture was allowed to decay, though a little was replaced by new construction. Many of the fine old buildings are visible from the Palace's arched windows, along with part of Port Townsend Bay.

A retired sea captain, Henry L. Tibbals, built the structure in 1889 to serve as part office space, part rented rooms. (At the very same intersection, of Water and Tyler streets, the original settlers in Port Townsend had built their log cabin.) The Palace's first floors, now an art gallery and shops, once held three saloons and a billiard parlor. From 1925 to 1933 Madame Marie M— operated what was euphemistically known as a "Palace of Sweets" on the upper floors, where alcohol was also served. Her lavishly decorated rooms are now called "Marie's Suite." Four rooms on the third floor were once lit only by a skylight, and had no source of outside air. These served as "cribs," small rooms for the "girls." After an early-morning raid by the sheriff, Marie was expelled from town, and her girls soon followed.

The remodeled third-floor "cribs" now serve as an apartment for the current owners, Ruth and Les Skogman. They've kept the guest rooms furnished with period pieces, and are especially proud of the restored two-storey stairway and lobby area, lit by a skylight.

Restrictions: Children O.K., no pets. Smoking in eight of the 11 rooms. Check-in after 1 p.m.
Beds: The 14 rooms accommodate up to five people per suite; some of the suites have kitchens. Nine rooms have private baths.
Extras: There's a coffeemaker in each room. In winter the hotel offers 20% discounts on dinners at nearby restaurants.
Rates: $35 (shared bath) to $56 ("Marie's Suite," fireplace, bath, kitchen), winter; $40 to $68, summer. Cots or cribs, no charge. Personal checks and credit cards accepted.

SEATTLE

**CHAMBERED NAUTILUS
BED & BREAKFAST INN**
Kate McDill and Deborah Sweet
5005 22nd Avenue NE
Seattle, WA 98105
(206) 522-2536
Year-round

1915 Neo-Georgian

LOCATION: The University of Washington is within walking distance; downtown Seattle is ten minutes away by car. Ravenia Park is nearby, and downhill and cross-country skiing an hour away. The house sits on a hill with maple trees and ivy.

This house came closer than most to the brink of disaster. After World War II the owners almost sold the place to a group of returning GIs for use as a fraternity house! Thankfully the sale was never completed, and the building was spared that cruel fate.

Many neo-Federal and neo-Colonial features ornament the house, including a columned entry porch, a pared-down Palladian window, and returning eaves. The overall effect is one of simplicity and solidity, enhanced by a coat of Williamsburg blue paint with white trim. The interior is marked by coved ceilings and unusual mouldings, especially those surrounding the dining room fireplace. Persian rugs cover the floors in both dining and living rooms, and the living room adjoins an enclosed sun porch with classical columns.

One guest room is panelled in cedar, and four of the six have porches or balconies. The furniture dates primarily from the late 19th and early 20th centuries, though there's a c. 1840 pie safe in the dining room. Varieties of wood give the rooms their decorating schemes: American golden oak in one, English inlaid mahogany in another, dark walnut and oak in still another.

The owners have met "all generations of previous owners," and from that "received an oral history of the house that we share with guests." For instance they know that the Gowens, the first owners, were "a lively and fun-loving family." The father, Dr. Herbert Gowen, established the Department of Oriental Studies at the then-fledgling University of Washington.

Restrictions: No smoking, no pets, children under 12 allowed by prior arrangement only.

Beds: For the six rooms—two queens, three doubles, and a queen with double—there are three baths.

Breakfast: Fresh scones or muffins, coffeecake, cinnamon rolls; fresh fruit, juice, and coffee, plus quiche, cheese, baked eggs, or soufflé. "No one goes hungry! One of the innkeepers is a professional baker."

Extras: "Personalized care for our guests" is provided, including excursions, travel arrangements to other inns, and ferry reservations.

Rates: $50 ("cozy" double with porch) to $75 (large, airy, double-and-queen suite). Cots, $10. Personal checks and credit cards welcome.

10% discount to OHJ members for stays of more than three nights.

SEATTLE

GALER PLACE BED & BREAKFAST GUEST HOUSE
Ms. Chris Chamberlain and McKinley T. Giles
318 West Galer
Seattle, WA 98119
(206) 282-5339
Year-round

1906 Shingle style/Foursquare

LOCATION: On the south slope of Queen Anne Hill, the house is near parks and views. Seattle Center is within walking distance, and downtown Seattle is a few minutes away.

The roof is hipped, even the chimney is "hipped." But by far the house's most unusual feature is the paired windows that ornament the facade: two tiny diamonds, atop two tiny squares.

Though the house was restored by previous owners, the current ones have added antique furnishings and what they call "British touches" to reflect their ancestry. Plentiful woodwork lines the high-ceilinged rooms.

Restrictions: Smoking only in downstairs lounge, no children under 12, pets welcome with prior approval.
Beds: One room has a private bath, one a half-bath, and the two others share.
Breakfast: "Expanded continental": freshly ground coffee or tea, choice of juice, fresh muffins or bread, fruit, yogurt, cottage cheese.
Extras: Freshly baked Scottish shortbread is offered at the complimentary afternoon tea. Tea, coffee, or a glass of wine are offered upon arrival.
Rates: $45 to $55, single; $50 to $65, double. 10% discount mid-week October to April. Personal checks and credit cards welcome.

10% discount to OHJ members.

WASHINGTON

SEATTLE

GASLIGHT INN
Steve Bennett and Trevor Logan
1727 15th Avenue
Seattle, WA 98122
(206) 325-3654
Year-round

1906 Foursquare with Mission details

LOCATION: The inn, in Seattle's Capitol Hill area, is near shopping districts and ten blocks from downtown and the waterfront.

An American Foursquare with flair, the Gaslight Inn has a standard shape but an unusual quantity of leaded, stained-glass, and arched windows. The windows are loaded with trim like tiny brackets and other ornaments; along the roofline and entry porch lie many exposed rafter ends.

Our recommending subscriber raved about the double parlors, living room, and library, all of which are panelled in oak. All nine bedrooms are furnished in antiques, but the television, video, and game table in the living room, beside the oak fireplace, provide a modern touch.

Restrictions: No children or pets.

Beds: The nine rooms have either double or queen beds, refrigerators, and TVs. There are six private baths; three other rooms share baths.

Breakfast: Continental.

Extras: Phone service and kitchenettes are available in some rooms; plus there's an in-ground heated pool.

Rates: $35 (shared bath, third floor) to $45 (second floor, private bath). Personal checks and credit cards welcome.

10% discount to OHJ members.

WASHINGTON

SEATTLE

1906 Foursquare

**WILLIAMS HOUSE BED &
BREAKFAST**
**Susan, Doug, and Danielle
Williams**
**1505 4th Avenue North
Seattle, WA 98109
(206) 285-0810
Year-round**

LOCATION: The house is at the top of Queen Anne Hill (named for the Victorian homes that dot it), within six blocks of Space Needle and Seattle Center. Downtown is within one mile, and the guest rooms afford "wonderful territorial views."

The classic tale of the "star boarder" came true here: In the 1940s, when the building became a boarding house for "gentlemen," one of the residents ended up marrying the older proprietress.

Before that, the house had remained in one family for 30 years, beginning in 1917. The daughter of the house was married before the bevelled-glass mirror that still stands in the living room. (Members of this family came back to see the Williamses at work on the house in 1983, and told them its history.)

Owners Susan and Doug had many original features to work with, including a tiled fireplace in the entry, some gas lighting fixtures, pressed-tin wallcoverings, and old distorted panes in the windows. But the woodwork needed a lot of cleaning, and some walls were covered by seven layers of wallpaper. Along with the cosmetic work they also restored the bathrooms with period fixtures. And finally they made a flower bed out of the garden which, when they bought the place, was strictly weeds.

Their taste in furniture runs to Victorian rococo, which, especially in the living room, makes a nice contrast with the simple post-Victorian woodwork and the wide, open rooms.

Restrictions: No smoking in the bedrooms. Children, but not pets, welcome. Check-in between 4 and 6 p.m., flexible. Check-out at noon.
Beds: There's one king, two queens, one double, and one room with twins. Three share a bath.
Breakfast: Hot breads, muffins, homemade jams, pitchers of juices, fresh fruit in season, granola and cereals, eggs, coffee, teas, hot cocoa.
Extras: Tours of the city can be booked through the innkeepers. A phone booth has a separate line for guests and offers free local calls.
Rates: $40 to $70. Cots, $10; cribs, $5. Personal checks and credit cards welcome.

WASHINGTON

SNOHOMISH

**COUNTRYMAN'S BED &
BREAKFAST**
Sandy and Larry Countryman
119 Cedar
Snohomish, WA 98290
(206) 568-9622
Year-round

1896 Queen Anne

LOCATION: Downtown Snohomish, a national landmark, is 30 minutes from Stevens Pass in the Cascades, 15 minutes to Puget Sound, and 30 miles north of Seattle.

"Since we remodelled and restored a six-unit apartment house into a 28-room Victorian home, and did most of the work ourselves, we have many experiences to share."

The Countryman's Inn has all the typical eclectic details of a Queen Anne extravaganza: fish-scale shingles, an asymmetrical tower, bay windows, porches with spindle rails. Inside on five different levels are 28 rooms, containing original staircases, sliding doors, and an oak-panelled library.

The house has a somewhat checkered past. The first owner, a doctor, went bankrupt and was forced to sell the property. Eventually it was divided into six apartments, and over the years it was mortgaged twice to Montgomery Ward to pay for the bathroom fixtures.

The Countrymans did some major work to reclaim the building. They had a house mover place the structure on pilings while they dug out and poured a full cement basement. They'd love to share this and other restoration stories.

They've filled the house with period oak furnishings, and there's a brass-and-iron bed in each sunny guest room.

Restrictions: Prior arrangements must be made for pets; no smoking preferred. Babies and children welcome. Check-in time flexible.
Beds: One room has a queen and two twins, two have twins, and three have queens. Three rooms have private baths.
Breakfast: Guests can choose what they want, usually eggs, hash browns, bacon, juice, and blueberry muffins fresh from the oven.
Extras: Babysitting is available for $1.50 per hour. Afternoon tea is provided, and the Countrymans offer a 30-minute tour of the town's historic homes, including the "folklore" of Snohomish.
Rates: $45 (single), $55 (double), all rooms. Cots, $5. Personal checks and credit cards accepted.

10% discount to OHJ members.

WISCONSIN

Wausau

Eau Claire

Green Bay

Madison

Milwaukee

Kenosha

BARABOO

THE HOUSE OF SEVEN GABLES
Ralph and Pamela Krainik
215 6th Street
Baraboo, WI 53913
(608) 356-8387
Year-round

1860 Carpenter Gothic

LOCATION: Nearby are antique shops, the North Freedom Railroad Museum, Ringling Theatre, Circus World Museum, and Devil's Lake State Park.

This ornate Carpenter Gothic is dripping with details: ornamental bargeboards with teardrop and acorn pendants, board-and-batten siding, latticework of diamonds and quatrefoils, oculus and Palladian windows, etched cranberry glass, and, of course, the seven steep gables that give it its name. Owners Ralph and Pamela Krainik have spent five years restoring the exterior of this house, which was built in 1860 for a banker named Terril Thomas. Pamela, an antique dealer, has furnished the house with Victorian furniture that dates from the 1860s to 1880s.

Restrictions: No pets. Check-in after 4 p.m., check-out at 10 a.m.
Beds: Two rooms with private baths.
Breakfast: Full breakfast is served in the dining room.
Extras: Guests get a free tour of the home and grounds.
Rates: $50 single, $55 double. Extra adults, $10 surcharge; extra child, $5. Personal checks and credit cards accepted.
Mailing Address: PO Box 204, Baraboo, WI 53913

BAYFIELD

COOPER HILL HOUSE
Phil and Sheree Peterson
33 South 6th Street
Bayfield, WI 54814
(715) 779-5060
Year-round (November to April
by reservation only)

1888 Vernacular

LOCATION: Bayfield (population 800) overlooks the Apostle Islands of Lake Superior. The town has a 60-block historic district, as well as many fresh-seafood (caught in the lake) restaurants. Ferry trips to the island are available; nearby are 50 miles of fine cross-country skiing trails.

Martin Johnson built this sturdy house of native hemlock and white pine from the lumber mill at which he was employed. It's an unassuming turn-of-the-century working man's home with two bay windows in the dining room and flooring of maple and Douglas fir. Though the house has been remodelled over the years, it still retains the simple lines characteristic of Bayfield architecture. It stands on top of a hill where the Cooper family once lived (and Bayfield residents often used to bobsled), hence the name.

Restrictions: Smoking on front porch only. Check-in after 2 p.m., check-out at 11 a.m.
Beds: Three doubles and one queen all have private baths.
Breakfast: "Expanded continental": homemade breads, jams, fresh fruit, juice; tea or coffee.
Rates: $44 to $49; personal checks and credit cards welcome.
    10% discount to OHJ members if paying by cash or check.
Mailing Address: PO Box 5, Bayfield, WI 54814

BAYFIELD

OLD RITTENHOUSE INN
Mary and Jerry Phillips
301 Rittenhouse Avenue
Bayfield, WI 54814
(715) 779-5765
May to October; weekends rest
of year except January

1890 Shingle Style/Neo-Colonial

LOCATION: Lake Superior is four blocks away, and much of Bayfield is a designated historic district. Tours of the Apostle Islands feature brownstone mines (where much of New York City's brownstone came from) and some of the few remaining nesting grounds of the bald eagle.

Guests can watch the sailboats crisscross Lake Superior from the wraparound porch of this 1890 Queen Anne. The Rittenhouse, in the Bayfield Historic District, sits on a hill just a few blocks from the shore. Allan Fuller, a general for Illinois during the Civil War, built the house—it was his summer "cottage." He finished it with the finest materials available. A cherry staircase leads to the guest rooms, eight of which have fireplaces. (There are four other fireplaces throughout the house.) Innkeepers Mary and Jerry Phillips have filled the house with antiques, and nearly doubled the size of the place with a compatible addition.

Restrictions: No smoking in the dining rooms, no pets.
Beds: Four doubles, five kings—all have private baths, and all but one have fireplaces.
Breakfast: Continental included in room rate; full is $3.50; these gourmet meals are served in the dining room.
Extras: Babysitting during dinner can be arranged. A variety of teas and coffee are served all day. The gourmet restaurant Mary runs on the first floor offers fresh specials that vary from day to day.
Rates: $69 (double) to $109 (king). Personal checks and credit cards accepted.
Mailing Address: PO Box 584, Bayfield, WI 54814

CEDARBURG

STAGECOACH INN
Brook and Liz Brown
W 61 N520 Washington Avenue
Cedarburg, WI 53012
(414) 375-0208
Year-round

1853 Greek Revival

LOCATION: Cedarburg, recently added to the National Register, has many antique shops, restored buildings, a covered bridge, plus a Pioneer Village (a collection of log and stone buildings). Milwaukee is 25 miles to the south.

This 1853 stone building was condemned when Brook and Liz Brown bought it in 1983. Known as the Central House Hotel and later the Nero Hotel, when Mr. Nero ran a bar and boarding house, the inn has only the essential modern conveniences—you won't find any televisions in the guest rooms. Many original details have survived its 131-year lifetime: the tin ceiling in the pub, the mouldings, plaster and lath; wide pine floors, the cherry bannister on the main staircase, original stencilling. The 100-year-old bar in the pub has bullet holes in it! (During prohibition, it was turned into a candy counter.) All of the furniture is antique, including brass, rope, and four-poster beds, wardrobes, and rocking chairs in the guest rooms.

Restrictions: Smoking outside only; no pets. Children welcome. Check-in after 4 p.m., check-out at noon.
Beds: Nine rooms, all with private baths, include four doubles, two singles, and three with two doubles and a twin.
Breakfast: Muffins/rolls, cereal, coffee, tea, orange juice, fruit in season.
Extras: The pub on the first floor offers a game room. Babysitting can be arranged with 24-hour notice.
Rates: $28 (single) to $35 (double). Cots and cribs, $5 each. Personal checks and credit cards welcome.
   10% discount to OHJ members.

CEDARBURG

THE WASHINGTON HOUSE INN
James Pape
W62 N573 Washington Avenue
Cedarburg, WI 53012
(414) 375-3550
Year-round

1886 Romanesque (commercial)

LOCATION: Shops, restaurants, the Cedarburg Settlement shops and a winery are nearby; the inn is located in the center of the town's historic district. Biking trails, golf courses, and cross-country skiing areas are within driving distance.

The Washington House was built on the site of Cedarburg's first inn, which it replaced in 1886. It was a hotel until the 1920s when it was converted into apartments and offices. The building, made from Milwaukee's "cream city" brick, has decorative brickwork and iron grillwork above the front entrance, features not to be missed. James Pape, who bought the building in 1982, has carefully reproduced the woodwork and wainscotting from surviving sections of originals. The walnut and maple floor in the lobby has been restored, and has the tin ceiling in the gathering room.

Restrictions: No pets. Check-in between 3 and 11 p.m.
Beds: Two twins, nine queens and three with two doubles or queens. All have private baths, and 12 of them have whirlpools.
Breakfast: Continental: fresh orange juice, variety of breads, cereal, fresh fruit, coffees and teas.
Extras: Telephones and televisions are provided in each room. A sauna is available for guest use. The "afternoon social" provides complimentary cheese, crackers, and grape juice.
Rates: $49 (queen bed, standard bath) to $89 (king bed, king-size whirlpool). Cots and cribs, $10 each. Personal checks and credit cards welcome.
   10% discount to OHJ members.

EPHRAIM

HILLSIDE HOTEL OF EPHRAIM

Dean S. and Evadne McNeil;
David M. and Karen J. McNeil
9980 Water Street
Ephraim, WI 54211
(414) 854-2417
December 30 to March 1

1858 to 1905 Vernacular

LOCATION: The inn, built on the shores of Green Bay's Eagle Harbor, is in a historic village close to many historic buildings and nature centers.

The Hillside Hotel is a wood-frame farmhouse with notched hickory sills and studs. The original structure was built by Reverend A. Iverson, founder of Ephraim and leader of the Moravian Church in America. O.M. Olsen purchased it in the late 1850s, and in the 1920s, after several additions and changes, the house eventually became a hotel. When more space was needed, the owners closed in lean-tos, hence the odd combinations of building materials.

Restrictions: Check-out at 10 a.m., check-in after 4 p.m. No pets; smoking only on the verandah.
Beds: One single, nine doubles, one room with two twins, one with a double and a single. One cottage, with three double bedrooms, and one with two double bedrooms are available. Six rooms in the main house share baths.
Breakfast: Scrambled eggs and bacon, eggs Benedict, spinach quiche, "scratch" waffles, seafood crepes, omelettes, clam soufflé; freshly smoked whitefish with Bernaise sauce.
Extras: Tea and lemonade are served on the verandah from 4 to 6 p.m. A private beach and boat moorings are available.
Rates: $45 (single) to $60 (double)—all rooms have large windows, some with bay views. No charge for cribs. Personal checks and credit cards welcome.

10% discount to OHJ members.
Mailing Address: PO Box 17, Ephraim, WI 54211

FISH CREEK

WHITE GULL INN
Andy and Jan Coulson
4225 Main Street
Fish Creek, WI 54212
(414) 868-3517
Year-round

1896 Vernacular Gothic Revival

LOCATION: The village of Fish Creek, in the heart of Wisconsin's Door Peninsula, offers shops, art galleries, summer stock theatre, music festivals and "every imaginable water and show sport." The inn stands a half-mile from Peninsula State Park.

Dr. Herman Welcker, the original owner, was determined to establish himself in the resort business, so he bought entire buildings in Marinette, Wisconsin. He then had them dragged by horse and sled across Green Bay in the wintertime. His guests then traveled to visit this fishing community via steamboat.

Although the plumbing and electricity has been upgraded recently, the inn is much the same as it was 90 years ago. The original staircase, windows, hardwood and pine floors, and the two-way native stone fireplace remain the same. Many of the furnishings belonged to the original owner; the rest are antiques from the same period.

Restrictions: No pets. Check-in after 3 p.m., check-out at 11 a.m.
Beds: The main house's 14 rooms include five with shared bath; the four cottages accommodate up to eight persons each.
Breakfast: A full breakfast—fresh berries in season, homemade coffeecake, buttermilk pancakes with Door County maple syrup—is included in the room rate only in winter.
Rates: $32 (main house, single) to $150 (eight people in the Lundberg House, one block from the main lodge), slightly higher in winter (for breakfast). Personal checks welcome.
Mailing Address: PO Box 159, Fish Creek, WI 54212

SISTER BAY

RENAISSANCE INN
John and JoDee Faller
414 Maple Drive
Sister Bay, WI 54234
(414) 854-5107
May 1 to November 1;
December 26 to March 15

C. 1884 Vernacular

LOCATION: The main highway is a half-block away, with assorted shops and restaurants. Three golf courses are nearby, along with Peninsula State Park, Newport and Whitefish Bay State Parks. Lake Michigan is five miles away, Green Bay a half-block away.

John and JoDee Faller turned this house into an inn in 1984, some 100 years after it was built. It's been a rooming house, a combination grocery store and sausage factory (ice was once stored in an upstairs bedroom), a bait shop, and a wood-burning stove store. There's an old store front on the main dining room, which also has a tin ceiling. The rooms are furnished with antiques.

Restrictions: Children over 14 are welcome if accompanied by parent. No pets. Check-in after noon, check-out at 10:30 a.m.
Beds: Four doubles and one room with a double and single all have private baths.
Breakfast: Full: fresh coffeecake, fresh fruit, juice, egg entree with meat or vegetables on the side, potatoes; English muffin, muffins, and coffee.
Extras: There's no charge for hot coffee and cider in winter, as well as popcorn. The Fallers operate a seafood restaurant in the first-floor dining rooms.
Rates: $55 to $70; personal checks and credit cards accepted.
  10% discount to OHJ members.

STURGEON BAY

WHITE LACE INN
Dennis and Bonnie Statz
16 North 5th Avenue
Sturgeon Bay, WI 54235
(414) 743-1105
Year-round

Main House - 1903 Queen Anne; Garden House - 1885 Vernacular

LOCATION: Two historic districts—one residential, one commercial—are nearby. All of Door County is within a 40-minute drive, including 250 miles of shoreline, apple and cherry orchards, and scenic places for cross-country skiing.

The leaded, bevelled-glass windows in this 1903 Queen Anne reflect rainbows throughout the house on sunny days. Other magical features: the three-storey tower and the wraparound verandah. The entire entry—even the ceiling—is entirely panelled in oak that was never painted. Innkeepers Dennis and Bonnie Statz had only to scrub the dirt off to make the oak gleam. There's panelling in the dining room, too (five feet high), and an oak archway and columns between the parlor and the sitting room. Behind the Queen Anne is the Garden House, a smaller building that would have been razed had the Statzes not bought it for $1 and moved it to their lot.

Restrictions: No pets, children "not recommended," smoking only in designated areas. Check-in after 2 p.m., check-out at 11 a.m.
Beds: Fifteen rooms, ten with fireplaces, all with private baths (some with whirlpools).
Breakfast: Homemade muffins and/or breads, coffee, tea, juice.
Extras: Coffee and tea are available anytime; in winter hot chocolate and apple cider are served.
Rates: $55 (ornate Victorian bed or canopied brass bed) to $120. Three-night packages (10-15% discount) available from November through mid-May. Personal checks and credit cards accepted.

INDEX